Praise for *The Challenge of History*

"The emergence of historical consciousness in the West has posed major challenges to Christian faith and theology over 300 years. Christophe Chalamet's expertly introduced thirty-seven excerpts from key figures from the Renaissance to Liberation Theologies brilliantly illuminate the development of biblical criticism and its impact. The international and ecumenical scope of this selection gives due recognition to the German masters while also retrieving valuable statements from some less well-known scholars. Excellent translations make crucial insights from European intellectual history available to new readers, and the editor's measured judgments on the necessity of critical investigation of the Bible are a refreshing contribution to contemporary debate."

—Robert Morgan, Linacre College (Oxford)

"Christophe Chalamet has curated a timely collection addressing the centrality of historical study in reading the Bible since the Protestant Reformation. *The Challenge of History* shows how Jewish, Protestant, and Roman Catholic theologians developed the historical approach to the Bible and why critical thinking continues to be an indispensable tool for resolving religious disputes today."

—Christine Helmer, Northwestern University

"Prefaced by a learned general introduction and rounded out with a thoughtful postscript, *The Challenge of History: Readings in Modern Theology* will introduce a new generation of students to the variety of ways in which the historical-critical study of the Bible has transformed the Christian theological tradition, especially in the last three centuries. Reaching back to the Renaissance and crossing over confessional lines, Christophe Chalamet has put together a fascinating set of primary sources and furnished each with a crisp and informative introduction. Student and teacher alike will be grateful for the appearance of this fresh anthology on a vital issue for the church and the academy alike."

—Brent W. Sockness, Stanford University

"The application of historical presuppositions and methods to the Bible constitutes one of the most significant sets of events in the history of Christianity. In this very helpful publication, Christophe Chalamet introduces his reader to vital publications stretching over more than five hundred years which in different ways show the never-easy relationship between history and theology. The two have rarely lived in any kind of harmony with each other, but as Chalamet makes clear, the tension which exists between them is both necessary and potentially fruitful."

—James Carleton Paget, Peterhouse, University of Cambridge

"The incisive and well-chosen excerpts in this volume offer readers a detailed yet accessible overview of a central problematic of modern Christian thought: the rise of historical and critical research methods. This outstanding collection makes clear not only the wide range of responses to the difficulties posed by this emerging historical consciousness but also the startling complexity of the challenge, the implications of which continue to reshape contemporary theological reflection."

—Kevin M. Vander Schel, Gonzaga University

"Interest in history and the critical study of historical sources has been one of the defining features of Western modernity. This outstanding volume brilliantly illustrates just how pervasively this intellectual concern has spanned centuries, nations, religions, and professions. Christophe Chalamet has edited a book that will be indispensable to those studying modern historical thought across the disciplines, as well as to those teaching it."

—Johannes Zachhuber, University of Oxford

The Challenge of History

The Challenge of History

Readings in Modern Theology

CHRISTOPHE CHALAMET, EDITOR

FORTRESS PRESS
MINNEAPOLIS

THE CHALLENGE OF HISTORY
Readings in Modern Theology

Print ISBN: 978-1-4514-9976-6
eBook ISBN: 978-1-5064-5892-2

Permissions information is located in back of book.

Cover image: Wassily Kandinsky, Composition Number 8 © 2019 Artists Rights Society (ARS), New York/ Bridgeman Images
Cover design: Laurie Ingram

Contents

Acknowledgments

Providing brief excerpts from so many different authors is a challenge, since it is impossible to gain real expertise on so many figures. Nevertheless, preparing such an anthology has been an exciting project to work on. Certainly, a number of other authors and thinkers could have been added to the (already long) list. My hope is that readers will be intrigued by some of the authors who are included here, and that they will look for their writings beyond the selections contained here.

The present anthology was supposed to be published as part of the new Shapers of Modern Theology series (before the cancellation of this series). I thank Michael Gibson and Scott Tunseth for their trust and their help. Andrea Lee did a marvelous job in the copy editing of the text: I am grateful for her assistance.

I also wish to thank Mathias Hassenfratz and Alessandra Maigre, my collaborators at the Institut romand de systématique et d'éthique (Faculté de théologie, University of Geneva), for helping me with the transcriptions of some of the texts. Kevin Bovier expertly translated the excerpts from Louis Cappel's *Critica sacra*. Fr. Joseph A. Komonchak generously gave me permission to use his translation of Marie-Dominique Chenu's text on Le Saulchoir. Elio Jaillet, my current collaborator at the Faculté de théologie at the University of Geneva, helped in a very efficient manner with the indexes. The Société des Amis de la Faculté de théologie (SAFT) has generously supported the present project through funding in the final stages, as we secured permission to reprint some of the excerpts.

At various stages in the preparation of this anthology, I asked colleagues and friends which author(s) they would include, and even though I was unable to always follow it, their advice was helpful: Frédéric Amsler, Nikolaos Asproulis, François Dermange, Thomas Guillemin, Timothy Nicholas-Twining, Enrico Norelli, Maria-Cristina Pitassi, Michael J. Thate, and Kevin Vander Schel. My thanks go to them.

I dedicate this book, with deep gratitude, to my *Doktorvater*, Olivier Fatio.

Introduction

The advent of the modern, historical, and critical methods of reading Scripture is one of the most significant events in the history of Christianity and Christian theology in the last five hundred years. New questions arose, which led to new answers. New ways of considering Scripture were articulated. The crisis in which academic Christian theology has found itself in the past approximately two hundred years is directly related to the emergence of new ways of studying—and criticizing—the Bible. In itself, a crisis is not necessarily bad: it can lead to new beginnings, to further clarifications and a deepened understanding of the matter at hand. It can, of course, also be seen as something that needs to be overcome. In recent decades, laments concerning the modern methods have commonly been voiced by theologians and exegetes alike. A certain nostalgia for premodern readings of Scripture, as well as a quest for other methods such as narrative exegesis, is evident, especially in anglophone theology.

The present volume seeks to trace and present key texts related to the birth of modern historical and critical exegesis and, more broadly, to the emergence, among theologians and biblical scholars, of a certain historical consciousness that characterizes vast segments of modernity. How did the historical and critical methods arise? How did they affect the study of Scripture? What are their implications for Christian theology? Should Christians and theologians deplore the advent of these methods—as many have and still do—or is there something of lasting value in the critical inquiry of Scripture and in the historical consciousness that modernity fostered?

The present book gives an unambiguous, positive answer to the last question—even while acknowledging the negative side effects of modern critical methods insofar as they entailed hegemonic claims and tended to curtail the very possibility of theological exegesis. There is no going back to premodern exegesis—even if we still have much to learn from it. There is also no controlling or blocking the progress of the critical inquiry about Scripture and the Christian tradition, as was attempted within Roman Catholicism at the Council of Trent and in much of the subsequent centuries, all the way until the middle of the twentieth century (the struggles were no less intense among Protestants, as the present anthology shows). Such endeavors are illusory and always fail. This does not mean that the critical study of Scripture is the be-all and end-all of biblical study and interpretation. If there is one thing that historical scholarship has taught us, it is that context matters. Not just the context of *production* of literary (and, more broadly, artistic) works, but also the context in which these works are read, studied, and so forth. Scripture is read—and needs to be read—differently in a parish, a monastery, and an academic setting. But the various ways of approaching Scripture should not be cordoned off from one another, and even more meditative readings of the *sacra pagina*, such as the ancient *lectio divina*, should not be unaware of the modern methods. Today's monks are *not* medieval monks! Reading Scripture intelligently presupposes knowledge of the various methods used in the history of Christianity. Among these methods, there are, of course, the modern, historical, and critical methods. We ignore or depreciate them at our own risk.[1]

FORERUNNERS

These methods, as they gradually emerged in the seventeenth century and were refined in subsequent centuries, were new with regard to the acuity and sharpness of the critical questions scholars who used them posed to the text. But, as Ernst Troeltsch argued at the end of the nineteenth century, is there ever anything absolutely new in human history? The modern methods of biblical inquiry indeed have their forerunners. Origen and other eminent biblical scholars were anything but naïve in their study of texts. The great Alexandrian theologian's *Hexapla*, in the first half of the third century, placed side by side no less than six versions of the Old Testament, precisely in order to allow textual comparison. "Nobody has taken so much pains about the Bible as he has," wrote Richard Simon in his 1678 *Critical History of the Old Testament* (Simon 1682, 49 rev.; Simon, himself a Catholic scholar and priest, became a key promoter of the rigorous, historical study of Scripture.) In his *De doctrina christiana* (book 2, ch. 14), Augustine of Hippo recommended correcting sacred texts—a point that was not lost on Simon, who quoted Augustine's recommendation in the opening pages of his *Critical History of the Old Testament* (Simon 1682, 2).

About four hundred years after Augustine, in 789, a key document of the Carolingian renaissance, Charlemagne's *Admonitio generalis*, a royal admonition, urged scholars to pay attention to philological issues and to use and provide sound editions of psalms, annotations, and hymns (Celenza 2012, 367). Around 812, Theodulf, bishop of Orleans, stated Charlemagne's intent this way: "For this is always dear to him: to exercise bishops in the thorough search (*indagatio*) of the Holy Scriptures and prudent and sound doctrine, every cleric in discipline, philosophers in knowledge of things divine and human" (Theodulf 2002, 2:281; McKitterick 2008, 307).

In the twelfth century, a formidable Jewish scholar who lived in Andalucía before years of wandering exile, Rabbi Abraham ben Meir Ibn Ezra (ca. 1089–1167), produced sig-

1. Interest in the relationship between history and theology, including as it affects the interpretation of Scripture, is still quite high, as can be seen with the following recent publications: Sarisky 2015; Riches 2015 and Cameron 2016; Hauser 2009, 2017; Reventlow 2010a; Reventlow 2010b; Wischmeyer 2016. For an older, still useful anthology of German texts on "the problem of New Testament theology," see Strecker 1975.

nal commentaries on the Hebrew Bible that in turn were often commented upon. Ibn Ezra stood out among Jewish commentators for his reluctance to harmonize contradictory passages and for making provocative comments concerning Moses's authorship of the Pentateuch—these comments were not lost on Baruch Spinoza, who was among the first scholars, following Thomas Hobbes (1588–1679) and Isaac La Peyrère (1596–1676), to argue in favor of a non-Mosaic authorship of the first five books of the Hebrew Bible. Several Christian scholars, too, such as Nicolò Maniacutia (d. ca. 1145), were working on textual criticism in the twelfth century (Linde 2012).

Later in the Middle Ages, Franciscan friar Roger Bacon (ca. 1220–94) and Nicholas of Lyra (ca. 1270–1349) were widely recognized masters of scriptural interpretation who also worked on collating manuscripts and who urged readers to learn the biblical languages. At the end of the medieval era, Gianozzo Manetti (1396–1459) called for a thorough revision and translation of the Bible and began to work on the Psalter (Bedouelle 1979, 98). His contemporary Lorenza Valla (ca. 1406–57) began examining the Vulgate and sought to improve on Jerome's Latin translation, thereby opening up new possibilities of questioning texts that were, up to that point and also later, often viewed as untouchable. As Valla put it in 1449, in the later version of the preface (§27) to his *Annotations to the New Testament*, he did "not always examin[e] the Greek words," for his intent was, rather, to lay bare "any ambiguities occurring in the Latin and illuminating any instances when the regular practice of literal translation may have made things more difficult to understand" (Celenza 2012, 373, 382). Such painstaking work was meant to serve the greatness of Scripture:

> For the individual words of divine scripture are like individual gems and precious stones, out of which the Heavenly Jerusalem is constructed. The "cities," so to speak, of other branches of learning, are constructed partly from bricks, like civil law, partly from tufa, like medicine, partly from marble, like astronomy, and there are likewise others. But the city of the Good News (*urbs evangelica*) is the only one made of gems, and the only city where it is more outstanding to be the humblest construction worker than it is to be the architect in other cities. (Preface, §30–31; Celenza 2012, 382)

Valla's work was a crucial contribution among the pioneering attempts that would eventually (significantly later; this is *longue durée* history) upset theology and indeed Christianity in many respects. Let us not forget that theology, during the final period of the medieval era and during the Renaissance, was often referred to simply as *sacras litteras*, "*sacred* letters." A theologian was a *magister in sacra pagina*, "a master in the *sacred* text." Calling into question the accuracy or adequacy of a text such as the Vulgate, and working at emending Jerome's text, as Valla and Erasmus did, was audacious, to say the least. Valla had to be careful, and so he stated that certainly he would dare "neither to say nor even to think anything against Jerome, who is both the holiest and the most learned of men, and who, when it comes to the Christian religion, is most worthy" (Celenza 2012, 386). Valla had to distinguish, as much as possible, his critical inquiry from any direct, personal criticism of Jerome himself. He did so by pointing out, in the earlier version of his preface, the difficulty of the very act of translating. If, in the Vulgate, "many things are translated in an obscure fashion," this is "not the fault of the translator but rather that of the rules and demands of translation, at least of that kind of translation that is not sense for sense but word for word" (Celenza 2012, 387). Valla enjoins his readers and potential critics not to "judge it unlawful that the freedom conferred on me (*mihi tribui libertatem*) is itself employed against someone [that is, Jerome] who himself employed it against everyone else" (Celenza 2012, 387). *Libertas*—"freedom": freedom to inquire and ask questions; freedom to challenge authorities, commonly accepted opinions, normative translations and texts! This is the program—which has not lost any of its importance, even if we think we have already assimilated much of it. Valla, Erasmus, and their followers still have something to teach us, and their legacy is very much part of Western culture.

FURTHER DEVELOPMENTS IN CRITICISM (SIXTEENTH THROUGH SEVENTEENTH CENTURIES)

Renaissance and early Reformation scholars produced countless editions, not only of ancient authors, such as Virgil or Homer, but also of the Bible. By facilitating access to the Bible through new editions and translations in the vernacular, these scholars contributed much to the rediscovery of the message of Scripture, including by those who would eventually be called Protestant Reformers. Besides Lorenzo Valla and Desiderius Erasmus, the name of Jacques Lefèvre d'Étaples (ca. 1460–1536) deserves to be mentioned. He is sometimes called the French Erasmus—certainly, he played a role analogous to Erasmus among scholars working in France and neighboring regions. Lefèvre d'Étaples's first work on the Bible was his *Quincuplex Psalterium*, a dense work of more than six hundred pages first published in Paris by Henri Estienne (the Elder) in 1509. In it, Lefèvre d'Étaples juxtaposed in as many columns five different versions of the Psalms, including three versions that Jerome corrected or established (*Psalterium gallicum*, *Psalterium romanum*, *Psalterium hebraicum*). In the second half of the book, he added two more versions: the *Psalterium vetus*, which Augustine used, and the *Psalterium conciliatum*, that is, Lefèvre's own version of the Psalter, in which, commenting upon the other four versions, he sought to harmonize them. His intent was to promote both rigorous philological work and sound theological interpretation: in his view, both needed to go hand in hand. His model, clearly, was Origen's *Hexapla*, which he mentions in the preface in order to defend his own work.[2] On the theological level, Lefèvre d'Étaples emphasized God's mercy and rejected any notion of human merit (Bedouelle 1979, 7, 14)—no wonder that some of the scholars close to Lefèvre d'Étaples, who in many cases belonged to the circle of Meaux around Bishop Guillaume Briçonnet (1470–1534), embraced Luther's

2. "Lest this appears too innovative and unusual, [let us say that] before us Origen composed for the people of Alexandria a quintuple Greek Psalter to which he added an epitome. Far from being criticized by anyone for this work, up to our time it has garnered much praise." "*Et ne hoc nimis novum aut insolitum videatur, ante nos graecam psalmorum pentaplum Alexandrinis fecit Origenes cui adjunxit Epitomen. Ex quo quidem opere tantum abfuit ut quis eum repraehenderit, ut etiam pro ea re laudes ejus ad tempora nostra perdurent.*" Bedouelle, 1979, 26 (lines 175–79), 31.

reformatory insights! Luther and Zwingli both used Lefèvre's *Quincuplex Psalterium*, at least since 1513 in Luther's case (Bedouelle 1979, 227–28).

Western scholarship of course did not stop with Renaissance scholarship and criticism. In 1555 Sebastian Castellio (1515–63) produced a new, idiosyncratic French translation of the entire Bible and Apocrypha, without verse division, titled *La Bible nouvellement translatée avec annotations*. Relying on Robert Estienne's (1503–59) work, Calvin's successor in Geneva—and a resolute contradictor of Castellio—Theodore Beza (1519–1605) published several editions of the Greek New Testament, which also included Latin translations (the Vulgate and his own). Immanuel Tremmelius (ca. 1510–80) studied the Hebrew and Syriac versions of the Bible and translated the Syriac New Testament into Latin (Geneva: Henri Estienne, 1569). A few generations later, Louis Cappel (1585–1658) became an acknowledged master of the new "criticism," mostly in line with the work of the humanists, even as his Reformed roots, and thus a specific theological approach, showed in his writings (Hardy 2017).

With Spinoza (1632–77), on the other hand, a radical shift begins. Spinoza, on the basis of a naturalistic metaphysics, treats Scripture as a human word *and only that*. The clash between this thesis and the forceful arguments in defense of the Bible's verbal inspiration (theopneusty) and infallibility, which were articulated precisely by some of Spinoza's contemporaries, is massive. What happened with Spinoza and his successors is clear: the Bible's unique status as God's own word was completely set aside (Preus 2001). And yet one of Spinoza's main intentions, interestingly, was to let Scripture speak for itself, to interpret Scripture through Scripture, rather than through certain theological (or philosophical) prejudgments. This is of course akin to certain hermeneutical guidelines that the Protestant Reformers had articulated in the sixteenth century—especially: *scriptura sui ipsius interpres*, "Scripture as its own interpreter." But Spinoza adapts this for his own ends (Preus 2001, 206). And his intention does not mean that he was able to avoid applying his own philosophical views to his interpretation of Scripture. Certainly, unlike Simon who was a pure critic and scholar and was practicing a new, critical kind of scholarship for its own sake, Spinoza had a political intention as he wrote his *Tractatus*: he envisioned a society in which the freedom to philosophize would be defended (Zac 1965, 41).

The pioneers of the modern critical methods were very much aware of their debt to Origen, Jerome, and other ancient scholars. But they also knew that much work remained to be done. As Jean Le Clerc put it, "neither in St. Jerome's time, nor afterwards, did any one, before our age, regard this advice [that is, paying close attention to context] as it deserved; so that our ancestors have left us a very ample harvest for this sort of learning" (see below, 61).

There were significant Roman Catholic historians and critics of the biblical text—the names of the two Oratorians Jean Morin (1591–1659), with his 1633 *Exercitationes biblicae: de Hebraei Graecique textus sinceritate* (Paris: Antoine Vitray), and Richard Simon come to mind—but for the most part it was Protestant scholars who fostered the new methods, as Alfred Loisy pointed out (see below, 155–56). At first sight, they seemed to have everything to lose: Wasn't Scripture the one and only basis for their understanding of the Christian faith? Protestant theologians were of course keenly aware of this problem. As the works of Simon demonstrate, Roman Catholics also knew full well that a challenge to Scripture, for Protestants, would be much more devastating to them than to the Roman Catholic Church and its twin pillars of Scripture and Tradition (with a capital T), two pillars that ought to be treated "with equal piety and reverence," according to the Council of Trent ("*pari pietatis affectu ac reverentia*"; Denzinger 2007, 783). What are the sources of this freedom, among certain Protestants, to criticize biblical texts? How is it that the word *criticism* came to be applied—first, apparently, by Joseph Scaliger (1540–1609; Grafton 1983)—to the study of Scripture?

Luther's way of handling Scripture must have had some influence in this regard. Unlike his early reformatory colleague Andreas Karlstadt (1486–1541), Luther maintained the authorship of Moses for the Pentateuch. But, again unlike Karlstadt, who was appalled by his arbitrariness, Luther famously disparaged the epistle of James, calling it "really an epistle of straw" (LW 35:362) and probably a text that had been written by St. Jerome (Barge 1905, 1:193–99).[3] Not every biblical book had the same worth in his eyes; there are highs and lows in Scripture. This seems hardly compatible with the view, promoted by later Protestant theologians, that the very letter of Scripture, from beginning to end, is divinely inspired (in fact, divinely dictated) and infallible. We are in a different theological world than the Westminster Confession of Faith (1647), which states, in its first chapter, section 8, "The Old Testament in Hebrew (which was the Native Language of the People of GOD of old) and the New Testament in Greek (which at the time of the writing of it was generally known to the Nations) being immediately inspired by God, and by his singular care and Providence kept pure in all Ages, are therefore Authentical" (see Popkin 1996, 388, 405). Still, even if he could not consider the book of Revelation as apostolic or the epistle to the Hebrews as Pauline, Luther refrained from modifying the canon. The important point, for our purpose—which explains why he is not among the thinkers who are included in this anthology—is that Luther expressed these views on theological, not historical, grounds. Again and again, Protestant theologians of all kinds would argue, against advocates of Scripture's infallibility even in its minutest details, that the letter of Scripture, far from being God's revelation as such, is a *human* witness to God's revelation. But modern scholars such as Joseph Scaliger, his disciple Hugo Grotius (1583–1645, who played a very important role in promoting critical readings of the Bible, though almost nothing of his numerous works has been translated from the Latin), and others went further than this and claimed Scripture not primarily as a "testimony" or "witness," but as a historical *source* for understanding Judaism and Christianity: a source that needs to be placed within its own historical, geographical, and cultural context if one is to understand it. As Le Clerc stated in 1683, "I would be eager to know which [scholar], in the last age, applied the histories of the old Oriental people who bordered upon the Hebrews, and what we find in ancient authors relating to their

3. Already in August 1519, in his *Resolutiones*, Luther writes, "*Stilus epistolae illius longe est infra Apostolicam maiestatem nec cum Paulino ullo modo comparandus*" (WA 2:425).

manners, opinions, and their country, towards the illustration of the Scriptures; two or three perhaps and no more" (see below, 61).

How scholars came to study and read Scripture strictly as one historical source among other sources, rather than as a witness, is an important thread in the story of the modern interpretation of the Bible. It should not blind us, however, to the fact that most of the seventeenth-century scholars who began to introduce critically the modern, scholarly study of the Bible were rooted in particular Christian confessions, were acutely aware of the intense polemical battles of their day, and operated, even in their supposedly detached scholarly works, with certain theological biases and agendas (Hardy 2017).

THE QUESTION OF THE CANON AND OF BIBLICAL THEOLOGY (EIGHTEENTH CENTURY)

One thing that happens when Scripture is read purely historically is that the grounds for maintaining these books together as a unit, or as two units (two Testaments), become problematic. The question of the canon, of its formation and boundaries, is not simply a historical question. It is also a theological question, which historical scholarship raises with new acuity: What is it that binds these books together? Johann Salomo Semler (1725–91) argued, quite rightly, that the answer to that question could only be a theological answer, not merely a historical one (see below, 76). But Semler went on to argue for a freedom of inquiry with regard to the various canonical books: "The freedom must exist, for people who have begun to experience the salutary power of basic truths, to judge, according to their own knowledge and experience, the basic moral value of certain books from these ancient collections, as well as the value of certain parts of these books" (see below, 75). Semler's critical work, and the distinction he introduced between the Bible, on the one hand, and the word of God, on the other, was soon furthered by Johann David Michaelis, whose *Introduction to the Divine Scriptures of the New Covenant* remains a landmark in New Testament scholarship (Kümmel 1973, 69–73).

Writing less than two decades after Semler's mature works on the canon, Johann Philipp Gabler (1753–1826) was still convinced of the inspiration of Scripture—an inspiration that, as he saw it, does not cancel out the intellectual and cultural habits of the inspired authors. His inaugural lecture in 1787 shows that he was very much aware of the various phases of Christian theology. He spoke of the presence of "a chronology and a geography to theology itself" (see below, 89) and searched for the transhistorical elements of truth in Scripture (Sandys-Wunsch 1980, 147). He called for clearer demarcations between biblical theology and dogmatic theology, but also between religion and theology, asking "that we distinguish carefully the divine from the human, that we establish some distinction between biblical and dogmatic theology" (see below, 89). The first step of a sound inquiry into Scripture had to be historical, and then, on that basis, certain elements could be retrieved by doctrinal theology. With this proposal, Gabler certainly contributed to the growing independence, in the course of the nineteenth century, of historical and critical exegesis from doctrinal considerations (Morgan 1986–87, 164).

LESSING AND HISTORICAL CONTINGENCY

Gotthold Ephraim Lessing (1729–81), too, was looking for the transhistorical, that is, the "necessary" truths of reason, and famously lamented that he was unable to reach these truths when starting with the contingency of history. His way of speaking about the "broad, ugly ditch" between historical contingency and the "necessary truths of reason" (an expression that is reminiscent of both Leibniz and Spinoza, and that might contain a dose of irony lost on most commentators; Nisbet 2013, 548–50) would prove very influential and signaled one of the key problems in modern theology, as can be seen in the selections below from Georg Wilhelm Friedrich Hegel, Søren Kierkegaard, Martin Kähler, and Karl Barth, among others. The crux of the problem, arguably, has to do with the question of the contemporaneity of past, contingent events. Lessing writes that "reports of fulfilled prophecies are not fulfilled prophecies"; "reports of miracles are not miracles" (see below, 78). Or, to quote one of the key sentences of Lessing's 1777 text on "The Proof of the Spirit and of Power," "Accidental truths of history can never become the proof of necessary truths of reason." The miracles may have happened—Lessing does not contest their factuality—but that does not mean their factuality is demonstrable today. Another miracle would need to happen in order for ancient miracles to affect us today. Until this takes place, reports of miracles are just that: *reports* of miracles. Such reports cannot be binding on anyone. How, then, does one make the leap from historical truths to the necessary truths? "That, then, is the ugly, broad ditch which I cannot get across, however often and however earnestly I have tried to make the leap. If anyone can help me over it, let him do it, I beg him, I adjure him. He will deserve a divine reward from me" (79). The problem of human mediations between God and our contemporary situation is thus a key issue for Lessing, who may have read Rousseau's similar line of reasoning in his fascinating "Profession of Faith of a Savoyard Vicar," in book 4 of his work *Émile, or on Education* (1762), where Rousseau writes:

> Apostle of truth, what have you to tell me of which I am not the sole judge? God himself has spoken; give heed to his revelation. That is another matter. God has spoken, these are indeed words which demand attention. To whom has he spoken? He has spoken to people. Why then have I heard nothing? He has instructed others to make known his words to you. I understand; it is people who come and tell me what God has said. I would rather have heard the words of God himself; it would have been as easy for him and I should have been secure from fraud. He protects you from fraud by showing that his envoys come from him. How does he show this? By miracles. Where are these miracles? In the books. And who wrote the books? People. And who saw the miracles? The people who bear witness to them. What! Nothing but human testimony! Nothing but people who tell me what others told them! How many human beings between God and me! (Rousseau 2013, 312–13)

How should Christian theology respond to this challenge? Various proposals have been made, ranging from a focus on the very contemporaneity of Christ to the believer and on the necessary "leap" of faith (Kierkegaard, who noted that Lessing already envisioned a "leap") and on the actual church proclamation of Christ in the present situation (Kähler), to the critique of Lessing's argument and its perception of a historical abyss between Jesus's life two millennia ago and us, as a way to avoid the scandal of Christ's presence to all times, including our own (Barth).

THE WATERSHED OF THE 1830S—FERDINAND CHRISTIAN BAUR AND DAVID FRIEDRICH STRAUSS

The struggle for and against what came to be called "higher criticism" reached a high point in the 1830s with the publication of important works by Ferdinand Christian Baur (1792–1860) and his student David Friedrich Strauss (1808–74). Of the two, it is Baur who was, by far, the most creative. But it is Strauss who scandalized the most, with his *Life of Jesus* (1835) and his claim that the bulk of the events narrated in the Synoptic Gospels is mythical in nature, and therefore not historical in the modern sense of the term. Strauss was also the first to argue, in contradiction to Friedrich Schleiermacher and Karl A. Hase, against the historical reliability of the fourth Gospel, claiming that John had imposed his way of speaking on John the Baptist and on Jesus. We thus owe Strauss the clear demarcation between the Synoptics and John's Gospel with regard to the traditions concerning Jesus (Kümmel 1973, 124).

With Baur and Strauss, and other lesser-known scholars, the modern historical and critical exegesis gained the upper hand within progressive Protestant academic theology (Morgan 1986–1987, 164). This did not go without massive resistance, as can be seen for instance (examples abound) with the preface and other anonymous articles published by the *Evangelische Kirchenzeitung* in 1836 (see below, 123). The "future of 'our' theology," as the editors of the conservative journal put it, was at stake. Soon, they thought, New Testament scholars would utterly undermine the authority of Scripture by considering the entire Pauline corpus as pseudepigraphic. The chronological proximity of Baur and Strauss should not deceive us: only one of them (Strauss) operated with the category of "myth," and only one of them (Baur) still wished to maintain a tight bond between history and theology (Morgan 2016, 75). Both were influenced by Hegel, but of the two it is Baur who made the most fruitful historical and theological use of the great philosopher's dynamic understanding of historical development, as he sought to locate each writing of early Christianity, including the books of the New Testament, within specific historical trajectories and as a progressive synthesis of two main original strands—namely, Jewish and Gentile Christian communities.

ERNST TROELTSCH'S CHALLENGE

Gabler had recommended a greater demarcation between biblical theology and dogmatic theology. Ernst Troeltsch, at the turn of the twentieth century, called for a major overhaul of dogmatic theology that should abandon all of its supranaturalistic presuppositions, for instance, about Jesus Christ as God's Son in the flesh, and opt for an entirely different starting point—namely, the history of religion. Thus, in Troeltsch's view, by beginning with human history one may discern, in the course of its development, traces of a transcendent reality that unfolds itself within it (Hegel's influence is again perceptible here). This call to a revolution within Christian theology, as Troeltsch summoned it to adjust to the new, modern historical consciousness, was immediately perceived for what it was—namely, a massive challenge—by some of the towering systematic theologians of the late nineteenth century, such as Julius Kaftan (1848–1926) and Wilhelm Herrmann (1846–1922), who were both indebted to Albrecht Ritschl (1822–89) at the time. Since Troeltsch too was somewhat influenced by Ritschl, the Ritschlian school came to be seen as comprising an older generation, represented by Herrmann, Kaftan, Ferdinand Kattenbusch (1851–1935), and others, and a younger one, of which Troeltsch was *the* systematic thinker.

Troeltsch's injunction was drastic and quite impressive: dogmatic theology as we know it no longer has any legitimacy. The modern historical consciousness calls for a full renovation of Christian doctrine. "Once applied to the scientific study of the Bible and church history, the historical method acts as a leaven, transforming everything and ultimately exploding the very form of earlier theological methods" (see below, 170). Its weak spot was, arguably, its use of a Hegelian metaphysic of history, which was Troeltsch's way of "overcoming history through history" (Troeltsch 2008, 1098), and thus of escaping full-blown historical relativism.

In October 1910, only one year after completing his theological studies and not long before his move from Geneva to the village of Safenwil (Aargau, Switzerland), the young Barth, who self-identified as a Herrmannian and thus as a modern theologian, took aim at Troeltsch's program and engaged this version of historicism. In "The Christian Faith and History" (1910), Barth articulated a radical critique of Troeltsch from not only a Ritschlian and a Herrmannian perspective but also from a Calvinist and a Schleiermacherian standpoint. Troeltsch's views on the topic were "totally unsatisfactory and insignificant" (*vollständig ungenügend und unwesentlich*), in the twenty-four-year-old pastor's opinion (Barth 1993, 150–51). The young theologian thought his article "entirely finished him [Troeltsch] up" (Barth 1993, 153). Clearly, Barth did not wait to become the leader of the new dialectical school of theology, in the 1920s, to oppose Troeltsch's program of a history of religion as a replacement of traditional dogmatic theology. Barth's opposition had to do not only with Troeltsch's way of drawing the systematic implications of the new history-of-religion school, but also with William Wrede's call for a New Testament theology, which, in Wrede's own words, "entirely surrenders its specifically theological character" so that the texts of the New Testament would no longer be treated "any differently from any other branch of intellectual history in general or the history of religion in particular" (see below, 166). But that does not mean Barth was simply opposed to modern historical exegesis as such. Other biblical scholars, such as Hermann Gunkel, who like Wrede was also a leading member of the history-of-religion school, certainly did not wish to "surrender" theological exegesis and called instead for new approaches of these texts within modern, historical scholarship:

> There [have] been times when theology had a low standing in the public sphere and when the Old Testament theologian preferred to present himself as an orientalist, as a philologue. Let us be proud of our theology and let us not forget that a commentary of a biblical book which is essentially philological is a deficient commentary, since it leaves out the main thing [*Hauptsache*]! (see below, 189)

It is thus not impossible to find accents before the First World War that anticipate the renewal of theological exegesis within academic theology in the 1920s and up to our day.

THE MODERNIST CRISIS

The challenge of history to Christian theology was not a purely intra-Protestant matter. Roman Catholicism was also severely shaken at the turn of the twentieth century as scholars were trying to overcome an absolutized and static understanding of revelation, dogma, and tradition. One of the key figures here is Alfred Loisy (1857–1940) who, as a Roman Catholic priest, was directly confronting his own church.

Loisy was attempting to more or less pick things up, with regard to biblical criticism, where they had been left since Richard Simon, at least as far as Catholic francophone biblical scholarship was concerned. The task was immense. Until Pope Gregory XVI (1765–1846), even if this rule was not strictly applied (the Gallican church ignored it throughout the seventeenth century), and even if Benedict XIV issued a decree in 1757 allowing for translations of the Bible, the indexes of prohibited books included all of the translations of the Bible in the vernacular (Mayeur 2001, 51). The 1893 encyclical *Providentissimus Deus*, issued by Leo XIII, while promoting the study of Scripture, defended its perfect infallibility, not just in matters of faith and morals but also in its entirety, due to the inspiration not just of its authors but also of the biblical letter itself:

> It is absolutely wrong and forbidden, either to narrow inspiration to certain parts only of Holy Scripture, or to admit that the sacred writer has erred. For the system of those who, in order to rid themselves of these difficulties, do not hesitate to concede that divine inspiration regards the things of faith and morals, and nothing beyond, because (as they wrongly think) in a question of the truth or falsehood of a passage, we should consider not so much what God has said as the reason and purpose which God had in mind in saying it—this system cannot be tolerated. For all the books which the Church receives as sacred and canonical, are written wholly and entirely, with all their parts, at the dictation of the Holy Spirit; and so far is it from being possible that any error can coexist with inspiration, that inspiration not only is essentially incompatible with error, but excludes and rejects it as absolutely and necessarily as it is impossible that God Himself, the supreme Truth, can utter that which is not true. (§20)

Not until Pius XII's encyclical *Divino afflante Spiritu* (1943), on the occasion of the fifty-year anniversary of Leo's encyclical, would Rome allow a greater freedom in the study of Scripture, including textual criticism, "by pointing out what seems necessary in the present day, in order to incite ever more earnestly all those sons of the Church who devote themselves to these studies, to so necessary and so praiseworthy an enterprise" (§2).

But in the final decades of the nineteenth century and the first years of the twentieth, Rome was simply not ready to accept the modern, historical study of Scripture, which it condemned simply as "rationalism."

Loisy was condemned and excommunicated (1908), but it is as a Catholic theologian—and a good one, who had read John Henry Newman's works on the development of doctrine—that he wrote his reply to Adolf von Harnack's *Essence of Christianity* (1901), with his little book *The Gospel and the Church* (1902; *L'Évangile et l'Église*). Loisy's way of siding with Harnack on certain points could not be accepted by Rome. He wrote, for instance, that the "entire gospel is bound up with a conception of the world and of history that is no longer ours" (Loisy 1912, 114). He was also convinced that "a considerable change in the state of knowledge might render necessary a new interpretation of old formulas, which, conceived in another intellectual atmosphere, no longer say what is necessary, or no longer say it suitably" (Loisy 1912, 216). Such pronouncements certainly did not sit well with the fixed and ahistorical interpretation of dogma in the neoscholastic Roman Catholic theology that was at its height at the time.

On February 11, 1903, Loisy wrote that his book did not lead "to the negation of any dogma," but to a "revision of the whole theological education from the standpoint of history, in order to make it positively more authentic" and more clear theoretically in relation to philosophy (Marlé 1960, 85). In 1907, Pope Pius X issued *Lamentabili sane exitu*, an encyclical that condemned sixty-five propositions thought to be typical of the modernists. Among the propositions that were condemned is the following one (twenty-seventh error), another obvious sign of Roman antihistoricism in those years: "*Dogmata quae ecclesia perhibet tamquam revelata, non sunt veritates e coelo delapsae*" ("The dogmas which the Church presents as revealed are not truths which fell from heaven"; Chenu 1985, 26n38). It would take decades, and hard work for many theologians, for the Roman Catholic Church to overcome such pronouncements.

OTHER TWENTIETH-CENTURY DEVELOPMENTS

Eschatology

The rediscovery of eschatology at the turn of the twentieth century was a decisive development within Protestant theology. The scholar behind this rediscovery, Johannes Weiss (1863–1914), did not quite know what to do with this insofar as constructive systematic theology was concerned. Albert Schweitzer ran with Weiss's insights and elaborated a radical interpretation of Jesus's message, retrieving along the way some of Hermann Samuel Reimarus's comments on Jesus's proclamation of the kingdom's imminent coming (see below, 82–83). But Schweitzer, too, struggled to integrate the eschatological nature of Jesus's message into a renewed theological orientation. It is Barth, mainly, with his *Epistle to the Romans* (1919), and Rudolf Bultmann, somewhat derivatively, who first articulated a thorough eschatological interpretation of the Christian faith. Barth found help in the writings of Johann Christoph Blumhardt (1805–80) and his son Christoph Blumhardt (1842–1919), two Pietist pastors of Southern Germany. They had a very keen sense for the ultimate horizon of the Christian faith, which they interpreted as the victory of God's reality. What mattered to them, and later to Barth as well, was not so much the "idea of God" (*Gottesidee*), as was the case of many liberal (and idealist) theologians of the time, but God's "reality" (*Wirklichkeit*) and actual power, which the elder Blumhardt believed he had witnessed in the healing of a parishioner at Christmas in 1843.

So eschatology became a key aspect of the new orientation within Protestant theology right after the First World War, thanks to a convergence of different influences. (Barth met Christoph Blumhardt in Bad Boll in 1915 and, like Bultmann, studied with Johannes Weiss at the University of Marburg.)

Bultmann was deeply impressed by the second edition of Barth's *Romans* commentary. For the rest of his life, Bultmann taught what Barth articulated in 1922 regarding eternity and time; namely, that God's eschatological act *continually* encounters time or becomes present at each present moment. Barth, for his part, alongside this "presentist" interpretation of eschatology, soon aimed to recover a sense of the futurity of the *eschaton*.

If Barth repeatedly claimed that, despite his predilection for theological exegesis, he did not reject the historical and critical method(s), Bultmann, for his part, remained a leading practitioner of these methods, even formulating a new one, which he and others called *Formgeschichte*, or "form criticism," that is, the identification and study of specific genres found especially in the Synoptic Gospels, such as "parables," "narrations," "logia," "parenetic speeches," and so on. Of the two, Bultmann remained more closely affiliated with liberal theology. The modern exegetical methods are useful insofar as they contribute, in Gustav Krüger's (1862–1940) words, "to imperil souls, to lead people into doubt, to shatter all naïve credulity" (see below, 204). Both Bultmann and Barth had no difficulty welcoming Strauss's radical criticism. Barth saw in it a good example of the results one arrives at when one is reading and studying Scripture *kata sarka* (according to the flesh), strictly as a historian.

Scripture and Tradition

The development of the ecumenical movement throughout the past century has led to significant changes in Christian theology. One change has to do with theologians' relationship to theological tradition. After the polemics of the nineteenth century (Friedrich Schleiermacher versus Johann Adam Möhler, Albrecht Ritschl versus mysticism in all of its forms, including Protestant ones), a new epoch began in the 1920s and 1930s as Protestant theologians entered into a fruitful dialogue with their Roman Catholic colleagues (the best example is Karl Barth's new interest in Catholic theology, in part in response to Catholic engagements with his own works, starting with his appointment at the University of Münster in 1925; Dahlke 2012). New ways of perceiving the theological past emerged, among Catholics as well as among Protestants, in each case thanks to the new ecumenical spirit. Roman Catholics began to see the limitations of their neo-Thomist concentration and sought to rediscover the Patristic tradition—including the Greek Fathers—in which rigorous theology and spirituality suffused each other. The launching of the *Sources chrétiennes* series in Lyon during the Second World War (1942) was a major event in this regard (see below, 213). In the 1960s, Catholic scholars began to read the Protestant Reformers constructively, taking them for what they are—namely, highly significant theologians—leaving the century-old polemics behind.

Some Protestant theologians, too, became dissatisfied with a certain narrowing of their key references to the sixteenth-century Protestant Reformers, even as these past voices continued to play a key role in their theological constructs. Barth warned that certain premodern and modern theological voices, which may be quite disagreeable to us, still need to be heard (see below, 200)—Barth was targeting of some his students and their antipathy toward liberal Protestant theology. All of this led to a vast movement, still lively today, especially in the anglophone Protestant world, that refuses superficial and clichéd oppositions to Catholicism (Protestants as people of Scripture versus Catholics as a church of Tradition), based for instance on erroneous interpretations of the Protestant motto *sola scriptura*, as if this means "*solitaria scriptura*" (Barth 1968a, 49). The results of this movement are numerous: Protestant scholars study the Fathers and medieval thinkers and are ready to learn from them—to the point where their theologies betray Thomist notes, as with the late John Webster, to the point even where some became Catholic themselves (a move Barth and his friends were never seriously inclined to make, even as he saw esteemed colleagues, such as Erik Peterson in 1930, make that decision). This broadening of theological sources among Catholics and Protestants is an important development in twentieth-century theology that continues to influence the field today. The vast history of Christian theology also challenges us today not to restrict it too quickly, not to focus too narrowly on our favorite authors, but to listen attentively to many of its voices.

Feminist Approaches

This vast history includes voices of women, which have often been ignored or even silenced and which feminist approaches have begun to recover. This new approach within Christian theology has taken various, more or less radical, forms. In the past fifty years or so—following nineteenth-century pioneers, such as Elizabeth Cady Stanton (1815–1902) and her *Woman's Bible* (1895)—feminist scholars have embarked on a huge effort to retrieve women's voices, in Scripture and in history. The past challenges us to listen to *all* of its voices, even those that male ecclesiastical leaders tried to marginalize or suppress in the course of history (see below, 228). The fact that the present anthology only includes one female voice is bound to provoke critical reactions. This can be interpreted as a failure of the kind of listening that was just mentioned and as a further example of the marginalizing of women. But isn't it the case that, until recently (roughly the middle of the twentieth century), almost all of the scholars who in the past five hundred years have contributed to the questions history addresses to theology have been males?

This of course only confirms the importance of fostering women voices in academic theology today.

HUMAN HISTORY AS HISTORY OF EVIL AND INJUSTICE

Theology and "the challenge of history" can mean different things: it can mean the emergence of historical scholarship as applied to Scripture (the present anthology places a big emphasis on this development in Christian thought), or the awareness of the historicity of any dogmatic pronouncement and indeed of any theological assertion—on this last aspect Troeltsch remains a compelling thinker. It can also mean, as we just saw, the retrieval of the Christian tradition, broadly conceived, for the sake of contemporary constructive efforts. But it can also mean the challenge that human history, as well as natural history, represents for certain traditional theological *loci*, such as, first and foremost, the topic of divine providence. In the sixteenth century, major theological voices had fairly clear answers to the problem of evil: in times of joy and prosperity, gratitude to God and solidarity with the less fortunate is in order, whereas in times of distress and trials the Christian must practice patience and endurance. The debates that developed in the wake of the Lisbon earthquake (November 1, 1755) signal that the old view of divine providence was no longer convincing, at least to those who had Deist tendencies, such as Voltaire. In a major shift with regard to ancient and modern theodicies, evil becomes an enigma, something that cannot be solved. As far as human responsibility is concerned, after Karl Marx and other socialist thinkers, Christian theology began to place a new emphasis on conversion, not just of the individual but also of the church and indeed of humanity as a whole. Human history is, to an extent, the history of evils committed by human beings on other human beings: that history too is a challenge to theology, not so much at the anthropological level, since Christian theology has often had a robust sense of human sinfulness, but rather in relation to the conviction that God is "in charge" of the world and providentially cares for it. Evils and injustice committed by humans have been nothing new, of course. But something happened in the modern era that led major thinkers no longer to accept the old answers. The atrocities of the twentieth century—the Cambodian killing fields, Rwanda in 1994, the Stalinist gulag, and especially Nazi Germany's death camps—mount a massive challenge to Christian theology and its trust in God who cares and provides for the world and especially for the little ones. Certainly, the Christian faith has significant resources, not for "solving" the problem but for considering the evil committed by human beings in relation to the one who is at the heart of what it believes in—namely, Jesus of Nazareth, the Christ of God. Christian theology since the end of the nineteenth century has repeatedly and rightly emphasized that the Christian faith is always a faith that orients itself toward history: not a salvation history which would be a specific strand distinct from "general" history, but rather a history that is part and parcel of human history, that irradiates far and wide within that history. Christian theology in the twentieth century has often, and rightly, moved away from notions of divine "timelessness" to emphasize instead the crucial historicity of God's revelation, as well as

God's faithfulness to humanity and the world, despite all the injustices and evils human beings inflict on one another, despite their unfaithfulness to God. If one thing stands out in the scriptural witness, it is that God does not simply hover above history. Incarnational motifs are found throughout the Bible, as God makes covenants with humanity and with Israel, as God's word comes out from God's mouth and does not return to God empty (Isa 55:10–11). And since this word is the word of One who is righteous, we should not be surprised to find in recent and contemporary theology stark reminders of God's involvement in history and of what that means for Christian communities around the world (in the present anthology, see the excerpts by Walter Rauschenbusch, Marie-Dominique Chenu, Elisabeth Schüssler Fiorenza, and Ignacio Ellacuría; a number of prominent political theologians, such as Jürgen Moltmann and Johann Baptist Metz, could also have been included in the volume). In this way too, then, human history, our history, has been and continues to be a challenge for theology.

Christophe Chalamet, editor

Notes on the Edition and the Translation of Texts

Pages in the original edition from which the selections are excerpted appear in square brackets (e.g.: [234]). Unless otherwise noted, all footnotes are those of this editor. Additionally, some of the footnotes in the original texts have been suppressed, especially when they concern references to scholarly literature of the time.

The selections have been modernized here and there, especially for works originally published in languages other than English but translated into English a century or more ago; for example, the word *Mensch* ("the human"), used by Germanophone scholars, was sometimes translated into English using the word *men*. In such cases a gender-neutral translation was introduced. Attempts at modernizing older text were much more limited with regard to selections from anglophone thinkers, such as John Locke or Thomas Hobbes, in order to respect their own prose. The decisive criterion for modifying their texts had to do with the intelligibility of their texts. The translations of selections by Sebastian Castellio, Johann Salomo Semler, Ferdinand Christian Baur, Alfred Loisy, and Hermann Gunkel were made by the volume editor. Some of the published translations of selected German or French texts included in the anthology were revised for a more accurate rendering of the original non-English versions.

1.

Erasmus of Rotterdam (1466–1536)

Having studied in France, England, and Italy, among other countries, Erasmus of Rotterdam moved to Basel in 1514 and soon planned, with printer Johannes Froben, the publication of his Greek and Latin New Testament and of his annotations to the New Testament. They were published in two volumes, totaling nearly one thousand pages, in 1516, with the title *Novum Instrumentum*, a title that became *Novum Testamentum* for the second, expanded edition (1519). While preparing this second edition, Erasmus became convinced of the need to present in greater detail the new methodology he had outlined in the first edition. In 1518, he wrote his *Ratio verae theologiae* to that effect, publishing it separately in 1518 as well as jointly with his exegetical notes a year later (Conroy 1974, 64). The original title of this work, in its first edition (published in November 1518 in Louvain by Theodorus Martinus), is *Ratio seu methodus compendio perveniendi ad veram theologiam* (The Procedure or Method of Concisely Arriving at True Theology). Only one complete copy of that edition has been preserved, at Oxford. The treatise was published a second time, in January 1519, with a shorter title: *Ratio seu compendium verae theologiae* (Method or Short Summary of True Theology) (Conroy 1974, 367).

The goal of the book, which has been somewhat neglected in Erasmian studies (Conroy 1974, 65), is simple: "to invite young men to the best method of studying" and to "enkindle the heart of people to the study of theology" (Conroy 1974, 99 and 71). As he was writing and publishing this treatise, Erasmus was associated with the creation of the Collegium Trilingue in Louvain (1518), an institution that, by promoting the study of the two biblical languages as well as Latin, was meant to profoundly reshape theological studies.

Erasmus built on Lorenzo Valla, whose pioneering work he praised (Oberman 1966, 308–15). What we see in this treatise is one of the earliest instances of the historical, philological exegesis that then became ubiquitous in the modern era. It is a "true hermeneutical manifesto of modern times" (Laplanche 1986, 44).

The following excerpts come from Donald B. Conroy, "The Ecumenical Theology of

Erasmus of Rotterdam: A Study of the 'Ratio Verae Theologiae'" (PhD diss., University of Pittsburgh, 1974). For a modern edition of the Latin original, with a German translation, see Erasmus 1967.

METHOD OR SHORT SUMMARY FOR REACHING TRUE THEOLOGY (1519)

[80] For truly theological wisdom, [Saint James] contends, is "above all pure and, in addition, it is modest, peaceful, obedient, full of [81] mercy and good fruits, and devoid of partiality and hypocrisy" [James 3:17]. Now with regard to those literary studies, with whose aid we more skillfully attain to these virtues, our primary concern must without question be to learn thoroughly the three languages of Latin, Greek, and Hebrew, because it is evident that all the Sacred Scriptures have been recorded in these languages. . . . For just as no one can decipher what is written without knowing the alphabet, so no one is able to understand what he reads without a knowledge of the languages. Indeed, my dear reader, do not immediately recoil from me as you are taken aback by the difficulty of the task, as if beaten back with a club. If the right spirit is present, if a capable teacher is available, these three languages can be learned [82] almost with less effort than required today when learning the detestable babbling of a single "half-language." The difficulty is undoubtedly due to the lack of knowledge and the incompetency of teachers. . . .

[83] It is sufficient if you arrive at some reasonable finesse and facility, that is, at a certain middling linguistic ability which is adequate for forming a judgment. For, setting aside all the other humane disciplines for now, on no account can it happen that you would come to understand the written text if you should be ignorant of the language in which it is written. . . .

[99] If someone in connection with this matter[1] is looking for a fitting proof, let him contrast and compare those old theologians such as Origen, Basil, Chrysostom, and Jerome with these more recent ones. He will see how with the former a golden river, so to speak, is flowing, whereas here among the latter some tiny rivulets flow and these are neither altogether pure nor commensurate with their source. Among the former thunder the oracles of eternal truth; with the latter you hear the little chatter of humans, whose narratives vanish like empty dreams the more closely you inspect them. With the former you will be directed on the right course toward the harbor of evangelical truth; with the latter you [100] tire yourself struggling among the windings of human questions or you dash yourself against the Scylla of pontifical power or into the Syrtes of scholastic teachings or into the Symplegades (unless you prefer to make it the Charybdis) of divine and human law. With the former, supported by the firm foundations of the Scriptures, the building rises upward; with the latter through the futile sophistry of man or, even at times, his cringing flattery is as fickle as a huge make-shift scaffolding which is built up to a monstrous size. With the former you will be, as it were, very delighted and satisfied in the gardens of supreme happiness; while with the latter you will lacerate and torture yourself among the barren thornbushes. With the former everything is filled with majesty, while with the latter there is just nothing magnificent so that you will find much shabbiness and so little worthy of theological dignity. . . .

[103] In other professions it is considered very laudable, as indeed it is, if one mentions his predecessors and his sources. Virgil expressly mentions Homer; Theocrites also refers to Hesiodes; Horace mentions Pindar and Anacreon; Avicenna mentions Galen; Galen, Hippocrates; Cicero, Demosthenes; Xenophon, Plato; Aristotle, who treated of many topics, mentions various authors for diverse arguments; Theophrastus, Themistius and Averroes in turn mention Aristotle. Why have we alone dared to leave out the predecessors of our philosophy from the whole procedure of our discussions? . . .

[108] Yet it is the extraordinary goal of theologians to recount the Holy Scriptures in a wise manner, to render an account of the faith and not of foolish questions, to discuss spirituality seriously

1. Erasmus is decrying "the thorny subtleties and the spiritless worries about problems" (98) which are rampant in scholastic theology.

and effectively, to elicit tears of contrition and to enflame hearts for the things of heaven. Already from the outset of his studies the future theologian should have exercise in these matters rather than grow old in strange scholarship. In my opinion it would pertain much more to the matter at hand if our young beginner be given the teachings written up in summary or in a concise form. This would be first of all from the evangelical sources, and then from the apostolic letters, so that in every matter he may have fixed objectives, which he can relate to that which he reads, such as, to mention one small example, that the heavenly Christ, [109] who is the new teacher, has instituted a new people on earth. . . .

[135] The same thing, I believe, that has been said about the laws instituted by men must be taught concerning the writings of the ancient and the recent doctors; we should not be so dependent upon them that we would consider it a crime to be of different opinion in some matters. . . . The authors themselves do not wish to be given such weight. . . .

[150] To a certain extent everything is to be venerated, but what endures must be read, and even imitated, with discretion and sound judgment. Nor would it, perhaps, be foolish to establish an authoritative order among the sacred books, too. This is something that Augustine was not afraid to do. For the first rank belongs to those books about which there never was any doubt among the ancients. In my opinion, Isaiah certainly carries more weight than Judith or Esther, the Gospel of Matthew more than the Apocalypse ascribed to John, the epistles of Paul to the Romans and the Corinthians more than the epistle written to the Hebrews. The place next in order to these is taken up by certain writings passed down to us, as it were, hand to hand either from the apostles themselves passed over to us or, indeed, [151] from those who were close to apostolic times. Among this number I especially place the Confession of faith published, if I am not mistaken, at the Council of Nicea, which is commonly designated as the Apostles'. . . .

[318] Indeed, the theological student must above all also be advised to learn thoroughly how to cite the testimony of Sacred Scripture in an appropriate fashion. This should not be from summaries and anthologies or shabby little essays or other collections of this type, which have for the hundredth time already been mixed up and redone somewhere by someone other than from the sources themselves. Nor should he imitate those who are unashamed to twist violently the prophetic utterances of divine wisdom into strange meanings, sometimes even into their contrary significances. To keep this from [319] happening, let it be our principal care to learn thoroughly from those ancient interpreters the teaching contained in all of the books of the Old and New Testament. . . .

[340] Therefore, we accord the primary honor to the New Testament through which we are Christians, and in which Christ is depicted for us much more distinctly than in the Old Testament. Then in the second place comes the Old Testament and within it those books which agree most with the New, such as the books of Isaiah. If, after arranging the passages as I have described above,[2] you frequently compare the Pauline epistles with the gospels and both of these with Isaiah and the remainder of the Old Testament, then it will happen that they will automatically and spontaneously adhere and be fixed in your memory. If this toil were to deter someone, I ask him to consider within himself the following. How does it happen that a future theologian can learn the sophistical pronouncements, that he can learn all sorts of commentaries on Aristotle or even a paraphrase of him, that he can learn the statements of Scotus which they call the *Argumenta*, and yet the same fellow is reluctant to expend some effort on the Holy Books from whose wellsprings all theology, that is true theology, gushes forth?

[341] But how much more worthwhile is it to devour at one time this amount of work (for I would never call it toil) than to be always running around in a circle with additional work to be done as often as something must be dealt with or quoted and to take refuge in dictionaries, summaries and anthologies! . . .

Consequently, when you have given up on these confused formularies and the muddy puddles of the summaries, then make your heart itself into a library of Christ [*bibliotheca Christi*; Erasmus

2. Erasmus recommends creating cards with the relevant biblical passages according to the theme(s) one is studying (Conroy 1974, 334–35).

1967, 462]. From it, like from the provident householder, you can bring forth "new things and old" as they should be needed. For these things which come from your own heart, as it were, practically alive, penetrate far more vividly into the souls of your listeners than those things which are gathered up from a hodge-podge of other authors. . . .

[342] In fact, the work of the [343] ancients should relieve us of part of the labor; we are aided by their commentaries so long as we only select the best among them, such as Origen, who is the foremost, so that no one else can be compared to him. Then after him there is Basil, Nazianzen, Athanasius, Cyril, Chrysostom, Jerome, Ambrose, Hilary, and Augustine. We should, hereafter, read even these authors with critical judgment and discretion, although I wish them to be read with reverence. They were human beings; some things they did not know; they were deceived in some matters; at times they got tired; they gave their utmost to overcoming heresies by whose arguments everything at that time was stirred up; they presented certain topics for the ears of those to whom they were then speaking.

Furthermore, there is scarcely anyone of them, under whose false signature quite a lot was circulated. . . . [344] Therefore, there should be discretion not only regarding authors but with respect to works as well. Also, among authors a differentiation exists not only in the fact that the Greeks are superior to the Latins and the ancients excel over the more modern ones, but also that even within the individual types one is superior to the other. For instance, no one teaches more fluently than Origen; none deals with common passages more successfully than John Chrysostom; in the interpretation of Sacred Literature Jerome has earned no ordinary praise; Thomas is more lucid and Scotus is more subtle. Take care in their works that you do not embrace the counterfeit and the substitute for the genuine and the true.

[345] However, with the number of books and the fleeting nature of life, one does not have the free time to read through everything; there is nothing left but to read the best first. Why then be concerned about spending valuable hours in an unprofitable manner with recent authors who are more accumulators than interpreters? . . . [346] If we are constantly involved in unproductive, indolent, superficial, thorny, and contentious writers, then we will necessarily become like them ourselves. If, on the contrary, we associate with those who truly know Christ, who are fervent, who are alive and active, who both teach and exemplify true devotion, then we should reflect them, at least to some extent.

But, you will say, if nothing else is added, I shall be poorly educated for scholastic debates. Truly, we are not developing prizefighters, but theologians, and that kind of theologian who prefers to express what he professes to be by living rather than by syllogisms. Nor is this something that you should fret about, namely, whether you should be [347] considered little among those theologians, since among these persons not even Jerome, and perhaps not Paul himself, would have an idea of what to answer. The fault does not lie with theology itself, which did not originate in this manner, but rather with the manner of treating it by certain people who have reduced the total study of theology to the subtleties of the dialecticians and the philosophy of Aristotle. In that situation it is more like philosophy than theology. . . .

[355] It was not said to them [students of theology] that they should add this: "Search the philosophy of Aristotle. Perhaps the resurrection of the dead can be taught with its assistance." But rather: "Search the Scriptures." . . . Therefore, we must deeply ponder Sacred Literature as far as our diligence leads us to those matters which Paul has mentioned. However, those who have not set this objective for themselves, but rather do this in order to bring forth some puzzles and novelties to capture the admiration of the population which always marvels at foolish things, become idle talkers instead of theologians. . . .

[356] Even these things could still be endured if this story telling were confined within the walls of college buildings. Now this foolish display has penetrated the sacred sermons. . . . How often I have felt ashamed of this state of affairs! How often I have lamented the situation of the people! I see the simple mass of people gaping and eagerly hanging on the words of the preacher and expecting nourishment for their soul as they are desirous of learning how they can return home in a better condition. There some theologaster—like a "sacred personage" to be venerated—brings forward some absurd and perplexing question from Scotus or

Occam, while showing how much he accomplished at the Sorbonne and pursuing the people's favor by this exhibition. Meanwhile, a large part of the assembly return home almost as "hungry as wolves," according to the Greek proverb. . . .

[364] Let whoever enjoys scholastic disputations really follow his own judgment on what has been accepted in the schools—only he should not do this exclusively, nor attribute too much to the teachings of a school, nor pursue these teachings too long. For I have seen several men who were already half gray trying to return to grace with that pristine theology. But anyone who attempted this task too late succeeded but little.

If, however, one wants to be more informed regarding devotion than disputation, then let him immediately and most importantly go to the sources, let him turn to those writers who most directly have drunk from the fonts. Should there have arisen any doubt in these matters which pertain to [365] true devotion, then an upright and prudent man will not lack an answer from the Sacred Prophecies which will lead to salvation. . . . The theologian derives his name from the word of God [*a divinis oraculis*], not from human theories [*ab humanis opinionibus*; Erasmus 1967, 492].

2.

Sebastian Castellio (1515–63)

Born in 1515 into a farming family of Savoy, between Lyon and Geneva, Sebastian Castellio studied the humanities in Lyon and, as three partisans of Luther's ideas were executed in Lyon in 1540, embraced the Reform movement. He first met John Calvin, who was six years older than him, in Strasbourg in 1540, even staying at Calvin's house. A year later, after Calvin's return to Geneva, Castellio was named rector of Geneva's gymnasium (Collège de Rive, now Collège Calvin). After a clash with Calvin, he moved to Basel in 1545, where he worked for a printer before becoming a professor of Greek in 1553. In 1551 he published a Latin translation of the Bible (*Biblia interprete Sebastiano Castalione una cum eiusdem annotationibus*), followed by a French version in 1555 (*La Bible nouvellement translatée* . . . ; Castellio 2005). After the death of Michael Servetus at the stake (October 27, 1553), he published a collection of texts opposing capital punishment for heretics (*De haereticis, an sint peresquendi* . . . , 1553). He also published editions of ancient Greek authors (Xenophon, Herodotus, Homer, Thucydides), the *Theologia deutsch*, the *Imitatio Christi*, and other works of medieval devotion.

Those who know anything about Castellio are usually familiar with him as a forerunner of modern interpretations of tolerance, rather than as a pioneer in the critical and historical interpretation of Scripture. His sentences, directed at Calvin and the Genevan authorities in the wake of Servetus's execution, are justly famous: "In killing a man, one does not protect a doctrine; one simply kills a man. When the Genevans killed Servetus, they did not defend a doctrine, they killed a man."[1] But there is another side to Castellio, insofar as he proposes a way of reading and interpreting Scripture that is quite sophisticated: he suggests Scripture contains four main types of discourses—namely, revelation (*patefactio*), knowledge (*cognitio*), prophecy (*vaticinatio*), and teaching (*doctrina*). This

1. "Hominem occidere, non est doctrinam tueri, sed est hominem occidere. Cum Genevenses Servetum occiderunt, non doctrinam defenderunt, sed hominem occiderunt." S. Castellio, *Contra Libellum Calvini in quo ostendere conatur Haereticos jure gladii coercendos esse*, §77. Written in 1555, this treatise was first published anonymously, without any mention of place or publisher, in Holland in 1612 (without pagination). The Latin quotation comes from this edition.

highly original argument for the sake of distinguishing between various genres within Scripture remained without any effect or influence at the time, for the simple reason that his treatise "On the art of doubting and trusting, ignoring and knowing" (*De arte dubitandi*), which he began to write in 1563, only months before his death, remained unpublished until 1937!

The text below is a translation, by the editor, of excerpts from Sébastien Castellion, *De l'art de douter et de croire, d'ignorer et de savoir*, French trans. Charles Baudoin (Geneva-Paris: Jeheber, 1953). The page numbers follow Baudoin's edition. For the critical Latin edition of this work, see Sébastien Castellion, *De arte dubitandi et confidendi, ignorandi et sciendi*, ed. Elisabeth Feist Hirsch (Leiden: Brill, 1981).[2]

ON THE ART OF DOUBTING AND TRUSTING, NOT KNOWING AND KNOWING (1563)

[57] §11. Here three difficulties arise. First, there are in the holy Scriptures certain things which seem absurd or unworthy of God's majesty. For instance when it is said of Moses (Exod. 33:18s) that he was put in a cleft of the rock, that God covered him with his hand and, God having passed, that Moses saw God's back, but not God's face. Or when God ordered the Israelites (Exod. 29:18 *passim*) to offer burnt animals, grilling their skin so that the odor would reach God's nostrils, as if God were feasting on the smell of flesh. The same is true of the tabernacle, the temple, clothing, and ceremonies, which God [58] prescribes as if God were enjoying the same kind of pleasures as human beings; and there are many passages which contain some kind of absurdity.

The second difficulty lies in the fact that the Scriptures seem, in certain places, to contradict themselves, in the narratives just as in the thoughts.

This leads to the third difficulty, namely that interpreters, through their words as well as their writings, teach certain theses which are not only different but which often contradict each other, and yet their theses are grounded on the authority of Scripture. As a result, people who do not lack in virtue and intelligence remain hesitant and perplexed.

On the first point, here is my answer. We see many things which are done, in nature as in art, and which, if we consider them in themselves, appear repugnant and absurd. And yet if you consider their end, you must conclude that they are done in the best fashion and very wisely—unless one wishes to simply repudiate nature and art. Let us first consider nature. How does it give birth, and does it nourish a human being? The human being is conceived in the woman's uterus, near organs which contain excrement and urine. . . . But if one considers the final end, if one considers what is a human being, if one thinks about this noble and divine animal to whom such destinies are promised, then one will conclude that nothing wiser can be imagined than this stupidity of nature, which [59] knows how to produce so wonderfully such a brave being from so much refuse.

§12. As concerns the second difficulty, namely the discordance or even the contradiction which seems to exist between different passages of Scripture, it must be known that such discordance may be found either in the words or in the things themselves. Let us first consider the words. The disagreement among words may come from copyists or from the authors. The discordance of copyists can be seen in various examples, where we see that the same passage may be read in different ways, as many [61] commentators have noted in very many passages. But this discordance must not shock us: to begin with, it comes from copyists, not from the authors, who thus cannot be held

2. A first, slightly incomplete Latin edition, already prepared by Elisabeth Feist Hirsch on the basis of Castellio's handwritten manuscript, was published in 1937 in *Per la storia degli eretici italiani del secolo XVI in Europa*, *Reale accademia d'Italia, Studi e documenti*, vol. 11, ed. Delio Cantimori and Elisabeth Feist (Rome: Reale accademia d'Italia), 307–403.

responsible for this; in addition, very often the discordance concerns one term or another, without compromising the meaning. Even if the meaning is compromised, it can be reestablished through the context—as long as the interpretation of the authors does not proceed through the scrupulous [*superstitiosus*][3] examination of each word, but rather, more often, by paying attention to the general tone of the speech—through the confirmation which comes from similar passages, or finally through reflection, as we shall argue later, God willing.

Similar discordances among copyists can be found in profane authors: in Plato, Aristotle, Homer, Cicero, Virgil, and all the others. Even though these authors have always been highly regarded among Gentiles, and recopied with extreme care, errors and divergences have made their way in the course of time. This fact does not discourage those who have a scholarly inclination, it does not lead them to think that the books which are attributed to Cicero are not good or are not Cicero's. When some of the shoots of a tree are crooked, or even broken, the farmer is not worried and the tree is not in trouble, for it flourishes in all directions in such a multitude of branches that such a small loss is compensated elsewhere without any harm. Similarly, if such an accident occurs in a passage of a text, a sound reader is not shocked and the author does not suffer from it. The trunk—the trunk of the author, if I may put it this way—remains; thanks to the general tone of his speech and to the abundance of his words, it is always possible to collect, without any harm, all of the fruits.

§13. But on this point two qualms arise. First, some find it inconceivable that God may have [62] accepted that even one word of Scripture became altered. Others fear that if this is conceded, then the authority of Scripture may collapse; for if we begin to doubt certain words here and there, are we not going to cast doubt on the authors as a whole? To the first difficulty, here is my reply: nowhere God has promised that he would direct the hand of the copyists in such a way that they would never err; God did not even promise to make sure none of the holy books would become lost. I therefore ask these contradictors to demonstrate the plausibility of their views. For we see that copyists have erred, we see some making mistakes today, and we see some of the holy books succumb to the hardship of time (even though we have reason to believe that God was more concerned about them than about a few isolated words). If they argue that God must show a concern for the holy Scriptures since God is their author, I will reply that God must show a much greater concern for God's children; namely, God's people, for whom God dictated the holy Scriptures. But God has tolerated not that this people should die (God has always preserved them from this), but that they may be decimated to such an extent that, out of this multitude, which is more numerous than grains of sand, only a feeble remnant remains. Must we be surprised, then, that God allowed Scripture to endure some mutilations? If reason shows that it could have happened, and if experience teaches that it did indeed happen, then I do not see why it is so difficult to admit this.

On the second point, I reply that the authority of authors does not reside in these or those words, which could have been adulterated or omitted, but rather in the general tone of the speech, a tone which remains unaltered. Cicero did not lose any of his authority, among those who studiously read him, because of several small passages which were adulterated or tweaked; in the same manner, the authority of the holy Scriptures must not suffer in any way if certain accidents, such as those we described, happened to them.

[63] Concerning discordances between words which come from authors and not from copyists, we do not need to worry either. What is true of testimonies is also true of authors: the wording which is used in order to report something is not important; what matters is the sincerity and accuracy of the report. For authors must be at the service of the realities [*rebus*], and words at the service of authors; not the other way around.

§14. But the discordance of things confronts us with a greater difficulty, about which I would rather remain silent, in order not to hurt the weak and also not to arouse the hatred of the malicious—something which, as a matter of fact, in this discussion, may scarcely be avoided, or indeed, let us admit it frankly, cannot be avoided. And

3. The Latin edition mentions a copy that replaces the word *superstitiosus* with *scrupulosos* (Feist Hirsch 1981, 41n22).

yet without this explanation I cannot fulfill my intention, nor can I bring to light, concerning the things which are necessary for the tranquility of conscience, the truth which until now is hidden: I must therefore dare. Often, at first sight, things are displeasing because they are new. But when one takes a closer look, they are pleasing and we approve of them. We must first know that there are four kinds of texts in the holy Scriptures. Since Paul alludes to this, I will quote here some words from the First Epistle to the Corinthians: "Indeed, my brethren," he writes, "if I came among you speaking unknown tongues, how would I be useful to you, if I did not make you hear what I would be saying to you through revelation [*patefactio*], through knowledge [*cognitio*], through prophecy [*vaticinatio*], or teaching [*doctrina*]?"[4] There can be talk of "revelation," according to the apostle, if something is revealed to the human being by God himself. "Prophecy" is the same thing as revelation, except that it is accompanied by an exaltation and a deep tremor of the spirit. I take "knowledge" to derive naturally from things which are seen or heard. Finally, I think that by "doctrine" Paul meant what human beings draw from the Scriptures and reason.

[64] But even if Paul and no one else had said this, the matter would not be any less true in itself, and we would have to acknowledge these four kinds of texts among the sacred authors. For they wrote as they were accustomed to speak among themselves of divine things; their intelligence, their science, and their spirit were not different as they wrote or as they spoke, and their writings are nothing but their conversations with absent people or with posterity. This can be shown easily. . . . That being said, we need to study the sacred authors in such a way as not to confuse these three things: revelation, knowledge, and doctrine; the parts which we have received from revelation must be taken to be God's own word; those which pertain to knowledge are testimonies; those which proceed from doctrine are human opinions. Let us then confer to each kind of text a value which corresponds to its nature. This way we will avoid the troubling questions which come from the ignorance of this distinction and which can be resolved only when this distinction is known and accepted. Therefore, if there are discordances or contradictions within the sacred texts, we will [65] have to carefully ponder whether it happens in God's word, in the testimonies, or in the human opinions.

If it happens in the word of God, we will have to examine with the greatest care all of the circumstances of time, place, people, occasions, and causes, until the apparent discordance is transformed to our eyes into a concord. If we are unable to reach that point, we will have to accuse our ignorance and recognize that we miss certain elements through which, if we possessed them, we would see the most perfect coherence reestablished. For the Spirit of truth, who is the author of these revelations, cannot be in discordance with himself, and neither forgetfulness, nor error, nor ignorance can be attributed to him.

If the difficulty pertains to the testimonies, we should not be too scrupulous and we do not need to consider so meticulously each word, confronting them with others; we will have to content ourselves with a general agreement. Laws, whether profane or sacred, rightly compel to accept the testimony of two or three witnesses even though testimonies of this sort, despite the witnesses' probity and truthfulness, seldom agree word for word (especially when they have to do with small or muddled matters). With regard to the testimonies of the sacred authors too, we must imitate this just prudence of the laws, we should not be too demanding. If we were demanding, what would happen? Two things might happen: no author, neither sacred nor profane, would satisfy us. Or, striving hard to reconcile minute details which cannot be reconciled, we would become foolish, even ridiculous people.

What I have said about testimonies also applies to human opinions: the same importance must be conferred to them as to the words of the saints, or the importance which the testimonies' authors themselves attribute to them; but they should not be placed at the same level as the word of God: they themselves do not expect this from us.

[66] §15. I do not doubt that some will be shocked by this! They will call it blasphemy. The

4. Castellio is quoting his own Latin translation of the Bible (1 Cor 14:6): *Biblia interprete Sebastiano Castalione una cum eiusdem annotationibus* (Basel: Jacob Parc and Johannes Oporin, 1551), 202. The Vulgate gives different, less surprising nouns, namely, *revelatio*, *scientia*, *prophetia*, and *doctrina*.

holy Scriptures, in their view, were written under the divine Spirit; they saw the light of day because of God's will, not because of human beings; and if one questions one single word, then the risk is that their entire authority may be denied. I ask these contradictors not to judge what I am saying before studying my statements with the necessary care. I am not inclined to devalue holy Scripture. Until now in my life I have shared the doctrine of those who might question me, and I hope to continue living like this until the end. I pray God to take my life rather than letting me live without abiding by such a holy and divine doctrine. At the same time, I think we need to steer clear of the scrupulous zeal of certain people, whom I would not consider evil, but who, fastening themselves quite stubbornly and unnecessarily to this or that word, imprudently trouble the Church; they have provoked discords, and I do not know how it might be possible to return to an agreement. . . .

[69] §16. This is not the place to consider the points which might be raised against my views. Someone might say that my arguments are likely to undermine the authority of the holy Scriptures and diminish the faith which is placed in them. To this I would answer that, even if this were the case, it does not yet address the truth of the opinions I have expressed; or, if someone considers the opinions I am presenting here to be false, then he should refute them. If they are true—as they indeed are—then it will be important to pay heed to them . . . . The authority of the holy Scriptures does not reside in some short passages which should be [70] scrupulously discussed, but rather in the tone and the body itself of the doctrine, as we have already indicated. . . .

[73] Such are the difficulties which this thesis raises; they are significant, it seems to me, and I do not see how they can be simply avoided. Let us then conclude that, in holy Scripture, the opinions and testimonies of human beings should not be placed on the same level as God's word.

3.

Louis Cappel (1585–1658)

Louis Cappel was a Calvinist (Reformed) scholar who dedicated much of his life to the *ars critica*, the art of criticism, as a student at Oxford for two years, at several universities in Germany and Holland, then in 1614 as a professor of Hebrew, and finally, starting in 1633, as a professor of theology at the Reformed Academy of Saumur, in the Loire valley, where he trained young biblical scholars, such as Samuel Bochart (1599–1667).[1] His *Critica sacra, or On the Various Readings which are Found in the Sacred Books of the Old Testament* (*Critica sacra, sive de variis quae in sacris veteris Testamenti libris occurrunt lectionibus libri VI*) (1650), which remains untranslated into any language, is a monument in the history of early biblical textual criticism. Since Protestant publishers in Switzerland and Holland refused to publish it, Cappel's son, Jean, who had become Catholic, secured support from French Catholics. No less than Hugo Grotius supported the publication of Cappel's work, which he thought surpassed what had been accomplished by previous scholars. In his *Annotationes ad Vetus Testamentum* from 1644, Grotius described Cappel as "most learned" (*eruditissimus*). But Grotius warned him, already in 1635 upon reading the completed manuscript, that Cappel would not find broad support for his results, even among eminent scholars (*paucos eminentes sequantur*) (Groetsch 2015, 129). French Catholic editors Sébastien and Gabriel Cramoisy thus published the book in Paris. Its title, with the daring juxtaposition of *critica* and *sacra*, is an event unto itself in the history of ideas (Delforge 1989, 330; Laplanche 1986, 229–30). And yet Cappel's intention, when compared to later criticism, was limited: his aim was to expunge Scripture of errors that had made their way into the text through the inattention of scribes. He was convinced that "every truth comes from God" and sought to apply to the text of Scripture the criticism of ancient literature practiced, for instance, by the Genevan printer and scholar

1. Bochart was a Reformed pastor in the city of Caen who became a phenomenal expert of more than a dozen (mostly ancient and Asian) languages. His *Geographia sacra, seu Phaleg et Canaan* (Caen: Pierre de Cardonel, 1646) made him famous in learned circles throughout Europe. In 1650, Queen Christina of Sweden invited him to reside in Stockholm (she invited René Descartes and Hugo Grotius as well). Two years later, Bochart spent a year as a guest in her royal palace. See Laplanche 1986, 250–53.

Henri Estienne (1528–98), the son of the well-known printer Robert Estienne. Cappel's aim certainly was not to undermine the authority of Scripture, but rather to provide a better, more accurate version of the biblical text. Knowing that his intent could easily be misconstrued, he tried to prevent outright rejection of his work, assuring that he was no *novatorem* (Cappel 1650, 396). Like other defenders of biblical criticism (see Meyer 1666, title page; Baur below, 135), Cappel was fond of quoting the apostle Paul's well-known injunction in order to defend his own scholarship: "Omnia probate, quod bonum est retinete" (test everything; hold fast what is good) (1 Thess. 5:21; Cappel 1650, 557).

The following selections come from *Critica sacra* (Paris: Sébastien & Gabriel Cramoisy, 1650). They were first translated into French by Kevin Bovier, then into English by the editor.

CRITICA SACRA, OR ON THE VARIOUS READINGS WHICH ARE FOUND IN THE SACRED BOOKS OF THE OLD TESTAMENT (1650)

Book 6, chapter 1

[384] §1. *That the current Hebrew text, with its letters and signs, does not always present to us the lesson which was found in the autographs of Holy Scripture themselves.*

On the basis of what we have examined up to this point in the five preceding books on the diversity of readings, we think that what we have suggested above, not just once, but quite frequently here and there, is quite obvious: in the current Hebrew text one does not always and everywhere find the original and the most ancient lesson; namely, the one which was found in the autograph[2] copies of Holy Scripture; rather—and this is the fate and condition of every single book in the world—because of the human weakness at play in the transcription of so many copies which have been made, each on the basis of others through so many centuries by people who are prone to errors and lapses, many different readings have found their way into the holy codices which are still extant; these copies' many variations, in the passages where they differ from one another, show a divergence and a deviation from the first autographs. This cannot be denied, unless we wish, knowingly and deliberately, to pull out our own eyes in order not to see the multiplicity of varying readings—a multiplicity that we have observed and noted. . . .

Book 6, chapter 3

[388] §1. *That the authority of Holy Scripture is not ruined by the varying readings, and that God's providence towards it is not refuted.*

We have already treated this topic in the first chapter of book 1, as we distinguished varying readings from the corruptions and depravations of Scripture which, being intentional and deliberate, result from malice. If the varying readings were depravations of this kind, purposely produced in order to falsify and corrupt authentic and salvific doctrine, since they are so frequent and numerous, it would certainly not be prudent to rest and sustain our faith on a book which is corrupted and vitiated in such a way in so many passages. However, even if the varying readings are of the same kind as those which we explained in the preceding chapter—as well as those which we mentioned in the previous five books—it is clear, to anyone who is not stubborn and does not deliberately wish to blur everything, that the authority of Scripture is not ruined and that our faith is not shaken nor threatened by these varying readings.

§2. Indeed, we must not doubt the authority of our sacred book, unless it contains, as may happen from time to time, a dangerous error, one of course which cannot be refuted or confounded using that very book. For if this happens in one or two passages, not more, in such a way that it can easily be confounded and discovered on the

2. This word appears in Greek letters in the original Latin version of Cappel's book.

basis of the unanimous consensus of Scripture as a whole and on the basis of the analogy of faith, the authority of the sacred books among us must not fall down because of this; the error, of course, must not be attributed and imputed to the sacred author, prophet, and apostle, but to the secretary, scribe, copyist, or printer; it must and can then all the more be confounded and expunged, following the consensus of Scripture. . . .

Book 6, chapter 12[3]

[439] §1. It now is manifest that he [Henri Estienne] points out and uncovers, in Greek and Latin authors, exactly the same sources of errors and mistakes which I have presented since the beginning of this Critique—he did this many years before I discovered that same passage in this learned man's work.

There is thus no reason to be surprised if, in the same manner and for the same reason, in the same way and for the same causes, so many varying readings have found their way into the sacred books of the Old and the New Testaments in Greek and Hebrew, as a result of indolence, slumber, carelessness, ignorance on the part of copyists or scribes, or also because of the temerity and boldness of correctors, since in this way too so many errors, so many considerable and shameful monstrosities have slipped into all sorts of Greek and Latin books, as we see that this learned man observed. Now, with regard to what is usually said about divine Providence which keeps watch over the sacred books, I have replied in several places in this Critique that divine Providence did not aim or did not have to aim to make all the scribes and copyists of the sacred books divinely inspired and infallible.[4] These men were without a doubt no different than all the other scribes, subject to missteps, errors, blunders, and all sorts of human deficiencies. On this point, the vigilance and rigor[5] of the Jewish Masoretes has not so far rendered the Hebrew text free of any variation, as we have shown above, be it with regard to the marginal Qere and Ketiv, the variations between Oriental and Occidental Jews, or with regard to what can be grasped of the Talmud, of Chaldean Paraphrases and rabbinic commentaries.

And so, on the basis of the observation made by this man, who is most learned on the origin and causes of errors, we may find an illustration, a confirmation of our Critique and a defense of our intent with regard to such errors (which ought not be taken lightly), since we wish for our sacred books to be free of the inexperience of uneducated copyists; not long ago, the most learned men have noted that this happened to all the other books and writings of all kinds.

These are precisely the passages which God made us annotate and comment upon as a result of the observation of divergent readings in the sacred books. Following the advice of the most learned and pious scholars (who consulted our work) [440], we considered it worthwhile to present our work to the public, since the numerous obscurities, ambiguities, and perhaps sometimes corruptions open a sure path in the sacred literature for its illustration, explanation, and even correction; if perchance not everything is already approved by all, one day this will change and become the case, as we hope, when the power of truth, which is the only power we tried to follow with our eyes, will by its own light demonstrate itself to human beings and persuade them. In order for this to become reality one day, anyone who really is a lover and devotee of truth will pray for it within oneself to God, with me, through silent pledges. Honor, praise, and glory to the Father, to the Son and to the Holy Spirit, one God, true and eternal, for ever and ever. Amen.

3. In "By Way of Illustration and Confirmation" ("Confirmatio et illustratio"; title of book 6, ch. 12), Cappel shows, in what immediately precedes chapter 12, how ancient texts (the edition of Cicero's works serves here as an example) have required a kind of critical editorial work that also needs to be applied to the Bible.

4. These last two words ("inspired" and "infallible") are written in Greek in the Latin original of Cappel's book.

5. In the Latin original: ἀκρίβεια.

4.

Thomas Hobbes (1588–1679)

One of the most prominent shapers of modern political thought as the author of *Leviathan* (1651), Thomas Hobbes studied in Oxford, worked alongside Francis Bacon, and in the course of his long life resided in various European countries, including a decade in Paris. While in France, Hobbes befriended Father Marin Mersenne (1588–1648), a prominent Catholic scholar. During a journey to Italy in 1636, he may have met Galileo (1564–1642), whose scientific method he admired (Hobbes never mentioned this meeting in writing). He later interacted with René Descartes (1596–1650). Hobbes's intellectual interests were wide ranging. He translated Thucydides's *History of the Peloponnesian War* (1629) and, in the last decade of his life, the *Odyssey* and the *Iliad* into English. Less known is that Hobbes was interested in biblical criticism. And yet chapter 33 of *Leviathan*'s book 3 contains some interesting claims on Moses's authorship of the Pentateuch. Hobbes suggests Moses is not the author of certain passages of the Pentateuch, especially the passages that concern his own death. Hobbes nevertheless maintains Moses's authorship for much of the first five books of the Old Testament.

The following excerpts are taken from *Leviathan*, vol. 3, *The English and Latin Texts (ii)*, ed. Noel Malcolm (Oxford: Clarendon, 2012), 588–92. Hobbes's English has been modernized.

LEVIATHAN (1651)

[588] Who were the original writers of the several Books of Holy Scripture, has not been made evident by any sufficient testimony of other History (which is the only proof of matter of fact); nor can be by any arguments of natural Reason: for Reason serves only to convince the truth (not of fact, but) of consequence. The light therefore that must guide us in this question, must be that which is held out unto us from the Books themselves: And this light, though it shows us not the writer of every book, yet it is not unuseful to give us knowledge of the time, wherein they were written.

[590] And first, for the *Pentateuch*, it is not argument enough that they were written by *Moses*, because they are called the five Books of *Moses*; no more than these titles, the Book of *Joshua*, the Book of *Judges*, the Book of *Ruth*, and the Books of the *Kings*, are arguments sufficient to prove that they were written by *Joshua*, by the *Judges*, by

Ruth, and by the *Kings*. For in titles of Books, the subject is marked, as often as the writer. The *History of Livy* denotes the writer; but the *History of Scanderbeg* is denominated from the subject. We read in the last Chapter of *Deuteronomy*, verse 6, concerning the sepulcher of Moses, *that no man knows of his sepulcher to this day*, that is, to the day wherein those words were written. It is therefore manifest that those words were written after his burial. For it were a strange interpretation, to say *Moses* spoke of his own sepulcher (though by Prophecy), that it was not found to that day, wherein he was yet living. But it may perhaps be alleged that the last Chapter only, not the whole *Pentateuch*, was written by some other man, but the rest not. Let us therefore consider that which we find in the Book of *Genesis*, ch. 12, verse 6: *And* Abraham *passed through the land to the place of* Sichem, *unto the plain of* Moreh, *and the* Canaanite *was then in the land*; which must be the words of one who wrote when the *Canaanite* was not in the land; and consequently, not of *Moses*, who died before he came into it. Likewise *Numbers* 21, verse 14: the Writer cites another more ancient Book, entitled: *The Book of the Wars of the Lord*, wherein were registered the Acts of *Moses*, at the Red Sea, and at the brook of *Arnon*. It is therefore sufficiently evident that the five Books of *Moses* were written after his time, though how long after it be not so manifest.

[592] But though Moses did not compile those Books entirely, and in the form we have them, yet he wrote all that which he is there said to have written: as for example, the Volume of the Law, which is contained, as it seems, in the 11 of *Deuteronomy*, and the following Chapters to the 27, which was also commanded to be written on stones, in their entry into the land of *Canaan*. And this did *Moses* himself write, and deliver to the Priests and Elders of *Israel*, to be read every seventh year to all *Israel*, at their assembling in the feast of Tabernacles.

5.

Baruch Spinoza (1632–77)

At the height of scholastic Protestant Orthodoxy and its promotion of the Bible as *the* infallible, inerrant foundation, as the divinely inspired (*theopneustos*) word of God in its minutest details, the publication of Baruch Spinoza's *Theological-Political Treatise*, in 1670, announced and shaped a new era in the study and interpretation of Scripture. Spinoza lived in a theological world in which the verbal or literal inspiration of Scripture was placed at the front and center of dogmatic constructs. Prominent theologians, such as J. A. Quenstedt, argued that, if even the smallest verse of Scripture is void of God's immediate inspiration, then all is lost, for Satan will claim the same for the entire chapter, for the book as a whole, and, ultimately, for the entire Bible, cancelling its authority.[1] Spinoza countered such views head-on. He called for a reading of the Bible that pays close attention to its language and context as well as to the personality of its authors. By focusing on the strictly natural and historical features of Scripture, to the exclusion of any supernatural or divinely inspired element, Spinoza sought to bring Scripture back "inside human history," thoroughly secularizing it "as a historical document" (Popkin 1996, 397, 403). This, undoubtedly, was revolutionary, since most of his forerunners in biblical criticism still presupposed the inspiration of Scripture. But Spinoza's most ardent desire was to let Scripture speak for itself, to interpret Scripture through Scripture (and not through any dogma or tradition, be it theological or philosophical) (Zac 1965, 28, 40).

In July 1656, Spinoza was banned from the Jewish community he belonged to in Amsterdam. He denounced those who, "under the false labels of holy devotion and ardent zeal," favored "the promotion of conflict and dissemination of senseless hatred" (see below, 38). Beyond Spinoza's personal difficulties with religious communities, we

1. "Si enim unicus Scripturae versiculus, cessante immediato Spiritus sancti influxu, conscriptus est, proptum erit Satanae, idem de toto capite, de integro libro, de universo denique codice Biblico excipere, et per consequens, omnem Scripturae auctoritatem elevare." Johannes Andreas Quenstedt, *Theologia didactico-polemica, sive systema theologicum, in duas sectiones, didacticam et polemicam, divisum* (Wittenberg: J. L. Quenstedt, 1691), part 1, ch. 4, sect. 2, p. 71. This passage is quoted by several modern theologians, including Karl Barth, *Church Dogmatics* I/2, §19.2, trans. G. T. Thomson and Harold Knight (London: T&T Clark, 2004), 525.

should not forget that he wrote in the wake of the enormous bloodshed and devastation of the Thirty Years' War (1618–48).

Going significantly further than Thomas Hobbes, Spinoza was among the first scholars to doubt Moses's authorship of the Pentateuch. This was in fact "plainer than the noonday," in his mind (Spinoza 2007, 122). But in certain regards he was still quite moderate: he believed the divine status of the Bible could be acknowledged in connection with its moral teachings, and he thought a sound reading of Scripture had to be docile and readers really strive to listen to its contents, rather than evaluate it from an external standpoint. Spinoza rejected the idea that a "supernatural light" is needed in order to understand Scripture: reason suffices.

The following excerpts come from Spinoza's *Theological-Political Treatise*, ed. Jonathan Israel, trans. Michael Silverthorne and Jonathan Israel (Cambridge: Cambridge University Press, 2007), ch. 7, 10, 12, and 15. The text has been slightly edited.

THEOLOGICAL-POLITICAL TREATISE (1670)

Chapter 7: On the interpretation of Scripture

[97] All people are ready to say that Holy Scripture is the word of God that teaches us true happiness or the way of salvation, but their actions betray a quite different opinion. For the common people, the last thing that they appear to want is to live by the teaching of Scripture. We see them advancing false notions of their own as the word of God and seeking to use the influence of religion to compel other people to agree with them. As for theologians, we see that for the most part they have sought to extract their own thoughts and opinions from the Bible and thereby endow them with divine authority. There is nothing that they interpret with less hesitation and greater boldness than the Scriptures, that is the mind of the Holy Spirit. If they hesitate at all, it is not because they are afraid of ascribing error to the Holy Spirit or straying from the path of salvation, but rather of being convicted of error by others and seeing themselves despised and their authority trodden underfoot.

If people truly believed in their hearts what they say with their lips about Scripture, they would follow a completely different way of life. There would be fewer differences of opinion occupying their minds, fewer bitter controversies between them, and less blind and reckless ambition to distort our interpretation of the Bible and devise novelties in religion. On the contrary, they would not dare to accept anything as biblical teaching which they had not derived from it in the clearest possible way. Sacrilegious persons, who have not been afraid to corrupt the Scriptures in so many places, would have been careful to avoid committing such a dreadful offense and kept their impious hands off them. But vice and ambition have in the end exercised so much influence that religion has been made to consist in defending purely human delusions [98] rather than in following the teachings of the Holy Spirit. Far from consisting of love, it has been turned, under the false labels of holy devotion and ardent zeal, into the promotion of conflict and dissemination of senseless hatred.

These bad things have been aggravated by superstition, which teaches people to despise reason, and nature, and revere and venerate only such things as conflict with these both. So it is hardly surprising that to enhance their admiration and reverence for Scripture, people seek to interpret it in such a way that it seems to conflict altogether with reason and with nature. They imagine that the most profound mysteries are hidden in Holy Scripture and put all their energy into investigating these absurd issues, while neglecting other matters which are useful. The fantasies they come up with they ascribe to the Holy Spirit, attempting to defend them with all the force and power of their passions. For this is how human beings are constructed: whatever they conceive purely with their intellects, they also defend purely with intellect and reason while, on the other hand, whatever opinions they derive from their passions, they defend with their passions.

To extricate ourselves from such confusion and to free our minds from theological prejudices and the blind acceptance of human fictions as God's teaching, we need to analyze and discuss the true method of interpreting Scripture. For if we do not know this, we can know nothing for certain regarding what the Bible or the Holy Spirit wishes to teach. To formulate the matter succinctly, I hold that the method of interpreting Scripture does not differ from the [correct] method of interpreting nature, but rather is wholly consonant with it. The [correct] method of interpreting nature consists above all in constructing a natural history, from which we derive the definitions of natural things, as from certain data. Likewise, to interpret Scripture, we need to assemble a genuine history of it and deduce the thinking of the Bible's authors by valid inferences from this history, as from certain data and principles. Provided we admit no other criteria or data for interpreting Scripture and discussing its contents than what is drawn from Scripture itself and its history, we will always proceed without any danger of going astray, and we shall have the same assuredness in discussing things that surpass our understanding as in discussing things that we learn by the natural light of reason.

[99] But in order to be perfectly clear that this method is not only the sure way but also the only way, and is consistent with the method of interpreting nature, we should note that the Bible is very often concerned with things that cannot be deduced from principles known by the natural light of reason. For the greater part of it is composed of historical narratives and revelations. In particular, these histories contain miracles, that is (as we showed in the previous chapters), narratives of things unknown to nature adapted to the beliefs and judgments of the chroniclers who compiled them. Revelations likewise are adjusted to the beliefs of the prophets . . . and really do transcend human understanding. Consequently, knowledge of all these things, that is, of almost everything in Scripture, must be sought from the Bible itself, just as knowledge of nature has to be sought from nature itself.

As for the moral teachings contained in the Bible, these can indeed be demonstrated from general concepts, but it cannot be demonstrated from general concepts that Scripture teaches them; this can only be made evident from Scripture itself. In fact, if we want to attest the divine character of Scripture objectively, we must establish from the Bible alone that it offers true moral doctrines. This is the only ground on which its divine character can be proven. For we have shown that this is principally what the assurance of the prophets derived from, that their minds were attuned to the right and the good; and this is what we need to be convinced of ourselves, if we are to have confidence in them. We have also already proven that God's divinity cannot be attested by miracles, not to mention the fact that miracles could also be performed by false prophets. Hence, the divine character of the Bible must needs be established by this one thing alone, that it teaches true virtue, something which can only be established from Scripture itself. Were this not the case, we could not acknowledge the Bible and its divine character without massively prejudging the issue. All of our knowledge of the Bible, hence, must be derived only from the Bible itself. Finally, Scripture does not offer definitions of the things which it speaks of, any more than does nature. Such definitions must be drawn from the various narratives about different things in Scripture, just as definitions of natural things are deduced from the different actions of nature.

The universal rule then for interpreting Scripture is to claim nothing as a biblical doctrine that we have not derived, by the closest possible [100] scrutiny, from its own [that is, the Bible's] history. What sort of thing a history of Scripture needs to be and what are the principal things it must deal with have now to be explained.

First, such a history must include the nature and properties of the language in which the biblical books were composed and which their authors were accustomed to speak. We can then investigate all the possible meanings that every single phrase in common usage can admit; and because all the writers of both the Old and the New Testament were Hebrews, undeniably the history of the Hebrew language is more essential than anything else, not only for understanding the books of the Old Testament which were first written in this language, but also those of the New Testament.

For while the latter were propagated in other languages, they are full of Hebrew idioms.

[Such a history] must gather together the opinions expressed in each individual book and organize them by subject, so that we may have available by this means all the statements that are found on each topic. We should then make note of any that are ambiguous or obscure or seem to contradict others. By obscure expressions I mean those whose sense is difficult to elicit from the context of a passage, while those whose meaning is readily elicited I call clear. I am not now speaking of how easily or otherwise their truth is grasped by reason; for we are concerned here only with their meaning, not with their truth. Moreover, in seeking the sense of Scripture we must take care especially not to be blinded by our own reasoning, insofar as it is founded on the principles of natural knowledge (not to mention our preconceptions). In order not to confuse the genuine sense of a passage with the truth of things, we must investigate a passage's sense only from its use of the language or from reasoning which accepts no other foundation than Scripture itself.

To make all this more clearly understood, I will give an example. Moses' statements, "God is fire" and "God is jealous," are as plain as possible so long as we attend exclusively to the meaning of the words, and therefore I class them as clear expressions, even though, with respect to truth and reason, they are exceedingly obscure. Moreover, even though their literal sense conflicts with the natural light of reason, unless it is also clearly in conflict with the principles and fundamentals derived from investigating the history of Scripture, we must still stick to this, the literal sense. Conversely, if the literal sense of these expressions is found to conflict with the principles drawn from Scripture, even if they are fully in agreement with reason, they will nevertheless need to be interpreted differently (i.e., metaphorically).

[101] In order to know whether or not Moses believed that God is fire, we certainly must not argue on the basis of whether this statement agrees or conflicts with reason, but only from other statements made by Moses himself. For example, since Moses also plainly teaches, in many passages, that God has no similarity with visible things in the sky or on earth or in the water, we must conclude that either this statement or all the others have to be interpreted metaphorically. But we should depart as little as possible from the literal sense, and therefore we must first ask whether this unique expression, "God is fire," admits any but a literal sense, that is, whether the word "fire" has any other meaning apart from natural fire. If we do not find it signifying anything else in normal linguistic usage, that is how we must interpret the expression, however much it may conflict with reason. All the others, however much they agree with reason, will have to be accommodated to this one. Where linguistic usage does not permit this, such statements are irreconcilable, and hence we must suspend judgment about them. Now the word "fire" also stands for anger and jealousy (see Job 31:12), and therefore Moses' statements are readily reconciled, and we are justified in concluding that they are one and the same. Again, Moses plainly teaches that God is jealous and nowhere teaches that God lacks emotions or mental passions. Hence, we must evidently deduce that this is what Moses believed, or at least what he wanted to teach, however much we may think this statement conflicts with reason. For, as we have already shown, we are not permitted to adjust the meaning of Scripture to the dictates of our reason or our preconceived opinions; all explanation of the Bible must be sought from the Bible alone.

Finally our historical inquiry must explain the circumstances of all the books of the prophets whose memory has come down to us: the life, character, and particular interests of the author of each individual book, who exactly he was, on what occasion he wrote, for whom and in what language. Then the fate of each book: namely how it was first received and whose hands it came into, how many variant readings there have been of its text, by whose decision it was received among the sacred books, and finally how all the books which are now accepted as sacred came to form a single corpus. All this, I contend, has to be dealt with in a history of the Bible.

It is important to know of the life, character, and concerns of each writer, so that we may know which statements are meant as laws and which as moral doctrine; we are more readily able to explain someone's words, the better we know his mind and personality. It is also crucial to know on what occasion, at what time, and for what people or age the various texts were written, so that we may not confuse eternal doctrines with those that are merely temporary or useful only to a few people. It is essential, finally, to [102] know all the other things mentioned above, so that, apart from the question of authorship, we may also discover, for each book, whether it may have been contaminated with spurious passages or not; whether mistakes have crept in, and whether the mistakes have been corrected by unskilled or untrustworthy hands. It is vital to know all this, so that we will not be carried away by blind zeal or just accept whatever is put in front of us. We must acknowledge exclusively what is certain and unquestionable.

Only when we have this history of Scripture before us and have made up our minds not to accept anything as a teaching of the prophets which does not follow from this history or may be very clearly derived from it, will it be time to begin investigating the minds of the prophets and the Holy Spirit. But this also requires a method and an order like we use for explaining nature on the basis of its history. In setting out to research natural history, we attempt first of all to investigate the things that are most universal and common to the whole of nature, namely motion and rest and their laws and rules which nature always observes and by which it continually acts; from these we proceed by degrees to others that are less universal. Similarly, we must first seek from the biblical history that which is most universal, the basis and foundation of the whole of Scripture, something affirmed by all the biblical prophets as eternal doctrine of supreme value for all people: for example, that there is a God, one and omnipotent, who alone is to be adored and cares for all people, loving most those who worship Him and love their neighbour as themselves, etc. These and similar things, I contend, Scripture teaches so plainly and so explicitly throughout that no one has ever called its meaning into question in these matters. But Scripture does not teach expressly, as eternal doctrines, what God is, and how God sees all things and provides for them, and so on. On the contrary, as we have already seen above, the prophets themselves have no agreed view about these matters, so that on these questions nothing can be regarded as the teaching of the Holy Spirit, even if they can be decided very well by the natural light of reason.

Once we have adequately got to know this universal doctrine of Scripture, we should then proceed to other less universal things which concern matters of daily life, flowing like rivulets from the universal teaching. Such are all the particular external actions of true virtue which can only be done when the opportunity arises. Anything found in the [103] Scriptures about these things which is obscure and ambiguous should be explained and decided only by the Bible's universal doctrine, and where such passages are self-contradictory, we must consider on what occasion, when, and to whom they were written. . . .

[104] So far we have explained only how to explore the meaning of biblical statements about questions of daily life. These are issues which are relatively easy to investigate since none of this was ever a subject of controversy for biblical writers. But other matters to be found in the Bible concerning purely philosophical questions, cannot be so easily resolved. The path to be followed here is thus more arduous. As we have already seen, the prophets disagreed among themselves in philosophical matters, and their narratives of things are very much adapted to the presuppositions of their respective times, and therefore we may not infer or explain the meaning of one prophet from clearer passages in another, unless it is absolutely evident that they both held exactly the same opinion. I will therefore now briefly explain how the mind of the prophets in such matters is to be investigated by an inquiry into Scripture.

Here too we must again begin from the most universal things, by inquiring first of all, from the clearest scriptural expressions, what prophecy or revelation is, what it chiefly consists in. Then we must ask what a miracle is, and continue thus with the most general questions. From these we must descend to the opinions of each individual prophet, and from these in turn proceed finally to the sense of each particular revelation or prophecy, of each narrative and miracle. We have given many examples above, in the appropriate places, showing how much care is needed not to confuse the minds of the prophets and historians with the mind of the Holy Spirit, so I do not think I need to discuss this at greater length. I should remark, however, with regard to the meaning of revelations, that our method only teaches us to investigate what the prophets actually saw or heard, not what they intended to signify or represent by these visions; that we can only conjecture, since we certainly cannot deduce it from the principles of Scripture.

[105] We have offered a method for interpreting Scripture and at the same time demonstrated that this is the most certain and only way to uncover its true meaning. I grant that certainty about this is easier to find for those, if they exist, who possess a solid tradition or a true exegesis inherited from the prophets themselves, such as the Pharisees claim to have, or those who possess a Pope who cannot err in the interpretation of Scripture, as Roman Catholics proclaim. Since, however, we cannot be certain either about that tradition or papal authority, nothing certain can be grounded on either of these. The latter was denied by the earliest Christians and the former by the most ancient Jewish sects; further, if we then examine the chronology (apart from any other arguments) which the Pharisees inherited from their rabbis by which they trace this tradition back to Moses, we shall find that it is false, as I show in another place.[2] . . .

[106] Since our method, based on the principle that knowledge of the Bible is to be sought from Scripture alone, is the only true method, wherever it is unable to yield what is needed for a complete knowledge of Scripture, we must simply give up. I must now therefore point out the limitations and difficulties in this method's capacity to guide us towards a full and certain knowledge of the sacred books.

Firstly, a major obstacle in this method is that it requires a perfect knowledge of the Hebrew language. But where is this to be sought? The ancient scholars of Hebrew have left nothing to posterity about the principles and structure of the language; at least we have absolutely nothing from them: no dictionary, no grammar, no book of rhetoric. The Jewish people have lost all their cultural and artistic accomplishments—no wonder, after suffering so many massacres and persecutions—and have held on to nothing but a few fragments of their language and a few books. Almost all of the names of fruits, birds, fish, and very many other words, have perished through the ravages of time. Thus the meaning of many nouns and verbs occurring in the Bible is either completely unknown or disputed. Not only do we lack all this but, worst of all, we have no phrase-book of the language; for almost all the idioms and modes of speech peculiar to the Hebrew people have been erased from man's memory by all-devouring time. We cannot therefore always discover, as we should, all the meanings of each and every phrase which usage of the language might yield, and there will be many statements expressed in distinctly known words whose sense will nevertheless still be highly obscure or utterly incomprehensible.

Besides our inability fully to reconstruct the history of Hebrew, the very nature and structure of the language create so many uncertainties that it is impossible to devise a method which will show us how to uncover the true sense of all the statements of Scripture with assurance. For besides the usual causes of ambiguity common to all tongues, there are certain other features of this language that produce a whole host of ambiguities. . . .

[108] To return to our point, one may easily discern from the structure and nature of the Hebrew language that numerous ambiguities are inevitable, and that no method will resolve them all. We cannot hope for this to be completely achieved by comparing expressions with each other, which we have shown is the only way of distinguishing the true sense from the many senses which an expression may admit in ordinary usage. This is because comparison of expressions can only throw light on an expression accidentally, since no prophet wrote with the intention of deliberately explaining either another's words or his own. It is also because we can only infer the mind of one prophet, Apostle, etc., from the mind of another in common, everyday matters, as we have already clearly shown, but not when they speak about philosophical things or when they narrate miracles or historical events. I could also give some examples to show that many expressions that occur in Holy Scripture are inexplicable, but I prefer to [109] pass this over for the present, and proceed to make some further remarks about the difficulties and limitations of this true method of interpreting Scripture.

A further problem with this method is that it requires a history of the vicissitudes of all the biblical books, and most of this is unknown to us. For either we have no knowledge whatever of the authors, or (if you prefer) the compilers, of many

2. In ch. 10, §17 of his *Treatise*.

of the books—or else we are uncertain about them, as I will demonstrate fully in the next chapters. Also, we do not know under what circumstances these books, whose compilers are unknown, were composed or when. Nor do we know into whose hands all these books subsequently came, or in whose copies so many variant readings occur, nor whether there may not have been many additional readings in others. I touched upon the need to know all this at one point, but purposely omitted a few things which we should deal with now. If we read any book that contains incredible or incomprehensible things, or is written in very obscure language, and if we do not know its author or when and under what circumstances he wrote it, our efforts to get at its true sense will be fruitless. For if all this is unknown, we cannot ascertain what the author intended or might have intended. When, on the other hand, all these things are adequately known, we determine our thoughts so as not to make prejudicial judgments or attribute to the author, or person on whose behalf he wrote, either more or less than is correct, or take anything else into consideration but what the author could have had in mind, or what the period and context demanded. . . .

[110] Another and final difficulty in interpreting some biblical books by our method is that we do not now have them in the same language in which they were originally written. The Gospel of Matthew and without doubt also the Letter to the Hebrews are commonly believed to have been composed in Hebrew, but these versions are not extant. There is also some doubt in what language the book of Job was written. Ibn Ezra[3] asserts in his commentary that it was translated into Hebrew from another language and that this is the cause of its obscurity. I will not discuss the apocryphal books, since they are of very different authority.

All these, then, are the difficulties of this method of interpreting Scripture on the basis of its own history which I undertook to describe. I think these difficulties are so great that I do not hesitate to affirm that in numerous passages, either we do not know the true sense of Scripture, or we can only guess at it without any assurance. However, we must also stress that all these problems can only prevent our understanding the minds of the prophets in matters that are incomprehensible and which we can only imagine, and not those topics that are accessible to the intellect and of which we can readily form a clear conception. For matters that by their nature are easily grasped can never be so obscurely phrased that they cannot be readily understood, according to the saying, a word is enough for [111] a wise man.[4] Euclid, who wrote nothing that was not eminently straightforward and highly intelligible, is easily explained by anyone in any language. In order to see his meaning and be certain of his sense there is no need to have a complete knowledge of the language in which he wrote, but only a very modest, even schoolboy, acquaintance with it, nor does one need to know the life, interests, and character of the author, nor in what language he wrote, to whom and when, nor the subsequent fate of his book or its variant readings, nor how or by what Council it was authorized.

What is true of Euclid we may also say about all who have written about things that are intelligible via their own nature. We thus conclude that we can readily discover the meaning of the Bible's moral teaching from the history of it that we are able to reconstruct, and can be certain about its true sense. For the teachings of true piety are expressed in the most everyday language, since they are very common and extremely simple and easy to understand. And since true salvation and happiness consists in our intellect's genuine acquiescence [in what is true], and we truly acquiesce only in what we understand very clearly, it most evidently follows that we can securely grasp the meaning of Scripture in matters necessary for salvation and happiness. Consequently, there is no reason why we should be concerned to the same extent about the rest, given that for the most part we are unable to grasp it by reason or the intellect and it is therefore something more curious than useful.

I have now explained, I think, the true method for interpreting Scripture, and sufficiently expounded my view of it. Moreover, I do not doubt that everyone now sees that this method requires no other light than that of natural reason. For the special character and excellence of this light chiefly consists in deducing and concluding

3. [*Original footnote*] Ibn Ezra, *Commentary on Job*, 2.11.

4. [*Original footnote*] Terence, *Phormio* 541; Plautus, *Persa* 729.

by valid inferences from things known or accepted as known, matters that are imperfectly understood, and this is all that our method requires. Admittedly, this procedure does not suffice to achieve certainty about everything in the biblical books, but this is due not to any defect in our methodology but because the path it shows to be the true and right one was never cultivated, or even ventured on, by people, so that owing to the passage of time, it became arduous and almost impassable, as is eminently clear, I think, from the difficulties that I have pointed out.

[112] It remains now to examine the views of those who disagree with us. First, I shall consider the opinion of those who hold that the natural light of reason does not have the power to interpret Scripture, and that for this a supernatural light is absolutely essential. What this light is which is beyond nature, I leave to them to explain. I, for my part, can only surmise that they have been trying to admit, in very obscure terms, that they are generally in doubt about the true sense of Scripture; for if we examine their interpretations, we shall find that they contain nothing supernatural, indeed nothing more than mere conjectures. Compare them if you will with the interpretations of those who frankly admit that they have no light beyond the natural light—they will be found to be entirely comparable to them; that is, they are just human conceptions, the result of hard work and much thought.

As for their claim that the natural light of reason is not adequate for this task, it is evident that this is false. We have already proved that none of the difficulties in the interpretation of Scripture arises from the inadequacy of the natural light, but only from human carelessness (not to mention malice) in neglecting to construct the history of the Bible when it would have been possible to do so. It is also due (as everyone, I think, would admit) to this supernatural light being a divine gift bestowed only on the faithful. But the prophets and Apostles used to preach not only to the faithful but, primarily, to unbelievers and impious persons, who were thus enabled to understand the meaning of the prophets and Apostles. Otherwise the prophets and Apostles would have appeared to be preaching to little children and infants, not to people endowed with reason; it would have been pointless for Moses to make laws if they could be understood only by the faithful who need no law. Hence those who postulate the need for a supernatural light to interpret the minds of the prophets and Apostles truly seem to be lacking in natural light themselves; so I am very far from believing that such people have a divine supernatural gift. . . .

[114] While our method requires a knowledge of Hebrew, and the common people likewise have no time to study that, no such objection weakens our position. For the Jewish and Gentile common people for whom in their day the prophets and Apostles preached and wrote, understood their language so that they also grasped the prophets' meaning. Yet they did not understand the reasons for what the prophets preached, though, according to Maimonides, they needed to know them if they were going to grasp their meaning. Under our methodological scheme, hence, it need not follow that the common people must accept the testimony of interpreters. I can point to the common people who understand very well the language of the prophets and Apostles, but Maimonides will not be able to point to any common people who understand the causes of things and grasp their meaning on that basis. As far as the common people of today are concerned, we have already shown that they can readily grasp, in any language, everything necessary for salvation, as this is all entirely normal and familiar, even if they are ignorant about the reasons for what is required; and the common people rely on this understanding, and certainly not on the testimony of interpreters. As for everything else, there they are in the same position as the learned.

[115] But let us return to Maimonides' stance and look at it more carefully. Firstly, it presupposes that the prophets agreed among themselves in everything and were consummate philosophers and theologians; for he insists that they reached conclusions from the truth of things which we showed in chapter 2 to be false. Then his position assumes that the sense of Scripture cannot be established from the Bible itself; for the truth of things is not established from Scripture, since it offers no demonstration of anything and does not teach the things about which it speaks by means of definitions and their own first causes. According to Maimonides, therefore, its true sense cannot be established from itself and should not be sought from the Bible itself. But it is evident from this

chapter that this too is incorrect. We have shown by both reason and examples that the sense of Scripture is established from the Bible itself and, even when it speaks about things known by the natural light of reason, is to be sought from the Bible alone. Finally, his view assumes that we are permitted to explain and distort the words of Scripture according to our own preconceived opinions, and to reject the literal sense, even when it is perfectly lucid and explicit, and bend it to some other sense. Apart from the fact that such liberty is diametrically opposed to what we have proved in this and other chapters, nobody can fail to see that it is excessively audacious.

But suppose we granted such great freedom, what does it achieve? Assuredly, nothing at all. For those things that are indemonstrable and which compose the larger part of Scripture cannot be investigated by this procedure nor explained or interpreted by this approach. Whereas, on the other hand, by following our method, we can explain many such things and discuss them with assurance, as we have already shown both by reason and by the fact itself. As for whatever is comprehensible from its nature, its sense—as we have already shown—can readily be derived from the context of what is said. Hence the method [of Maimonides] is plainly useless. It also utterly deprives the common people of the assurance they derive from conscientious reading, and which everyone can have of the sense of Scripture by following a different method. This is why we dismiss this opinion of Maimonides as harmful, useless, and absurd.

As for the tradition of the Pharisees, we have already noted above that it is inconsistent with itself, while the authority of the Roman Popes requires clearer evidence, and for this reason I reject it. For if they could prove [their authority] to us from Scripture itself and with the same [116] certainty as the Hebrew high priests could once do, it would not worry me that among the Roman Popes there have been a number of heretics and impious men. For formerly among the Hebrews heretics and impious, men were also to be found who acquired the supreme pontificate by dubious means and yet nevertheless wielded, by edict of Scripture, the supreme power of interpreting the law. See Deut 17:11–12 and 33:10 and Mal 2:8. But as they produce no such testimony, their authority remains wholly suspect.

In case anyone is misled by the example of the Hebrew High Priest to believe that the Catholic religion too requires a high priest, one must remark that the laws of Moses were the public laws of a country and necessarily needed therefore a public authority for their preservation. If every individual had the liberty to interpret the public laws at his own discretion, no state could survive; it would immediately be dissolved by this very fact, and public law would be private law. It is wholly different with religion. Since it does not consist so much in external actions as in simplicity and truth of mind, it does not belong to any public law or authority. For simplicity and truth of mind are not instilled in people by the power of laws or by public authority, and absolutely no one can be compelled to be happy by force of law. It requires, rather, pious and fraternal advice, a proper upbringing and, more than anything else, one's own free judgment. Since therefore the supreme right of thinking freely, about religion also, belongs to each and every individual, and it cannot be conceived that anyone could surrender this right, every individual will also possess the supreme right and authority to judge freely about religion and to explain it and interpret it for himself. The reason why the supreme authority in interpreting the laws and the supreme judgment on public questions lie with the magistrate is simply because they are matters of public right. For the same reason, the authority to interpret religion and make judgments about it will lie with each individual person, because it is a question of individual right.

It is therefore far from being the case that the authority of the Roman Pontiff to interpret religion can be inferred from the authority of the Hebrew High Priest to interpret the laws; on the contrary, one may more readily conclude from this that it is principally the individual who possesses this authority. And as the highest authority to interpret Scripture rests with each individual, the rule of interpretation must be nothing other than the natural light of reason which is common to all people, and [117] not some light above nature or any external authority. The criterion should not be so difficult that it cannot be applied by any but the most acute philosophers, but should be adapted to the natural and common intelligence and capacity of [all] human beings, as we have shown that our norm is; for we have seen that the difficulties which it continues to present have their origin not in the nature of the method, but in people's carelessness.

Chapter 10: Where the remaining books of the Old Testament are examined in the same manner as the earlier ones

[152] §15–17: As for the other deficiencies I spoke of, I do not plan to detail them all here, since I could not do so without making this extremely tedious for the reader, especially as they have already been pointed out by others. For Rabbi Shlomo[5] was compelled by the very evident contradictions he observed in the genealogies I have discussed, to utter these candid words (in his commentary on 1 Chronicles 8): "The fact that Ezra" (who he thinks wrote the books of Chronicles) "calls the sons of Benjamin by other names, and gives him a different genealogy from the one we have in the book of Genesis, and finally lists most of the Levites' cities differently from Joshua, derives from the fact that he found his sources disagreeing." Slightly further on, he adds: "the fact that the genealogy of Gibeon and others is given twice, but differently each time," (is) "because Ezra found [153] several divergent epistles of genealogy for each man, and in copying from them, followed the majority version, but when the number of discrepant genealogies was equal on either side, then he copied out both versions."

He thus concedes without reservation that these books were compiled from originals which had not been adequately corrected or were less than altogether certain. Furthermore, the commentators themselves, when attempting to reconcile passages, very often do nothing but reveal how these errors arise. In any case, I do not think that anyone with a sound judgment believes that the sacred chroniclers had the deliberate intention of writing in such a way that they would be seen as continually contradicting themselves.

Possibly someone will say that I am completely undermining Scripture by my manner of proceeding, since it may lead everyone to suspect that the Bible is everywhere full of mistakes. But, on the contrary, I have shown that my methodology works in favour of Scripture by preventing passages which are clear and pure from being corrupted to fit defective passages, and simply because some passages are defective we are not justified in placing every passage under suspicion. There has never ever been a book without mistakes: has anyone (I ask) therefore ever supposed that they were defective throughout? Of course not, especially when the expression is lucid and the meaning of the author is clearly evident.

This completes what I wanted to say about the history of the books of the Old Testament. Our conclusion is evident: no canon of sacred books ever existed before the time of the Maccabees. The books we now possess were selected, in preference to many others, by the Second Temple Pharisees who also set out the forms for prayers, and these have been accepted purely as a consequence of their decisions. Hence, those who seek to demonstrate the authority of Holy Scripture must prove the authority of each individual book. It is insufficient to demonstrate the divine character of just one book, if one wishes to prove the divinity of all. Otherwise we would be obliged to suppose that the council of the Pharisees could not have erred in their selection of books, and no one will ever demonstrate that.

Chapter 12: On the true original text of the divine law, and why holy Scripture is so called, and why it is called the word of God, and a demonstration that, in so far as it contains the word of God, it has come down to us uncorrupted

[163] §1. Those who consider the Bible in its current state a letter from God, sent from heaven to people, will undoubtedly protest that I have sinned "against the Holy Spirit" [Matt 12:31; Mark 3:29; Luke 12:10] by claiming the word of God is erroneous, mutilated, corrupt, and inconsistent, that we have only fragments of it, and that the original text of the covenant which God made with the Jews has perished. However, if they reflect upon the facts, I have no doubts that they

5. [*Original footnote*] Rabbi Solomon ben Isaac of Troyes (1040–1105), otherwise known by his acronym Rashi.

will soon cease to protest. For both reason and the beliefs of the prophets and Apostles evidently proclaim that God's eternal word and covenant and true religion are divinely inscribed upon the hearts of human beings, that is, upon the human mind. This is God's true original text, which God himself has sealed with God's own seal, that is, with the idea of himself as the image of his divinity.

Chapter 15: What faith is, who the faithful are, the foundations of faith defined, and faith definitely distinguished from philosophy

§3–6. It is [188] indeed true that Scripture must be explained by Scripture, so long as we are only deriving the sense of the passages and the meaning of the prophets, but after we have arrived at the true sense, we must necessarily use our judgment and reason before giving assent to it. If reason must be entirely subject to Scripture despite its protest against it, I ask whether we should do this in accordance with reason or, like blind people, without reason. If the latter, then we are certainly acting stupidly and without any judgment. But what of the former? We are in that case accepting Scripture solely at the command of reason, and therefore we would not accept it where it is in conflict with reason. I also ask, who can accept anything with his mind if his reason protests against it? For what is it to reject something with your mind but a protest of reason?

Assuredly, I am utterly amazed that people should want to subject reason, the greatest gift and the divine light, to ancient words which may well have been adulterated with malicious intent. I am amazed that it should not be thought a crime to speak disparagingly of the mind, the true text of God's word, and to proclaim it corrupt, blind, and depraved, while deeming it the highest offense to think such things of the mere letter and image of God's word. They consider it pious not to trust their reason and their own judgment, and deem it impious to have doubts concerning the reliability of those who have handed down the sacred books to us. This is plain stupidity, not piety. But I ask, why does the use of reason worry them? What are they afraid of? Can religion and faith not be defended, unless we make ourselves ignorant of everything and reason is totally dispensed with? If they believe that, then surely such people fear Scripture more than they trust it. Religion and piety should not wish to have reason for a servant, nor should reason wish to have religion for a servant. Both should be able to rule their own realms in the greatest harmony. I will explain this directly, but I want first to examine the rule of this rabbi [that is, Al-Fakhar].

As we said, he wants us to be bound to accept as true everything that Scripture affirms, and reject as false everything Scripture denies, and he holds that the Bible never affirms or denies in explicit terms anything contrary to what it affirms or denies in another passage. Yet everyone must see how very rash these two positions are. I will omit here what he did not remark, that Scripture consists of a variety of different books, of different periods and for different people, and compiled by a variety of authors; I will also pass over the point that he makes these assertions on [189] his own authority, and that neither reason nor Scripture assert anything comparable. He ought to have shown, from the character of the language and the purpose of the passage, that all passages that are in conflict with others only by implication can be properly construed metaphorically, as well as that Scripture has come down to us uncorrupted.

But let us examine the issue methodically and consider the first point: what if reason protests? Are we still obliged to accept as true what Scripture affirms, and reject as false whatever Scripture denies? Perhaps he will say that nothing is found in Scripture which is in conflict with reason. But Scripture, I contend, expressly affirms that God is jealous (namely in the Ten Commandments and at Exod 24:14 and Deut 4:24 and several other passages). This is in conflict with reason, despite which we should supposedly regard this as true. Any passages in Scripture implying that God is not jealous would then necessarily have to be explained metaphorically, so that they would not appear to assume anything of the sort. Likewise, the Bible expressly states that God descended to Mount Sinai (see Exod 29:10, etc.), and ascribes other local motions to God, and nowhere explicitly asserts that God does not move. Thus, this too would have to be admitted by all people as true, while Solomon's assertion that God is not contained in any place (see 1 Kgs 8:27), not being a direct statement but just a consequence of deducing that God does not move, will therefore have to be explained in such a way that it does not deny local motion to God. Equally, the heavens would have to be considered the dwelling-place and throne of God, since Scripture expressly affirms it. There are very many things phrased in this way, in accordance with the beliefs of the prophets and the common people, which reason and philosophy, though not Scripture, reveal to be false. Yet all of them, in the view of al-Fakhar, must be accepted as true, since there is no consultation with reason concerning these questions.

Secondly, he is mistaken in claiming that one passage contradicts another passage only by implication, and never directly. For Moses directly asserts that "God is fire" (see Deut 4:24) and flatly denies God has any similarity to visible things (see Deut 4:12). If he responds that the latter does not deny God is fire directly but only by implication, and that we must reconcile it with the other passage, so that it may not seem to deny it, well then, let us concede that God is fire, or rather, in order not to participate in such nonsense, let us discard this example and proceed [190] to another. Samuel clearly denies that God repents of his decisions (see 1 Sam 15:29), while Jeremiah by contrast maintains that God repents of the good and evil which he has decreed (see Jer 18:8–10). Now, are these two passages not plainly contradictory to each other? Which, then, of the two propositions does he propose to interpret metaphorically? Both are universal but contrary to the other; what one plainly affirms, the other directly denies. Thus, by his rule he must both accept the fact as true, and reject it as false.

But again, what does it matter that a passage does not contradict another directly but only by implication, if the implication is clear and the context and nature of the passage does not admit metaphorical interpretation? There are very many such passages in the Bible. See chapter 2 (where we showed that the prophets held different and contrary opinions), and especially look at the numerous contradictions we pointed out in the histories (in chapters 9 and 10).

I need not go through them all again here, for what I have said suffices to demonstrate the absurdities that follow from this opinion and such a rule, how false these are, and how superficial the author.

We must therefore dismiss both this theory and that of Maimonides. We have established it as absolutely certain that theology should not be subordinate to reason, nor reason to theology, but rather that each has its own domain. For reason, as we said, reigns over the domain of truth and wisdom, theology over that of piety and obedience. For the power of reason, as we have shown, cannot extend to ensuring that people may be happy by obedience alone without understanding things, while theology tells us nothing other than this and decrees nothing but obedience. Theology has no designs against reason, and cannot have any. For the dogmas of faith (as we showed in the previous chapter) determine only what is necessary for obedience, and leave it to reason to determine how precisely they are to be understood in relation to truth. Reason is the true light of the mind, without which it discerns nothing but dreams and fantasies.

By theology here I mean precisely revelation insofar as it proclaims the purpose which we said that Scripture intends, namely the method and manner of obedience that is the dogmas of true piety and faith. This is [191] what is properly termed the word of God, which does not consist in a specific collection of books (on this see chapter 12). If you consider the commands or moral advice of theology understood in this way, you will find that it agrees with reason, and if you look at its intent and purpose, you will see that in fact it does not conflict with reason in anything. Hence, it is universal to all people.

As regards Scripture generally, when considered as a whole, we have already shown in chapter 7 that its sense must be determined solely from its own history and never from the universal history of nature which is the sole ground of philosophy. If we find, after we have investigated its true sense in this way, that in places it conflicts with reason, this should not trouble us at all. For we know for certain that nothing of this sort encountered in the Bible, and nothing people can be ignorant of without loss of charity, has the least effect on theology or on the word of God. Consequently, everyone may think whatever they like about such matters without doing wrong. We conclude therefore without hesitation that Scripture is not to be accommodated to reason nor reason to Scripture.

6.

Richard Simon (1638–1712)

Richard Simon's work on both the Old and the New Testament represents a key moment in the emergence of the modern historical and critical exegetical methods. A Catholic (Oratorian) priest, his *Histoire critique du Vieux Testament* (Critical History of the Old Testament) is a landmark of modern biblical scholarship, even if others before him, such as Louis Cappel and fellow Oratorian Jean Morin (1591–1659), had already reached similar results. But Cappel had written his *Critica sacra* in Latin. Now the word *criticism* found its way in the title of a scholarly book about Scripture written in French (Auvray 1974, 42). Only six of the 1,300 copies, which were first printed in Paris in 1678, escaped destruction. Jacques-Bénigne Bossuet (1627–1704), the most influential person on religious matters in France at the time, and other prominent figures within French Catholicism tried to suppress Simon's work. The book was subsequently published in Holland, first in Amsterdam in 1680 by Daniel Elzevier, a defective edition, and then, more reliably, in 1685 in Rotterdam by Reinier Leers. Simon was excluded from the Oratory in May 1678.

Cappel's *Critica sacra* was one of Simon's key resources: "[It] ought to be preferred before all others upon this subject," as Simon put it (Simon 1682, preface). Despite all of the polemics of the time across Christian confessions, Simon considered Cappel's work "the most learned work which we have upon the several readings and other changes of the Old Testament" (Simon 1682, 10). On the other hand, in his preface (and only there), Simon explicitly opposed the consequences Baruch Spinoza drew from his analysis of Scripture. Simon had completed his *Histoire critique* before discovering Spinoza's *Tractatus* (Auvray 1968).

Simon sought to achieve three aims with his critical history of the Old Testament: in Book 1 he addresses questions related to the text of the Hebrew Bible: Did the text evolve? Who are its authors? Simon reached the conclusion that Moses was not the author of the entire Pentateuch. In Book 2 he examines the main ancient and modern translations of the Old Testament. Finally, in Book 3 Simon considers the commentators of the Old Testament. Not just Catholic thinkers—Bossuet as well as prominent members of

Port-Royal—but also Protestants opposed Simon for various reasons: certain Protestants perceived Simon's work as a direct threat to the authority of the one and only basis of Protestant theology and ecclesiology, namely Scripture, which they viewed as inspired in its very letter.

The selections below come from *A Critical History of the Old Testament*, trans. anonymous [Henry Dickinson?] (London: Walter Davis, 1682). This English translation is based on the 1680 Elzevier edition of Richard Simon's book. Certain details have been modernized and modified, also on the basis of the original 1678 French edition.[1]

A CRITICAL HISTORY OF THE OLD TESTAMENT (1678; 1685)

Preface[2]

. . . The great alterations which have happened, as we have shown in the first Book of this work, to the copies of the Bible since the first originals have been lost, utterly destroy the Protestant and Socinian principle, who consult only these same copies of the Bible as we at present have them. If the truth of religion remained not in the Church, it would be unsafe to search for it at present in Books which have been subject to so many alterations, and have in many things depended upon the pleasure of transcribers. It is certain that the Jews, who have written out these Books, have taken the liberty of adding and leaving out certain letters according as they thought fit, and yet the sense of the Text often depends upon these letters; to this we may add the uncertainty of the Hebrew Grammar, which could never be perfectly restored since its being lost. This has been explained at length at the end of the first Book, where we have given an account of the rise and progress of the Jewish Grammar.

Besides, the Criticism we have made of the chief Translations of the Bible is an evident proof that it is almost impossible to translate the Holy Scripture, especially if we join herewith the project of a new Translation set down at the beginning of the third Book. Those Protestants without doubt are either ignorant or prejudiced who affirm that the Scripture is plain of itself. As they have laid aside the Tradition of the Church, and will acknowledge no other principle of Religion but the Scripture itself, they were obliged to suppose it plain and sufficient for the establishing the truth of Faith without any Tradition.

But if we but consider the conclusions which the Protestants and Socinians draw from the same principle, we shall be convinced that their principle is not so plain as they imagine, since these conclusions are so different and the one absolutely denies what the other affirms.

Instead of believing with the Protestants that the shortest and most certain way of deciding the questions of Faith is to consult the Holy Scriptures, we shall on the contrary find in this Work that if we join not Tradition with the Scripture, we can hardly affirm anything for certain in Religion. We cannot be said to quit the word of God by joining therewith the Tradition of the Church, since he who refers us to the Holy Scriptures has also referred us to the Church whom he has entrusted with this holy pledge. . . .

To conclude, although the Council of Trent ordained that we should not in interpreting of the Scripture deviate from the explanations of the Fathers, it has not for all that prohibited private persons from searching out of other explanations of places not relating to matters of Faith. We may on the contrary say that men never endeavoured so much to find out new interpretations of the Scripture Text as since this Council. They thought not that the Fathers had thoroughly sifted the matter. Wherefore I have made bold to give my opinion upon their Commentaries in the third Book. I have observed both their failures and perfections; and lastly I have examined their Works according to the rules of Criticism, because in those places

1. For Richard Simon's work on the New Testament, see his *Critical History of the Text of the New Testament. Wherein Is Established the Truth of the Acts on which the Christian Religion Is Based*, trans. Andrew Hunwick (Leiden: Brill, 2013).

2. No pagination.

there is no mention made of matters of Faith. We however at present find some learned persons who collect only whatever they can find out of the Fathers' books upon the Scripture, as if the Fathers had better succeeded than the other interpreters of the Bible.

They who search after truth itself without prejudice value not persons' names nor their antiquity, especially in things not relating to Faith; and it is certain that most of the Fathers have not had all the necessary helps nor time enough to search into the great difficulties in the Scripture. The Commentaries of the modern Interpreters ought in many places to be preferred before those of the ancient ones, and we ought rather to search for Religion in the Fathers' interpretation than literal explanations of the Scripture text. There are few who have applied themselves to this sort of study, and amongst the Latin Fathers there have been none except S. Jerome who were capable of doing it. Wherefore for the carrying on of my design of observing what I thought was necessary for the understanding of the Scripture, it was convenient that I should consult the Jewish commentaries as well as those of the Catholic Doctors, that everyone might be instructed as well in the method which has been observed even to this time in the Synagogue, as in the Church, for the explaining of the Holy Scriptures: I have joined with the latter the Protestant and Socinian Authors, to the end one may profit by their new discoveries in this study, as the Fathers heretofore consulted the Greek translations of the Bible which had been made by the greatest enemies of the Church. . . .

But after all I found that no one had hitherto thoroughly searched into the Criticism of the Scriptures; everyone has commonly spoken according to his prejudice. The Jews, for example, who consulted only their authors, have had but a very slender knowledge herein, and they have contented themselves with admiring what they did not understand. As for the Christians, most of the Fathers have been so much prejudiced in favor of the ancient translations of the Church, that they have wholly neglected the Hebrew Text, besides that they have not had all the necessary helps for the thorough examining of what belongs to the Criticism of the Bible.

As for the writers of our times, whether Catholics or Protestants, I have found none who were wholly free from prejudice. The two Buxtorfs, who have got much reputation, especially among the Protestants, have in most of their works only shown they were biased in favor of the Rabbins' opinions, without having consulted any other authors.[3] Father Morin on the contrary was prejudiced against the Rabbins before he had read them, and under pretense of defending the ancient translations of the Church, he has collected all the proofs he could find to destroy the originals of the Bible.[4]

There is indeed much more judgment in Cappel's Criticism, but as he endeavours hardly anything else but to find out the various readings, he has multiplied them. Wherefore I have in this History laid down some principles for the explaining of several various readings, without blaming the transcribers for being mistaken in all those places. Besides Cappel has taken for various readings some downright errors of transcribers, which might be easily corrected by good copies. Lastly, he has not, as I see it, given authority enough to the Massoret, which has fixed the way of reading the Hebrew text of the Bible. For although the Jews have not been infallible in their Massoret or Criticism, we ought not however to reject or despise it only because it comes from the Jews. As the question is about the custom of reading, we ought to consult them amongst whom this custom has been preserved. But notwithstanding these faults and some others which I do not mention here, Cappel's work ought to be preferred before all others upon this subject, and although he was a Protestant he was not prejudiced in favor of those of his Religion. They of Geneva, Sedan and Leyden opposed the publishing of this Book for

3. [*Original footnote*] Johannes Buxtorf (1564–1629) and his son, also named Johannes (1599–1664), who both taught at the University of Basel. Both debated with Louis Cappel on specific issues such as Hebrew vocalization and the chronological origin of vowel-points in Hebrew.

4. [*Original footnote*] Jean Morin (1591–1659), like Richard Simon, was a French scholar and an Oratorian priest. He edited the Samaritan Pentateuch for Guy Michel Le Jay's (1588–1674) polyglot Bible, a sumptuous 10 vol. marvel which is unfortunately filled with errors. Its title: *Biblia 1. Hebraica, 2. Samaritana, 3. Chaldaica, 4. Græca, 5. Syriaca, 6. Latina, 7. Arabica quibus textus originales totius Scripturæ sacræ … exhibentur* (Paris: Antoine Vitré, 1645).

ten years together, being persuaded it destroyed the principle of their Religion, and obliged them to have recourse to the Tradition of the Catholics. Father Pétau, a Jesuit, Father Morin of the Oratory and Father Mersenne, a Minime, got the King's license for the printing of it.[5]

This so alarmed the Court of Rome that it had almost condemned it, it being a thing without precedent that heretical books wherein matters of Theology are treated of, should be printed in France with the King's license. But Father Morin, who had helped forward the printing of it, and perhaps had not foreseen all the consequences, wrote to Cardinal Francis Barberini, that they at Rome did Cappel a kindness in condemning his Criticism which had created him the hatred of those of his Sect, and that at the same time they did the Catholics injury, who made use of this book to show that the Protestants have no certain principle of their Religion, having rejected the Tradition of the Church; Cappel however never intended to draw this consequence from his book.

Lastly, Vossius, who could not allow of the ignorance of some Protestants, whom he calls half Jews, undertook in a work for that purpose to defend the Septuagint translation, but, under pretense of rejecting the Massoret copies, he has flown into another extreme concerning the Septuagint, so that we may say there are very few persons who have been able to keep the medium which was necessary for the finding out of the truth.[6] This I have endeavoured to do in this work, by preserving as much as possibly I could the authority of the original Hebrew, and translations. I have had no prejudice either for the Greek, Latin, Hebrew, or any other language. But I have carefully examined according to the rules of Criticism the Hebrew text and all the translations; and after having observed the various readings, I have shown how we might correct the faults in the present copies.

If we ought to reject the original Hebrew because of the faults which are therein, we ought also for the same reason to reject all the ancient translations of the Church which have been made from the Hebrew, because they are also faulty as well as the Hebrew text, and consequently we ought to admit of no copy of the Scripture. But these extremes are very dangerous.

Origen and S. Jerome, who found many faults in the ancient Greek copies of the Septuagint translation, would not for all that reject it; they endeavoured only to restore it according to the common rules of Criticism. I have followed the example of these two great men, and as there has been nothing upon this subject as yet in French, no one ought to wonder why I make use sometimes of certain expressions which are not altogether exact in French; every art has peculiar terms which are in a manner consecrated to it. Thus we shall often find in this work the word *Critique*, and some other like it, which I have been forced to use the better to express myself according to the terms of the art I treated of. Besides persons who are scholars are already used to these terms in our tongue. When we speak, for example, of Cappel's book, printed under the title *Critica Sacra*, and of the English commentaries called Critici Sacri, we say in French *la Critique de Cappel, les Critiques d'Angleterre. . . .*

But I have spoken enough of the design and profit of this work, I am now only to desire those who will take the pains to read it carefully, to tell me charitably of my faults, to the end that I may profit by their admonitions. It is but reasonable that after having criticized upon so many authors I should submit myself to the censure of others.

Book 1, chapter 5

[36] It is not difficult to bring other proofs to show that Moses is not the only author of the whole Pentateuch after the manner as we now have it. S. Jerome, as we have before remarked, does not ascribe wholly to him; and Massius, who is one of the learned and judicious interpreters of the Scripture we have had in recent centuries, did not hesitate to say that several things have been added to the Books of Moses. He acknowledges those public writers which we before spoke of, and

5. [*Original footnote*] Fathers Denis Pétau (1583–1652) and Marin Mersenne (1588–1648) were two towering intellectuals within 17th century French Catholicism.

6. [*Original footnote*] Isaac Vossius (1618–1689), the son of the Calvinist theologian Gerard Vossius, was a Dutch scholar.

Pererius, a Jesuit, is of Massius' opinion, because it seems extremely reasonable to him. . . . Shall we say for example that Moses is the author of the last chapter of Deuteronomy where his death and burial are described? I know that Josephus and Philo upon this occasion have recourse to prophecy, but we ought not to believe him more than other Jews who ascribe the whole Law to Moses to render it more authentic.

We have already observed that Joshua added something to the Law, and moreover if Moses was the author of the Pentateuch, [37] after the manner of speaking as it is at present written, would he have used this way of speaking: *the Canaanite was then in the land?* . . .

Besides these ways of speaking and many others like this, of which Moses could never be the author, there is an infinite number of repetitions of the same thing in the Pentateuch which are apparently not Moses', but rather theirs who have made a collection of the holy Scriptures, and have joined together several readings or explanations of the same words, not thinking it convenient to leave out of their copies what might illustrate the text. . . .

[39] *In fine*, the Books of Moses are full of these sorts of repetitions, whereof some are rather explanations of what went before than repetitions, as in the same Ex 16:36 . . . .

But there is another sort of repetition in the Books of Moses which renders the text obscure, which is when the same thing is repeated in different places, at little distance one from the other, for then to find out the order in the words the sense is often changed, whereas it is supposed as certain that the order is very often neglected in the Scripture. For example, the history of the Deluge is very confused, chiefly in what related to the time that the waters remained upon the earth; and [40] it is likewise the same in the narration of the Rods which Jacob used to divide his flocks from Laban's, and abundance of similar places, the explanation of which is hard, by reason of certain repetitions with some changes, that make one believe they are different things, although for the most part it is one and the same thing differently expressed in several places.

It may be nevertheless that good part of these repetitions belong to the Genius of the Hebrew tongue, which is a very plain language, and repeats often the same thing by different terms, which appears in almost all the Books of the Scripture, and which we find even in the Ordinances of our Kings, and in the style of the Chancery of Rome, as well as in the style of our Courts for civil Affairs, where several words are placed after one another which signify the same thing. When these repetitions are not immediate after one another S. Augustine calls them recapitulations, and in this most interpreters have followed him, but whether these repetitions proceed from him who has collected the records, and has let them alone because they serve for explanation, or whether they proceed from the genius of the Hebrew tongue, it is convenient to observe them for the better understanding the Scripture style.

I question likewise whether one should attribute to Moses or to the public writers which were in his time the lack of order which is to be found in some places of the Pentateuch, it is more probable that as in those times the books were written upon little scrolls or separate sheets that were sewed together, the order of these sheets might be changed. And besides the Books of the Bible we have now, being only an abridgment, the order of matters contained in them has not always been regarded. The Rabbins have endeavoured to excuse this by a figure, which they call *Mukedam Meuhar*, and is the same thing with *Hysteron Proteron* with the Greeks. It is true that the best authors sometimes fall into little mistakes, so likewise do we not pretend to draw from thence an infallible consequence to prove that Moses could not be the author of the Pentateuch in the order that it is. It seems to me that the Jews themselves did not much regard writing in method, as it would be easy to prove by the style of the Epistles of S. Paul: and Haron, a Caraite Jew, who has made literal commentaries on the whole Pentateuch, observes often this confusion of order, which he calls *Haphuck*, and says [40] that it is usual enough in Scripture to begin with one thing, then to pass to another, and afterwards to resume again the first. A great many places in the Books of the Law where the order is confused make me think that those Books were not originally composed in that method. For example, can anyone believe that a historian should write the history of the creation of man with so little order as there is in the first chapter of Genesis, where the same things are several times repeated without method, and as it were besides the purpose? And moreover after the man and the woman were created in chapter 1, verse 27, the woman is supposed not to be made, and in the following chapter the manner how she was taken from Adam's side is described, nevertheless in the same chapter it was before forbidden him, as he was her husband, whom she accompanied in the Garden, to eat the fruit of a certain tree.

There is not more method observed in the other part of the narration, which explains the creation of other things, than in that of man, and I do not know whether it is sufficient to say that all these repetitions are recapitulations, because they are very little remote one from the other. To understand the Books of Moses one must often join many verses together by beginning with the last and coming up to the first. . . .

Book 3, Chapter 1: A project for a new translation of the Scripture, where the faults of other translations are also shown

[1] The criticism which we have already made, as well of the *Hebrew* text, as of the different translations, plainly shows that we have at present no exact translation of the Holy Scripture: If we consider the difficulties which have already been observed, it seems impossible for us to succeed. We shall nevertheless, to the best of our power, chalk out the way [2] which ought to be observed in the making of a translation of the Bible, which may come closer to a true one than anything that has yet been made upon this subject.

Every translation ought as much as it can to be like the original; and therefore it is necessary first of all to show which is this original by which the translations of the Bible are to be regulated. If the *Hebrew* text had not suffered so many alterations, it would without doubt be the only true original: But because several translators of the Scripture look upon it at present as a work altered by the Jews, especially by the Massorets of Tiberias, they have recourse to the ancient translations of the Bible. Some think that for want of the first and true original, we ought to keep to the Septuagint; and others think we ought to acknowledge no other Holy Scripture but the ancient Latin translation, commonly called the Vulgate.

But after having considered the reasons alleged both on one side and the other, I have found a great deal of prejudice, and that it was very hard to reconcile all these different opinions. Nobody can deny but that the *Hebrew* text is the original, although we have at present none but imperfect copies; and therefore it is necessary to join the ancient translations of the Bible with the *Hebrew* text, if we intend to restore as well as we can this first original.

We ought nevertheless to prefer the *Hebrew* text before these ancient translations; because when a work is to be translated, it is more proper to translate from the text, than from translations made from that very text. It is only necessary to consult them in places where we find the *Hebrew* text may be helped out by them; and thus we may consider them only as serviceable to render the original more plain. It is true that the *Hebrew* text at present is very faulty; but on the other side, the ancient translations, whether *Greek* or *Latin*, are much more defective. Wherefore we shall join with the *Hebrew* text ancient translations which have been made from this text, and by this means we may in some sort restore the first original.

For the further clearing of this matter, we may observe that many diverse readings have happened to the Holy Scriptures, as well as to all other books. As the first original, by which we ought to regulate these diverse readings, has been lost, the *Jews* [3] have had recourse to another rule which they esteem infallible, and call it the *Massoret*. This *Massoret*, as we have already observed, is a criticism of the *Hebrew* text, the reading of which they have limited as we at present find it; which criticism they have called *Massoret*, which signifies "tradition," because they affirm that in this they have only followed the tradition of their Fathers, and have innovated nothing at all. But as we have already shown, that the *Massoret* is not divine, and that the *Massorets* may have been deceived in many places, we are not to give credit to the *Hebrew* text at present, as to a first and true original. We shall consider it then only as an excellent copy corrected by the *Jews* of *Tiberias*, called *Massorets*, which were indeed very understanding in the *Hebrew* tongue, but neither prophets, nor infallible in their criticism, or review of the *Hebrew* text.

Wherefore a translator of the Scripture ought not to follow the Hebrew text at present too exactly, but to examine according to all the rules of criticism the various readings which may be found out both by the help of ancient copies, and by ancient translations. One would do well to print a *Hebrew* text with all these variations, as other books are usually printed. I acknowledge that this is hard, because we want at present ancient *Hebrew* copies, and that it would be difficult to find any above seven or eight hundred years old, and besides, most of them have been corrected by the *Massorets*. Besides, it is hard to find good ones; and therefore it is to be feared that the various readings would be increased by being confounded with the errors of transcribers.

Notwithstanding all these difficulties, we ought first of all to establish a *Hebrew* text, and observe the various readings according to the rules of criticism, as we use to do in other books. In the translation these same variations may be translated, and put in the margin, and the best reading may be kept for the body of the translation, without following too closely the *Massoret* text; and therefore care is to be taken of confounding a different interpretation with a various reading, which several authors have done who have explained the Scripture. . . .

Book 3, chapter 2: Continuation of the same project for a new translation of the Holy Scripture

[7] It is not sufficient to have a text by which we may regulate our translation; besides that, we ought to understand thoroughly the tongue in which the text is written. Now we must suppose, as indeed it is true, that most of the Hebrew words are equivocal, and their signification altogether uncertain. Thus when a translator makes use of, as he thinks, the best interpretation, we cannot for all that absolutely say that this interpretation expresses truly what the original means. We have reason to doubt whether the sense of the Hebrew words be truly expressed, since there are other senses as probable. This can only be remedied by comparing together the best interpreters of the Holy Scriptures, as well Jews as Christians. That which one supposes to be the best interpretation of the Hebrew words, may be put into the body of the translation, and the others may be placed in the margins.

Most of the Protestants have understood this rule which they have in some measure observed in their translations; but so seldom, and after so negligent a manner, that in reading their translations one would think that the words of the Scripture could be differently interpreted, only in those places which are marked; which is not true. Considering they allege the Scripture to be the only rule of their religion, they had reason sometimes in their translations not to take notice of the different significations of the Hebrew words. This method could only make the people doubt of the certainty of their religion, which was grounded upon so uncertain a principle. On the contrary, the Catholic Church, who besides the Scripture acknowledges true Tradition as a principle of its religion, is not ashamed to confess that the Hebrew text of the Bible may be interpreted several ways by reason of the equivocation of the Hebrew words.

7.

Jean Le Clerc (1657–1736)

Jean Le Clerc may have been largely forgotten by posterity, but his scholarship remains a very important moment in the advent of critical methods of scriptural interpretation. His exegetical work began with his commentary on the Pentateuch (1693–96), followed by his *Ars critica* in 1697.

Le Clerc studied philosophy and theology in Geneva, the city of his birth, where he became a pastor in 1678. Soon after that, he embarked on a journey that led him to the Protestant Academy of Saumur, in France's Loire valley, and to Holland and England. In 1683, having returned to Geneva, he had a conflict with François (Francis) Turretini, a prominent Genevan theologian who was an adherent of Protestant Orthodoxy. He then moved to Amsterdam, taught philosophy and the humanities for more than four decades at the Arminian seminary, and befriended John Locke, who was in exile in Holland at the time.

During his studies in Geneva, Le Clerc was repelled by the Orthodox scholasticism of Turretini: metaphysical speculations and other subtleties were obfuscating the simpler language of Scripture itself. He wrote, "Since Scripture is not a work of philosophy, understanding what it says depends less on long reasonings than on the study of the languages in which it was written."[1] This was of course directly related to Erasmus's program for theology. Le Clerc knew this program very well and even edited Erasmus's treatise on theological method (*Methodus*) in Leiden in 1703 (Conroy 1974, 69n1). Le Clerc also read the Leiden theologian André Rivet (1572–1651), Hugo Grotius, Baruch Spinoza, and Richard Simon with profit, but deemed Simon's focus on copies, translations, interpreters, and commentators to be too narrow (Simon and Le Clerc disliked each other; Auvray 1974, 80–84): "Many agree with me that this cannot be taken to be the History of a book, unless we may consider it as a history of a prince a small narrative in which is presented the kinds of clothing the prince was ordinarily wearing, which

1. "Avertissement" to *Entretiens sur diverses matieres de Théologie*, published in Amsterdam by H. Wettstein in 1685, written in collaboration with Charles Le Cène. Maria Cristina Pitassi, *Entre croire et savoir: Le problème de la méthode critique chez Jean Le Clerc* (Leiden: Brill, 1987), 12.

painters produced his portraits, and which authors have reflected upon his deeds" (Le Clerc 1686, 14; Pitassi 1987a, 112n78). Against the Roman Catholic Simon, the Calvinist Le Clerc also argued in favor of the clarity of Scripture with regard to matters of salvation. Le Clerc was fonder of Spinoza's biblical hermeneutics, especially his proposal for a biblical interpretation through Scripture itself, rooted in the rigorous examination of historical facts. Like Spinoza, Le Clerc sought to read and study texts, including Scripture, without philosophical and theological constraints, paying attention to the meaning of a given passage or book. In many ways, Le Clerc's practice of the *ars critica* resembles Hugo Grotius's, who, in his *Annotata ad Vetus Testamentum* (1644) and other works, already sought to combine philology, textual criticism, and history (Pitassi 1987b, 76).

The source of the excerpts below is "On the Best Manner of Interpreting the Bible. Dissertation II," in *Twelve Dissertations Out of Monsieur Le Clerk's Genesis* [...], trans. Thomas Brown (London: R. Baldwin, 1696). Original title: *Genesis sive Mosis prophetae liber primus. Ex translatione Joannis Cleric, cum ejusdem paraphrasi perpetua, commentario philologico, dissertationibus criticis et tabulis Chronologicis* (Amsterdam: A. Wolfgang & J. Waesbergios, 1693). The English translation has been modernized.

ON THE BEST MANNER OF INTERPRETING THE BIBLE. DISSERTATION II (1696)

[51] Since after the labours of so many learned men, who both in this, and especially the last age, have endeavoured to interpret the [52] Holy Scriptures, it is my lot also to undertake the same province; I think it but necessary to acquaint the reader upon what motives I attempted, and after what manner I have performed it. I am sensible that I have engaged not only in a very difficult, but a most invidious affair, by reason of the different parties and factions that disturb the repose of the Christian world. For in a business of this nature, if a man does not do something singular to distinguish him from the rest, he must expect to meet with the contempt and laughter of the learned and unlearned, and if he advances any thing unheard of, and untouched before (which I dare presume to say is no easy matter), for his recompense he is sure to incur the hatred and malice of the world, especially as it is managed by the divines nowadays. Nevertheless after I had seriously revolved all this in my mind, I was at last determined by the authority of *Philo Judæus*,[2] who after he has commended the divine volumes of *Moses* as they deserve, and shown what a fatigue and trouble his interpreters must expect, says[:] "Yet we must not therefore desist, but for the sake of piety, strive to say something above our power, and advance as far as it is lawful for human minds to aspire, that are possessed with the love and desire of wisdom." In the beginning of his Book Περὶ κοσμοποιίας.[3]

Having therefore with God's assistance, as I hope, undertaken this difficult affair, I have all [53] along endeavoured neither to disgust the nice reader with any nauseous repetitions, nor disoblige the lovers of antiquity with any new doctrines. After what manner I have accomplished it, I design to lay open in this dissertation as plainly as I can; but first of all I shall show with what difficulties I struggled, and by what means I was able to overcome them; and in this age particularly better than could be done in the last; not that we pretend to a greater share of judgment; but because we have much better helps now to enable us to surmount them.

II. Before we come to the interpretation of the holy Books, it will be necessary to remind the reader as briefly as we can, what is meant by the word *interpret*, for we do not here design to deliver all the rules of that art. Now since those who speak make use of certain words or forms of speaking

2. Philo of Alexandria.

3. *Peri kosmopoiias*, or *On the Creation of the Cosmos*.

in order to be understood by others, and to raise the same motions and affections of the mind in their hearers as they feel themselves, those may be said to interpret other people's words (if we take the word in a large acceptation) who so express them in another tongue, that they who hear the interpreter speak, think altogether the same things, in the very same order and manner, as the person who spoke first would have them. If all languages were equally copious, and furnished with words of the same force and energy, we might safely then render word for word, and phrase for phrase, and consequently we should only have [54] occasion for a literal simple translation. But since languages do not answer one another so exactly, it is impossible to make a verbal translation if the narration is somewhat long. Many things must of necessity be explained in fewer or more words, as the occasion demands, if the interpreter has a mind to be understood, and to gain that point in the minds of his hearers, as he whose interpreter he is desires he should. Sometimes, though we increase or diminish the number of words, the same notion cannot be expressed in two languages, by reason of the diversity of the idiom. An infinite number of words and expressions, whether figurative or proper, are so peculiar to their own tongues that they can by no means be transfused into another, without a long and troublesome circumlocution, which cannot be inserted into a translation.

From hence it is easy to conclude that no translation can be in all respects complete, that is to say, such a translation, that after the perusing of it, the reader shall think the very same things, and be affected after the same manner, as if he understood the language out of which the version was made, and was able to draw for himself out of the original fountain. And as this holds certainly true in all languages in the world, so it is most sensibly perceived in the Latin translations of the Hebrew books, by reason of the vast disagreements between the Hebrew and Latin tongues, as we shall more [55] fully demonstrate below. We know indeed that the ancient Jews and Christians, who were ignorant of the Hebrew tongue, thought the Greek version of the Old Testament—but especially that of the Pentateuch, commonly said to be done by the LXX interpreters—to be the most absolute thing in its kind that ever was . . . [:] "Whether the Chaldeans learn the Greek tongue, or the Greeks the Chaldean tongue, and light upon both Scriptures, the Chaldean, and that into which it is translated, they admire and adore them as Sisters, or rather as one and the same both in words and things; not content to call them interpreters, but prophets, and revealers of heavenly things, who happily expressed the genuine thoughts of Moses with a most pure Spirit." These are Philo's words in his book *De vitâ Mosis*, which we could heartily wish were as true as they are remote from truth.[4] We should then have the best and surest interpreters of Moses, and the exemplar of a perfect translation, which they were very far from obliging the world with.

But since it is evident that, what Philo pretends was done by the LXX interpreters, is impossible to be performed, by reason of the great difference of languages, as it has been already observed, we did not therefore attempt to translate the Old Testament, because we hoped that those who were only well skilled in Latin, might be able, after the reading of our translation, to [56] reach the meaning of the prophets, as well as those who understand Hebrew, and hear them speak in their own native tongue; we thought it was enough to aspire towards it, as far as the most different idioms of the two languages would give us leave; and since without taking too great a liberty, we could not bend the Hebrew phrase to the genius of the Latin tongue, we often expressed the hebraisms word for word, especially such as the Christian world has been long accustomed to, or whenever we did not certainly understand the meaning of any place. Of which more thereafter.

But because the Hebrew phrases, and manner of expression, being different from all others, would give a great deal of trouble to those who are only acquainted with Latin, we have added a plain paraphrase more suited to the nature of that tongue; by the reading of which, if they cannot attain to the very words of Moses, yet since we have in the same order expressed that in Latin, which Moses did in Hebrew, they will in some measure comprehend his sense, and not as I imagine, deviate much from the true meaning of the text. By this means what we were not able to compass by one single version, perhaps we may perform by the help of the paraphrase.

4. [*Original footnote*] Philo, *Life of Moses* II, 20.

But after all, we thought we should not fully satisfy the curiosity, if not of the most learned, yet of those who were not altogether strangers to Hebrew, if we did not in our annotations explain the hebraisms, opinions, customs, rites, [57] the allusions to them, and the nature of places, as far as we could arrive to the knowledge of them, and give an account of our whole translation and paraphrase. Thus in our paraphrase we have in a few words shown what our opinion was; and in our annotations more at large why we were of that opinion . . . .

[58] In our annotations we have only endeavoured to open and illustrate that which is called the *grammatical*, and by the schoolmen the *literal* sense. We have there laid down no theological or theoretical, no moral or practical conclusions, as well because it would have too much swelled the bulk of the work, as because after the grammatical sense is once fully understood, it is the easiest matter in the world to find out the theoretical or practical doctrines, especially to those that have read any systems of divinity or morality. We have also meddled with no theological controversies, because it was not our intention to gratify this or that party, but (what all good Christians ought to agree in) the lovers of the Holy Scriptures and of the truth. As for those persons who take a delight to know these squabbles, which it were better for the interest of mankind that they were extinguished, they may have books and comments more than enough, written merely to gratify a faction, and these they may turn over at their leisure.

Perhaps some people will censure me, that I have not handled every thing more like a divine, [59] but let them know, whoever they be, that I purposely left that province, to be managed by their sublimer wits. We might indeed be justly blamed, if we omitted any thing we promised to perform, but since it was never in our thoughts, as we have solemnly affirmed, to retail theological dogmas, it would be hard measure to condemn us for what we never promised. No, they have our leave to despise these our performances in comparison of theological and abstruser contemplations. We'll not disown, if they please, that we did not penetrate into the obscure meaning of the Holy Writers, that lurks under the *cortex grammaticus*.[5] Let us be thought to understand no more in the Sacred Books of the Hebrews, than the *authors were willing the people should understand* . . . . If we have been able to attain but to this small pittance everywhere, we shall mightily congratulate ourselves, and others of vulgar understanding, to whose apprehension this was suited.

But as we had often occasion to doubt whether our conjectures were right, and could not make out the meaning clear enough by the help of grammar and criticism alone, or else several meanings of equal probability offered themselves: the reader may observe, that both in our paraphrase and commentary, we use a doubtful and no dogmatical style, and perhaps he will there discover more frequent reasons for suspending [60] his opinion, than in most writings of this nature. But since every man believes and doubts for himself, I must inform those learned gentlemen who have a greater insight in these matters, that I write for myself, and such as stand upon the same level, and may they hug themselves with the sweet contemplation that they know more than their neighbours. Lest we should betray anyone into mistakes, we made a scruple to assert some things positively, when neither by the assistance of others, nor by our own endeavours, we were able to fix any certain judgment: However it does not follow that people do not invent, because they do not affirm. As we vastly disagree from the opinion of those persons who believe that nothing can be made out in Scripture with the help of grammar alone, unless tradition comes in for a share; so we do not believe that it can explain and clear everything: We are sure we have found it so. Now where the matter was not evident beyond all possibility of dispute, we have taken care to restrain all rash determinations, which could be an unpardonable imposition on the world, if we should affirm things false, or things unknown; besides that, nothing can be more scandalous, than to let our approbation run before our knowledge.

III. So much we thought ourselves obliged to say, concerning our manner of interpreting in general, now we shall proceed to lay before our reader the difficulties that gave us no little [61] pain, when we first began to set pen to paper. If we rendered word for word, it was apparent that the version would become unserviceable to those who were unacquainted with Hebrew, for

5. Or "under the grammatical layer."

whose use it was principally intended: For it had been utterly impossible for them to understand it, unless they perpetually consulted the comments, where nevertheless many grammatical criticisms of small importance are omitted: And frequently too, those who are unskillful in hebraisms, would have wrested them in a wrong sense. And now, if to avoid these inconveniencies, we had followed a different conduct, allowing ourselves too great a latitude; it was to be feared, lest in obscure places we might impose our own conjectures upon the reader, instead of the meaning of the sacred Writers. I know it will be replied to all this, that a middle way is then to be observed, whereby the translation shall neither be made so servile and close as to become obscure, and mislead those who are only skilled in Latin, nor too lax or redundant, so as to show the interpreter rather than the writer himself. But so severe an undertaking is much harder to be well performed, than it is easy to talk of it, as we shall show by a few examples. . . .

[102] XIII. Furnished with these helps especially, not to mention any more, we begin our translation and commentary upon the Old Testament. It is true, several learned men have gone the same way before us, especially in the last age, and the beginning of this, who deserve great commendation for their performances. But if we may be allowed to speak the truth, though they neither lacked abilities nor diligence, yet two things stood in their ways, which hindered them from giving any lasting satisfaction to those who came after them.

The first was the lack of due helps, which we now enjoy; for we may justly say of the writers of this age, that they have taken more pains in illustrating and cultivating the sacred philology, than was done in two thousand years before. Hence it comes to pass, that we have such vast numbers of excellent works to assist us to understand the holy Volumes. The truth of this sufficiently appears by the Polyglott Bibles, the lexicons, and treatises of all sorts that adorn our libraries, which before had no such treasures in them, and the reading of our work, wherein they are so often commended, will undeniably evince this.

The other was, the general bent of the last age, rather towards theological than grammatical learning, by reason of the new controversies that then employed the whole Christian world; [103] so that interpreters rather busied themselves to confute errors than give us a plain and critical enarration of the words. I will not say that, by thus inclining their studies, men of skill and learning have been so far led out of the way that they have sought out doctrines, which were true indeed, and agreeable to religion, in improper places, though nothing be more certain; however it is manifest, that by so doing, they have neglected several helps necessary for the understanding of languages, since it is impossible for anyone to grasp everything at the same time. They who have read the most celebrated commentaries of the divines of the last age, and examined their translations, know how true this is, and to prove it to those who never looked upon them, would be labour lost.

They who employed their time most this way, chiefly depended upon some late grammarians of the Jews and modern Rabbis, but were in a manner destitute of all other assistances of critical learning. I would be eager to know which of them, in the last age, applied the histories of the old Eastern people who bordered upon the Hebrews, and what we find in ancient authors relating to their manners, opinions, and their country, towards the illustration of the Scriptures; two or three perhaps and no more. Nevertheless St. Jerome had long ago advised, though nobody would regard him, that "it was one thing to compose books of our own, as for instance covetousness, faith, virginity, widows, and upon each of these heads to [104] produce testimonies from all parts of the Bible, and set them off with a little secular eloquence, and make a magnificent appearance upon such common subjects; and another thing to dive into the sense of the prophets and apostles, to know why they wrote so, by what reasons they support their opinions, what peculiar things the Idumeans, the Moabites, the Ammonites, the Tyrians, the Philistines, the Egyptians and Assyrians have to themselves in the Old Testament. For it is necessary," he continues, "that they should have different causes, and arguments, and originals, according to the diversity of places, and times, and people, to whom they were written." But neither in St. Jerome's time, nor afterwards, did anyone, before our age, regard this advice as it deserved; so that our ancestors have left us a very ample harvest for this sort of learning; upon this account we may pretend to set out more accurate translations and annotations upon the Scriptures than they did, though we are otherwise inferior to them in wit, learning and industry. In their times theological and moral precepts could hardly be inculcated enough, but now since they are known to all, we lie under no necessity to dwell upon them any longer. Therefore have we employed ourselves in that way of interpretation which we have described in this dissertation, and have endeavoured to observe the laws we enjoined ourselves very religiously. How we have succeeded in our performance, let other persons judge, who have pursued these studies out of a desire to find out the [105] truth, to whose censure we most willingly submit our undertaking, and shall be always ready to receive their instruction and emendations, with all imaginable gratitude.

8.

John Locke (1632–1704)

A key figure in the advent of modernity, born into a Puritan family, John Locke lived in an age of deep social and political turmoil: the end of the British monarchy with the execution of Charles I in 1649, the restoration of the monarchy with Charles II (1660), and the Glorious Revolution of 1688. In 1689–90, Locke published three great works that exercised a deep influence on modern thought: *An Essay Concerning Human Understanding*, in which he promotes empiricism and reflects on the boundaries of human understanding; the *Second Treatise of Government*, published anonymously, which makes a case for the sovereignty of the people, presenting government in terms of social contract; his *Letter Concerning Toleration*, which was translated from Latin into English that year, also published anonymously, in which he argues for the separation of church and state. These writings already exhibit Locke's interest in the Scriptures. In the course of his studies, he became familiar with the scholarship of Sebastian Castellio, whom he admired (Backus 2012, 144), Richard Simon, and Jean Le Clerc, among others.

Educated at Christ Church (Oxford), Locke later served that institution as a lecturer in Greek (1660) and rhetoric (1663), before studying medicine and becoming a doctor. Discovering René Descartes's philosophy was a turning point, as it helped him move past the Aristotelian and scholastic philosophy he had been taught at Christ Church. In 1688 he returned to England after five years of exile in Holland, where he witnessed the arrival of thousands of Protestant refugees from France, as the 1598 Edict of Nantes, which had secured some toleration for French Protestants, had been revoked in 1685. After his return to England, he befriended Isaac Newton and encouraged him to write an anti-Trinitarian treatise. Newton read the section on Corinthians in Locke's *Paraphrase and Notes on the Epistles of St. Paul* and thought it was "done with very great care and judgment" (Wainwright 1987, 5). Among Locke's last works is his *Reasonableness of Christianity* (1695), a treatise that belongs to what may be called "rational theology" (Ashcraft 1992).

Le Clerc befriended Locke in Holland. He read early chapters of *An Essay Concerning*

Human Understanding and translated and published an abridged version in French. After Locke's death, Le Clerc penned a detailed biographical eulogy titled, "Éloge de feu Mr. Locke," (Le Clerc 1705) in which he wrote, "Some years before his death, he applied himself entirely to the study of the holy Scriptures, and found so much pleasure therein, that he was very much troubled he had applied his mind to that study no sooner" (Le Clerc 1706, 24). A close study of Locke's *Paraphrase* indicates clearly, and somewhat surprisingly, his emphasis on the primacy of revelation over reason and his views on the limitations of reason and philosophy (Wainwright 1987, 31–33). Locke did not live to see his *Paraphrase and Notes on the Epistles of St. Paul* published as a book: they were published posthumously in 1705–7.

What follows is Locke's preface to a 1707 version of his *Paraphrases and Notes*, as found in *An Essay for the Understanding of St. Paul's Epistles, by Consulting St. Paul Himself* (London: Black Swan, 1707). (For a modern edition, see John Locke, *A Paraphrase and Notes on the Epistles of St. Paul*, vol. 1, ed. Arthur W. Wainwright [Oxford: Clarendon, 1987].) This text introduces the reader to Locke's method for reading Scripture and attaining knowledge of its "sense" or meaning. Sound interpretation of Paul's Epistles depends on close and repeated readings of the entire Epistles—not just of short passages that appear in our versions of the text as verses and chapters. As Locke put it, he "endeavoured to make St. Paul an interpreter to me of his own epistles" (see below, 70). Pressed by friends to publish the result of his studies of Scripture, Locke consented, hoping that his paraphrases and notes may help Christians understand what they believe, for "if I must believe for myself, it is unavoidable that I must understand for myself" (see below, 72).

Locke's English has been slightly modernized; for instance, many uppercase letters, used for nouns, are now lowercase.

PREFACE TO *A PARAPHRASE AND NOTES ON THE EPISTLES OF ST. PAUL*

[iii] To go about to explain any of St. Paul's Epistles, after so great a train of expositors and commentators, might seem an attempt of vanity, censurable for its needlessness, did not the daily and approved examples of pious and learned men justify it. This may be some excuse for me to the public, if ever these following papers should chance to come abroad: But to my self, for whose use this work was undertaken, I need make no apology. Though I had been conversant in these epistles, as well as in other parts of sacred Scripture, yet I found that I understood them not; I mean the doctrinal and discursive parts of them: Though the practical directions, which are usually dropped in the latter part of each epistle, appeared to me very plain, intelligible, and instructive.

I did not, when I reflected on it, very much wonder that this part of sacred Scripture had difficulties in it, many causes of obscurity did readily occur to me. The nature of epistolary writings in general, disposes the writer to pass by the mentioning of many things, as well known to him to whom his letter is addressed, which are necessary to be laid open to a stranger, to make him comprehend what is said: And it not seldom falls out, that a well penned letter which is very easy and intelligible to the receiver, is very obscure to a stranger, who hardly knows what to make of [iv] it. The matters that St. Paul wrote about were certainly things well known to those he wrote to, and which they had some peculiar concern in, which made them easily apprehend his meaning, and see the tendency and force of his discourse. But we having now at this distance no information of the occasion of his writing, little or no knowledge of the temper and circumstances those he wrote to were in, but what is to be gathered out of the epistles themselves, it is not strange that many things in them lie concealed to us, which no doubt they who were concerned in the letter understood at first sight. Add to this, that in many places it is manifest he answers letters sent, and questions proposed to him, which if we had, would much better clear those passages that relate to them, than all the learned notes of critics and commentators, who in aftertimes fill us with their conjectures; for very often, as to the matter in hand, they are nothing else.

The language wherein these epistles are written, are another; and that no small occasion of their obscurity to us now. The words are Greek; a language dead many ages since: A language of a very witty volatile people, seekers after novelty, and abounding with variety of notions and sects, to which they applied the terms of their common tongue with great liberty and variety. And yet this makes but one small part of the difficulty in the language of these epistles; there is a peculiarity in it, that much more obscures and perplexes the meaning of these writings, than what can be occasioned by the looseness and variety of the Greek tongue. The terms are Greek, but the idiom or turn of the phrases may be truly said to be Hebrew or Syriac. The custom and familiarity of which tongues do sometimes so far influence the expressions in these epistles, that one may observe the force of the Hebrew conjugations, particularly that of *hiphil* given to Greek verbs, in a way unknown to the Grecians themselves. Nor is this all; the subject treated of in these epistles [v] is so wholly new, and the doctrines contained in them so perfectly remote from the notions that mankind were acquainted with, that most of the important terms in it have quite another signification from what they have in other discourses. So that putting all together, we may truly say that the New Testament is a book written in a language peculiar to itself.

To these causes of obscurity common to St. Paul, with most of the other penmen of the several books of the New Testament, we may add those that are peculiarly his, and owing to his style and temper. He was, as it is visible, a man of quick thought, warm temper, mighty well versed in the writings of the Old Testament, and full of the doctrine of the New. All this put together, suggested matter to him in abundance on those subjects which came in his way: So that one may consider him when he was writing, as beset with a crowd of thoughts, all striving for utterance. In this posture of mind it was almost impossible for him to keep that slow pace, and observe minutely that order and method of ranging all he said, from which results an easy and obvious perspicuity. To this plenty and vehemence of his may be imputed those many large parentheses which a careful reader may observe in his epistles. Upon this account also it is, that he often breaks off in the middle of an argument, to let in some new thought suggested by his own words; which having pursued and explained as far as conduced to his present purpose, he reassumes again the thread of his discourse, and goes on with it, without taking any notice that he returns again to what he had been before saying, though sometimes it be so far off that it may well have slipped out of his mind, and requires a very attentive reader to observe, and so bring the disjointed members together, as to make up the connection, and see how the scattered parts of the discourse hang together in a coherent well-agreeing sense, that makes it all of a piece.

[vi] Besides the disturbance, in perusing St. Paul's Epistles, from the plenty and vivacity of his thoughts, which may obscure his method, and often hide his sense from an unwary, or over-hasty reader; the frequent changing of the personage he speaks in, renders the sense very uncertain, and is apt to mislead one who has not some clue to guide him; sometimes by the pronoun I, he means himself; sometimes any Christian; sometimes a Jew, and sometimes any man, etc. If speaking of himself in the first person singular has so various meanings, his use of the first person plural is with a far greater latitude, sometimes designing himself alone, sometimes those with himself whom he makes partners to the epistle; sometimes with himself comprehending the other apostles, or preachers of the Gospel, or Christians: no, sometimes he in that way speaks of the converted Jews, other times of the converted Gentiles, and sometimes of others, in a more or less extended sense, every one of which varies the meaning of the place, and makes it to be differently understood. I have forborn to trouble the reader with examples of them here. If his own observation has not already furnished him with them, the following paraphrase and notes I suppose will satisfy him in the point.

In the current also of his discourse, he sometimes drops in the objections of others, and his answers to them, without any change in the scheme of his language, that might give notice of any other speaking besides himself. This requires great attention to observe, and yet if it be neglected or overlooked, will make the reader very much mistake and misunderstand his meaning, and render the sense very perplexed.

These are intrinsic difficulties arising from the text itself, whereof there might be a great many other named, as the uncertainty, sometimes, who are the persons he speaks to, or the [vii] opinions or practices which he has in his eye, sometimes in alluding to them, sometimes in his exhortations and reproofs. But those above mentioned being the chief, it may suffice to have opened our eyes a little upon them, which, well examined, may contribute towards our discovery of the rest.

To these we may subjoin two external causes that have made no small increase of the native and original difficulties that keep us from an easy and assured discovery of St. Paul's sense, in many parts of his epistles, and those are, first, the dividing of them into chapters and verses, as we have done, whereby they are so chopped and minced, and as they are now printed, stand so broken and divided, that not only the common people take the verses usually for distinct aphorisms, but even people of more advanced knowledge, in reading them lose very much of the strength and force of the coherence, and the light that depends on it. Our minds are so weak and narrow, they have need of all the helps and assistances that can be procured, to lay before them undisturbedly the thread and coherence of any discourse; by which alone they are truly improved and lead into the genuine sense of the author. When the eye is constantly disturbed with loose sentences that, by their standing and separation, appear as so many distinct fragments, the mind will have much to do to take in and carry on in its memory an uniform discourse of dependent reasonings, especially having from the cradle been used to wrong impressions concerning them, and constantly accustomed to hear them quoted as distinct sentences, without any limitation or explication of their precise meaning from the place they stand in, and the relation they bear to what goes before, or follows. These divisions also have given occasion to the reading these epistles by parcels and in scraps, which has farther confirmed the evil arising from such partitions. And I doubt not but [viii] every one will confess it to be a very unlikely way to come to the understanding of any other letters, to read them piecemeal, a bit today, and another scrap tomorrow, and so on by broken intervals; especially if the pause and cessation should be made as the chapters the apostle's epistles are divided into do end sometimes in the middle of a discourse, and sometimes in the middle of a sentence. It cannot therefore but be wondered, that that should be permitted to be done to Holy Writ, which would visibly disturb the sense, and hinder the understanding of any other book whatsoever. If Tully's epistles were so printed, and so used, I ask whether they would not be much harder to be understood, less easy and less pleasant to be read by much than now they are?

How plain soever this abuse is, and what prejudice soever it does to the understanding of the sacred Scripture, yet if a Bible was printed as it should be, and as the several parts of it were written, in continued discourses where the argument is continued, I doubt not but the several parties would complain of it, as an innovation, and a dangerous change in the publishing those holy Books. And indeed those who are for maintaining their opinions, and the systems of parties by sound of words, with a neglect of the true sense of Scripture, would have reason to make and foment the outcry. They would most of them be immediately disarmed of their great magazine of artillery wherewith they defend themselves, and fall upon others, if the Holy Scripture were but laid before the eyes of Christians in its due connection and consistency, it would not then be so easy to snatch out a few words, as if they were separate from the rest, to serve a purpose, to which they do not at all belong, and with which they have nothing to do. But as the matter now stands, he who has a mind to it, may at a cheap rate be a notable champion for the truth, that is, for the doctrines [ix] of the sect that chance or interest has cast him into. He need but be furnished with verses of sacred Scripture, containing words and expressions that are but flexible (as all general obscure and doubtful ones are) and his system that has appropriated them to the orthodoxy of his church, makes them immediately strong and irrefragable arguments for his opinion. This is the benefit of loose sentences, and Scripture crumbled into verses, which quickly turn into independent aphorisms. But if the quotation in the verse produced were considered as a part of a continued coherent discourse, and so its sense were limited by the tenor of the context, most of these forward and warm disputants would be quite stripped of those, which they doubt not now to call spiritual weapons, and they would have often nothing to say that would not show their weakness, and manifestly fly in their faces. . . . [x] Nothing is more acceptable to fancy than pliant terms and expressions that are not obstinate, in such it can find its account with delight, and with them be illuminated, orthodox, infallible at pleasure, and in its own way. But where the sense of the author goes visibly in its own train, and the words, receiving a determined sense from their companions and adjacents, will not consent to give countenance and color to what is agreed to be right, and must be supported at any rate, there men of established orthodoxy do not so well find their satisfaction. And perhaps if it were well examined, it would be no very extravagant paradox to say that there are fewer that bring their opinions to the sacred Scripture to be tried by that infallible rule, than bring the sacred Scripture to their opinions, to bend it to them, to make it as they can a cover and guard of them. And to this purpose its being divided into verses, and brought as much as may be into loose and general aphorisms, makes it most useful and serviceable. And in this lies the other great cause of obscurity and perplexedness, which has been cast upon St. Paul's Epistles from without.

[xi] St. Paul's Epistles, as they stand translated in our English Bibles, are now by long and constant use become a part of the English language, and common phraseology, especially in matters of religion; this every one uses familiarly, and thinks he understands, but it must be observed that if he has a distinct meaning when he uses those words and phrases, and knows himself what he intends by them, it is always according to the sense of his own system, and the articles or interpretations of the society he is engaged in. So that all this knowledge and understanding which he has in the use of these passages of sacred Scripture, reaches no further than this, that he knows (and that is very well) what he himself says, but thereby knows nothing at all what St. Paul said in them. The apostle wrote not by that man's system, and so his meaning cannot be known by it. This being the ordinary way of understanding the epistles, and every sect being perfectly orthodox in its own judgment: What a great and invincible darkness must this cast upon St. Paul's meaning to all those of that way, in all those places where his thoughts and sense run counter to what any party has espoused for orthodox, as it must unavoidably to all but one of the different systems, in all those passages that any way relate to the points in controversy between them.

This is a mischief which, however frequent and almost natural, reaches so far that it would justly make all those who depend upon them, wholly diffident of commentators, and let them see how little help was to be expected from them in relying on them for the true sense of the sacred Scripture, did they not take care to help to cozen themselves, by choosing to use and pin their faith on such expositors as explain the sacred Scripture in favor of those opinions that they before hand have voted orthodox, and bring to the sacred Scripture not for trial, but confirmation. Nobody can think that any text of St. Paul's Epistles [xii] has two contrary meanings, and yet so it must have to two different men, who taking two commentators of different sects for their respective guides into the sense of any one of the epistles, shall build upon their respective expositions. . . .

[xiii] This indeed seems to make the case desperate: For if the comments and expositions of pious and learned men cannot be depended on, where shall we go for help? To which I answer, I would not be mistaken, as if I thought the labours of the learned in this case wholly lost, and fruitless. There is great use and benefit to be made of them, when we have once got a rule to know which of their expositions, in the great variety there is of them, explains the words and phrases according to the apostle's meaning. Until then it is evident, from what is above said, they serve for the most part to no other use, but either to make us find our own sense, and not his, in St. Paul's words; or else to find in them no settled sense at all.

Here it will be asked, how shall we come by this rule you mention? Where is that touchstone to be had, that will show us whether the meaning we ourselves put, or take as put by others upon St. Paul's words in his epistles, be truly his meaning or no? I will not say the way which I propose, and have in the following paraphrase followed, will make us infallible in our interpretations of the apostle's text: But this I will own, that until I took this way, St. Paul's Epistles to me, in the ordinary way of reading and studying them, were very obscure parts of Scripture, that left me almost everywhere at a loss; and I was at a great uncertainty in which of the contrary senses, that were to be found in his commentators, he was to be taken. Whether what I have done has made it any clearer and more visible now, I must leave others to judge. This I beg leave to say for myself, that if some very sober judicious Christians, no strangers to the sacred Scriptures, indeed [xiv] learned divines of the church of England, had not professed that by the perusal of these following papers, they understood the epistles better much than they did before, and had not with repeated instances pressed me to publish them, I should not have consented they should have gone beyond my own private use, for which they were at first designed, and where they made me not repent my pains.

If anyone be so far pleased with my endeavours, as to think it worthwhile to be informed, what was the clue I guided myself by through all the dark passages of these epistles, I shall minutely tell him the steps by which I was brought into this way, that he may judge whether I proceeded rationally, upon right grounds or no, if so be anything in so mean an example as mine may be worth his notice.

After I had found by long experience that the reading of the text and comments in the ordinary way proved not so successful as I wished to the end proposed, I began to suspect that in reading a chapter as was usual, and thereupon sometimes consulting expositors upon some hard places of it, which at that time most affected me, as relating to points then under consideration in my own mind, or in debate amongst others, was not a right method to get into the true sense of these epistles. I saw plainly, after I began once to reflect on it, that if anyone now should write me a letter as long as St. Paul's to the Romans, concerning such a matter as that is, in a style as foreign, and expressions as dubious as his seem to be, if I should divide it into fifteen or sixteen chapters, and read of them one today, and another tomorrow, etc., it was ten to one I should never come to a full and clear comprehension of it. The way to understand the mind of him who wrote it, every one would agree, was to read the whole letter through from one end to the other, all at once, to see what was the main subject and tendency of it: or if it had several views and purposes in it, not dependent one of another, nor [xv] in a subordination to one chief aim and end, to discover what those different matters were, and where the author concluded one, and began another; and if there were any necessity of dividing the epistle into parts, to make the boundaries of them.

In prosecution of this thought, I concluded it necessary, for the understanding of any one of St. Paul's Epistles, to read it all through at one sitting, and to observe as well as I could the drift and design of his writing it. If the first reading gave me some light, the second gave me more; and so I persisted on reading constantly the whole epistle over at once, until I came to have a good general view of the apostle's main purpose in writing the epistle, the chief branches of his discourse wherein he prosecuted it, the arguments he used, and the disposition of the whole.

This, I confess, is not to be obtained by one or two hasty readings; it must be repeated again and again, with a close attention to the tenor of the discourse, and a perfect neglect of the divisions into chapters and verses. On the contrary, the safest way is to suppose that the epistle has but one business, and one aim, until by a frequent perusal of it you are forced to see there are distinct independent matters in it, which will forwardly enough show themselves.

It requires so much more pains, judgment and application, to find the coherence of obscure and abstruse writings, and makes them so much the more unfit to serve prejudice and preoccupation when found, that it is not to be wondered that St. Paul's Epistles have with many passed rather for disjointed, loose pious discourses, full of warmth and zeal, and overflows of light, rather than for calm, strong, coherent reasonings, that carried a thread of argument and consistency all through them.

[xvi] But this muttering of lazy or ill disposed readers hindered me not from persisting in the course I had begun; I continued to read the same epistle over and over, and over again, until I came to discover, as appeared to me, what was the drift and aim of it, and by what steps and arguments St. Paul prosecuted his purpose. I remembered that St. Paul was miraculously called to the ministry

of the Gospel, and declared to be a chosen vessel; that he had the whole doctrine of the Gospel from God by immediate revelation, and was appointed to be the apostle of the Gentiles, for the propagating of it in the heathen world. This was enough to persuade me that he was not a man of loose and shattered parts, uncapable to argue, and unfit to convince those he had to deal with. God knows how to choose fit instruments for the business he employs them in. A large stock of Jewish learning he had taken in at the feet of Gamaliel, and for his information in Christian knowledge, and the mysteries and depths of the dispensation of grace by Jesus Christ, God himself had condescended to be his instructor and teacher. The light of the Gospel he had received from the fountain and Father of light himself, who, I concluded, had not furnished him in this extraordinary manner, if all this plentiful stock of learning and illumination had been in danger to have been lost, or proved useless, in a jumbled and confused head; nor have laid up such a store of admirable and useful knowledge in a man, who for want of method and order, clearness of conception, or pertinency in discourse, could not draw it out into use with the greatest advantages of force and coherence. That he knew how to prosecute his purpose with strength of argument and close reasoning, without incoherent sallies, or the intermixing of things foreign to his business, was evident to me from several speeches of his recorded in the Acts: [xvii] And it was hard to think that a man who could talk with so much consistency and clearness of conviction, should not be able to write without confusion, inextricable obscurity, and perpetual rambling. The force, order and perspicuity of those discourses could not be denied to be very visible. How then came it that the like was thought much wanting in his epistles? And of this there appeared to me this plain reason: The particularities of the history in which these speeches are inserted, show St. Paul's end in speaking, which being seen, casts a light on the whole, and shows the pertinency of all that he says. But his epistles not being so circumstantiated; there being no concurring history that plainly declares the disposition St. Paul was in, what the actions, expectations, or demands of those to whom he wrote, required him to speak to, we are nowhere told. All this and a great deal more necessary to guide us into the true meaning of the epistles, is to be had only from the epistles themselves, and to be gathered from thence with stubborn attention, and more than common application.

This being the only safe guide (under the Spirit of God, that dictated these sacred Writings) that can be relied on, I hope I may be excused if I venture to say that the utmost ought to be done to observe and trace out St. Paul's reasonings; to follow the thread of his discourse in each of his epistles; to show how it goes on still directed with the same view, and pertinently drawing the several incidents towards the same point. To understand him right, his inferences should be strictly observed; and it should be carefully examined from what they are drawn, and what they tend to. He is certainly a coherent, argumentative, pertinent writer, and care I think should be taken in expounding of him, to show that he is so. But though I say he has weighty aims in his epistles, which he steadily keeps in his eye, and drives at in all that he says, yet I do not say that he puts his discourses into an artificial method, or leads his reader into a distinction of his arguments, or gives them notice of [xviii] new matter by rhetorical or studied transitions. He has no ornaments borrowed from the Greek eloquence; no notions of their philosophy mixed with his doctrine to set it off. The "inticing words of man's wisdom," whereby he means all the studied rules of the Grecian schools, which made them such masters in the art of speaking, he, as he says himself (1 Cor 2:4), wholly neglected. The reason whereof he gives in the next verse, and in other places. But though politeness of language, delicacy of style, fineness of expression, laboured periods, artificial transitions, and a very methodical ranging of the parts with such other embellishments as make a discourse enter the mind smoothly, and strike the fancy at first hearing, have little or no place in his style, yet coherence of discourse, and a direct tendency of all the parts of it, to the argument in hand, are most eminently to be found in him. This I take to be his character, and doubt not but he will be found to be so upon diligent examination. And in this if it be so, we have a clue, if we will take the pains to find it, that will conduct us with surety through those seemingly dark places, and imagined intricacies in which Christians have wandered so far one from another, as to find quite contrary senses.

Whether a superficial reading, accompanied with the common opinion of his invincible obscurity, has kept off some from seeking in him the coherence of a discourse tending with close strong reasoning to a point; or a seemingly more honourable opinion of one that had been wrapped up into the third heaven,[1] as if from a man so warmed and illuminated as he had been, nothing could be expected but flashes of light, and raptures of zeal hindered others to look for a train of reasoning, proceeding on regular and cogent argumentation from a man raised above the ordinary pitch of humanity to a higher and brighter way of illumination; or else whether others were loath to beat their heads about the tenor and coherence in St. Paul's discourses, which, if found out, possibly might set him at a manifest and irreconcilable [xix] difference with their systems, it is certain that whatever has been the cause, this way of getting the true sense of St. Paul's Epistles seems not to have been much made use of, or at least so thoroughly pursued as I am apt to think it deserves.

For, granting that he was full stored with the knowledge of the things he treated of: For he had light from heaven, it was God himself [who] furnished him, and he could not want: Allowing also that he had ability to make use of the knowledge [that] had been given him for the end for which it was given him, namely the information, conviction, and conversion of others; and accordingly that he knew how to direct his discourse to the point in hand, we cannot widely mistake the parts of his discourse employed about it, when we have anywhere found out the point he drives at: Wherever we have got a view of his design, and the aim he proposed to himself in writing, we may be sure that such or such an interpretation does not give us his genuine sense, it being nothing at all to his present purpose. Indeed among various meanings given a text, it fails not to direct us to the best, and very often to assure us of the true. For it is no presumption, when one sees a man arguing for this or that proposition, if he be a sober man, master of reason or common sense, and takes any care of what he says, to pronounce with confidence in several cases, that he could not talk thus or thus.

I do not yet so magnify this method of studying St. Paul's Epistles, as well as other parts of sacred Scripture, as to think it will perfectly clear every hard place, and leave no doubt unresolved. I know expressions now out of use, opinions of those times, not heard of in our days, allusions to customs lost to us, and various circumstances and particularities of the parties, which we cannot come at, etc. must needs continue several passages in the dark now to us at this distance, which shone with full light to those they were directed to. But for all that the studying of St. Paul's Epistles in the way I have proposed, will, I humbly conceive, carry us a [xx] great length in the right understanding of them, and make us rejoice in the light we receive from those most useful parts of divine revelation, by furnishing us with visible grounds that we are not mistaken, while the consistency of the discourse, and the pertinency of it to the design he is upon, vouches it worthy of our great apostle. At least I hope it may be my excuse for having endeavoured to make St. Paul an interpreter to me of his own epistles.

To this may be added another help which St. Paul himself affords us towards the attaining the true meaning contained in his epistles. He who reads him with the attention I propose, will easily observe, that as he was full of the doctrine of the Gospel, so it lay all clear and in order open to his view. When he gave his thoughts utterance upon any point, the matter flowed like a torrent, but it is plain it was a matter he was perfectly master of: he fully possessed the entire revelation he had received from God, had thoroughly digested it; all the parts were formed together in his mind into one well contracted harmonious body. So that he was no way at uncertainty, nor ever in the least at a loss concerning any branch of it. One may see his thoughts were all of a piece in all his epistles, his notions were at all times uniform, and constantly the same, though his expressions very various. In them he seems to take great liberty. This at least is certain, that no one seems less tied up to a form of words. If then having by the method before proposed got into the sense of the several epistles, we will but compare what he says, in the places where he treats of the same subject, we can hardly be mistaken in his sense, nor doubt what it was, that he believed and taught concerning those points of the Christian religion. I know it is not unusual to find a multitude of texts heaped up for the maintaining of an espoused proposi-

1. See 2 Cor 12:2–4.

tion, but in a sense often so remote from their true meaning that one can hardly avoid thinking that those who so used them, either sought not, or valued not, the *sense*, and were satisfied with the *sound*, where [xxi] they could but get that to favor them.[2] But a verbal concordance leads not always to texts of the same meaning; trusting too much thereto will furnish us but with slight proofs in many cases, and anyone may observe how apt that is to jumble together passages of Scripture not relating to the same matter, and thereby to disturb and unsettle the true meaning of Holy Scripture. I have therefore said that we should compare together places of Scripture treating of the same point. Thus indeed one part of the sacred Text could not fail to give light unto another. And since the providence of God has so ordered it, that St. Paul has written a great number of epistles, which though upon different occasions, and to several purposes, yet are all confined within the business of his apostleship, and so contain nothing but points of Christian instruction, amongst which he seldom fails to drop in, and often to enlarge on the great and distinguishing doctrines of our holy religion; which, if quitting our own infallibility in that analogy of faith[3] which we have made to ourselves, or have implicitly adopted from some other, we would carefully lay together, and diligently compare and study, I am apt to think would give us St. Paul's system in a clear and indisputable sense, which everyone must acknowledge to be a better standard to interpret his meaning by, in any obscure and doubtful parts of his epistles, if any such should still remain, than the system, confession, or articles of any church or society of Christians yet known, which however pretended to be founded on Scripture, are visibly the contrivances of men (fallible both in their opinions and interpretations) and as is visible in most of them, made with partial views, and adapted to what the occasions of that time, and the present circumstances they were then in, were thought to require for the support or justification of themselves. Their philosophy also has its part in misleading men from the true sense of the sacred Scripture. He who shall attentively read the Christian [xxii] writers after the age of the apostles will easily find how much the philosophy they were tinctured with influenced them in their understanding of the books of the Old and New Testament. In the ages wherein Platonism prevailed, the converts to Christianity of that school, on all occasions, interpreted Holy Writ according to the notions they had imbibed from that philosophy. Aristotle's doctrine had the same effect in its turn, and when it degenerated into the Peripateticism of the Schools, that too brought its notions and distinctions into divinity, and affixed them to the terms of the sacred Scripture. And we may see still how at this day every one's philosophy regulates everyone's interpretation of the Word of God. Those who are possessed with the doctrine of aerial and aetherial vehicles, have thence borrowed an interpretation of the first four verses of 2 Cor 5 without having any ground to think that St. Paul had the least notion of any such vehicles. It is plain that the teaching of men philosophy, was no part of the design of divine revelation; but that the expressions of Scripture are commonly suited in those matters to the vulgar apprehensions and conceptions of the place and people where they were delivered. And as to the doctrine therein directly taught by the apostles, that tends wholly to the setting up the Kingdom of Jesus Christ in this world, and the salvation of men's souls, and in this it is plain their expressions were conformed to the ideas and notions which they had received from revelation, or were consequent from it. We shall therefore in vain go about to interpret their words by the notions of our philosophy, and the doctrines of men delivered in our schools. This is to explain the apostles' meaning by what they never thought of while they were writing, which is not the way to find their sense in what they delivered, but our own, and to take up from their writings not what they left there for us, but what we bring along with us in ourselves. He who would understand [xxiii] St. Paul right, must understand his terms in the sense he uses them, and not as they are appropriated by each man's particular philosophy, to conceptions that never entered the mind of the apostle. For example, he who shall bring the philosophy now taught and received to the explaining of Spirit, soul, and body, mentioned 1 Thess 5:23, will I fear hardly reach St. Paul's sense, or represent to himself the notions St. Paul then had in his mind. That is what we

2. Editor's emphasis.
3. See Rom 12:6: κατὰ τὴν ἀναλογίαν τῆς πίστεως.

should aim at in reading him, or any other author, and until we from his words paint his very ideas and thoughts in our minds, we do not understand him.

In the divisions I have made, I have endeavoured the best I could to govern myself by the diversity of matter. But in a writer like St. Paul, it is not so easy always to find precisely where one subject ends, and another begins. He is full of the matter he treats and writes with warmth, which usually neglects method, and those partitions and pauses which men educated in the schools of rhetoricians usually observe. Those arts of writing, St. Paul, as well out of design as temper, wholly laid by: The subject he had in hand, and the grounds upon which it stood firm, and by which he inforced it, was what alone he minded, and without solemnly winding up one argument, and intimating any way that he began another, let his thoughts, which were fully possessed of the matter, run in one continued train, wherein the parts of his discourse were woven one into another. So that it is seldom that the scheme of his discourse makes any gap; and therefore without breaking in upon the connection of his language, it is hardly possible to separate his discourse, and give a distinct view of his several arguments in distinct sections.

I am far from pretending infallibility in the sense I have anywhere given in my paraphrase or notes; that would be to erect myself into an apostle, a presumption of the highest nature in anyone who cannot confirm what he says by miracles. I have for my own information sought the true meaning as far as my poor abilities [xxiv] would reach. And I have unbiasedly embraced what upon a fair inquiry appeared so to me. This I thought my duty and interest in a matter of so great concernment to me. If I must believe for myself, it is unavoidable that I must understand for myself. For if I blindly and with an implicit faith take the pope's interpretation of the sacred Scripture, without examining whether it be Christ's meaning, it is the pope I believe in, and not in Christ; it is his authority I rest upon; it is what he says I embrace: For what it is Christ says, I neither know nor concern myself. It is the same thing when I set up any other man in Christ's place, and make him the authentique interpreter of sacred Scripture to myself. He may possibly understand the sacred Scripture as right as any man, but I shall do well to examine myself, whether that which I do not know, indeed (which in the way I take) I can never know, can justify me in making myself his disciple, instead of Jesus Christ's, who of right is alone and ought to be my only Lord and Master: and it will be no less sacrilege in me to substitute to myself any other in his room, to be a prophet, to me, than to be my king or priest.

The same reasons that put me upon doing what I have in these papers done, will exempt me from all suspicion of imposing my interpretation on others. The reasons that led me into the meaning which prevailed on my mind are set down with it; as far as they carry light and conviction to any other man's understanding, so far I hope my labour may be of some use to him; beyond the evidence it carries with it, I advise him not to follow mine, nor any man's interpretation. We are all men liable to errors, and infected with them; but have this sure way to preserve ourselves, every one, from danger by them, if laying aside sloth, carelessness, prejudice, party, and a reverence of men, we betake ourselves in earnest to the study of the way to salvation, in those holy Writings wherein God has revealed it from heaven, and proposed it to the world, seeking our religion where we are sure it is in truth to be found, comparing spiritual things with spiritual things.

9.

Johann Salomo Semler (1725–91)

Throughout the seventeenth century, francophone scholars, especially Louis Cappel and Richard Simon, were at the forefront of textual criticism of the Bible, that is the critical inquiry concerned with the text and versions of Scripture. These pioneers did not find any successors in their regions, perhaps because of the troubles they had encountered. The entire movement stopped, at least in French-speaking countries. German scholars took over in the eighteenth century. Johann Salomo Semler was one of them.

The son of a Lutheran pastor, Semler studied theology at the University of Halle. In 1751 he became a professor of history and of Latin poetry in Altdorf. Two years later at the University of Halle, Siegmund Jacob Baumgarten (1706–57), who had taught Semler and encouraged him to study history, offered him a faculty position teaching theology. Halle was an important center for Pietism; Semler advocated a different approach for theology, one much more attentive to other fields of human knowledge, especially history and philosophy, and to the modern critical and historical methods. Selmer's interests were quite broad within theology: not just biblical studies but also the history of Christianity and of dogma, and dogmatics. He took a critical stance not just against late Orthodox Lutheran theologians, such as Johann Melchior Goeze, but also against Hermann Samuel Reimarus and certain Deist positions (Hornig 2000, 143).

Against Lutheran Orthodoxy (or Lutheran scholasticism), Semler argues that the Scriptures are not verbally inspired; they are also not to be considered as all having the same weight or value. The most decisive biblical texts, according to Semler, are Paul's Epistles to the Galatians, to the Romans, to the Corinthians and the Gospel of John. In these texts, Semler finds the very heart of the Christian faith, namely, the Easter message of reconciliation and salvation, a message he was ready to defend against Reimarus and others. For Semler there is no contradiction between the message of Jesus of Nazareth and the Christian message about him as Savior (Hornig 2000, 144–45). Following his teacher Baumgarten, Semler reflected on the "essence of Christianity" and had no inclination to take the Bible's talk of "demons," "the devil," and of a "descent to hell" literally. He thus had a sense for what scholars would eventually call the "mythical picture of the world" that comes to expression in the Bible. And he was hopeful that, in its future course, Christian theology would gain a better understanding of Christianity's true essence as a religion. Semler advocated a greater freedom—not just docility, as Calvin, alongside many others, recommended—for Christians in relation to the Bible: "The freedom must exist, for people who have begun to experience the salutary power of basic truths, to judge, according to their own knowledge and experience, the basic moral value of certain books from these ancient collections, as well as the value of certain parts of these books" (see below, 75).

Semler's treatise on the canon, titled "Free Investigation of the Canon" (*Abhandlung von freier Untersuchung des Canon*), is perhaps his most important contribution. Gotthold Ephraim Lessing responded to it by envisioning, in a private letter, a book that he would call "an even freer examination of the canon" (Nisbet 2013, 543).

Semler paved the way for many other scholars, in Germany and beyond, who pursued a rigorous, critical examination of the Christian sources while maintaining lively attention to the existential message these sources convey (Johann Philipp Gabler, Friedrich Schleiermacher, Ferdinand Christian Baur, Johannes Weiss, Adolf von Harnack).

What follows is the editor's English translation of excerpts from Johann Salomo Semler, *Abhandlung von freier Untersuchung des Canon*, ed. Heinz Scheible (Gütersloh: Mohn, 1967; 2nd ed. 1980). Scheible's edition is based on Semler's second edition but helpfully signals the changes made by Semler to the first edition.

TREATISE ON A FREE INQUIRY OF THE CANON (1771, 1776)

[27] §5. Undoubtedly, [Christians] will discover with interior joy and great affection the basic teachings which come across some of the books of the Jews, in the acts or examples from some of the figures these books present; but the question is the following: Should pious and honest people, who are acquainted with the inner Christian virtue—a virtue they have reached through the teaching of Christ—accept the content of all of these books, which the Jews are used to numbering in this or that way, as divine?[1] And also: is there an internal or external *historical* ground on the basis of which Christians must make that decision, just as the Jews do, who with regard to *moral* practice and aptitude are far from matching these Christians, to the point where they must still be described as being in a state of *minority* as long as they do not accept the Christian doctrine? Must Christians who are honestly committed to their own spiritual improvement—as taught by Christ and the apostles and confirmed by new exemplars of these kinds—following the standard axioms of true perfection, find and accept the books of Ruth, Esther, Esdras, and Nehemiah as containing clear signs of the divine, salvific, and indispensable truth? Or must they accept these books simply because the Jews have been in the habit of gathering them, alongside other ancient documents and scriptural records of their nation, under this or that main concept, such as the *Scripture*, or the *holy Scripture*? Moreover, should Christians really find in the *narratives* and the description of the history of the exodus out of *Egypt*, of the setting up of the administration and the entire state of the Israelites, of their wars against neighboring peoples, of the creation of the twelve tribes and of the inner breakdown of both kingdoms, of the *Babylonian* captivity, of the repeated edification of the city of Jerusalem and of the temple, the distinguishing marks of the kinds of occurrences which God's [28] extraordinary, unfamiliar action usually carries, as it pertains to God's specific, new revelation? Are not all of the events which are narrated there common human events? Is it therefore correct to conclude that, since the Jews consider these books

1. Semler is discussing the twenty-four books of the Jewish canon and their normativity for Christians.

as *divine* and *holy* books, therefore other peoples too must also view their content as divine and as much more worthy than the account of stories and particular events of other peoples? As far as I can see, and even though many theologians claim it is possible, a general, affirmative answer cannot be given to this question . . . .

The same applies to some of the books of the New Testament, when one keeps in mind the significant diversity of so many readers which it presupposes. Just as the accounts of the gospel writers make it clear that Jesus, in his speeches and in the level he selected for his teaching, took into consideration the varying capacities of those who were listening to him on any given occasion, in the same way it is quite certain that it was a primary concern of the writers, as they arranged their narration or their teaching, to be useful to their contemporary readers, in their own contexts. Consequently, certain things which would have been much more useful with regard to the aptitude and training of today's actual readers were not written down. Or should we claim that it would have been the same if Paul had sent his Romans epistle to the Thessalonians, and his Galatians epistle to Corinth? A difference remains, among these Christians, whereby some already have a greater knowledge, which does not make it necessary to adjust and condescend to them, unlike what needed to be done with regard to other readers in other writings. These proficient Christians, all the more, have the right not to exchange their insights and their basic principles, which are good and really useful to them and others, with insights which are of no great benefit to them or which are basic in nature. Suppose certain readers have already reached the dignified way of thinking about specific matters such as the ones about Onesimus that Paul wishes to bring up to Philemon; how are they supposed to view the letter to Philemon as authentically divine, or as written through a particular inspiration from God? How should they do this, since they already have within themselves this humane disposition and thus cannot learn anything, for themselves and others, from this text? If certain readers are already acquainted with the *moral* truths, their intrinsic value, and their use for themselves; if these readers are already practicing [29] these precepts; if they are humane to the point where they help all people attain the kind of inner regulation which is the beginning of the experience of authentic felicity; if they find the tone in poems, psalms, and in the book of Revelation disagreeable and abhorrent when these texts call for the annihilation of Pagans and so forth, how should these readers find in this book [Revelation], and in its fiery threats and wishes, the expression of genuine divine universal love and beneficence which aims at the renovation of all human beings? Absent this love and beneficence, how can these readers regard such severe curses, pronounced against people who were not Jewish, as having God, who is genuine love for human beings, as their particular and authentic originator? The freedom must exist, for people who have begun to experience the salutary power of basic truths, to judge, according to their own knowledge and experience, the basic moral value of certain books from these ancient collections, as well as the value of certain parts of these books. In the same way, the freedom must also exist, for other readers, to accept and affirm as divine all of the books of the entire Old and New Testaments, as they were written or published as a whole, and to do so following their real or independent insight, without positing any particular difference (even though it is great) between the contents of these books. This judgement concerning divine books, moreover, may also be more remote for others, or it may be left, in one's conscience, undecided.

§6. [31] It is certain that the decision really cannot be made—including for others who inquire about this matter—through a mere historical report and notice, that *these are divine books*, that nothing more and nothing less must be accepted by upright lovers of what is true or of the best religion.[2] . . . Therefore, for someone who searches what is true in relation to these books, any *witness* from the so-called *Jewish* and *Christian Church* is wholly inadequate and cannot ground one's own conviction. . . . The *witness* of the so-called

2. This excerpt is found in a larger section in which Semler addresses the question of the criteria that may be used to determine the divine origin of particular books. Semler seeks to show that, already within ancient Christianity, there were several "parties" (Alexandria, Antioch, Jerusalem, Judeo-Christians, Gnostics, etc.), which all had their own canon.

Church can thus, like *any historical* witness, accept or deny something only on the basis of an *external* occurrence; the question whether one or several books have a divine origin, or whether a book's author was *prompted* by God, *does not concern any external occurrence*; there is thus also no *external* or *historical* witness of that. The following fact, on the other hand, can always be made patent *historically*, namely that the Samaritans have accepted and usually accept, for their religious institution, only the five books of Moses, the Jews in Palestine or Syria only 22 or 24 books, *hellenistic* Jews even more than these. But that, back then, these books may *have had* a divine origin is precisely not something *history* can examine, unlike history which relies on witnesses from other human beings, such as the destruction of Jerusalem or the feast of Pessah and other similar events.

§9. [40] In the oral teaching much was directed simply to the very specific circumstances of the audience of that time—other listeners, from another time and with different qualities, did not yet exist—and so it is clear that, also in the written composition, which was directed at readers back then, at a specific time and in specific places (if one presupposes these were real conditions), there must be certain parts of the text which are of limited and of very different suitability and usability. There are no real reasons why these parts could be seen as possessing a continued universality in their good, proper application on all readers *of all other epochs* and other regions of the world. There is quite certainly in all of the texts of this so-called *canon certain passages and parts of what is being stated and formulated which are outdated*, just as the time in which they arose has passed, for they relate to a time and to certain circumstances which, along with their immediate hearers or readers, have also passed.

10.

Gotthold Ephraim Lessing (1729–81)

The son of a Lutheran pastor and a mother who was herself the daughter of a Lutheran pastor, Gotthold Ephraim Lessing was raised in a somewhat orthodox Lutheran family. A towering figure of the German Enlightenment, he was a multifaceted writer: an author of poems; of historical, philosophical, and theological essays (see for instance his last work, *The Education of the Human Race* [1777, 1780]) and studies; and of plays (see for example *Nathan the Wise* [1779], a plea for religious toleration) and literary reviews. Lessing lived and worked in Berlin, Breslau, and Hamburg (1767–70)—where he met Hermann Samuel Reimarus—before accepting a position at the ducal Wolfenbüttel library, located between Hannover and Magdebourg, in 1770.

Lessing produced significant theological and philosophical works during his years in Wolfenbüttel. Starting in 1777, he began publishing anonymous fragments of a manuscript that had supposedly been found in the Wolfenbüttel library. The author was in fact Reimarus, who, in one of the fragments titled "On the Intentions of Jesus and His Disciples" (May 1778), claimed that Christianity's Easter message was the result of a subterfuge by Jesus's disciples. The publication of this fragment unleashed a storm of protest (known in Germany as the *Fragmentenstreit*), including a vigorous debate between Lessing and Johann Melchior Goeze (1717–86), the most prominent Lutheran pastor in Hamburg at the time. Lessing was subsequently forbidden to publish anything dealing with religion without first submitting his texts to the censors.

Lessing's text "On the Proof of the Spirit and of Power" (1777), which is a brief reply to a book published in September 1777 by Johann Daniel Schumann titled "On the Evidence of the Proofs of the Truth of Christianity" (*Über die Evidenz der Beweise für die Wahrheit der christlichen Religion*), is reprinted in full below. The original source for this English translation is *Lessing's Theological Writings*, ed. and trans. Henry Chadwick (Stanford: Stanford University Press, 1956), 51–56.

ON THE PROOF OF THE SPIRIT AND POWER (1777)

[51] Fulfilled prophecies, which I myself experience, are one thing; fulfilled prophecies, of which I know only from history that others say they have experienced them, are another.

Miracles, which I see with my own eyes, and which I have the opportunity to verify for myself, are one thing; miracles, of which I know only from history that others say they have seen them and verified them, are another.

That surely, is beyond controversy? Surely there is no objection to be made against that?

If I had lived at the time of Christ, then of course the prophecies fulfilled in his person would have made me pay great attention to him. [52] If I had actually seen him do miracles; if I had had no cause to doubt that these were true miracles; then in a worker of miracles who had been marked out so long before, I would have gained so much confidence that I would willingly have submitted my intellect to his, and I would have believed him in all things in which equally indisputable experiences did not tell against him.

Or: if I even now experienced that prophecies referring to Christ or the Christian religion, of whose priority in time I have long been certain, were fulfilled in a manner admitting no dispute; if even now miracles were done by believing Christians which I had to recognize as true miracles: what could prevent me from accepting this proof of the spirit and of power, as the apostle calls it [1 Cor 2:4]?

In the last instance Origen was quite right in saying that in this proof of the spirit and of power the Christian religion was able to provide a proof of its own, more divine than all Greek dialectic. For in his time there was still "the power to do miraculous things which still continued" among those who lived after Christ's precept; and if he had undoubted examples of this, then if he was not to deny his own senses, he had of necessity to recognize that proof of the spirit and of power.

But I am no longer in Origen's position; I live in the 18th century, in which miracles no longer happen. If I even now hesitate to believe anything on the proof of the spirit and of power, which I can believe on other arguments more appropriate to my age: what is the problem?

The problem is that this proof of the spirit and of power no longer has any spirit or power, but has sunk to the level of human testimonies of spirit and power.

The problem is that reports of fulfilled prophecies are not fulfilled prophecies; that reports of miracles are not miracles. These, the prophecies fulfilled before my eyes, the miracles that occur before my eyes, are immediate in their effect. But those—the reports of fulfilled prophecies and miracles, have to work through a medium which takes away all their force.

To quote Origen and to cite his words that "the proof of power is so called because of the astonishing miracles which have happened to confirm the teaching of Christ," is of little use if one keeps from one's readers what Origen says immediately thereafter. For the readers will [53] also turn up Origen and find with surprise that he argues for the truth of the miracles which happened with the foundation of Christianity ἐκ πολλῶν μὲν ἄλλων [for many other reasons], thus, from the narrative of the evangelists; chiefly and particularly, however, he argues their truth on the basis of miracles which were still happening.

If then this proof of the proof has now entirely lapsed; if the historical certainty is much too weak to replace this apparent proof of the proof which has lapsed: how is it to be expected of me that the same inconceivable truths which sixteen to eighteen hundred years ago people believed on the strongest inducement, should be believed by me to be equally valid on an infinitely lesser inducement?

Or is it invariably the case, that what I read in reputable historians is just as certain for me as what I myself experience?

I do not know that anyone has ever asserted this. What is asserted is only that the reports which we have of these prophecies and miracles are as reliable as historical truths ever can be. And then it is added that historical truths cannot be demonstrated: nevertheless we must believe them as firmly as truths that have been demonstrated.

To this I answer: *First*, who will deny (not I) that the reports of these miracles and prophecies are as reliable as historical truths ever can be? But if they are only as reliable as this, why are they treated as if they were infinitely more reliable?

And in what way? In this way, that something quite different and much greater is founded upon them than it is legitimate to found upon truths historically proved.

If no historical truth can be demonstrated, then nothing can be demonstrated by means of historical truths.

That is: *accidental truths of history can never become the proof of necessary truths of reason.*

I do not for one moment deny that in Christ prophecies were fulfilled; I do not for one moment deny that Christ performed miracles. But since the truth of these miracles has completely ceased to be demonstrable by miracles still happening at the present time, since they are no more than reports of miracles (however incontroverted and incontrovertible they may be), I deny that they can and should bind me in the least to a faith in the other teachings of Christ. These other teachings I accept on other grounds.

Then *secondly*: what does it mean to accept an historical proposition [54] as true? to believe an historical truth? Does it mean anything other than this: to accept this proposition, this truth as valid? to accept that there is no objection to be brought against it? to accept that one historical proposition is built on one thing, another on another? that from one historical truth another follows? to reserve to oneself the right to estimate other historical things accordingly? Does it mean anything other than this? Or something more? Let us examine ourselves carefully.

We all believe that an Alexander [the Great] lived, who in a short time conquered almost all Asia. But who, on the basis of this belief, would risk anything of great, permanent worth, the loss of which would be irreparable? Who, in consequence of this belief, would forswear forever all knowledge that conflicted with this belief? Certainly not I. Now I have no objection to raise against Alexander and his victory: but it might still be possible that the story was founded on a mere poem of Chœrilus just as the ten-year siege of Troy depends on no better authority than Homer's poetry.

If on historical grounds I have no objection to the statement that Christ raised to life a dead man; must I therefore accept it as true that God has a Son who is of the same essence as himself? What is the connection between my inability to raise any significant objection to the evidence of the former and my obligation to believe something against which my reason rebels?

If on historical grounds I have no objection to the statement that this Christ himself rose from the dead, must I therefore accept it as true that this risen Christ was the Son of God?

That the Christ, against whose resurrection I can raise no important historical objection, therefore declared himself to be the Son of God; that his disciples therefore believed him to be such; this I gladly believe from my heart. For these truths, as truths of one and the same class, follow quite naturally on one another.

But to jump with that historical truth to a quite different class of truths, and to demand of me that I should form all my metaphysical and moral ideas accordingly; to expect me to alter all my fundamental ideas of the nature of the Godhead because I cannot set any credible testimony against the resurrection of Christ: if that is not a μετάβασις εἰς ἄλλο γένος [a change into another kind of genus or category], then I do not know what Aristotle meant by this phrase.

It is said: "The Christ of whom on historical grounds you must [55] allow that he raised the dead, that he himself rose from the dead, said himself that God had a Son of the same essence as himself and that he is this Son." This would be quite excellent! if only it were not the case that it is not more than historically certain that Christ said this.

If you press me still further and say: "Oh yes! this is more than historically certain. For it is asserted by inspired historians who cannot make a mistake."

But, unfortunately, that also is only historically certain, that these historians were inspired and could not err.

That, then, is the ugly, broad ditch which I cannot get across, however often and however earnestly I have tried to make the leap. If anyone can help me over it, let him do it, I beg him, I adjure him. He will deserve a divine reward from me.

And so I repeat what I have said above in the same words. I do not for one moment deny that in Christ prophecies were fulfilled. I do not for one moment deny that Christ did miracles. But since the truth of these miracles has completely ceased to be demonstrable by miracles still happening now, since they are no more than reports of miracles (even though they be narratives which have not been, and cannot be, impugned), I deny that they can and should bind me to the very least faith in the other teachings of Christ.

What then does bind me? Nothing but these teachings themselves. Eighteen hundred years ago they were so new, so alien, so foreign to the entire mass of truths recognized in that age, that nothing less than miracles and fulfilled prophecies were required if the multitude were to attend to them at all.

But to make the multitude attentive to something means to put common sense onto the right track.

And so it came about, so it now is. And what it hunted out to the left and right of this track are the fruits of those miracles and fulfilled prophecies. These fruits I may see before me ripe and ripened, and may I not be satisfied with that? The old pious legend that the hand which scatters the seed must wash in snails' blood seven times for each throw, I do not doubt, but merely ignore it. What does it matter to me whether the legend is false or true? The fruits are excellent.

Suppose that a very useful mathematical truth had been reached by the discoverer through an obvious fallacy. (Even if such an instance [56] does not exist, yet it could exist.) Should I deny this truth? Should I refuse to use this truth? Would I be on that account an ungrateful reviler of the discoverer, if I were unwilling to prove from his insight in other respects, indeed did not consider it capable of proof, that the fallacy through which he stumbled upon the truth *could* not be a fallacy?

I conclude, and my wish is: May all who are divided by the Gospel of John be reunited by the Testament of John. Admittedly it is apocryphal, this testament. But it is not on that account any the less divine.

11.

Hermann Samuel Reimarus (1694–1768)

Born in Hamburg, Hermann Samuel Reimarus first studied theology, later languages and philosophy, at the University of Jena (1714) and two years later in Wittenberg. In 1727, he became a professor of Middle Eastern languages at the gymnasium in Hamburg, where he taught for forty years, refusing a call to a professorship at the University of Göttingen. During three decades (1736–68), Reimarus secretly worked on a massive manuscript titled "Apology or Defense of the Rational Worshippers of God" (Apologie oder Schutzschrift für die vernünftigen Verehrer Gottes).[1] Reimarus rejected several offers, made by friends who had seen the manuscript, to publish it.

Reimarus was a Deist and, as such, as fond of natural theology as he was suspicious of revealed doctrines. In 1754, he published a treatise on the principal truths of natural religion (*Abhandlungen von den vornehmsten Wahrheiten der natürlichen Religion*) that was highly regarded by many, including Kant (Nisbet 2013, 539).

Reimarus, alongside university professors such as Eichhorn and Semler, is part of the shift that began in the second half of the eighteenth century, as Germany replaced France as the country where textual criticism of the Bible was making its most important progress (Gibert 2008, 55).

The texts below were published by Gotthold Ephraim Lessing in 1777 and 1778. They are three fragments that were published separately but that in fact belong together. They are titled "Concerning the Intention of Jesus and His Teaching," "On the Resurrection Narratives," and "On the Intentions of Jesus and His Disciples."

Albert Schweitzer regarded Reimarus as a pioneer in the rediscovery of the eschatological tenor of Jesus of Nazareth's message. Indeed, Reimarus's insights are remarkable on this point. His theory of a trick played by Jesus's disciples, who stole his dead body and began announcing his resurrection, on the other hand, has long lost much of its appeal among scholars. But this thesis, as well as other arguments he articulates in the fragments, made him one of the first voices of radical biblical criticism (Schultze 1997, 472) and

1. The first publication of Reimarus's full manuscript occurred only in 1972: *Apologie oder Schutzschrift für die vernünftigen Verehrer Gottes*, 2 vols., ed. Gerhard Alexander (Frankfurt a. M.: Insel, 1972).

indeed of the modern attacks on Christianity (his manuscript has even been described as "a systematic assault on the Bible"; Nisbet 2013, 538).

The selections below come from: *Reimarus: Fragments*, ed. Charles H. Talbert, trans. Ralph S. Fraser (Philadelphia: Fortress Press, 1970).

"CONCERNING THE INTENTION OF JESUS AND HIS TEACHING" (1777)

§3–4. [64] Hence, just as there can be no doubt that Jesus in his teaching referred man to the true great goal of religion, namely, eternal salvation, we are concerned now with just this one question: What sort of purpose did Jesus himself see in his teaching and deeds? Jesus left us nothing in writing; everything that we know of his teaching and deeds is contained in the writings of his disciples. Especially where his teaching is concerned, not only the evangelists among his disciples, but the apostles as well undertook to present their master's teaching: However, I find great cause to separate completely what the apostles say in their own writings from that which Jesus himself actually said and taught, for the apostles were themselves teachers and consequently present their own views; indeed, they never claim that Jesus himself said and taught in his lifetime all the things that they have written. On the other hand, the four evangelists represent themselves only as historians who have reported the most important things that Jesus said as well as did. If now we wish to know what Jesus' teaching actually was, what he said and preached, that is a *res facti*—a matter of something that actually occurred; hence this is to be derived from the reports of the historians. Now since [65] there are four of them and since they all agree on the sum total of Jesus' teaching, the integrity of their reports is not to be doubted, nor should it be thought that they might have forgotten or suppressed any important point or essential portion of Jesus' teaching. Thus it is not to be assumed that Jesus intended or strove for anything in his teaching other than what may be taken from his own words as they are found in the four evangelists. Everyone will grant, then, that in my investigation of the intention of Jesus' teaching I have sufficient reason to limit myself exclusively to the reports of the four evangelists who offer the proper and true record. I shall not bring in those things that the apostles taught or intended on their own, since the latter are not historians of their master's teaching but present themselves as teachers. Later, when once we have discovered the actual teaching and intention of Jesus from the four documents of the historians, we shall be able to judge reliably whether the apostles expressed the same teaching and intention as their master.

§4. Jesus' discourses in the four evangelists can not only be read through quickly, but we also immediately find the entire content and intention of his teaching expressed and summarized in his own words: "Repent, and believe in the gospel" [Mark 1:15]. Or, in another place, "Repent, for the kingdom of heaven is at hand:" [Matt 4:17]. And in another place he says, "I have come to call sinners to repentance" [Mark 2:17; Matt 9:13; Luke 5:32]. Further, "I must preach the good news of the kingdom of God . . . for I was sent for this purpose" [Luke 4:43]. And it is this very thing that impelled John, Jesus' forerunner, to prepare the way for him, "Repent, for the kingdom of [66] heaven is at hand" [Matt 3:2]. Both these things, the kingdom of heaven and repentance, are so connected that the kingdom is the goal, while repentance is the means or preparation for this kingdom. By the kingdom that was at hand, announced to the Jews by the gospel or "joyful news," we understand (to use the Jewish expression) the kingdom of the Christ or Messiah for which the Jews had so long waited and hoped. The matter is self-evident: Since Jesus had come as the Messiah and since John specifically proclaimed this, it is expressed in the figure of speech actually used among the Jews of that day so that, when they heard of the kingdom of heaven that was to come, they understood nothing other than the kingdom of the Messiah. Since Jesus and John do not explain this term in any other way they wanted to have it understood in the familiar and customary meaning. Thus when it is said that the kingdom of heaven is near at hand, that means the Messiah will soon reveal himself and establish his kingdom. When it says believe in the gospel, that is another way of saying, believe in the joyful news of the imminent coming of the Messiah and his kingdom. The people were thus to prepare and make themselves ready through repentance for this now imminent kingdom of the Messiah, that is, by a change in thinking and spirit, in that they leave off wickedness and the tendency to commit it and with all their hearts turn to good and godliness. This demand was not only reasonable in all ages, but also was considered necessary among the Jews for the advent of the Messiah, just as they indeed believe to this present day that it is particularly the lack of repentance and betterment that delays the Messiah's advent, so that if they once were to do the proper penance the Messiah would come immediately. The person who reads and reflects upon all Jesus' words will find that their content applies collectively to these two things: either he describes the kingdom of heaven and commands his disciples to proclaim it, or he shows how men must undergo a sincere repentance and not cling to the sanctimonious nature of the Pharisees. . . .

§16–17. [93] And just as Cornelius saw an angel in a vision and heard it speak to him, and when Peter soon thereafter in a vision saw heaven opened and all sorts of animals descending and heard a voice speaking to him, so John also saw the heaven opened and a dove descending and also heard a voice [Acts 10:3–7, 10–16]. And how in fact could the heavens open? How can rational people think such a thing? But the power of imagination by which these visions take form can portray such pictures. Grotius indeed notes *id velut solenne signum praevium* παῖς ὀπτασίαις, the opening of heaven was a customary sign of visions, such as is already noted in Ezekiel: "The heavens were opened, and I saw visions of God" [Ezek 1:1]. In reality the heavens can open just as little as God can be seen with physical eyes or a human being can take his place at God's right hand in heaven. Similarly, a cloth tied in its four corners can so little contain all the animals and descend from heaven with them; or heaven, in which and from which all this is supposed to have been seen and heard, can just as little actually open or a dove fly down from the opened heavens. Also, it was not even the idea and intent of the Hebrew writers to understand these things as actual events; he who understands their language knows very well that in such cases and with such expressions they intend merely to recount prophetic visions and dreams, even if they do dress them up in the form of a [94] story or a narrative. Again, this is an indication of how a person unfamiliar with the Hebrews' style of writing may be deceived about the true meaning of their words.

§17. Thus we may assume that it has been sufficiently shown that the things reported about Jesus' baptism are no more than a vision of John the Baptist, even according to the purpose and understanding of the evangelists. . . .

§33 [133–34]. Since the story of Jesus as told by the disciples differs in its most important points according to the change in doctrine; since the disciples speak of things taking place that are the mainstays of their new doctrine and which they could not possibly have known about before the change; and since they omit other things that they must necessarily have thought of before the change, the new doctrine is not controlled by history, but just the opposite.[2] That is, as long as they had Jesus' actual words and deeds before them they hoped that he would redeem Israel temporally, and their doctrine was based on actual fact. Now, however, that their hope is disappointed, in a few days they alter their entire doctrine and make of Jesus a suffering savior for all mankind; then they change their facts accordingly and Jesus must now say and promise during his lifetime things that they could not have known of before. Indeed, the whole council must also have acted in the same way. Now, where the doctrine is not controlled by the history but vice versa, both history and doctrine are to this extent unfounded; the history because it is not taken from events themselves and the experiences and reminiscences thus brought about, but is told as having happened simply so that it will agree with the new and altered hypotheses or the new doctrine, and the doctrine because it refers to facts that originated in the writers' thinking only after the doctrine was altered and which were simply fabricated and false. Accordingly, to the extent that from the dual and completely altered behavior of Jesus' disciples and especially the evangelists anything can be concluded concerning the actual intention of Jesus in his words and deeds, we can think only that their

2. In section 33, Reimarus writes about the passion narrative, Jesus's death, and the claim that he rose from the dead.

first doctrine had been based on an intended temporal redemption of Israel and that they invented another doctrine concerning his intention, namely, of his becoming a suffering spiritual savior of men, only when their hopes had been disappointed after his death, and that they afterwards composed the narrative of his words and deeds. Consequently, this story and this doctrine are unfounded and false to this extent.

Part 2, §20.

[174] The first thing that we notice concerning the consistency of the four evangelists is that their stories diverge from each other in almost each and every point of the affair, and each one reads differently. Although this does not straightaway show a contradiction, still it certainly does not make a unanimous story, especially since the difference is expressed in the most important elements of the event. And I am definitely assured that if today in court four witnesses were heard in a case and their testimony was as different in all respects as is that of our four evangelists', the conclusion would at least have to be made that no case could be constructed on such conflicting testimony. Here it is a question of the truth of Jesus' resurrection, and insofar as it is to be judged by the mere testimony of witnesses, a unanimity of their testimony is necessary as to who saw him, where and how often, what he said and did in the meantime, and finally, what became of him.

Part 2, §36.

[211–12] It has hitherto been shown that the new system adopted by the apostles, of a spiritual suffering Savior, who was to arise from the dead, and after his ascension to return from heaven with great power and glory, is false in its first main principle, namely, the resurrection from the dead: 1. Because the previously cited evidence of the Roman guards, in Matthew, is highly incongruous, and is nowhere alluded to by any other evangelists or apostles. On the contrary, it is contradicted by many circumstances. So that the saying, which had become current among the Jews, namely, "that the disciples had come by night and stolen the body, and afterwards said he was risen," remains not only quite possible, but highly probable. 2. Because the disciples themselves, as witnesses of the resurrection of Jesus, not only vary outrageously in the principal points of their assertion, but they also, in manifold ways, distinctly and grossly contradict one another. 3. Their proof of the resurrection and of their whole system by the Old Testament writings, and by a number of things which have nothing to do with it, is made up of scolding and scoffing, distortion of Scripture sentences, false conclusions, and *petitionibus principii.*

Part 2, §53.

[243] . . . We have, a short time ago, examined the foundation of this new structure thoroughly and by itself, and we have found it sham and fictitious throughout. And thus we see how impossible it is that the apostles could have had any other object in promulgating a new doctrine than their old one, namely, that of ultimately obtaining power and worldly advantages. For an intentional, deliberate fabrication of a false occurrence can only spring from a preconceived resolve and from an object or motive harbored in the mind. He who diligently fabricates an untruth must have conceived a motive for so doing before he can concoct anything that will further his object; and the more bold and important this fabrication is, the deeper must the intention have been previously rooted in his mind, and of the more vital consequence must it have been to him. As, then, the new doctrine of the apostles was an undoubted fabrication, they must have invented it with a preconceived motive in their mind and will. Now as the former motives of the apostles, invariably and up to the time of the fabrication, had been aimed as worldly wealth and power, it follows with all moral certainty that the possession of worldly wealth and power was also the object of the apostles in the fabrication of their new doctrine. Nor can we doubt that all the circumstances attending their conduct will verify this conclusion.

Part 2, §56.

[249–250] Above all things, it was necessary to get rid of the body of Jesus as speedily as possible, in order that they might say he had arisen and ascended into heaven, and would promptly return from thence with great power and glory. This design of disposing of the body of Jesus was easy to carry out. . . . and when it became known that the body of Jesus was gone, they pretended to be full of astonishment, and ignorant of any resurrection, and proceeded with others to the spot in order to survey the empty tomb.

12.

Johann Philipp Gabler (1753–1826)

Johann Philipp Gabler studied theology during six years at the University of Jena (1772–78)—where Johann Gottfried Eichhorn (1752–1827) and Johann Jakob Griesbach (1745–1812) were instrumental in convincing him to focus on biblical scholarship (Gabler 1790, xiii)—before becoming a tutor (*Repetent*) in Göttingen and a high school teacher in Dortmund. In 1785 he began teaching in Altdorf, where he obtained his doctorate in theology two years later. He became a professor at the University of Jena (1804), where he would eventually serve five times as vice rector.

His inaugural lecture, included below, and given in Altdorf on March 30, 1787, is among his best known works.[1] Besides editing both *Neuesten theologischen Journal* (18 volumes, 1798–1811), to which he contributed most of the articles, and, in three volumes, Eichhorn's doctoral dissertation, *Urgeschichte* (1790–93), Gabler did not publish much, preferring to focus on his university lectures, which he scrupulously prepared.

Gabler's program centers on the idea of "biblical theology," which must in his opinion be grounded in exegesis and avoid as much as possible being influenced by "dogmatic prejudgments" that might "obfuscate the simple and natural meaning of the original text; and so, exegesis must ground dogmatics, but dogmatics should not influence exegesis," in Gabler's opinion.[2] From dogmatics, Gabler writes, "I expect only *petitiones principii*, whereby absolutely nothing will be gained for the truth. History teaches this: as long as dogmatics was the touchstone of theological and biblical studies, people were constantly moving within a circle without making progress toward truth even by one step."[3]

1. The Latin title of this lecture is "De iusto discrimine theologiae bibliae et dogmaticae regundisque recte utriusque finibus."

2. "Ich redete auch nur da zuweilen etwas stark und mit Wärme, wo dogmatische Vorurtheile den leichten und natürlichen Sinn der Urkunde verdunkelten, und dogmatische und physikalische Künste den wahren Gesichtspunkt derselben ganz verrückten. Auch der grosse Mann [Eichhorn] wird in meinen Augen klein, sobald ihn dogmatisches Interesse in seinen Untersuchungen leitet. Dogmatik muss von Exegese, und nicht umgekehrt Exegese von Dogmatik abhängen." Johann Philipp Gabler, "Vorrede" (preface) to *Johann Gottfried Eichhorns Urgeschichte*, ed. J. P. Gabler (Altdorf: Monath-Kussler, 1790), xv.

3. "Denn von daher erwarte ich lauter *petitiones principii*, wodurch schlechterdings nichts für die Wahrheit gewon-

The text below is excerpted from John Sandys-Wunsch and Laurence Eldredge, "J. P. Gabler and the Distinction Between Biblical and Dogmatic Theology: Translation, Commentary, Discussion of His Originality," *SJT* 33 (1980): 133–58.

AN ORATION ON THE PROPER DISTINCTION BETWEEN BIBLICAL AND DOGMATIC THEOLOGY AND THE SPECIFIC OBJECTIVES OF EACH . . . .

[134] All who are devoted to the sacred faith of Christianity, most worthy listeners, profess with one united voice that the sacred books, especially of the New Testament, are the one clear source from which all true knowledge of the Christian religion is drawn. And they profess too that these books are the only secure sanctuary to which we can flee in the face of the ambiguity and vicissitude of human knowledge, if we aspire to a solid understanding of divine matters and if we wish to obtain a firm and certain hope of salvation. Given this agreement of all these religious opinions, why then do these points of contention arise? Why these fatal discords of the various sects? Doubtless this dissension originates in part from the occasional [135] obscurity of the sacred Scriptures themselves; in part from that depraved custom of reading one's own opinions and judgments into the Bible, or from a servile manner of interpreting it. Doubtless the dissension also arises from the neglected distinction between religion and theology; and finally it arises from an inappropriate combination of the simplicity and ease of biblical theology with the subtlety and difficulty of dogmatic theology.

Surely it is the case that the sacred books, whether we look at the words alone or at the concepts they convey, are frequently and in many places veiled by a deep obscurity—and this is easily demonstrated; for one thing it is self-evident, and for another a host of useless exegetical works proclaims it. The causes of this state of affairs are many: first the very nature and quality of the matters transmitted in these books; second, the unusualness of the individual words and of the mode [136] of expression as a whole; third, the way of thinking behind times and customs very different from our own; fourth and finally, the ignorance of many people of the proper way of interpreting these books, whether it is due to the ancient characteristics of the text as a whole or to the language peculiar to each scriptural writer. But before this audience it is of little importance to describe each and every one of these causes, since it is self-evident that the obscurity of the Holy Scriptures, whatever its source, must give rise to a great variety of opinion. Also one need not discuss at length that unfortunate fellow who heedlessly dared to attribute some of his own most insubstantial opinions to the sacred writers themselves—how he increased the unhappy fate of our religion! There may even be some like him who would like to solidify the frothiness of such opinions about the sacred authors; for it is certainly something to give a divine appearance to their human ideas. Those completely unable to interpret correctly must inevitably inflict violence upon the sacred books; truly we even notice that often the wisest and most skilled of interpreters goes astray, so much so that, disregarding the laws of correct interpretation, they indulge their own ingenuity for its own sake. And let us not think then that it is suitable and legitimate for those who use the sacred words to tear what pleases them from its context in the sacred Scriptures; for it happens again and again that, when they cling to the words and do not pay attention to the mode of expression peculiar to the sacred writers, they express something other than the true sense of these authors. And if they continue to use metaphors when the context demands universal notions, then they may persuade themselves to say that some meaning which they brought to the sacred texts in the first place, actually comes from the sacred texts.

Another cause of discord, a most serious one, is the neglected distinction between religion and theology; for if some people apply to religion what is proper to theology, it is easy to understand that there would be enormous room for the sharpest differences of opinion, and these differences will

nen wird. Dies lehrt die Geschichte: so lange Dogmatik der Probierstein theologischer und biblischer Untersuchungen war; so drehte man sich unaufhörlich in einem Kreise herum, ohne in der Wahrheit nur um einen Schritt weiter zu kommen." Gabler, "Vorrede" (preface), xvi.

be even more destructive because each party to the quarrel will only with great reluctance surrender what he considers to pertain to religion. However, after the work of Ernesti, Semler, Spalding, Toellner, and others, most recently the venerable Tittmann has shown us brilliantly that there is considerable difference between religion and theology. For, if I may quote this excellent scholar, religion is passed on by the doctrine in the Scriptures, teaching what each Christian ought to know and believe and do in order to secure happiness in this life and in the life to come.

Religion then, is everyday, transparently clear knowledge; but theology is subtle, learned knowledge, surrounded by a retinue of many disciplines, and by the same token derived not only from the sacred Scripture but also from elsewhere, especially from the domain of philosophy and history. It is therefore a field elaborated by human discipline and ingenuity. It is also a field that is advanced by careful and discriminating observation that experiences various changes along with other fields. Not only does theology deal with things proper to the Christian religion, but it also explains carefully and fully all connected matters; and finally it makes a place for them with the subtlety and rigor of logic. But religion for the common man has nothing to do with this abundance of literature and history.

[137] But this sad and unfortunate difference of opinion has always been and, alas, always will be associated with that readiness to mix completely diverse things, for instance the simplicity of what they call biblical theology with the subtlety of dogmatic theology; although it certainly seems to me that the one thing must be more sharply distinguished from the other than has been common practice up to now. And what I should like to establish here is the necessity of making this distinction and the method to be followed. This is what I have decided to expound in this brief speech of mine insofar as the weakness of my powers allows and insofar as it can be done. Therefore, most honored listeners of all faculties, I strongly beg your indulgence. Would you grant me open ears and minds and be so kind as to follow me as I venture to consider these increasingly important matters. I pray and ask each and every one of you for your attention as far as is necessary so that I may speak my mind as clearly as possible.

There is truly a biblical theology, of historical origin, conveying what the holy writers felt about divine matters; on the other hand there is a dogmatic theology of didactic origin, teaching what each theologian philosophizes rationally about divine things, according to the measure of his ability or of the times, age, place, sect, school, and other similar factors. Biblical theology, as is proper to historical argument, is always in accord with itself when considered by itself—although even biblical theology when elaborated by one of the disciplines may be fashioned in one way by some and in another way by others.

But dogmatic theology is subject to a multiplicity of change along with the rest of the humane disciplines; constant and perpetual observation over many centuries shows this enough and to spare. How greatly the churches of the learned differ from the first beginnings of the Christian religion; how many systems the fathers attributed to each variety of era and setting! For history teaches that there is a chronology and a geography to theology itself. How much the scholastic theology of the Middle Ages, covered with the thick gloom of barbarity, differs from the discipline of the fathers! Even after the light [138] of the doctrine of salvation had emerged from these shadows, every point of difference in theology was endured even in the purified Church, if I may refer to Socinian and Arminian factions. Or if I may refer to the Lutheran Church alone, the teaching of Chemnitz and Gerhard is one thing, that of Calov another, that of Museus and Baier another, that of Buddeus another, that of Pfaff and Mosheim another, that of Baumgarten another, that of Carpov another, that of Michaelis and Heilmann another, that of Ernesti and Zachariae another, that of Teller another, that of Walch and Carpzov another, that of Semler another, and that of Doederlein finally another. But the sacred writers are surely not so changeable that they should in this fashion be able to assume these different types and forms of theological doctrine. What I do not wish to be said, however, is that all things in theology should be considered uncertain or doubtful or that all things should be allowed according to human will alone. But let those things that have been said up to now be worth this much: that we distinguish carefully the divine from the human, that we establish some distinction between biblical and dogmatic theology, and after we have separated those things which in the sacred books refer most immediately to their own times and to the men of those times from those pure notions which divine providence wished to be characteristic of all times and places, let us then construct the foundation of our philosophy upon religion and let us designate with some care the objectives of divine and human wisdom. Exactly thus will our theology be made more certain and more firm, and there will be nothing further to be feared for it from the most savage attack from its enemies. The late Professor Zachariae did this very capably, but I hardly need to remind you of the fact that he left some things for others to emend, define more correctly, and amplify. However, everything comes to this, that on the one hand we hold firmly to a just method for cautiously giving shape to our interpretations of the sacred authors; and on the other that we rightly establish the use in dogmatics of these interpretations and dogmatics' own objectives.

The first task then in this most serious matter is to gather [139] carefully the sacred ideas and, if they are not expressed in the sacred Scriptures, let us fashion them ourselves from passages that we compare with each other. In order that the task proceed productively and that nothing is done fearfully or with partiality, it is necessary to use complete caution and circumspection in all respects. Before all else, the following will have to be taken into account: in the sacred books are contained the opinions not of a single man, nor of one and the same era or religion. Yet all the sacred writers are holy men and are armed with divine authority; but not all attest to the same form of religion; some are doctors of the Old Testament of the same elements that Paul himself designated with the name "basic elements" [Gal 4:9]; others are of the newer and better Christian Testament. And so the sacred authors, however much we must cherish them with equal reverence because of the divine authority that has been imprinted on their writings, cannot all be considered in the same category if we are referring to their use in dogmatics. I would certainly not suggest that a holy man's own native intelligence and his natural way of knowing things are destroyed altogether by inspiration. Finally, since especially in this context it is next asked what each of these men felt about divine things (this can be understood not from any traditional appeal to divine authority but from their books), I should judge it sufficient in any event that we do not appear to concede anything which lacks some proof. I should also judge that when it is a case of the use in dogmatics of biblical ideas, then it is of no consequence under what authority these men wrote, but what they perceived this occasion of divine inspiration clearly transmitted and what they perceived it finally meant. That being the case it is necessary, unless we want to labour uselessly, to distinguish among each of the periods in the Old and New Testaments, each of the authors, and each of the manners of speaking which each used as a reflection of time and place, whether these manners are historical or didactic or poetic. If we abandon this straight road, even though it is troublesome and of little delight, it can only result in our wandering into some deviation or uncertainty. Therefore we [140] must carefully collect and classify each of the ideas of each patriarch—Moses, David, and Solomon, and of each prophet with special attention to Isaiah, Jeremiah, Ezekiel, Daniel, Hosea, Zachariah, Haggai, Malachi, and the rest; and for many reasons we ought to include the apocryphal books for this same purpose; also we should include the ideas from the epoch of the New Testament, those of Jesus, Paul, Peter, John, and James. Above all, this process is completed in two ways: the one is in the legitimate interpretation of passages pertinent to this procedure; the other is in the careful comparison of the ideas of all the sacred authors among themselves.

The first of these two involves many difficulties. For not only must we consider here the linguistic problem of the language then in use, which in the New Testament is both graeco-Hebrew and the vulgar Greek of the time; we must also consider that which is peculiar to each writer; that is, the uses of the meaning that a particular word may have in one certain place, whether that meaning be broader or narrower. Also we should add the reason for the divergence of these uses and explain, if possible, the common meaning in which several instances of the same word fall together. But we must also investigate the power and reason of the meaning itself; what is the primary idea of the word, and what merely added to it. For the interpreter who is on his guard must not stop short at the primary idea in the word, but he must also press on to the secondary idea which has been added to it either through long use or through ingenuity or through scholarly use of the word, and in so doing one may certainly make the most egregious of blunders. Let us not by applying tropes forge new dogmas about which the authors themselves never thought. Not only in prophetic or poetic books, but also in the writings of the Apostles, there are often improper uses of words which should be traced either to an abundance of genius or to the traditional usage of opponents, or to the use of words familiar to the first [141] readers. Up to now this is mostly done when we are comparing carefully many opinions of the same author, such as Paul; in comparing many things and words, we reduce to one idea and thing the many passages which, although variously expressed, show the same meaning. Morus recently showed and illustrated all this in a distinguished fashion—a very great man whose reputation is his monument. Finally one must properly distinguish whether the Apostle is speaking his own words or those of others; whether he is moved only to describe some opinion or truly to prove it; and if he wants to do the latter, does he repeat the argument from the basic nature of the doctrine of salvation, or from the sayings of the books of the Old Testament, and even accommodating them to the sense of the first readers? For although the opinions of the Apostles deserve our trust, so that we may easily get along without some part of their argument, the first readers nonetheless wanted the proofs that were appropriate to their own sense and judgment. Therefore, it is of great interest whether the Apostle proposes some opinion as a part of Christian doctrine, or some opinion that is shaped to the needs of the time, which must be considered merely premises, as the logicians call them. If we rightly hold on to all these things, then indeed we shall draw out the true sacred ideas typical of each author; certainly not all the ideas, for there is no place for everything in the books that have come down to us, but at least those ideas which the opportunity or the necessity for writing had shaped in their souls. Nonetheless, there is a sufficient number of ideas, and usually of such a kind that those that have been omitted can then be inferred without difficulty, if they constitute a single principle of opinion expressly declared, or if they are connected to the ideas that are stated in some necessary fashion. This process, however, requires considerable caution.

At this point we must pass on to the other part of the task, namely to a careful and sober comparison of the various parts attributed to each testament. Then, with Morus, the best of men, as our guide, each single opinion must be examined for its [142] universal ideas, especially for those which are expressly read in this or that place in the Holy Scriptures, but according to this rule: that each of the ideas is consistent with its own era, its own testament, its own place of origin, and its own genius. Each one of these categories which is distinct in cause from the others should be kept separate. And if this cautionary note is disregarded, it may happen that the benefit from the universal ideas will give way to the worst sort of damage to the truth, and it will render useless and will destroy all the work which had been brought together in diligently isolating the opinions of each author. If, however, this comparison with the help of the universal notions is established in such a way that for each author his own work remains unimpaired, and it is clearly revealed wherein the separate authors agree in a friendly fashion, or differ among themselves; then finally there will be the happy appearance of biblical theology, pure and unmixed with foreign things, and we shall at last have the sort of system for biblical theology that Tiedemann elaborated with such distinction for Stoic philosophy.

When these opinions of the holy men have been carefully collected from Holy Scripture and suitably digested, carefully referred to the universal notions, and cautiously compared among themselves, the question of their dogmatic use may then profitably be established, and the goals of both biblical and dogmatic theology correctly assigned. Under this heading one should investigate with great diligence which opinions have to do with the unchanging testament of Christian doctrine, and therefore pertain directly to us; and which are said only to men of some particular era or testament. For among other things it is evident that the universal argument within the holy books is not designed for men of every sort; but the great part of these books is rather restricted by God's own intention to a particular time, place, and sort of man. Who, I ask, would apply to our times the Mosaic rites which have been invalidated by Christ, or Paul's advice about women veiling themselves in church? Therefore the ideas of the Mosaic law have not been designated for any dogmatic use, neither by Jesus and his Apostles nor by reason itself. By the same token we must diligently investigate what in the books of the New Testament was said as an accommodation to the ideas or the [143] needs of the first Christians, and what was said in reference to the unchanging idea of the doctrine of salvation; we must investigate what in the sayings of the Apostles is truly divine, and what perchance merely human. And at this point finally the question comes up most opportunely of the whys and wherefores of *theopneustia*. This matter, to be sure very difficult, is, in my opinion at least, rather incorrectly inferred from the sayings of the Apostles, in which they make mention of a certain divine inspiration, since these individual passages are very obscure and ambiguous. However, we must beware, if we wish to deal with these things with reason and not with fear or bias, not to press those meanings of the Apostles beyond their just limits, especially since only the effects of the inspirations, and not their causes, are perceived by the senses. But if I am judge of anything, everything must be accomplished by exegetical observation only, and that with constant care, and compared with the things spoken of and promised by our Saviour in this matter. In this way it may finally be established whether all the opinions of the apostles, of every type and sort altogether, are truly divine, or rather whether some of them, which have no bearing on salvation, were left to their own ingenuity.

Thus, as soon as all these things have been properly observed and carefully arranged, at last a clear sacred Scripture will be selected with scarcely any doubtful readings, made up of passages which are appropriate to the Christian religion of all times. These passages will show with unambiguous words the form of faith that is truly divine; the *dicta classica* properly so called, which can then be laid out as the fundamental basis for a more subtle dogmatic scrutiny. For only from these methods can those certain and undoubted universal ideas be singled out, those ideas which alone are useful in dogmatic theology. And if these universal notions are derived by a just interpretation from those *dicta classica*, and those notions that are derived are carefully compared, and those notions that are compared are [144] suitably arranged, each in its own place, so that the proper connexion and provable order of doctrines that are truly divine may stand revealed; truly then the result is biblical theology in the stricter sense of the word which we know the late Zachariae to have pursued in the preparation of his well-known work. And finally, unless we want to follow uncertain arguments, we must so build only upon these firmly established foundations of biblical theology, again taken in the stricter sense as above, a dogmatic theology adapted to our own times. However, the nature of our age urgently demands that we then teach accurately the harmony of divine dogmatics and the principles of human reason; then, by means of art and ingenuity by which this can happen, let us so elaborate each and every chapter of doctrine that no abundance is lacking in any part—neither subtlety, whether in proper arrangement of passages or the correct handling of arguments, nor elegance in all its glory, nor human wisdom, primarily philosophy and history. Thus the manner and form of dogmatic theology should be varied, as Christian philosophy especially is, according to the variety both of philosophy and of every human point of view of that which is subtle, learned, suitable and appropriate, elegant and graceful; biblical theology itself remains the same, namely in that it deals only with those things which holy men perceived about matters pertinent to religion, and is not made to accommodate our point of view. . . .

13.

Friedrich D. E. Schleiermacher (1768–1834)

Friedrich Schleiermacher undoubtedly ranks among the most significant theologians between the sixteenth-century Protestant Reformers and the towering figures of theology in the twentieth century. A translator of Plato's works, a gifted and beloved preacher, a participant alongside Wilhelm von Humboldt (1767–1835) in the creation of Berlin's university, a brilliant philosopher and intra-Protestant ecumenist, he helped reshape the study of theology with his *Brief Outline of Theology as a Field of Study* (1811, 1830), and articulated a highly sophisticated and creative presentation of the Christian faith, *Der christliche Glaube*, or *Christian Faith* (1821–22; Schleiermacher 2016). In addition, Schleiermacher was the first scholar to give academic lectures on the life of Jesus, first in 1819 and then four more times in the ensuing years, at the University of Berlin (Schleiermacher 1975). His lectures, however, were published in 1864, nearly thirty years after his death, amidst a flurry of books, some of them sensational, on the historical Jesus.[1] In these lectures, besides expressing his (to us, puzzling) conviction concerning the historical reliability of the fourth Gospel and its authorship by Jesus's disciple John the son of Zebedee, he stated that "we cannot achieve a connected presentation of the life of Jesus" (Schleiermacher 1975, 43).

With his scholarship, Schleiermacher demonstrated that it is possible to combine deep, rigorous constructive theological reflection with a no-less rigorous and deep interest in historical criticism. It is an understatement to say that Schleiermacher's historical scholarship has not stood the test of time in the same way his dogmatic work has, and several critics have objected that his presentation of the life of Jesus is dogmatically and philosophically determined (Baur 1828; Strauss 1977; Verheyden 1975, li–lii). But the significance conferred to historical and critical scholarship in his *Brief Outline*, in relation to Scripture as well as the Christian tradition up to the present, is quite remarkable, and still worth pondering today. In his own way, Schleiermacher exemplifies the "eter-

1. Ernest Renan, *Vie de Jésus* (Paris: Michel Lévy, 1863); Daniel Schenkel, *Das Charakterbild Jesu: Ein biblischer Versuch* (Wiesbaden: C. W. Kreidel, 1864); Carl Weizsäcker, *Untersuchungen über die evangelische Geschichte, ihre Quelle und den Gang ihrer Entwicklung* (Gotha: Rudolf Besser, 1864).

nal covenant" he wished to promote between modern science and the Christian faith (Schleiermacher 1981, 64).

The excerpts that follow come from Friedrich D. E. Schleiermacher, *Brief Outline of Theology as a Field of Study*, 3rd ed., revised translation of the 1811 and 1830 editions by Terrence N. Tice (Louisville: Westminster John Knox, 2011); *On the* Glaubenslehre*: Two Letters to Dr. Lücke*, 1829, trans. James Duke and Francis Fiorenza (Atlanta: Scholars Press, 1981).

BRIEF OUTLINE OF THEOLOGY AS A FIELD OF STUDY (1811, 1830)

Part Two: Regarding historical theology

Introduction

[31] §69. In accordance with its content, historical theology . . . is part of the modern study of history; and thus all the natural divisions of that science are coordinate with it.

Historical theology belongs especially to the inner core of these studies, that is, to the modern history of culture and customs, into which Christianity has plainly introduced a development of its own. It belongs there, for it is clear that the sort of outlook that presents Christianity merely as a source of perversions and retrogressions is out of date.

§70. Insofar as it comprises a theological discipline, historical information about Christianity is, first and foremost, the indispensable condition of all intelligent effort toward the further cultivation of Christianity, and in this connection all the other parts of historical study are then strictly subservient to it.

Based on these observations, it is already evident what a different turn the study of the same mass of "facts" would take, and even the manner of handling them, when these facts were assigned to historical theology, as compared with placing them within the general study of history. This is true even though the basic principles of historical research do not cease to be the same for both areas of study. . . .

[34] §79. Accordingly, the career of Christianity can also be treated in two ways: (a) as a single period within one branch of religious development, but also (b) as a particular historical whole that arises as something new and that pursues its own separate course in a series of periods divided by epochs. . . . [35] [The] Christian faith . . . could not be what it is were not the basic fact of it established, unexceptionably, as something original [*ein Ursprüngliches*]. . . .

[36] §85. The whole of historical theology is included within these three divisions: information about primitive Christianity, information about the [37] total career of Christianity, and information about the state of Christianity at the present time. . . .

[43] §100. Each student of theology must form one's own clear historical vision for oneself, concerning both information about the total career of Christianity and information about the moment of history in which one lives. . . .

§101. Since one has to use historical presentations by scholars for this purpose, presentations that can never be wholly divested of the scholar's own distinctive viewpoints and opinions, every student must possess the art of separating out the material to be used for one's own work in the purest state possible.

§102. Historical criticism is the all-pervasive and indispensable organ for the work of historical theology, as it is for the entire field of historical studies.

I. Exegetical theology

[46] §110. The Protestant church necessarily claims to be continually occupied in determining the canon more exactly; and this is the greatest theological-exegetical task for higher criticism.

The New Testament canon has obtained its present form through the decision of the church, though this decision cannot be found expressed in any one particular act or declared with exactness. This is not a decision to which we attribute an authority exalted above all inquiry, and thus we are quite justified in starting fresh investigations in connection with earlier waverings of the boundary. This is the greatest task for higher criticism, because it is more important to determine whether a piece of writing is canonical or not than to determine whether it is to be assigned to this or that author, in which case it could still be canonical no matter what decision is made.

§111. Textual criticism has two kinds of investigation to undertake: (a) concerning whether certain material found within the canon is not, strictly taken, uncanonical, and (b) concerning whether there might be some canonical material outside the canon not yet recognized as such. Investigations of the second kind have been in process again quite recently; those of the first kind have actually never ceased. . . .

[47] §112. . . . An uncanonical book may contain new canonical passages, just as most of what has been interpolated by a later hand within a canonical book will be uncanonical.

§113. Higher criticism carries out its task, for the most part, only by approximation; and there is no other measure of the soundness of its decisions than the congruence of internal and external evidence. Thus, what is in question here is simply this: (a) how definitely do external signs indicate that a questionable piece of literature belongs either to the times of the apostolic fathers, later on, or to the area of apocryphal treatment, which is remote from the center of the church, and (b) how definitely do internal signs indicate that it is not apprehended and thought out in exact agreement with what is essential in the canonical presentation?

So long as both kinds of evidence conflict, or some signs stand on one side and some on the other of each kind, no critical decision will be possible.

That by "center of the church" neither any given realm nor any official post is to be understood here, but only the fullness of Christian sensibility and insight, doubtless needs no further explanation. . . .

[48] §118. The definitive task of lower criticism, everywhere to separate out the original reading as accurately and convincingly as possible, is entirely the same within the area of exegetical theology as it is elsewhere.

The terms "lower criticism" and "higher criticism" are employed here according to established usage, without any intention either of justifying [49] their appropriateness or of defining the boundaries between them more exactly.

§119. Thus, the New Testament critic has both the duty to follow the same rules and the right to employ the same means as those used elsewhere. . . .

[57] §145. Thus far, the major task of exegetical theology is in no way to be regarded as completely executed.

This is true even when one discounts the fact that there are particular passages some of which will never be emended with complete surety and others of which will never be explained to the satisfaction of all. . . .

§147. Any ongoing occupation with the New Testament canon that is not motivated by a genuine interest in Christianity can only be directed against the canon.

This is true, for the purely philological and historical gain of which the canon gives promise is not rich enough to attract a person to such an [58] occupation. Still, even the investigations of opponents . . . have been very useful, and they will continue to be so in future.

§148. Every occupation with the canon that lacks philological spirit and art must remain within the bounds of general edification, for in the theological field it could only produce confusion by its pseudo-dogmatic tendency.[2]

The reason is that such a procedure cannot be founded on a pure and firm desire to understand.

ON THE GLAUBENSLEHRE*: TWO LETTERS TO DR. LÜCKE* (1829)

[63] When I think about the impending crisis, I realize that, unless I were to exclude all science from my life, I would have to choose between two

2. Schleiermacher alludes here to the hermeneutical task, that is, the art of understanding. See *Brief Outline*, §132: "The full understanding of a discourse or piece of writing is a kind of artistic achievement and thus requires an 'art doctrine' [*Kunstlehre*] or technique [*Technik*], which we designate by the term 'hermeneutics'" (53, rev.). For Schleiermacher's views on hermeneutics and criticism, see Schleiermacher 1998.

alternatives. I can throw the origin of Christianity in with the infinite accumulation of common experience and present it as raw material for science, which will then decide whether it is right and worth the trouble to lift out especially this item from the mass. Or I can take my faith on loan from speculation, which may safeguard it from natural science, but which will likewise set the rules and subject it to its general constructions. Given these two alternatives, I would truly not know which I wanted to select. For myself alone, I would promptly choose the latter, although I fear my sense of joy would be dulled if I were called upon to explain in detail how the truth of the absolute filiation of God in the person of Jesus finds its certitude in knowledge. Moreover, I suspect that there would not remain much more of the historical person of the redeemer than there is in the Ebionitic view. . . .

[64] Neither the one approach nor the other is our way. Unless the Reformation from which our church first emerged endeavors to establish an eternal covenant between the living Christian faith and completely free, independent scientific inquiry, so that faith does not hinder science and science does not exclude faith, it fails to meet adequately the needs of our time and we need another one, no matter what it takes to establish it. Yet it is my firm conviction that the basis for such a covenant was already established in the Reformation. It is necessary only that we become more precisely aware of the task at hand so that we can resolve it. This awareness is not lacking, for each of us is sufficiently warned and doubly challenged to contribute to the resolution, that is, to participate actively in the building up of both the church and science.

Precisely this position, my dear friend, represents that of my *Glaubenslehre*. . . .

[65] But we will have to deal not only with the natural sciences and knowledge of the world. Historical research and criticism, both indispensable to our field, also threaten us with the same danger. Do you know already what the final verdict will be about the Pentateuch and the Old Testament canon? Do you hope that the traditional views of the messianic prophecies and even of the forerunners [*Vorbilder*] will be found credible by those who have come to a sound and lively view of historical matters? If I correctly read the signs of the times, I cannot believe it. . . . The belief in a special inspiration or revelation of God that continued up to a certain point of time in the Jewish nation is one that contemporary studies of Jewish history do little to corroborate. Nor do I think it very likely that the results of these studies will lend that belief much more support. Consequently, it seems to me to be essential that I state as clearly as possible my view and strong feeling that faith in God's revelation in Christ is not dependent upon such belief. If our doctrine of faith were a collection or system of decisions about all the authentic [66] or alleged facts of revelation, then of course a decision would have to be made about this point, too. But, since it consists only in giving an account of the Christian faith as such, we ought not to place this additional burden on ourselves. The need must always arise from within, and we do not need a prophetic plea for that. I believe that the one who would have allowed himself to be led to a correct answer to the question "where I am to go?" by the study of the Old Testament prophecies is still to come. . . .

I cannot regard the attempt to prove Christ from prophecies as a joyful task, and I regret that so many distinguished scholars still bother with it. For this reason I cannot help but suspect that such an attempt always rests on something wrong, and that placing great value on these external proofs is due at least to a lack of unworn trust in the inner power of Christianity [*frischer Zuversicht zu der innern Kraft des Christenthums*]. . . .

And, to take up this issue immediately, the question can be raised: how will criticism affect our view of the New Testament canon? You do not want to restrain criticism any more than I do. Who would not be happy to see the previously scattered comments about the character of the Gospel of John presented in the proper form of a critical hypothesis? Indeed, this seems inevitable. And how long do you think it will be before Dr. Schulz's view of [67] Matthew, though stated much too briefly, gains general acceptance, especially since its further elaboration will make it far more convincing?[3] And should we not also come back to the doubt that earlier prevailed in the church about several of the epistles? We would not

3. David Schulz, "Beilage: Bemerkungen über den Verfasser des Evangeliums nach Matthäus," in *Die christliche Lehre vom heiligen Abendmahl nach dem Grundtexte des Neuen Testaments: Ein Versuch* (Leipzig: Johann Ambrosius

lose anything essential: Christ remains the same and our faith in him remains the same. But as for our doctrine of the canon and of inspiration as a special activity of the Spirit producing the canon, we must take care not to make any claims that conflict with the universally recognized results of historical research. It will become increasingly difficult to adhere to the principle that everything in Scripture is divine teaching, and so it will be hard to determine which texts are Holy Scriptures and what distinguishes them from all others. . . . in times such as these our primary concern should be to take into account what appears to me to be the inevitable and immediate future. To be sure, we ought not to sacrifice or even obscure anything essential to Protestant Christianity. But we must in good time rid ourselves of everything that is obviously only secondary and based on presuppositions that are no longer valid, so that we might avoid becoming ensnared in useless controversies that might lead many easily to give up hope of ever grasping what is essential. . . .

Barth, 1824), 302–22. Schulz (1779–1854), who taught in Breslau, argued that the Gospel of Matthew was written after the other Synoptic Gospels and questioned its historical reliability.

14.

Johann Sebastian Drey (1777–1853)

Born into an impoverished family between Stuttgart and Nuremberg, Johann Sebastian Drey became a priest in the Roman Catholic Church in 1801. In 1812, he began teaching dogmatics and the history of dogma at the newly founded Friedrichsuniversität, a Catholic university in Ellwangen. Five years later, this university was transferred to the University of Tübingen. In 1819 he published a *Brief Introduction to the Study of Theology*, which remains a key document of Roman Catholic theology in the last two centuries or so.[1] This work, which provides an encyclopedic introduction to academic theology and its subfields, or "an overview of the whole field of the science in its external boundaries and internal divisions" (Drey 1994, xxxiii), is often—rightly—compared to Friedrich Schleiermacher's *Brief Outline of Theology as a Field of Study* (1811).[2] But it would be a mistake to consider Drey's encyclopedia to be a direct fruit of Schleiermacher's work, even if Drey certainly studied the 1811 *Brief Outline* closely.

Drey is the founder of the Tübingen school of theology in its Catholic version (there was a Protestant Tübingen school counterpart, for a shorter period of time, led by Ferdinand Christian Baur). Except for a manual of apologetics and his *Brief Introduction*, his literary production amounted mostly to journal articles.[3] With his *Brief Introduction*, a programmatic work that called for a reform of theological study, Drey signaled the possibility of a new beginning for Catholic theology after the deep trauma of the French Revolution. Drey had two main goals: first, to integrate a philosophical approach to the academic study of theology in order to reconstruct philosophically the essence of the Christian faith (Seckler 2007, 114–15); second, to show how the subject matter of theology is related to the student's "own innermost being, how knowledge of it is identi-

1. *Kurze Einleitung in das Studium der Theologie mit Rücksicht auf den wissenschaftlichen Standpunct und das katholische System* (Tübingen: Heinrich Laupp, 1819).

2. *Kurze Darstellung des theologischen Studiums zum Behuf einleitender Vorlesungen* (1811/1830), ed. Dirk Schmid (Berlin: W. de Gruyter, 2012).

3. J. S. Drey, *Die Apologetik als wissenschaftliche Nachweisung der Göttlichkeit des Christentums in seiner Erscheinung*, 3 vols. (Mainz: Kupferberg, 1838–47).

cal in its origin with the human spirit" (Drey 1994, xxxiv). Was this program ever put into practice? To a certain extent, yes, in Tübingen, especially with Drey, Johann Adam Möhler and other members of the school, and certainly since the middle of the twentieth century with the "nouvelle théologie" of Yves Congar, Henri de Lubac, Marie-Dominique Chenu, and others. But, starting with the second half of the nineteenth century, a different school, namely, neo-Scholasticism or neo-Thomism, became dominant, whereas Drey, due in part to the closeness of his *Brief Introduction* with Schleiermacher, began to be suspected of semi-rationalism (Seckler 2007, 65–67).

The following excerpts are drawn from Johann Sebastian Drey, *Brief Introduction to the Study of Theology. With Reference to the Scientific Standpoint and the Catholic System* (1819), trans. Michael J. Himes (Notre Dame: University of Notre Dame Press, 1994).

BRIEF INTRODUCTION TO THE STUDY OF THEOLOGY (1819)

§141.

b) Biblical Criticism

No historical study—including the history of biblical literature—can be conducted without the use of criticism. Under this heading are understood first of all certain general principles and rules by which we can distinguish historical truth from falsehood. Criticism is exercised when these principles and rules are employed on any given historical question. So it is not surprising that there is a theory of historical criticism, that is, that its principles and rules can be expressly set down and that in well-organized studies the theory of criticism must precede its exercise.

§142. Theoretically viewed, criticism is in itself a very general science and belongs by nature to the domain of philosophical sciences. When exercised on a *particular* subject, its general principles and rules must be more precisely defined in terms of this subject. Thus there are many kinds of specialized criticism. One of these is *biblical* criticism, whose historical subject is the Bible.

*In all criticism the specialized aspects are the result of the particular characteristics of the historical events which are its subject matter, of the historical agents who were the active parties in this material, of the author of the narrative who is the transmitter of the history, of the historical period, etc. Thus it is clear what the specialized aspects of biblical criticism are.

**If the lack of almost any biblical criticism in earlier times was a great problem, the lack of a foundational theory of biblical criticism is no less a problem in modern times. Endless confusion in biblical history and diametrically opposed positions among critics are only the most obvious results of this deficiency in a biblical discipline which should be especially open to systematic treatment. How much has happened since Richard Simon and how little has been accomplished toward a satisfactory theory of criticism!

§143.

The subject matter of biblical criticism is the history of this literature in terms of the three key issues which have been mentioned, and its task to find the truth of that history. But because the history of the Christian canon is not very hard to establish and, although thorough proof of authenticity is more difficult, this problem is resolved thanks to canonicity, textual history remains the most pressing concern for criticism and textual correction its most problematic task. The critical perspective is all the more indispensable since looking on these books as canonical can no more render scrutiny of the books unnecessary than their canonical quality can protect them from the vicissitudes common to every other kind of literature.

*Any worry which the immensity of critical

work on the Bible may inspire in theologians is dispelled by reflecting that no distortion has taken place in the text in any essential regard and that correction of non-essentials are of no immediate importance for theology.

§144.

In recent times a distinction has been drawn between lower and higher criticism, but there is no unanimity on the idea. By analogy to the way these terms are employed in other sciences, less rigorous tasks would have to be assigned to lower criticism and more rigorous to higher criticism; yet textual emendation, which is for the most part as demanding as any other task, is often ascribed to lower criticism. Others have dealt with the question as one of relative importance of the material and so have ascribed to higher criticism questions involving authenticity and the origin and early history of biblical sources. And still others have added to the importance of the material the distinctive more of operation and tools of criticism, which in ordinary criticism are simply given (historical data) but in higher criticism are reflective and comparative and even speculative. This last use of the terms may in fact be the historically correct one, for the originator of higher criticism began in that way.—A careful theory of biblical criticism has to clarify this notion.

§145.

Tools and evidence in criticism, which determine critical procedures, are either simply given and historical or consequent on what is given, drawn from it, built upon it. The first can be called historical evidence, the second philosophical evidence. The first is like witnesses speaking from other times and in other tongues who testify to the primitive history, such as manuscripts, traditions, quotations, etc., whose values as a rule is decided by their antiquity. The philosophical evidence is like an invocation of the spirit of the ancient author to speak on his own behalf and give testimony—through compiling and comparing his thoughts, the character of his language, his literary style, etc.

*Older criticism confined itself mostly to evidence of the first sort and was deficient even in this. Modern criticism made good use of such evidence at first, and after it had done so began almost to disdain this resource and to seek something more. The strictly historical route now satisfies few, and yet its tools lead directly to the fact which is sought. Now facts must be established first of all by the method of combination and what one wants to find must be sought in these combinations by deduction. But in these complicated procedures there is greater chance of error. Indeed, this aversion to the straightforwardly empirical and this complication of simple operations into multiple steps are a product of the age, like so many other examples of the same sort. They are an integral part of the same phenomenon.

§146.

c) Biblical Philology

In dealing with a biblical source, even if one grants that all important steps in its evaluation have been done correctly and one now has the source exactly as it was when it was first written and so, from the historical point of view, a perfectly unimpeachable source but written in a foreign language, the understanding of its language is still a necessary condition for making use of it. Training and deeper study in the languages in which the biblical sources were written are thus necessary for exegetical studies.

*Translations of the Bible cannot make skills in biblical languages superfluous. A) No translation perfectly corresponds to the original, least of all biblical translations, given the many peculiarities of the original languages and of the authors of the books. B) Only the originals have *actual* canonical authority. C) Without study of the original languages no translations, let alone good ones, are possible.

15.

Georg Wilhelm Friedrich Hegel (1770–1831)

As a speculative philosopher—including as a philosopher of religion—Georg Wilhelm Friedrich Hegel was far less interested in biblical criticism than in the question of the unfolding of the absolute Spirit (*Geist*) in history, in the world. His lectures on the philosophy of religion, given at the University of Berlin in the 1820s, are in fact lectures on the progressive *historical* self-expression of the absolute in contingent reality. Religion pertains to the realm of "representation" (*Vorstellung*) of the absolute; it is called to attain a higher level, that of the "concept" (*Begriff*). In order to attain that level, religion needs to be subsumed (*aufgehoben*) or integrated (no disappearing here!) into a higher plane through a thorough philosophical reinterpretation that alone may elucidate religion's true meaning beyond its inadequate, religious expressions. These views, as well as other aspects of Hegel's philosophy of religion, made a lasting and deep impact on Protestant theology, all the way to the present (for echoes in the present volume, see below, 121).

Hegel decried a certain historical method and a certain theology, which keep their distance from what they study and which focus on their "external features" rather than on "their content" (see below, 104). Against such tendencies, Hegel called for a theology (and a philosophy) that "engage[s] the needs of our spirit" and that deals with "the thing itself," that is, with the subject matter itself. Engaging "the thing itself," for Hegel, means considering God's own history as it unfolds in human history: philosophy of religion, as well as theology, should never lose sight of the double aspect of all history, as a human history, certainly, but also as the history of God's action.

The sources of what follows are *Lectures on the Philosophy of Religion*, vol. 1: *Introduction and The Concept of Religion* (1824 and 1827), ed. Peter Hodgson, trans. R. F. Brown, P. C. Hodgson, and J. M. Stewart with J. P. Fitzer and H. S. Harris (Berkeley: University of California Press, 1984). *Lectures on the Philosophy of Religion*, vol. 3, *The Consummate Religion*, ed. Peter Hodgson, trans. R. F. Brown et al. (Berkeley: University of California Press, 1985).

LECTURES ON THE PHILOSOPHY OF RELIGION (1824, 1827)

[From 1824 Lectures]

[128] It is to be noted that there is a type of theology that wants to adopt *only a historical attitude* toward religion; it even has an abundance of cognition, though only of a historical kind. This cognition is no concern of ours, for if the cognition of religion were merely historical, we would have to compare such theologians with counting-house clerks, who keep the ledgers and accounts of other people's wealth, a wealth that passes through their hands without their retaining any of it, clerks who act only for others without acquiring assets of their own. They do of course receive a salary, but their merit lies only in keeping records of the assets of other people. In philosophy and religion, however, the essential thing is that one's own spirit itself should enter with the utmost interest into an inner connection, not only occupying itself with something alien to it but drawing its content from what is essential and deeming itself worthy of cognition. Here human beings are dealing with the value of their own spirit and are not permitted to stay humbly outside it, standing about at a distance.[1]

This is therefore the relationship [of the philosophy of religion to the theology of our time]. In view of this plague the more explicit need that arises is that of regaining, for the true, essentially through philosophy, a fullness, a content, and an import.

[From 1827 Lectures]

[158–59] The most important sign that these positive dogmas[2] have lost much of their importance is that in the main these doctrines are treated *historically*. [This theology, which adopts only a historical attitude with respect to the cognition of God, and which is indeed a cornucopia of cognitions but only of an external sort, clings tightly to merely historical perspectives and piles up a mass of content as external information.][3] As far as this historical procedure is concerned, it deals with thoughts and representations that were had, introduced, and fought over by others, with convictions that belong to others, with histories that do not take place within our spirit, do not engage the needs of our spirit. What is of interest is rather how these things have come about in the case of others, the contingent way in which they were formed. [The subject is there dealing not with its own commitments to believe, with a cognition that should belong to it and be for its own benefit, but with a cognition of the opinions and views of others, not with the thing itself; the thing itself would benefit anyone concerned with it.][4] The absolute way in which these doctrines were formed—out of the depth of spirit—is forgotten, and so their necessity and truth is forgotten, too, and the question what one holds as one's own conviction meets with astonishment. The historical procedure is very busy with these doctrines, though not with their content but rather with the external features of the controversies about them, with the passions that have attached themselves to them, etc.

For this reason [philosophy seems to be in little danger when it is reproached for treating the Christian dogmas in a thoughtful way, or indeed for opposing the Church doctrines themselves. If there are now only a few dogmas, or if these dogmas are now only a matter of history, then philosophy could no longer be opposed to them, and then][5] philosophy no longer has to face the reproach that it devalues the dogmas. Instead it suffers the reproach of containing within itself too much of the teachings of the Church, more than the generally prevailing theology of our time.

1. Much of this sentence comes from a different version of the text (2nd ed., published in Berlin in 1840), which is included in a footnote in Peter C. Hodgson's 1984 edition of *Lectures on the Philosophy of Religion*, vol. 1, p. 128n36).

2. Hegel is referring to "eternal damnation" and "eternal blessedness."

3. This last sentence is found in a different version of the text (Georg Lasson, ed., Leipzig, 1925–29), which the editors of Hegel's lectures have included in a footnote (158, note 22).

4. Lasson ed., Leipzig, 1925–29.

5. The bracketed portion of the sentence is found in the first edition of the text, published by Philipp Marheinecke in Berlin in 1832.

[From 1827 Lectures]

[399] Something can be expounded in a historical mode and yet we do not take that to be its serious sense; we certainly do attend to the story with our imagination, but we do not ask whether it is meant seriously. We enjoy the narratives of Jupiter and the other deities, but we do not in the main inquire further about what Homer reports of them to us, we do not take it in the way we do some other historical report. Still, there is also something historical that is a divine history—a story, indeed, that is supposed to be history in the proper sense, namely the story of Jesus. This story does not merely count as a myth, in the mode of images. Instead it involves sensible occurrences; the nativity, passion and death of Christ count as something completely historical. Of course it therefore exists for representation and in the mode of representation, but it also has another, intrinsic aspect. The story of Jesus is something twofold, a divine history. Not only [is there] this outward history, which should only be taken as the ordinary story of a human being, but also it has the divine as its content: a divine happening, a divine deed, an absolutely divine action.

This absolute divine action is the inward, the genuine, the substantial dimension of this history, and this is just what is the object of reason. Just as a myth has a meaning or an allegory within it, so there is this twofold character generally in every story.

[From 1827 Lectures]

[469–70] This is the explication of reconciliation: that God is reconciled with the world, or rather that God has shown himself to be reconciled with the world, that even the human is not something alien to him, but rather that this otherness, this self-distinguishing, finitude as it is expressed, is a moment in God himself, although, to be sure, it is a disappearing moment.

For the community, this is the history of the appearance of God. This history is a divine history, whereby the community has come to the certainty of truth. From it develops the consciousness that knows that God is triune. The reconciliation in Christ, in which one believes, makes no sense if God is not known as the triune God, [if it is not recognized] that God *is*, but also is as the other, as self-distinguishing, so that this other is God himself, having implicitly the divine nature in it, and that the sublation of this difference, this otherness, and the return of love, are the Spirit.

These are the moments with which we are here concerned and which establish that humanity has become conscious of the eternal history, the eternal movement, which God himself is. . . . In order that it should become a certainty for humanity, it had to be a sensible certainty, which, however, at the same time passes over into spiritual consciousness, and likewise is converted into the immediately sensible—in such a way that the movement and history of God is seen in it, the life that God himself is.

[From 1824 Lectures, in vol. 3]

[186–87] The next point is to explicate the idea [of God in its self-development] as follows. Universal spirit—the totality that it is—posits itself [*setzt sich*] in its three determinations, namely, it develops itself, realizes itself; and it is complete only at the end, which is at the same time its presupposition [*Voraussetzung*]. At first, it is in itself as the totality; [then] it sets itself forth [*setzt sich voraus*], and likewise it *is* only at the end.

We thus have to consider spirit in the three forms, *the three elements*, into which it posits itself. These three forms are: (1) Eternal being, within and present to itself—the form of universality. (2) The form of *appearance*, that of *particularization*, of being for others. (3) The form of return from appearance into itself, the form of absolute singularity, of absolute presence-to-self.

It is in these three forms that the divine idea explicate itself. Spirit is divine history, the process of self-differentiation, of diremption [*Aufhebung*] and return into self; it is the *divine* history and therefore is to be viewed in each of the three forms.

16.

David Friedrich Strauss (1808–74)

David Friedrich Strauss was only twenty-seven years old when his two-part *Life of Jesus* (*Das Leben Jesu*) was published in June and November 1835. It almost immediately unleashed a storm of protest.[1] Strauss had studied under Ferdinand Christian Baur (see chapter 17), who greeted the publication of Strauss's work with interest, noting, however, in private letters that it did not contain anything new and that its destructive criticism should have been balanced with a constructive one (Köpf 2014, 18). Like Baur, Strauss was deeply influenced by Georg Wilhelm Friedrich Hegel's philosophy, as can be seen in the last pages of his book (see below, 121).

Strauss achieved several important things with his massive work on the life of Jesus. He made a convincing case against rationalizing or naturalizing interpretations and supranaturalist interpretations of many aspects of Jesus's life: it simply will not do to rationalize biblical narratives and to imagine for instance that the three magi were traveling to Jerusalem anyway when they saw a star that, as astronomical records at the time show, was particularly bright, and so on. It is equally impossible to simply maintain a divine supernatural intervention that contradicts all that we know about how stars shine, move, and so forth. To a large extent, Strauss's appeal to an interpretation of the four canonical Gospels that seeks the meaning especially of miraculous events, beyond their alleged historical and factual veracity, has arguably now become standard procedure in New Testament academic exegesis.

Friedrich Schleiermacher had advocated a "pact" between scientific inquiry and faith. Strauss all but destroyed such endeavors by describing large segments of the Gospel narratives as "mythical"; that is, as imaginative formulations typical of premodern cultures that had not yet reached the level of conceptualization or rational thought (Frei 1985, 221, 235).

The excerpts that follow come from George Eliot's translation, *The Life of Jesus Crit-*

1. See for instance "Vorwort," *Evangelische Kirchenzeitung* 18, no. 1 (January 2, 1836):1–6; no. 2 (January 6, 1936):9–14; no. 3 (January 9, 1836):17–23; no. 4 (January 13, 1836):25–31; no. 5 (January 16, 1836):33–38; no. 6 (January 20, 1836):41–45.

ically Examined (Philadelphia: Fortress Press, 1972). Some words have been modernized (for instance, in the preface to the first edition, "superannuated" was replaced with "obsolete"). The original footnotes, which for the most part refer to the scholarship of Strauss's time, have been removed.

THE LIFE OF JESUS (1835)

Preface to the First German Edition, Volume 1

[li] It appeared to the author of the work, the first half of which is herewith submitted to the public, that it was time to substitute a new mode of considering the life of Jesus, in the place of the antiquated systems of supranaturalism and naturalism. This application of the term "antiquated" will in the present day be more readily admitted in relation to the latter system than to the former. For while the interest excited by the explanations of the miracles and the conjectural facts of the rationalists has long ago cooled, the commentaries now most read are those which aim to adapt the supernatural interpretation of the sacred history to modern taste. Nevertheless, in point of fact, the orthodox view of this history became obsolete earlier than the rationalistic, since it was only because the former had ceased to satisfy an advanced state of culture, that the latter was developed, while the recent attempts to recover, by the aid of a mystical philosophy, the supernatural point of view held by our forefathers, betray themselves, by the exaggerating spirit in which they are conceived, to be final, desperate efforts to render the past present, the inconceivable conceivable.

The new point of view, which must take the place of the above, is the mythical. This theory is not brought to bear on the evangelical history for the first time in the present work: it has long been applied to particular parts of that history, and is here only extended to its entire tenor. It is not by any means meant that the whole history of Jesus is to be represented as mythical, but only that every part of it is to be subjected to a critical examination, to ascertain whether it have not some admixture of the mythical. The exegesis of the ancient church set out from the double presupposition: first, that the Gospels contained a history, and secondly, that this history was a supernatural one. Rationalism rejected the latter of these presuppositions, but only to cling the more tenaciously to the former, maintaining that these books present unadulterated, though only natural, history. Science cannot rest satisfied with this half-measure: the other presupposition also must be relinquished, and the inquiry must first be made whether in fact, and to what extent, the ground on which we stand in the Gospels is historical. This is the natural course of things, and thus far the appearance of a work like the present is not only justifiable, but even necessary.

It is certainly not therefore evident that the author is precisely the individual whose vocation it is to appear in this position. He has a very vivid consciousness that many others would have been able to execute such a work with incomparably superior erudition. Yet on the other hand he believes himself to be at least possessed of one qualification which especially fitted him to undertake this task. [lii] The majority of the most learned and acute theologians of the present day fail in the main requirement for such a work, a requirement without which no amount of learning will suffice to achieve anything in the domain of criticism—namely, the internal liberation of the feelings and intellect from certain religious and dogmatical presuppositions; and this the author early attained by means of philosophical studies. If theologians regard this absence of presupposition from his work as unchristian, he regards the believing presuppositions of theirs as unscientific. Widely as in this respect the tone of the present work may be contrasted with the edifying devoutness and enthusiastic mysticism of recent books on similar subjects; still it will nowhere depart from the seriousness of science, or sink into frivolity; and it seems a just demand in return, that the judgments which are passed upon it should also confine themselves to the domain of science, and keep aloof from bigotry and fanaticism.

The author is aware that the essence of the Christian faith is perfectly independent of his criticism. The supernatural birth of Christ, his miracles, his resurrection and ascension, remain eternal truths, whatever doubts may be cast on their reality as historical facts. The certainty of this can alone give calmness and dignity to our criticism, and distinguish it from the naturalistic criticism of the last century, the design of which was, with the historical fact, to subvert also the religious truth, and which thus necessarily became frivolous. A dissertation at the close of the work will show that the dogmatic significance of the life of Jesus remains inviolate: in the meantime let the calmness and insensibility with which, in the course of it, criticism undertakes apparently dangerous operations, be explained solely by the security of the author's conviction that no injury is threatened to the Christian faith. Investigations of this kind may, however, inflict a wound on the faith of individuals. Should this be the case with theologians, they have in their science the means of healing such wounds, from which, if they would not remain behind the development of their age, they cannot possibly be exempt. For the laity the subject is certainly not adequately prepared; and for this reason the present work is so framed, that at least the unlearned among them will quickly and often perceive that the book is not destined for them. If from curiosity or excessive zeal against heresy they persist in their perusal, they will then have, as Schleiermacher says on a similar occasion, to bear the punishment in their conscience, since their feelings directly urge on them the conviction that they understand not that of which they are ambitious to speak.

A new opinion, which aims to fill the place of an older one, ought fully to adjust its position with respect to the latter. Hence the way to the mythical view is here taken in each particular point through the supranaturalistic refutation, with an acknowledgment of what is true in the opinions combated, and an adoption of this truth into the new theory. This method also brings with it the extrinsic advantage, that the work may now serve as a repertory of the principal opinions and treatises concerning all parts of the evangelical history. [liii] The author has not, however, aimed to give a complete bibliographical view of this department of theological literature, but, where it was possible, has adhered to the chief works in each separate class of opinions. . . .

Tübingen, 24 May 1835.

§13: The Possibility of the Existence of Myth in the New Testament Considered in Reference to the External Evidences

[69] The assertion that the Bible contains myth is, it is true, directly opposed to the convictions of the believing Christian. For if his religious view be circumscribed within the limits of his own community, he knows no reason why the things recorded in the sacred books should not literally have taken place; no doubt occurs to him, no reflection disturbs him. But, let his horizon be so far widened as to allow him to contemplate his own religion in relation to other religions, and to draw a comparison between them, the conclusion to which he then comes is that the histories related by the heathens of their deities, and by the Muslim of his prophet, are so many fictions, while the accounts of God's actions, of Christ and other Godlike human beings contained in the Bible are, on the contrary, true. Such is the general notion expressed in the theological position: that which distinguishes Christianity from the heathen religions is this: they are mythical, it is historical.

But this position, thus stated without further definition and proof, is merely the product of the limitation of the individual to that form of belief in which he has been educated, which renders the mind incapable of embracing any but the affirmative view in relation to its own creed, any but the negative in reference to every other—a prejudice devoid of real worth, and which cannot exist in conjunction with an extensive knowledge of history. For let us transplant ourselves among other religious communities; the believing Muslim is of opinion that truth is contained in the Quran alone, and that the greater portion of our Bible is fabulous; the Jew of the present day, while admitting the truth and divine origin of the Old Testament, rejects the New; and, the same exclusive belief in the truth of their own creed and the falsity of every other was entertained by the professors of most of the heathen religions before the period of syncretism. But which community is right? Not all, for this is impossible, since the assertion of each excludes the others. But which particular one? Each claims for itself the true faith. The pretensions are equal; what shall decide? The origin of the several religions? Each lays claim to a divine origin. Not only does the Christian religion profess to be derived from the Son of God, and the Jewish from God himself, through Moses; the Muslim religion asserts itself to be founded by a prophet immediately inspired by God; in like manner the Greeks attributed the institution of their worship to the gods.

"But in no other religion," it is urged, "are the vouchers of a divine origin so unequivocal as in the Jewish and the Christian. The Greek and Roman mythologies are the product of a collection of unauthenticated legends, while the Bible history was written by eyewitnesses; or by those whose connexion with eyewitnesses afforded them opportunities of ascertaining the truth; and whose integrity is too apparent to admit of a doubt as to the sincerity of their intentions." It would most unquestionably be an argument of decisive weight in favour of the credibility of the biblical history, could it indeed be shown that it was written by eyewitnesses, or even by persons nearly contemporaneous with the events narrated. For though errors and false representations may glide into the narrations even of an eyewitness, there is far less probability of unintentional mistake (intentional deception may easily be detected) than where the narrator is separated by a long interval from the [70] facts he records, and is obliged to derive his materials through the medium of transmitted communications.

But this alleged ocular testimony, or proximity in point of time of the sacred historians to the events recorded, is mere assumption, an assumption originating from the titles which the biblical books bear in our Canon. Those books which describe the departure of the Israelites from Egypt, and their wanderings through the wilderness, bear the name of Moses, who being their leader would undoubtedly give a faithful history of these occurrences, unless he designed to deceive; and who, if his intimate connexion with Deity described in these books be historically true, was likewise eminently qualified, by virtue of such connexion, to produce a credible history of the earlier periods. In like manner, of the several accounts of the life and fate of Jesus, the superscriptions assign one to Matthew and one to John: two men who, having been eyewitnesses of the public ministry of Jesus from its commencement to its close, were particularly capable of giving a report of it; and who, from their confidential intercourse with Jesus and his mother, together with that supernatural aid which, according to John, Jesus promised to his disciples to teach them and bring all things to their remembrance, were enabled to give information of the circumstances of his earlier years; of which some details are recorded by Matthew.

But that little reliance can be placed on the headings of ancient manuscripts, and of sacred records more especially, is evident, and in reference to biblical books has long since been proved. In the so-called books of Moses mention is made of his death and burial: but who now supposes that this was written beforehand by Moses in the form of prophecy? Many of the Psalms bear the name of David, which presuppose an acquaintance with the miseries of the exile; and predictions are put into the mouth of Daniel, a Jew living at the time of the Babylonian captivity, which could not have been written before the reign of Antiochus Epiphanes. It is an incontrovertible position of modern criticism that the titles of the biblical books represent nothing more than the design of their author, or the opinion of Jewish or Christian antiquity respecting their origin; points the first of which proves nothing; and as to the second, everything depends upon the following considerations: 1. the date of the opinion and the authority on which it rests; 2. the degree of harmony existing between this opinion and the internal character of the writings in question. The first consideration includes an examination of the external, the second of the internal grounds of evidence respecting the authenticity of the biblical books. To investigate the internal grounds of credibility in relation to each detail given in the Gospels (for it is with them alone we are here concerned), and to test the probability or improbability of their being the production of eyewitnesses, or of competently informed writers, is the sole object of the present work. . . .

[74] Admitting however that we do not possess the immediate record of an eyewitness in any one of the four Gospels, it is still very incomprehensible, replies the objector, how in Palestine itself, and at a time when so many eyewitnesses yet lived, unhistorical legends and even collections of them should have been formed. But, in the first place, the fact that many such compilations of narratives concerning the life of Jesus were already in general circulation during the lifetime of the

Apostles, and more especially that any one of our gospels was known to an Apostle and acknowledged by him, can never be proved. With respect to isolated anecdotes, it is only necessary to form an accurate conception of Palestine and of the real position of the eyewitnesses referred to, in order to understand that the origination of legends, even at so early a period, is by no means incomprehensible. Who informs us that they must necessarily have taken root in that particular district of Palestine where Jesus tarried longest, and where his actual history was well known? And with respect to eyewitnesses, if by these we are to understand the Apostles, it is to ascribe to them absolute ubiquity, to represent them as present here and there, weeding out all the unhistorical legends concerning Jesus in whatever places they had chanced to spring up and flourish. Eyewitnesses in the more extended sense, who had only seen Jesus occasionally and not been his constant companions, must, on the contrary, have been strongly tempted to fill up their imperfect knowledge of his history with mythical representations.

But it is inconceivable, they say, that such a mass of myth should have originated in an age so historical as that of the first Roman emperors. We must not however be misled by too comprehensive a notion of an historical age. The sun is not visible at the same instant to every place on the same meridian at the same time of year; it gleams upon the mountain summits and the high plains before it penetrates the lower valleys and the deep ravines. No less true is it that the historic age dawns not upon all people at the same period. The people of highly civilized Greece, and of Rome the capital of the world, stood on an eminence which had not been reached in Galilee and Judaea. Much rather may we apply to this age an expression become trite among historians, but which seems in the present instance willingly forgotten: namely, that incredulity and superstition, scepticism and fanaticism go hand in hand. . . .

§15: Definition of the evangelical myth[2] and its distinctive characteristics

[86] The precise sense in which we use the expression *myth*, applied to certain parts of the gospel history, is evident from all that has already been said; at the same time the different kinds and gradations of the myths which we shall meet with in this history may here by way of anticipation be pointed out.

We distinguish by the name *evangelical myth* a narrative relating directly or indirectly to Jesus, which may be considered not as the expression of a fact, but as the product of an idea of his earliest followers: such a narrative being mythical in proportion as it exhibits this character. The myth in this sense of the term meets us, in the Gospel as elsewhere, sometimes in its pure form, constituting the substance of the narrative, and sometimes as an accidental adjunct to the actual history.

The pure myth in the Gospel will be found to have two sources, which in most cases contributed simultaneously, though in different proportions, to form the myth. The one source is, as already stated, the messianic ideas and expectations existing according to their several forms in the Jewish mind before Jesus, and independently of him; the other is that particular impression which was left by the personal character, actions, and fate of Jesus, and which served to modify the messianic idea in the minds of his people. The account of the transfiguration, for example, is derived almost exclusively [87] from the former source; the only amplification taken from the latter source being—that they who appeared with Jesus on the Mount spoke of his decease. On the other hand, the narrative of the rending of the veil of the temple at the death of Jesus seems to have had its origin in the hostile position which Jesus, and his Church after him, sustained in relation to the Jewish temple worship. Here already we have something historical, though consisting merely of certain general features of character, position, etc.; we are thus at once brought upon the ground of the historical myth.

The historical myth has for its groundwork a definite individual fact which has been seized upon by religious enthusiasm, and twined around with mythical conceptions culled from the idea of the Christ. This fact is perhaps a saying of Jesus such as that concerning "fishers of men" or the barren fig tree, which now appear in the Gospels transmuted into marvellous histories: or, it is perhaps

2. The 1835 English translation has "mythus" here and in the pages that follow.

a real transaction or event taken from his life; for instance, the mythical traits in the account of the baptism were built upon such a reality. Certain of the miraculous histories may likewise have had some foundation in natural occurrences, which the narrative has either exhibited in a supernatural light, or enriched with miraculous incidents.

All the species of imagery here enumerated may justly be designated as myths, even according to the modern and precise definition of George, inasmuch as the unhistorical which they embody—whether formed gradually by tradition, or created by an individual author—is in each case the product of an *idea*.[3] But for those parts of the history which are characterized by indefiniteness and want of connexion, by misconstruction and transformation, by strange combinations and confusion,—the natural results of a long course of oral transmission; or which, on the contrary, are distinguished by highly coloured and pictorial representations, which also seem to point to a traditionary origin;—for these parts the term *legendary* is certainly the more appropriate.

Lastly. It is requisite to distinguish equally from the myth and the legend, that which, as it serves not to clothe an idea on the one hand, and admits not of being referred to tradition on the other, must be regarded as *the addition of the author*, as purely individual, and designed merely to give clearness, connexion, and climax, to the representation.

It is to the various forms of the unhistorical in the Gospels that this enumeration exclusively refers: it does not involve the renunciation of the *historical* which they may likewise contain.

§16: Criteria by which to distinguish the unhistorical in the Gospel narrative

Having shown the possible existence of the mythical and the legendary in the Gospels, both on extrinsic and intrinsic grounds, and defined their distinctive characteristics, it remains in conclusion to inquire how their actual presence may be recognised in individual cases?

The myth presents two phases: in the first place it is not history; in the second it is fiction, the product of the particular mental tendency of a certain community. These two phases afford the one a negative, the other a positive criterion, by which the myth is to be recognised.

I. *Negative*. That an account is not historical— that the matter related could not have taken place in the manner described—is evident,

[88] *First*. When the narration is irreconcilable with the known and universal laws which govern the course of events. Now according to these laws, agreeing with all just philosophical conceptions and all credible experience, the absolute cause never disturbs the chain of secondary causes by single arbitrary acts of interposition, but rather manifests itself in the production of the aggregate of finite causalities, and of their reciprocal action. When therefore we meet with an account of certain phenomena or events of which it is either expressly stated or implied that they were produced immediately by God himself (divine apparitions—voices from heaven and the like), or by human beings possessed of supernatural powers (miracles, prophecies), such an account is *insofar* to be considered as not historical. And inasmuch as, in general, the intermingling of the spiritual world with the human is found only in unauthentic records, and is irreconcilable with all just conceptions; so narratives of angels and of devils, of their appearing in human shape and interfering with human concerns, cannot possibly be received as historical. . . .

Secondly. An account which shall be regarded as historically valid, must neither be inconsistent with itself, nor in contradiction with other accounts.

The most decided case falling under this rule, amounting to a positive contradiction, is when one account affirms what another denies. Thus, one gospel represents the first appearance of Jesus in Galilee as subsequent to the imprisonment of John the Baptist, while another Gospel remarks, long after Jesus had preached both in Galilee and in Judea, that "John was not yet cast into prison."

When, on the contrary, the second account, without absolutely contradicting the first, differs

3. Strauss is referring to Johann Friedrich Leopold George, author of *Mythus und Sage: Versuch einer wissenschaftlichen Entwickelung dieser Begriffe und ihres Verhältnisses zum christlichen Glauben* (Berlin: Schroeder, 1837).

from it, the disagreement may be merely between the incidental particulars of the narrative; such as *time* (the clearing of the Temple), *place* (the original residence of the parents of Jesus); *number* (the Gadarenes, the angels at the sepulchre); *names* (Matthew and Levi); or it may concern [89] the essential substance of the history. In the latter case, sometimes the character and circumstances in one account differ altogether from those in another. Thus, according to one narrator, the Baptist recognizes Jesus as the Messiah destined to suffer; according to the other, John takes offence at his suffering condition. Sometimes an occurrence is represented in two or more ways, of which one only can be consistent with the reality; as when in one account Jesus calls his first disciples from their nets while fishing on the sea of Galilee, and in the other meets them in Judea on his way to Galilee. We may class under the same head instances where events or discourses are represented as having occurred on two distinct occasions, while they are so similar that it is impossible to resist the conclusion that both the narratives refer to the same event or discourse.

It may here be asked: is it to be regarded as a contradiction if one account is wholly silent respecting a circumstance mentioned by another? In itself, apart from all other considerations, the argumentum *ex silentio* is of no weight; but it is certainly to be accounted of moment when, at the same time, it may be shown that had the author known the circumstance, he could not have failed to mention it, and also that he must have known it had it actually occurred.

II. *Positive*. The positive characters of legend and fiction are to be recognized sometimes in the form, sometimes in the substance of a narrative.

If the form be poetical, if the actors converse in hymns, and in a more diffuse and elevated strain than might be expected from their training and situations, such discourses, at all events, are not to be regarded as historical. The absence of these marks of the unhistorical do not however prove the historical validity of the narration, since the myth often wears the most simple and apparently historical form: in which case the proof lies in the substance.

If the contents of a narrative strikingly accords with certain ideas existing and prevailing within the circle from which the narrative proceeded, which ideas themselves seem to be the product of preconceived opinions rather than of practical experience, it is more or less probable, according to circumstances, that such a narrative is of mythical origin. The knowledge of the fact that the Jews were fond of representing their great men as the children of parents who had long been childless, cannot but make us doubtful of the historical truth of the statement that this was the case with John the Baptist; knowing also that the Jews saw predictions everywhere in the writings of their prophets and poets, and discovered types of the Messiah in all the lives of holy men recorded in their Scriptures; when we find details in the life of Jesus evidently sketched after the pattern of these prophecies and prototypes, we cannot but suspect that they are rather mythical than historical.

The more simple characteristics of the legend, and of additions by the author, after the observations of the former section, need no further elucidation.

Yet each of these tests, on the one hand, and each narrative on the other, considered apart, will rarely prove more than the possible or probable unhistorical character of the record. The concurrence of several such indications, is necessary to bring about a more definite result. The accounts of the visit of the magi, and of the murder of the innocents at Bethlehem, harmonize remarkably with the Jewish messianic notion, built upon the prophecy of Balaam, respecting the star which should come out of Jacob; and with the history of the sanguinary command of Pharaoh. Still this would not alone suffice to stamp the narratives as mythical. But we have also the corroborative facts that the described appearance of the star is contrary to the physical, [90] the alleged conduct of Herod to the psychological laws; that Josephus, who gives in other respects so circumstantial an account of Herod, agrees with all other historical authorities in being silent concerning the Bethlehem massacre; and that the visit of the magi together with the flight into Egypt related in the one Gospel, and the presentation in the temple related in another Gospel, mutually exclude one another. Wherever, as in this instance, the several criteria of the mythical character concur, the result is certain, and certain in proportion to the accumulation of such grounds of evidence. . . .

In these last remarks we are, to a certain extent, anticipating the question which is, in conclusion, to be considered: viz., whether the mythical character is restricted to those features of the narrative upon which such character is actually stamped; and whether a contradiction between two accounts invalidate one account only, or both? That is to say, what is the precise boundary line between the historical and the unhistorical?—the most difficult question in the whole province of criticism. . . . [91]

The boundary line, however, between the historical and the unhistorical, in records, in which as in our Gospels this latter element is incorporated, will ever remain fluctuating and unsusceptible of precise attainment. Least of all can it be expected that the first comprehensive attempt to treat these records from a critical point of view should be successful in drawing a sharply defined line of demarcation. In the obscurity which criticism has produced, by the extinction of all lights hitherto held historical, the eye must accustom itself [92] by degrees to discriminate objects with precision; and at all events the author of this work wishes especially to guard himself in those places where he declares he knows not what happened, from the imputation of asserting that he knows that nothing happened.

§105: The Transfiguration of Jesus Considered as a Miraculous External Event

[535] The history of the transfiguration of Jesus on the mountain could not be ranged with the narratives of miracles which we have hitherto examined; not only because it relates to a miracle which took place *in* Jesus instead of a miracle performed *by* him; but also because it has the character of an epoch in the life of Jesus, which on the score of resemblance could only be associated with the baptism and resurrection. Hence Herder has correctly designated these three events as the three luminous points in the life of Jesus, which attest his heavenly mission.

According to the impression produced by the first glance at the synoptical narrative (Matt 17:1ff; Mark 9:2ff; Luke 9:28ff)—for the history is not found in the fourth gospel—we have here a real, external, and miraculous event. Jesus, six or eight days after the first announcement of his passion, ascends a mountain with his three most confidential disciples, who are there witnesses how all at once his countenance, and even his clothes, are illuminated with supernatural splendour; how two venerable forms from the realm of spirits, Moses and Elias, appear talking with him; and lastly, how a heavenly voice, out of the bright cloud, declares Jesus to be the Son of God, to whom they are to give ear.

These few points in the history give rise to a multitude of questions, by the collection of which Gabler has done a meritorious service. In relation to each of the three phases of the event—the light, the apparition of the dead, and the voice—both its possibility, and the adequacy of its object, may be the subject of question. First, whence came the extraordinary light with which Jesus was invested? Let it be remembered that a *metamorphosis* of Jesus is spoken of (μεταμορφώθη ἔμπροσθεν αὐτῶν): now this would appear to imply, not a mere illumination from without, but an irradiation from within, a transient effulgence, so to speak, of the beams of the divine glory through the veil of humanity. Thus Olshausen regards this event as an important crisis in the process of purification and glorification, through which he supposes the corporeality of Jesus to have passed, during his whole life up to the [536] time of his ascension. But without here dilating further on our previous arguments, that either Jesus was no real man, or the purification which he underwent during his life, must have consisted in something else than the illumination and subtilization of his body; it is in no case to be conceived how his clothes, as well as his body, could participate in such a process of transfiguration. If, on this account, it be rather preferred to suppose an illumination from without, this would not be a metamorphosis, which however is the term used by the Evangelists: so that no consistent conception can be formed of this scene, unless indeed we choose, with Olshausen, to include both modes, and think of Jesus as both radiating, and irradiated. But even supposing this illumination possible, there still remains the question, what purpose could it serve? The answer which most immediately suggests itself is: to glorify Jesus; but compared with the spiritual glory which Jesus created for himself by word and deed, this physical glorification, consisting in the investing of his body with a brilliant light, must appear very insignificant, nay, almost childish. If it be said that, nevertheless, such a mode of glorifying Jesus was necessary for the maintenance of weak faith: we reply that in that case, it must have been effected in the presence of the multitude, or at least before the entire circle of the disciples, not surely before just the select three who were spiritually the strongest; still less would these few eyewitnesses have been prohibited from communicating the event precisely during the most critical period, namely, until after the resurrection. These two questions apply with enhanced force to the second feature in our history, the apparition of the two dead men. Can departed souls become visible to the living? And if, as it appears, the two men of God presented themselves in their former bodies, only transfigured, whence had they these—according to biblical ideas—before the universal resurrection? Certainly in relation to Elijah, who went up to heaven without laying aside his body, this difficulty is not so great; Moses, however, died, and his corpse was buried. But further, to what end are we to suppose that these two illustrious dead appeared? The evangelical narrative, by representing the forms as talking with Jesus, συλλαλοῦντες τῷ *'I.*, seems to place the object of their appearance in Jesus; and if Luke be correct, it had reference more immediately to the approaching sufferings and death of Jesus. But they could not have made the first announcement of these events to him, for, according to the unanimous testimony of the synoptists, he had himself predicted them a week before (Matt 16:21 par). Hence it is conjectured, that Moses and Elias only informed Jesus more minutely concerning the particular circumstances and conditions of his death: but, on the one hand, it is not accordant with the position which the gospels assign to Jesus in relation to the ancient prophets, that he should have needed instruction from them; and on the other hand, Jesus had already foretold his passion so circumstantially, that the more special revelations from the world of spirits could only have referred to the particulars of his being delivered to the Gentiles, and the spitting in his face, of which he does not speak till a subsequent occasion (Matt 20:19; Mark 10:34). If, however, it be suggested, that the communication to be made to Jesus consisted not so much in information, as in the conferring of strength for his approaching sufferings: we submit that at this period there is not yet any trace of a state of mind in Jesus, which might seem to demand assistance of this kind; while for his later sufferings this early strengthening did not suffice, as is evident from the fact, that in Gethsemane a new impartation is necessary. [537] Thus we are driven, though already in opposition to the text, to try whether we cannot give the appearance a relation to the disciples; but first, the object of strengthening faith is too general to be the motive of so special a dispensation; secondly, Jesus, in the parable of the rich man, must on this supposition have falsely expounded the principle of the divine government in this respect, for he there says that he who will not hear the writings of Moses and the prophets,—and how much more he who will not hear the present Christ?—would not be brought to believe, though one should return to him from the dead: whence it must be inferred that such an apparition, at least to that end, is not permitted by God. The more special object, of convincing the disciples that the doctrine and fate of Jesus were in accordance with Moses and the prophets, had been already partly attained; and it was not completely attained until after the death and resurrection of Jesus, and the outpouring of the Spirit: the transfiguration not having formed any epoch in their enlightenment on this subject. Lastly, the voice out of the bright cloud (without doubt the *Shechinah*) is, like that at the baptism, a divine voice: but what an anthropomorphic conception of the Divine Being must that be, which admits the possibility of real, audible speech on his part! Or if it be said, that a communication of God to the spiritual ear, is alone spoken of here, the scene of the transfiguration is reduced to a vision, and we are suddenly transported to a totally different point of view.

§106: The Natural Explanation of the Narrative in Various Forms

It has been sought to escape from the difficulties of the opinion which regards the transfiguration of Jesus as not only a miraculous, but also an external event, by confining the entire incident to the internal experience of the parties concerned. In adopting this position, the miraculous is not at once relinquished; it is only transferred to the internal workings of the human mind, as being thus more simple and conceivable. Accordingly it is supposed, that by divine influence the spiritual nature of the three apostles, and probably also of Jesus himself, was exalted to a state of ecstasy, in which they either actually entered into intercourse with the higher world, or were able to shadow forth its forms to themselves in the most vivid manner; that is, the event is regarded as a vision. But the chief support of this interpretation, namely, that Matthew himself, by the expression ὅραμα, *vision* (v. 9), describes the event as merely subjective and visionary, gives way so soon as it is remembered, that neither is there anything in the signification of the word ὅραμα which determines it to refer to what is merely mental, nor is it exclusively so applied even in the phraseology of the New Testament, for we also find it, as in Acts 7:31, used to denote something perceived externally. . . .

[538] To avoid the above difficulty, others, still confining the event to the internal experience of the parties, regard it as the product of a natural activity of soul, and thus explain the whole as a dream. During or after a prayer offered by Jesus, or by themselves, in which mention was made of Moses and Elias, and their advent as messianic forerunners desired, the three disciples, according to this interpretation, slept, and (the two names mentioned by Jesus yet sounding in their ears) dreamed that Moses and Elias were present, and that Jesus conversed with them: an illusion which continued during the first confused moments after their awaking. . . .

Not only, however, does the interpretation which sees in the transfiguration only a natural dream of the apostles, fail as to its main support, but it has [539] besides a multitude of internal difficulties. It presupposes only the three disciples to have been dreaming, leaving Jesus awake, and thus not included in the illusion. But the whole tenor of the evangelical narrative implies that Jesus as well as the disciples saw the appearance; and what is still more decisive, had the whole been a mere dream of the disciples, he could not afterwards have said to them: *Tell the vision to no man*, since by these words he must have confirmed in them the belief that they had witnessed something special and miraculous. Supposing however that Jesus had no share in the dream, it still remains altogether unexampled, that three persons should in a natural manner have had the same dream at the same time. This the friends of the above interpretation have perceived, and hence have supposed that the ardent Peter, who indeed is the only speaker, alone had the dream, but that the narrators, by a synecdoche attributed to all the disciples what in fact happened only to one. But from the circumstance that Peter here, as well as elsewhere, is the spokesman, it does not follow that he alone had the vision, and the contrary can by no figure of speech be removed from the clear words of the Evangelists. But the explanation in question still more plainly betrays its inadequacy. Not only does it require, as already noticed, that the audible utterance of the name of Moses and Elias on the part of Jesus, should be blended with the dream of the disciples; but it also calls in the aid of a storm, which by its flashes of lightning is supposed to have given rise in them to the idea of supernatural splendour, by its peals of thunder, to that of conversation and heavenly voices, and to have held them in this delusion even for some time after they awoke. But, according to Luke, it was on the waking of the disciples (διαγρηγορήσαντες δὲ εἶδον κ. τ. λ.) that they saw the two men standing by Jesus: this does not look like a mere illusion protracted from a dream into waking moments . . . . By giving this turn to the circumstances, all those occurrences which on the interpretation based on the supposition of a dream, should be regarded as mere mental conceptions, are again made external realities: for the idea of supernatural brilliancy is supposed to have been produced by a flash of lightning, the idea of voices, by thunder, and lastly, the idea of two persons in company with Jesus, by the actual presence of two unknown individuals. All this the disciples could properly perceive only when they were awake; and hence the supposition of a dream falls to the ground as superfluous.

Therefore, since this interpretation, by still retaining a thread of connexion between the alleged character of the event and a mental condition, has the peculiar difficulty of making three partake in the same dream, it is better entirely to break this thread, and restore all to the external world: so that we now have a natural external occurrence before us, as in the first instance we had a supernatural one. Something objective presented itself to the disciples; thus it is explained how it could be perceived by several at once: they deceived themselves when awake as to what they saw; this was natural, because they were all born within the same circle of ideas, were in the same frame of mind, and in the same situation. According to this opinion, the essential fact in the scene on the mountain is a secret interview which Jesus had preconcerted, and with a view to which he took with him the three most confidential of his disciples. Who the two men were with whom Jesus held this interview, Paulus does not venture to determine. . . . [540] On hearing strange voices talking with Jesus, they awake, see Jesus, who probably stood on a higher point of the mountain than they, enveloped in unwonted brilliancy, proceeding from the first rays of morning, which, perhaps reflected from a sheet of snow, fell on Jesus, but were mistaken by them in the surprise of the moment for a supernatural illumination; they perceive the two men, whom, for some unknown reasons, the drowsy Peter, and after him the rest, take for Moses and Elias; their astonishment increases when they see the two unknown individuals disappear in a bright morning cloud, which descends as they are in the act of departing. . . . The disciples must have been so far acquainted with the appearance of the morning beams on the mountains of their native land, as to be able to distinguish them from a heavenly glory; how they came to have the idea that the two unknown individuals were Moses and Elias, is not easy to explain on any of the former views, but least of all on this;—why Jesus, when Peter, by his proposal about the building of the three tabernacles, gave him to understand the delusion of the disciples, did not remove it, is incomprehensible, and this difficulty has induced Paulus to resort to the supposition, that Jesus did not hear the address of Peter;—the whole conjecture about secret allies of Jesus has justly lost all repute; and lastly, the one of those allies who spoke the words to the disciples out of the cloud, must have permitted himself to use an unworthy mystification.

§107: The History of the Transfiguration Considered as a Myth

Thus here, as in every former instance, after having run through the circle of natural explanations, we are led back to the supernatural; in which, however, we are precluded from resting by difficulties equally decisive. Since [541] then the text forbids a natural interpretation, while it is impossible to maintain as historical the supernatural interpretation which it sanctions, we must apply ourselves to a critical examination of its statements. These are indeed said to be especially trustworthy in the narrative before us, the fact being narrated by three Evangelists, who strikingly agree even in the precise determination of the time, and being moreover attested by the Apostle Peter (2 Pet 1:17). The agreement as to the time . . . is certainly striking; and besides this, all the three narrators concur in placing immediately after the transfiguration the cure of the demoniacal boy, which the disciples had failed to effect. But both these points of agreement may be accounted for, by the origin of the synoptical gospels from a fixed fund of evangelical tradition, in relation to which, we need not be more surprised that it has grouped together many anecdotes in a particular manner without any objective reason, than that it has often preserved expressions in which it might have varied, through all the three editions. The attestation of the history by the three synoptists is, however, very much weakened, at least on the ordinary view of the relation which the four gospels bear to each other, by the silence of John; since it does not appear why this Evangelist should not have included in his history an event which was so important, and which moreover accorded so well with his system, nay, exactly realized the declaration in his prologue (v. 14): *We beheld his glory, the glory as of the only begotten of the Father*. The worn-out reason, that he might suppose the event to be sufficiently known through his predecessors, is, over and above its general invalidity, particularly unavailable here, because no one of the synoptists was in this instance an eyewitness, and consequently there must be many things in their narratives which one who, like John, had participated in the scene, might rectify and explain. Hence another reason has been sought for this and similar omissions in the fourth gospel; and such an one has been supposed to be found in the anti-gnostic, or, more strictly, the anti-docetic tendency which has been ascribed to the gospel, in common with the epistles, bearing the name of John. It is, accordingly, maintained that in the history of the transfiguration, the splendour which illuminated Jesus, the transformation of his appearance into something more than earthly, might give countenance to the opinion that his human form was nothing but an unsubstantial veil, through which at times his true, superhuman nature shone forth; that his converse with the spirits of ancient prophets might lead to the conjecture, that he was himself perhaps only a like spirit of some Old Testament saint revisiting the earth; and that, rather than give nourishment to such erroneous notions, which began early to be formed among gnosticising Christians, John chose to suppress this and similar histories. But besides that it does not correspond with the apostolic *plainness of speech* (παρρησία) to suppress important facts in the evangelical history, on account of their possible abuse by individuals, John, if he were guided by the above consideration, must at least have proceeded with some consistency, and have excluded from the circle of his accounts all narratives which, in an equal degree with the one in question, were susceptible of a docetic misinterpretation. Now, here, every one must at once be reminded of the history of the walking of Jesus on the sea, which is at least equally calculated with the history of the transfiguration, to produce the idea that the body of Jesus was a mere phantom, but which John nevertheless records. It is true that the relative importance of events [542] might introduce a distinction; so that of two narratives with an equally strong docetic aspect, John might include the one on account of its superior weight, while he omitted the less important. But no one will contend that the walking of Jesus on the sea surpasses, or even equals, in importance the history of the transfiguration. John, if he were intent on avoiding what wore a docetic appearance, must on every consideration have suppressed the first history before all others. As he has not done so, the above principle cannot have influenced him, and consequently can never be advanced as a reason for the designed omission of a history in the fourth gospel; rather it may be concluded, and particularly in relation to the event in question, that the author knew nothing, or at least nothing precise, of that history. It is true that this conclusion can form an objection to the historical character of the narrative of the transfiguration, to those only who suppose the fourth gospel to be the work of an apostle; so that from this silence we cannot argue against the truth of the narrative. On the other hand, the agreement of the synoptists proves nothing in its favour, since we have already been obliged to pronounce unhistorical more than one narrative in which three, even all four gospels agree. Lastly, as regards the alleged testimony of Peter, from the more than doubtful genuineness of the second Epistle of Peter, the passage which certainly refers to our history of the transfiguration is renounced as a proof of its historical truth even by orthodox theologians.

On the other hand, besides the difficulties previously enumerated, lying in the miraculous contents of the narrative, we have still a further ground for doubt in relation to the historical validity of the transfiguration: namely, the conversation which, according to the two first Evangelists, the disciples held with Jesus immediately after. . . . The doctrine of the scribes, namely, had taught them to anticipate that Elias on his second appearance would exert a reforming influence on the life of the nation; whereas in the appearance which they had just beheld he had presently vanished again without further activity. . . . [543]

In order next to understand how such a narrative could arise in a legendary manner, the first feature to be considered, on the examination of which that of all the rest will most easily follow, is the sun-like splendour of the countenance of Jesus, and the bright lustre of his clothes. To the oriental, and more particularly to the Hebrew imagination, the beautiful, the majestic, is the luminous. . . . [544] But especially in the Messiah himself, it was expected that there would be a splendour which would correspond to that of Moses, and even outshine it; and a Jewish writing which takes no notice of our history of the transfiguration, argues quite in the spirit of the Jews of the first Christian period, when it urges that Jesus cannot have been the Messiah, because his countenance had not the splendour of the countenance of Moses, to say nothing of a higher splendour. Such objections, doubtless heard by the early Christians from the Jews, and partly suggested by their own minds, could not but generate in the early church a tendency to introduce into the life of Jesus an imitation of that trait in the life of Moses, and even, in one respect to surpass it, and instead of a shining countenance that might be covered with a veil, to ascribe to him a radiance, though but transitory, which was diffused even over his garments.

That the illumination of the countenance of Moses served as a type for the transfiguration of Jesus, is besides proved by a series of particular features. Moses obtained his splendour on Mount Sinai: of the transfiguration of Jesus also the scene is a mountain; Moses, on an earlier ascent of the mountain, which might easily be confounded with the later one, after which his countenance became luminous, had taken with him, besides the seventy elders, three confidential friends, Aaron, Nadab, and Abihu, to participate in the vision of Jehovah (Exod 24:1.9–11); so Jesus takes with him his three most confidential disciples, that, so far as their powers were adequate, they might be witnesses of the sublime spectacle. . . . [545]

By the transfiguration on the mount Jesus was brought into contact with his type Moses, and as it had entered into the anticipation of the Jews that the messianic time, according to Isa 52:6ff, would have not merely one, but several forerunners, and that among others the ancient lawgiver especially would appear in the time of the Messiah: so no moment was more appropriate for his appearance than that in which the Messiah was being glorified on a mountain, as he had himself once been. With him was then naturally associated the prophet, who, on the strength of Mal 3:23, was the most decidedly expected to be a messianic forerunner, and, indeed, according to the rabbis, to appear contemporaneously with Moses. If these two men appeared to the Messiah, it followed as a matter of course that they conversed with him; and if it were asked what was the tenor of their conversation, nothing would suggest itself so soon as the approaching sufferings and death of Jesus, which had been announced in the foregoing passage, and which besides, as constituting emphatically the messianic mystery of the New Testament, were best adapted for the subject of such a conversation with beings of another world. . . .

According to this, we have here a myth, the tendency of which is twofold: first, to exhibit in the life of Jesus an enhanced repetition of the glorification of Moses; and secondly, to bring Jesus as the Messiah into contact with his two forerunners,—by this appearance of the lawgiver and the prophet, of the founder and the reformer of the theocracy, to represent Jesus as the perfecter of the kingdom of God, and the fulfilment of the law and the prophets; and besides this, to show a confirmation of his messianic dignity by a heavenly voice.

[546] Before we part with our subject, this example may serve to show us with peculiar clearness, how the natural system of interpretation, while it seeks to preserve the historical certainty of the narratives, loses their ideal truth—sacrifices the essence to the form: whereas the mythical interpretation, by renouncing the historical body of such narratives, rescues and preserves the idea which resides in them, and which alone constitutes their vitality and spirit. Thus if, as the natural explanation would have it, the splendour around Jesus was an accidental, optical phenomenon, and the two appearances either images of a dream or unknown men, where is the significance of the incident? Where the motive for preserving in the memory of the Church an anecdote so void of ideas, and so barren of inference, resting on a common delusion and superstition? On the contrary, while according to the mythical interpretation, I do not, it is true, see in the evangelical narrative any real event,—I yet retain a sense, a purpose in the narrative, know to what sentiments and thoughts of the first Christian community it owes its origin, and why the authors of the gospels included so important a passage in their memoirs.

§152: Relation of the Critical and Speculative Theology to the Church

[781] Schleiermacher has said, that when he reflected on the approaching crisis in theology, and imagined himself obliged to choose one of two alternatives, either to surrender the Christian history, like every common history, as a spoil to criticism, or to hold his faith in fee to the speculative system; his decision was that for himself, considered singly, he would embrace the latter, but that, regarding himself as a member of the Church, and especially as one of its teachers, he should be induced rather to take the opposite course. For the idea of God and of man on which, according to the speculative system, the truth of the Christian faith rests, is indeed a precious jewel, but it can be possessed only by a few, and he would not wish to be that privileged individual in the Church, who alone among thousands held

the faith on its true grounds. As a member of the church, he could have no satisfaction but in [782] perfect equality, in the consciousness that all receive alike, both in kind and manner, from the same source. And as a teacher and spokesman to the Church, he could not possibly attempt the task of elevating old and young, without distinction, to the idea of God and of man: he must rather attack their faith as a groundless one, or else endeavour to strengthen and confirm it while knowing it to be groundless. As thus in the matter of religion an impassable gulf would be fixed between two parties in the Church, the speculative theology threatens us with the distinction of an esoteric and exoteric doctrine, which ill accords with the declaration of Christ, that all shall be taught of God. The scientific alone have the foundation of the faith: the unscientific have only the faith, and receive it only by means of tradition. If the Ebionite view, on the contrary, leave but little of Christ, yet this little is equally attainable by all, and we are thereby secured from the hierarchy of speculation, which ever tends to merge itself in the hierarchy of Rome.

Here we see presented, under the form of thought belonging to a cultivated mind, the same opinion which is now expressed by many in a less cultivated fashion: namely, that the theologian who is at once critical and speculative, must in relation to the Church be a hypocrite. The real state of the case is this. The Church refers her Christology to an individual who existed historically at a certain period: the speculative theologian to an idea which only attains existence in the totality of individuals; by the Church the evangelical narratives are received as history: by the critical theologian, they are regarded for the most part as mere myth. If he would continue to impart instruction to the Church, four ways are open to him:

First, the attempt already excluded by the above observations of Schleiermacher, namely, to elevate the Church to his own point of view, and for it, also, to resolve the historical into the ideal:—an attempt which must necessarily fail, because to the Church all those premises are wanting on which the theologian rests his speculative conclusions; and upon which, therefore, only an enthusiast for interpretation would venture.

The second and opposite measure would be to transport himself to the point of view of the Church, and for the sake of imparting edification ecclesiastically, to descend from the sphere of the ideal into the region of the popular conception. This expedient is commonly understood and judged too narrowly. The difference between the theologian and the Church is regarded as a total one; it is thought that in answer to the question, whether he believes in the history of Christ, he ought to say exactly, no; whereas he says yes: and this is a falsehood. It is true, that if in the discourses and instructions of the spiritual teacher, the main interest were an historical one, this would be a correct representation of the case: but, in fact, the interest is a religious one,—it is essential religion which is here communicated under the form of a history; hence he who does not believe in the history as such, may yet appreciate the religious truths therein contained, equally with one who does also receive the history as such: the distinction is one of form merely, and does not affect the substance. Hence it is an evidence of an uncultivated mind, to denounce as a hypocrite a theologian who preaches, for example, on the resurrection of Christ, since, though he may not believe in the reality of that event as a single sensible fact, he may, nevertheless, hold to be true the representation of the process of spiritual life, which the resurrection of Christ affords. Strictly considered, however, this identity of the substantial truth [783] exists only in the apprehension of him who knows how to distinguish the substance from the form of religion, that is, of the theologian, not of the Church, to whom he speaks. The latter can conceive no faith in the dogmatical truth of the resurrection of Christ, for example, apart from a conviction of its historical reality: and if it come to discover that the theologian has not this conviction, and yet preaches on the resurrection, he must appear in the eyes of the Church a hypocrite, and thus the entire relation between the theologian and the Church would be virtually cancelled.

In this case, the theologian, though in himself no hypocrite, would appear such to the Church, and would be conscious of this misconstruction. If notwithstanding this, he should continue to instruct the Church under the form of its own conceptions, he would ultimately appear a hypocrite to himself also, and would be driven to the third, desperate course, of forsaking the ministerial office. It avails nothing to say, he has only to descend from the pulpit, and mount the professor's chair, where he will not be under the necessity of withholding his scientific opinions from such as are destined to science; for if he, whom the course of his own intellectual culture has obliged to renounce the ministerial office, should by his instructions lead many to the same point, and thus render them also incapable of that office, the original evil would only be multiplied. On the other hand, it could not be held good for the Church, that all those who pursue criticism and speculation to the results above presented, should depart from their position as teachers. For no clergyman would any longer meddle with such inquiries, if he thus ran the risk of being led to results which would oblige him to abandon the ministerial office; criticism and philosophy would fall into the hands of those who are not professed theologians, and to the theologian nothing would remain but the faith, which then could not possibly long resist the attacks of the critical and speculative laity. But where truth is concerned, the possible consequences have no weight; hence the above remark ought not to be made. Thus much, however, may be maintained in relation to the real question: he whom his theological studies have led to an intellectual position, respecting which he must believe, that he has attained the truth, that he has penetrated into the deepest mysteries of theology, cannot feel either inclined or bound just at this point in his career to abandon theology: on the contrary, such a step would be unnatural, and even impossible.

He will therefore seek another expedient; and as such there presents itself a fourth, which is not, like the two first, one-sided, nor like the third, merely negative, but which offers a positive mode of reconciling the two extremes—the consciousness of the theologian, and that of the Church. In his discourses to the Church, he will indeed adhere to the forms of the popular conception, but on every opportunity he will exhibit their spiritual significance, which to him constitutes their sole truth, and thus prepare—though such a result is only to be thought of as an unending progress—the resolution of those forms into their original ideas in the consciousness of the Church also. Thus, to abide by the example already chosen, at the festival of Easter, he will indeed set out from the sensible fact of the resurrection of Christ, but he will dwell chiefly on the being buried and rising again with Christ, which the Apostle himself has strenuously inculcated. This very course every preacher, even the most orthodox, strictly takes, as often as he draws a moral from the evangelical text on which he preaches: for this is nothing else than the transition from the externally historical to the inward and spiritual. It is true, we must not overlook the distinction, that the orthodox preacher builds [784] his moral on the text in such a way, that the latter remains as an historical foundation; whereas, with the speculative preacher, the transition from the biblical history or the Church doctrine, to the truth which he thence derives, has the negative significance of a sublation [*Aufhebung*] of the former.[4]

Viewed more closely, however, the transition of the orthodox preacher from the evangelical text to the moral application, is not free from this negative moment; in proceeding from the history to the doctrine he implies at least thus much: the history is not enough, it is not yet truth, it must be transmuted from a past fact into a present one, from an event external to you, it must become your own intimate experience: so that with this transition, the case is the same as with the proof of the existence of God, in which worldly existence, which is the point of departure, apparently remains as a foundation, but is in fact negated [*negiert*] as a true existence, and sublated [*aufgehoben*] in the absolute. Nevertheless, there remains a marked distinction between these two propositions: since, and insofar as, this has happened, so and so is your duty and your consolation—and: this is indeed related as having happened once, but the truth is, that it always so happens, and both in and by you ought to happen. At least, the community will not receive both as identical; and thus, here again, in every excess or diminution which the more or less spontaneous relation of the teacher to critical theology, together with the variety in the degrees of culture of the community, introduces—the danger is incurred that the community may discover this difference, and the preacher appear to it, and consequently to himself, a hypocrite.

In this difficulty, the theologian may find him-

4. This sentence as well as the following ones are revised.

self driven either directly to state his opinions, and attempt to elevate the people to his ideas: or, since this attempt must necessarily fail, carefully to adapt himself to the conception of the community; or, lastly, since, even on this plan, he may easily betray himself, in the end to leave the ministerial profession.

We have thus admitted the difficulty with which the critical and speculative views are burdened, with reference to the relation of the clergyman to the Church; we have exhibited the collision into which the theologian falls, when it is asked, what course remains for him insofar as he has adopted such views? And we have shown that our age has not arrived at a certain decision on this subject. But this collision is not the effect of the curiosity of an individual; it is necessarily introduced by the progress of time and the development of Christian theology; it surprises and masters the individual, without his being able to guard himself from it. Or rather he can do this with slight labour, if he abstain from study and thought, or, if not from these, from freedom of speech and writing. Of such there are already enough in our day, and there was no need to make continual additions to their number through the calumniation of those who have expressed themselves in the spirit of advanced science. But there are also a few who, notwithstanding such attacks, freely declare what can no longer be concealed—and time will show whether by the one party or the other, the Church, mankind, and truth are best served.

17.

Ferdinand Christian Baur (1792–1860)

Ferdinand Christian Baur (1792–1860) is undoubtedly one of the giants of historical criticism in theology. Some even call him "the father of historical theology" since, with him, for the first time, a New Testament theology was presented "on the basis of a fully critical evaluation of the sources and reconstruction of early Christian history" (Morgan 1973, 13). Recent editions, translations, and studies help us identify the nature and scope of his contribution with greater precision. A major purpose of his scholarship consisted in assessing the theological purpose and intention of early Christian texts (and of *all* early Christian texts, including noncanonical and apocryphal), situating them in relation to each other and as part of a larger historical process. Baur thus went far beyond David Friedrich Strauss's concern to check the factual veracity of Gospel stories: his aim was to locate the "tendency" (as he put it) or historical trajectory of the Gospels (Frei 1982, 236; Baur 1847, 43). Methodologically speaking, Baur was formulating theological questions as historical questions. This task has not lost its relevance in the study of the New Testament and early Christianity (Koester 1975, 8–9).

What follows is an English translation, by the editor, of excerpts from his 1836 "Abgenöthigte Erklärung," or "Declaration compelled by and directed against an article of the *Evangelische Kirchenzeitung*, edited by Dr. E. W. Hengstenberg, Prof. of Theology at the University of Berlin. May 1836."[1] The German title adds that this "Declaration" was "wrung from" (*abgenöthigt*) the author by an attack he was subjected to. The attack came from the *Evangelische Kirchenzeitung*, in a brief, three-column article titled "The Future of Our Theology."[2] Baur had recently published his book on the Pastoral Epistles, and this publication, in which Baur argued that not only the Pastoral Epistles but also

1. "Abgenöthigte Erklärung gegen einen Artikel der *Ev. Kirchenzeitung*, herausgegeben von D[oktor] E. W. Hengstenberg, Prof. der Theol. an der Universität zu Berlin. Mai 1836," first published in *Tübinger Zeitschrift für Theologie* 8, no. 3 (1836):59–178, reprinted in Baur, *Ausgewählte Werke in Einzelausgaben*, ed. Klaus Scholder (Stuttgart-Bad Cannstat: Friedrich Frommann-Holzboog Verlag, 1963), 1:267–320 (what follows is an English translation of pages 288–320).

2. "Die Zukunft unserer Theologie," *Evangelische Kirchenzeitung* 18, no. 36 (May 4, 1836):281–85, and no. 37 (May 7, 1836):289–91.

the First Epistle of Peter were pseudepigraphs written in the second century, evidently incensed the circles of the *Evangelische Kirchenzeitung*.[3] Baur assumed Hengstenberg had authored the attack, when in fact it was August Tholuck who had written it, out of grave concern for the future of theology, certainly, but also, in all likelihood, to help block Baur from a professorship at the University of Halle, where Tholuck was on the faculty and did not wish to be surrounded by too many colleagues who did not embody his favored kind of evangelical theology. Tholuck's authorship would have surprised many; he convinced Hengstenberg not to disclose it, and so very few knew who exactly had attacked Baur. It appears that Baur too never found out (Kramer 1972, 167–83).

DECLARATION COMPELLED BY AND DIRECTED AGAINST AN ARTICLE OF THE *EVANGELISCHE KIRCHENZEITUNG*, EDITED BY DR. E. W. HENGSTENBERG, PROF. OF THEOLOGY AT THE UNIVERSITY OF BERLIN. MAY 1836

[288] But this too is not enough!

Since the entire article seeks to place me in the same category with Strauss, and since a main aspect of the anger which Strauss' work has provoked circles around his rejection of the apostolic authority of the fourth Gospel, it was to be expected that my inquisitor would be compelled to denounce me publicly as one who shares Strauss' opinion on the Gospel of John. He did not quite succeed in this, insofar as he was not able to do what he did for the rest of his denunciations, namely to adduce a quote from my writing. I did mention, on page 105 of my writing, an omitted legend which is found at the end of the Gospel of John, but his critical conscience seems not to have allowed him, on the basis of what I write there, to bring me to the courtroom, since he must be aware of the way in which the conclusion of John's Gospel is viewed nowadays, and how unjustified it is to apply such judgments concerning the conclusion in the direction of the Gospel as such. This concession to modern criticism is inconsistent, since it is made by a theologian who is convinced one should never even begin to doubt and classify, so as not to concede anything to disbelief [289]—it is a basic principle of this theologian that everything which is found in the canon must be considered equally authentic and unquestionable. Be that as it may, he has in this way relinquished the possibility to substantiate his accusation with regard to the Gospel of John. What does he do, instead? He says: "Having read this study on the pastoral epistles we must in fact believe that Mister Baur, like Strauss, has already thrown overboard the historical authority of the Gospel of John." On what basis does the author make such pronouncement? For my part, I have not once said this about the Gospel of John in my text. From the fact that I cannot consider the pastoral epistles as authentic letters of the apostle Paul, does it follow that I must already have thrown overboard the historical authority of the Gospel of John? Given the nature of the matter, does the former imply the latter, or do the reasons which undermine the authenticity of the pastoral epistles also apply when dealing with the fourth Gospel? Nowhere in my book on the pastoral epistles, nowhere in my other publications have I allowed myself a judgment concerning the historical authority of the Gospel of John, not only because my critical research so far as not been directed to this text, but also because I have absolutely no interest in depriving it of its historical authority or in declaring something for which I could not bring evidence. My work does not consist in simply expressing critical doubt, but to express it only when it compels me as something objectively given [*als etwas objectiv Gegebenes*]. How could I in any given manner earn the reputation of being a level-headed man—something the author of the article himself affirms—if I could follow the kind of method which he implies here? Concerning the historical authority of the Gospel of John I have therefore said absolutely nothing which [290]

3. Ferdinand Christian Baur, *Die sogenannte Pastoralbriefe des Apostels Paulus aufs neue kritisch untersucht* (Stuttgart-Tübingen: Cotta, 1835).

could be brought forth, even with the slightest legitimacy, for the accusation that I have already, like Strauss, thrown it overboard. It is thus him, the author of the article, who wishes in this case to read something not only in my writings, but also in my soul, something of which I myself know nothing. Therefore I now declare, in all seriousness, as the level-headed man he himself thinks I am, that the accusation which is made against me concerning the Gospel of John is not simply false, but also, considering the spiteful intention which here appears clearly, a calumny. It is up to him, my inquisitor, when he will have to hear this publicly from me, who has been accused by him, to comport himself in the way he wishes. It is his responsibility, if he can, to respond against this as firmly as I am, defending myself against all his groundless accusations and spiteful insinuations.

This should suffice, concerning the texts which, once fully accepted, are incidentally eroded by doubt in my book! I now turn to the main object of the attack which is directed against me, namely my book: *Die sogenannte Pastoralbriefe des Apostels Paulus aufs neue kritisch untersucht*, Stuttgart and Tübingen, published by J. G. Cotta, 1835. The accusation which is levelled against me on account of my book is the following: "There is in it an arbitrary skepticism (*eine Willkühr des Skeptizismus*) which in fact can only be compared to Strauss'; the two letters to Timothy and the one to Titus are presented in the book as a botch from the second century; this is done with an arbitrariness and brazenness of criticism (*Dreistigkeit der Kritik*) which one would not have expected from a man who otherwise is so level-headed (*so besonnenen Manne*)."[4] It is true, I have written the book in question, I have thoroughly articulated in it the reasons for which I do not consider these letters to be authentic letters of the apostle but only as literary productions of a later period. Which crime have I thereby committed? It is well-known how, among Protestant theologians, these letters have long been [291] considered; I am certainly not the first one to doubt and deny their authenticity. Not to mention Schleiermacher, even scholars such as Neander and Lücke have very recently expressed a skeptical judgment on the first letter to Timothy, so that I do not see why I should not be allowed to make the same judgment. Respected critics have also long delivered judgements on the other two epistles. What distinguishes me from most of my predecessors is only this: what they stated without demonstration, at least without sufficient demonstration, I believe I now have demonstrated, through a range of reasons rooted in history. But this should not lead me to become the object of strong reproaches—reproaches which none of these scholars had to face—such as the grave accusations of practicing an arbitrary and brazen criticism, an unstable (*schwindelnde*) and indeed intoxicated (*berauschte*) critical skepticism.[5] Rather, if a difference can be found between my predecessors and I, then those who are displeased to such a profound degree with the publication of my book and with the results of my inquiry should see in this a challenge to counter all the more rigorously the reasons I put forward. And what could be easier than this? An arbitrary and brazen criticism, an unstable, even intoxicated skepticism, an unfathomable frivolity, all of this can only mean that weapons are placed in the opponent's hands, against oneself. Such criticism would only expose its perfect nudity and nullity, and it would not even be necessary to make the effort of refuting the entire book; it would suffice to point out a few examples which are particularly striking and on the basis of which the inanity of such a criticism would be precisely and definitively demonstrated. Then the book could simply be left to its own destiny. But how has my accuser behaved, in this particular respect? The divine voice of his conscience did not leave him completely unforewarned about this. He, as can readily be seen, had [292] secretly to say to himself that whoever accuses someone else so gravely becomes accountable and must prove what he is stating, if he otherwise wishes to claim to be a person of integrity, so that he does not become guilty of an apparent sin against the decalogue's eighth commandment.[6] But if what is claimed was not so easy to demon-

4. Baur quotes "Die Zukunft unserer Theologie," 289, skipping one sentence from the original article.

5. The article in the *Evangelische Kirchenzeitung* indeed spoke of Baur's criticism in these terms. "Wenn bereits solche Theologen wie Baur einer so schwindelnden, ja berauschten kritischen Skepsis sich hinzugeben vermögen, was sollen Jüngere, Unerfahrenere thun!" (291).

6. [Original footnote] "You shall not bear false witness against your neighbor" (Exod 20:16).

strate, then what could be done? Would the natural man, as a consequence of this, let himself fall to the level of rendering a false witness against his neighbor? One could assuage the warning voice of conscience by giving the impression that in itself it would be quite possible to also demonstrate the accusations which are made, but that the point of the attack is precisely not to provide such a demonstration. This is precisely the way in which the author solves this conflict between his conscience and his natural man. He writes: "If this were the place for thorough and erudite pronouncements, it would not be difficult at all to show how such a criticism can be retained only through an arbitrary fastening onto Strauss' results." I must admit that no other passage, in the entire article, has filled me with a stronger impression of the moral indignity of such a reproach than this sentence. The author of the article wishes thus to give the impression that he could without effort prove what he is stating. Why then does he not do it? I myself have urged others to refute me. Why would it not be the place, here, to demonstrate the accusations which are being made to the detriment of someone else? Where else should we expect such a demonstration, if not precisely where the accusations are stated? Is the *Evangelische Kirchenzeitung*, in its basic outlook, only a journal for reproaches and accusations, for suspicions and calumnies, so that, as a consequence of this, it may excuse itself from the requirement to provide a demonstration? Or is the honor and reputation [293] of a fellow human being and fellow Christian something so unimportant to its editor and author that he does not believe it warranted to take this into consideration, not even through a single column of his journal? But certainly, if one considers it one's entire business, as a self-appointed plenipotentiary, to conduct supervisory control over everything and everybody within the Protestant Church, to then denounce whatever does not perfectly fit in the straightjacket of the *Evangelische Kirchenzeitung*'s dogmatics (the only salvific dogmatics there is), and to depict it with the crudest colors as the greatest scandal in all of Christendom, then one has no time for detailed, learned discussions, since learned discussions—as it appears—require not only tranquility and sobriety, but also learned studies. But who needs such studies? The lovely hope, which is sufficiently confirmed by experience, that with such accusations, and in the eyes of those who have made them, at the end of the day plenty enough of these accusations will stick, at least in the eyes of one's supporters and other like-minded comrades, this hope will, in this case as well, not be deceived!

The entire direction of the accusation against my book on the pastoral epistles aims at merging my criticism fully with Strauss'. That, at least, is the judgment one must reach, when one is in advance convinced that all the results of criticism, without even the smallest urge to examine them, are absolutely objectionable in that they contradict the opinion which was accepted until now. From this standpoint, criticism is nothing else than arbitrariness, brazenness, unfathomable frivolity, intoxicated dizziness, and there is thus nothing easier than to throw together all possible expressions coming from the field of criticism. But this is also the most superficial and frivolous judgment which can be thought of. With regard to my criticism and Strauss' criticism, no one who is able to judge in these matters, no one who has no particular [294] interest, out of ill will, in repudiating the truth, will miss the difference (*Unterschied*) between my approach in treating the matter and Strauss' own approach. The specificity of Strauss' criticism lies, as is well-known, in the mythical explanation of facts from the Gospel history, and how this explanation unfolds partly from the nature of the Gospel accounts, and partly from the untenability of the supranaturalist and rationalist approaches. And so I ask: Where does my criticism rely, even in one instance in my book, on the mythical interpretation? Where do I reject even one historical fact, which might be of importance for the critical judgment of these epistles, simply on the grounds that it is a miracle? Where do I argue solely on the basis of the inner contradiction of the content? Everywhere I proceed from specific, historically compiled facts, and then only, namely on the basis of this groundwork, do I seek to draw together the various threads of my critical combinations into one whole. This way of clinging to what is historically given is the specificity of my criticism, and it seemed timely to me to apply the principles of this historical criticism, not just in relation to the criticism which has been used until now (and whose deficiencies are nowhere more obvious in New Testament criticism than precisely with the pastoral epistles), but precisely even in confrontation with Strauss' criticism—we should also note that the particularity of the subject matter is not conducive to a perfectly adequate comparison between his criticism and my own. Whoever reads my book carefully sees that I not only aim to state only things which can be historically supported, but also, and above all, that I seek to reach a historically complete picture (*historischen Totaleindruck*) which guides the entire inquiry. In the Preface of my book I have already indicated, in detail and clearly, the objective standpoint of the criticism (*objectiven Standpunkt der Kritik*) I pursue, and so it is either a severe blindness or a very ill will which must be blamed for the fact that no attention whatsoever was paid to this. Without boasting, I may state that no [295] other critic of the pastoral epistles has engaged with the same effort in the thorough research—a research which seeks to provide a solution to this critical question—of the entire literary sources. When one considers this onerous study of the sources, then it is in fact not a big affair if someone comes up with the reproach of arbitrariness and brazenness, of unfathomable frivolity and so forth, thinking that in this way the entire work is discredited; only one thing is passed over, namely that all of this is simply ridiculous. I am convinced that nothing can be objected with good reason against the principles of historical criticism which I have articulated. I could not have arrived at any other result concerning the pastoral epistles, as I applied the principles of my stipulated methods. I could only arrive at the result which provoked such an aversion from the part of the editor of the *Evangelische Kirchenzeitung*. It is not my fault. He should argue about this with history, which made it possible for me to find such proofs in itself, and ultimately with divine providence, which meant for history to take this particular course. Or he should learn how good it is also in such matters to subject one's human subjectivity, which in the end is only the seat of the natural man, to the objectivity which is determined and ordained by God.

In putting my undemanding book on the pastoral epistles on an equal footing with Strauss' works on the life of Jesus, the author of the article has given—beyond what was just noted and if one disregards the malignity of his intention (which in any case can no longer be doubted)—a remarkable sign of the narrowness and inner insecurity of his entire position. Not only are the principles of criticism different, but also the object of the critical inquiry at hand is essentially different, as must be instantly obvious to everyone. Is the entire objective foundation of Christianity challenged in my research in the same manner as through Strauss' research, or is it not [296] possible to let this foundation remain in its full integrity and simultaneously realize that, concerning the authenticity of this or that of our canonical epistles, things might be different than what we commonly thought until now? Just as it might be quite possible to reach an always greater consensus and learn to realize how little alarm may be caused when we admit that certain epistles, such as—to name one—the Second Epistle of Peter, illegitimately found their place in the canon, in the same way it might be possible to give up, if it must happen, the authenticity not just of the pastoral epistles, but also of several other smaller letters of our canon, without undermining in any way the historical foundation of Christianity. But my accuser confronts me with this appeal (after having said, immediately before: if theologians such as Baur are able to surrender themselves to such an unstable, indeed intoxicated critical skepticism, what then might younger, more inexperienced ones do!): "It should not surprise us if someone comes and strikes the final *coup*, which Strauss himself did not strike, namely denying their authenticity to the entire corpus of Pauline letters." This is precisely what I mean when I describe this position as extremely narrow as well as innerly insecure and objectionable, and I will now show my opponent how, behind the fear he expresses, lurks a truly awful faithlessness, how he is very much and equally lacking both in true faith and true science.

What is, in fact, a faith which is each moment afraid and anxious that the foundation (*Grundlage*) upon which it rests what it wishes to cling to as its most prized and holy content, may be taken and snatched away forever, a faith which considers every new occurrence in philosophy and theology, every critical question and inquiry which comes to the light of day about the canonical books, with the constant concern and apprehension that these might [297] in the long run bring its fatal end? Faith is, in the authentic Protestant sense, the surest consciousness of what one holds as true (*das gewisseste Bewusstsein dessen, was man für wahr hält*). If, consequently, faith cannot exist without the Christian foundation upon which it rests, then this foundation too must rest on rock-solid grounds, and if it were possible for this foundation to be shaken and taken away from faith, then the consequence would only be the following: not that it would be the end of faith, but rather that there is yet another ground of faith, one which cannot be shaken, or that the ground of our faith, which can be shaken and invalidated, is still not yet the true and correct one. Whoever knows what true faith is, knows also that faith is, according to its essence, what is surest and steadiest, that when everything else around it falters and dissolves, faith itself never falters and dissolves. And so, where such a fear and anxiety is still present within faith, when one still thinks it possible that a final strike may be fatal to it, what is such a faith if not faithlessness within faith, the doubt which has not yet been overcome and according to which everything which one believes may be completely different, the bad conscience that such a faith bears in itself and which it cannot hide to itself or to others? As a matter of fact, the German public in recent times has not given a good witness as regards the strength of its faith, when one looks at the true panic and terror with which it has been seized since the publication of Strauss' life of Jesus. As if we could imagine one instant that the book of a young scholar (even if its scientific quality and significance cannot be doubted, as was recognized even by Neander) would rob the world of its God, of its Christ, of its all, of its final consolation in time and in eternity! But this is how it always goes when faith holds fast only to the letter, that is, when, from the letter, which kills, it has not attained the Spirit, who alone enlivens. Whoever clings to the mere letter [298] must in fact live in constant agitation and worry that, with Scripture's first letters, simultaneously the last ones may be taken away from him, that the final *coup* may occur, that the terrible discovery, which had been feared since the beginning, will finally be made and released publicly, namely that behind Christianity and the Christian faith stands a really awful and evil deceit. Where would be the joyfulness, which the Protestant faith is supposed to foster in us and in others, where would be the free and joyous faith in God and in God's eternal Word, if one were afflicted with such anxieties, and who would not think here of the Indian myth in which disbelief leads to the world's end because a leviathan has stolen the sacred scriptures and has thus deprived the world of God's Word?

This is how the matter stands, if one considers it from the standpoint of faith. But it is no different if we view it from the standpoint of science. What kind of science would it be, whose only interest would be to deliver a *coup*, and which, guided by this one intent, would deny the authenticity of this or that epistle, and eventually also of the entire Pauline corpus? As any person who can think would see, whoever speaks like this reveals that in him the very idea of science has not yet even begun to dawn. Only someone who does not know what science wants and what it must want in order to be conform to its nature, only someone who thinks that his personal activity and effort may be called scientific even though, far from being purely concerned with the subject matter (*aus dem reinen Interesse für die Sache selbst*) it serves the subject matter with a concern which is foreign to it, only such a person will presuppose that all the scientific publications which go beyond his own perspective and which obviously contradict his own agenda (and which contradict it all the more as the scientific concern which underpins these publications is purer) have something to do with dishonest and selfish [299] interests.

And so what happens here is that one is projecting one's own base and menial view of science onto others. One suspects others of being guided by impure motivations, such as the attempt to create an irritated and sour atmosphere, when they publish a piece of writing. And since, within the field of theology, there is nothing one may be more suspicious of than disbelief, then all of the publications of this kind must be the product of disbelief: they must come from what best characterizes disbelief, namely arbitrariness and brazenness, an unfathomable frivolity, an unstable, indeed intoxicated critical skepticism. Hence the confidence such people have that all of the publications of this sort can be disposed of in the simplest and easiest manner. They do not know that science always renews itself from itself, that it is caught up in a forward-looking, living movement. It is driven by itself, without the possibility of any human power blocking its way. It always creates new paths for itself, in order to follow to its final goal what it has already attained and comprehended. This they do not know, and even if they knew it, this knowledge would still be insufficient. In order to participate in science's living, developing process as a real actor, one must enter in it in such a way that one is ready to give science the sacrifice it requires. One may not stipulate in advance what one wishes to receive from it and the conditions under which one is willing to commit to it. Rather, one must be ready, when necessary, to relinquish one's subjective representations and interests in order to welcome, in return, through the rebirth of science, whatever is true and tenable about them. Here too it is necessary to kill the natural man, to die to the flesh, so that we may recognize what is not of the flesh but spiritual, so that the old may pass and all things may be new. [300] No wonder, therefore, that the natural man also resists against science and that much about it seems inopportune or acrid to him, or that he simply does not wish to have anything to do with it. It is only folly to him. He cannot understand it, for it can only be understood spiritually. But he can also not completely conceal to himself the fact that there is indeed something to it; his natural sense tells him that. False, misguided and inane science, the kind of science which does not deserve the name, never causes much worry. Worry happens only with the kind of science about which I must say to myself, in secret, that its results are not entirely made out of thin air, even if I have difficulties agreeing with them as I realize I was mistaken in my previous views (views which had become sweet habits of thoughts), as I feel hurt because my concern is being contradicted. But this conflict places the natural man all the more in a state of turmoil and passion, since on the one hand he senses what takes place in science, but on the other hand he is unable, with his mind marked by the flesh, to commit to it—in order to correctly understand it—and to examine it conscientiously. Hence, what is always easiest and most convenient, his accusation, his suspicion, his sentence and condemnation, his uproar and rage, his entire unruly nature, as we know it only too well. It is only on the basis of this inner contradiction that I can understand, on a psychological level, why the author of the article, alongside all the hard and offending words with which I must put up, then also adds lovely and positive comments about me—comments for which I must state my gratitude. In itself I can only see the clearest contradiction here, and I would be the greatest enigma to myself, a sort of truly Manichean two-sided being, if I were simultaneously scholarly, competent and level-headed, and arbitrarily brazen, unfathomably frivolous, unstable and, indeed, intoxicated—and all of that to the same degree.

And so only a false faith and false science can comport themselves in such a way. Nothing of the sort happens with true faith and true science. On the contrary, the two stand in perfect harmony. Both nourish and refresh themselves through each other, and just as science only profits from faith, faith only profits from science. From faith, and only from faith, science learns to purify itself of anything foreign and corrupt, to dedicate itself undividedly and unconditionally to the holy reality of truth (*der heiligen Sache der Wahrheit*). Conversely, thanks to science, faith does not fall into sluggish quiescence, but maintains a fresh and living dynamism, becoming always more clearly and immediately conscious of its divine content. Even if science appears to be in a position of enmity with regard to faith, as science always unsettles it anew, shakes all of its foundations and erodes the ground on which it takes root, by so doing science renders it the greatest service. For the point is not how much one believes, but only what one believes and how one believes, whether one believes in such a way that one knows how to distinguish, in one's faith too, the true and the false, what is certain and what is not, what is essential and what is less so. True faith is content with little, whereby the little it has remains a steadier and more secure possession. If one gives it only a sliver of good ground in which it may place its grain of mustard seed, even in these conditions it will become a tremendous tree, high above all other plants of the earth and reaching up to the sky, under whose shadow we may dwell. One single passage of Scripture was enough for the greatest doctor of the Church of ancient times to ground his faith, and to transform him into a pillar of the Church. All of the doubts which the new criticism creates are extremely salutary and fruitful for faith, they must be considered as a powerful educational and formative instrument. For faith should never be inactive and secure, but should always grow more and become stronger. How else is that possible, however—as the extensive and the intensive always stand [302] in a reciprocal relation—if not as faith learns to better distinguish between what is essential and what is less essential, between content and form, as faith learns to separate more sharply the inner core, the very essence of the matter (*das Wesen der Sache*), from the external envelope and husk, as faith learns to abandon and let go always more of certain particular aspects, it learns to hold on all the more, with full inner intensity and steadfastness (*Innigkeit und Festigkeit*), on what abides for it, in its unity. Science helps faith in this regard, insofar as faith must maintain itself against science and at the same time also must acknowledge its legitimacy. As a living faith—that is, a faith which does not stand still but which, in the peace it holds within itself, constantly seeks to attain an always higher certainty—becomes more and more important to our Church, our Church has considered the free inquiry (*die freie Forschung*) into Scripture and about Scripture as its most inestimable gem. Which guidance, however, does Scripture itself provide for distinguishing between what is essential to faith and what is less essential, including in relation to the historical dimension of the gospel story? Who has better articulated the whole depth and fullness of the Christian faith than the apostle Paul in his letters? But does he abide by the most minute details of Jesus' life history, does he privilege certain miracles and occurrences, does he come back, again and again, to the historical dimension of Jesus' life? Does he not presuppose, does he not take his point of departure, rather, only in the most general facts (*allgemeinsten Thatsachen*) of the gospel story, which everyone must recognize and presuppose in one way or in another, and which after all are certain even without the Gospels? There is much to be learned, also in this respect, from Paul's understanding of the gospel, from the apostle who did not see the Lord sensuously and bodily, but who asserted most decidedly the legitimacy of his apostolic vocation against the apostles who had walked, day in and day out, with the Lord! Whether one considers this or that aspect of the gospel story as historically less reliable [303], as the product of the tradition, has thus no relevance for faith. This has long been acknowledged, without concern, by the most distinguished theologians. It has to do, ultimately, only with the relation between the historical and what comes from traditions in the gospel story and the balance between them. It would be a good thing to finally realize this, to limit the quarrel with the new criticism to this, in order to quarrel with what can be successfully quarreled over, namely the question of the point at which it goes too far, instead of transforming the quarrel with it into a conflict over principles, which leads to nothing at all. Who would dare to argue that, in the case of these old accounts—which go back so far in time and which have been transmitted in ways which are quite unknown to us; accounts which must be always tackled according to the rules of historical criticism—the usual phenomenon did not happen and that absolutely no trace of elements coming from the tradition have been associated with properly historical elements?[7] [304] And why is such a demonstration—whereby not even the least non-historical element will be granted,[8] since this would amount to dissolving the principle which must be fought for—not actually made by those who take it to be an easy task? Isn't it a task which can be fulfilled—this much

7. [Original footnote] It is easy to state, as is done in the *Evangelische Kirchenzeitung*'s "Preface," on p. 43: "The NT is thoroughly based on history; all aspects of the setting in which it appeared, among which it began and developed itself, are known to us." So speak all who contentedly develop such a satisfying idea of human knowledge concerning historical matters generally, as well as, more specifically, of their own knowledge—a view which is quite pleasing to human vanity. As they have no idea concerning what belongs to such a knowledge, they are ready to complete what is positively missing out with matters springing out of their own arbitrariness. It is quite astonishing to dare to say, in good conscience, of any single occurrence of that time, that *all aspects of its setting are known to us*! Whoever has taken a look at these settings knows how much is unknown to us, and how it befits Christian humility to acknowledge, also here, the fragmentariness of our knowledge. Only human delusion can ignore this. But whoever, having acknowledged this, attempts to distinguish between Jesus' public life and what preceded it, or between the historical and the pre-historical (*Vorhistorischen*), must realize how much, by so doing, is conceded to Strauss' criticism. I note this simply in order to recall how necessary it is, in every debate involving principles, to consider rigorously the implications of each of the two opposing principles.

is obvious—with a clarity and evidence which far surpass the clarity and evidence of the opponents, since the truth must let itself be demonstrated much more clearly and evidently than its opposite? The basic axiom according to which the rules of historical criticism, which otherwise apply to everything which pertains to history, find no application in this particular instance (which concerns what is most important and holy for human beings), the axiom which declares that, in this particular case and only here, the free examination which Protestantism demands is not valid: this basic axiom can only result from an *a priori* presupposition. But which presupposition can it be, if not one in which something purely arbitrary has been mixed in? Here too let us only consider, above all, the Protestant point of view. A Protestant differs from a Catholic not only in that he does not believe in anything else than in the Word of God, but also in that he gives an account concerning the grounds of his faith. But faith itself cannot give such an account; only science, the knowledge of faith (*das Wissen vom Glauben*), can do it. When it is not determined by certain general, static truths of the religious and Christian consciousness, science is an inquiry which is never at rest, without definite limits. It does not allow its results to be predetermined, for an inquiry whose results are settled in advance is not an inquiry. The difference between Protestantism and [305] Catholicism also lies in the rejection of the authority of the tradition. Protestants reject the tradition because, as a human construction, it falsely presents itself as the divine truth and it wishes to put what emerged later on a par with what is original. Only the pure word of Scripture, not the tradition, is valid. In the performing of the critical principle of Protestantism—a principle which aims at the strictest separation of the divine and the human—is it consistent, or is it possible to justify, on the basis of the Protestant principle, the practice of progressing toward Scripture, but then of making a full stop in front of it, and thus to neglect to ask, also in relation to Scripture, whether here too perhaps something human and traditional may have to be separated from Scripture's divine content? The highest principle of Protestantism does not prohibit this, on the contrary it demands it, and whoever does not abide by this Protestant critical principle, applying his best capacities, pays tribute to the Catholic principle of authority (*Auktoritätsprincip*). This is the reason why in the Protestant Church, since its beginning, historical and critical studies have always existed (this critical principle already comes into view, in its full significance, in Luther). And if, in recent times, these studies have led theologians whose disinterested love of truth cannot be doubted, such as Neander, to declare certain canonical books of the New Testament to be either inauthentic or at least very dubious, this, far from damaging faith, benefits it. When faith is placed in a purely human word in Scripture, it is a false faith, because as faith ascends to a higher consideration of the word of Scripture, the more it will matter for faith not to treat as God's Word what cannot be demonstrated to be such. When, with the assistance of science, faith knows how to distinguish the authentic from the inauthentic, it demonstrates its strength, its illuminating power, its penetration in the inner spirit of Scripture. Whoever [306] knows how to conduct such inquiries in a true scientific manner, that is, with motives which signal an accurate and consistent thinking and a thorough knowledge of the matter, not only is fully entitled to do so, but also adequately fulfills his task as a Protestant Christian and theologian. Anyone who, instead of carefully examining and correcting these inquiries, obstructs them, anyone who, more mildly, seeks to curtail them on the basis of a general principle, namely the axiom according to which knowledge should not come into conflict with faith: anyone who acts in this way acts in an anti-Protestant way and pays tribute, once again, to the Catholic principle of authority—a principle which, to put it in a Kantian way, is also the principle of lazy reason. For, indeed, why does someone like that wish to let science conflict with faith? Simply because knowledge threatens *his own* faith: it does not let him rest peacefully with what he believed until then. The agitation in which he finds himself, instead of leading him to get rid of this state quickly by appealing to this axiom, should have led him to see himself entrusted with the task of finding an agreement between faith and science (whose results, even if they must be circumscribed

8. In other words, following Baur's distinction between "historical" and "traditional," elements that have been created by the subsequent tradition.

and corrected in many ways as regards their details, cannot be refuted in their broad scope). Such agreement should only be sought in the form of a higher position (*eine höhere Vermittlung*) of one's faith, instead of considering the former position as the only possible position for faith. If, on the one hand, one cannot prevent the progress of science, and if, on the other hand, one cannot adjust the result of science to *one's own* faith, then one should beware of having science carry the burden which comes from the subjective incapacity of an individual person, or from the smugness of someone who is convinced his own position must abide forever and is the only salvific one. [307] Such reactions, which have to do with the limitations of subjective standpoints and concerns, and all the anathemas which are issued by those to whom the very idea of historical criticism is a life and death question,[9] will not detract historical criticism from following its own way, the way which is clarified and prescribed through all the preceding stages of the development of science.

With this I believe I have provided an adequate reply to my opponent and his accusation, namely that a critical inquiry of canonical letters, such as my book on the pastoral epistles, will eventually lead to the full carrying out of the final *coup*, namely the denial of the authenticity of the entire Pauline corpus. Already in my book I have made clear what I think about such a *coup*, to use my opponent's language. The more I study the questions of the authenticity of Paul's letters, the more such ideas strike me as totally inconsistent. If someone considers such a *coup* feasible, let him attempt to do with an unquestionably authentic Pauline epistle what I have done with the pastoral epistles—but let him do it in the same manner, [308] with arguments which are as historically documented as mine! Any doubt which has no basis disintegrates at once, whereas doubt which has support carries within itself its own measure and rule; believing this belongs to the faith which is linked with science. Anyone who totally rejects in principle any doubt and inspection should explain—if his thinking is not contradictory and inconsistent—how this attitude can lead to any progress in science and to any reform in the Church, how anything else follows from it than absolute standstill, the death of faith and of knowledge.

The entire article from the *Evangelische Kirchenzeitung*, insofar as it deals with me, not only seeks to place my book on the pastoral epistles exactly in the same category as Strauss' *Life of Jesus*, so that all of the anathema which have been made concerning Strauss' work in the Preface of the *Evangelische Kirchenzeitung* may also apply to my book;[10] it also describes me as a theologian who stands "under Strauss' influence" (a spiteful accusation, without proof, which questions my theological independence and offends my honor, an accusation which I could only qualify by using a word which I already used above[11]). And so, in addition to the rest, it is momentously announced to the public that I stand in a "friendly rapport" with D. Strauss. Here I could ask: how does the author of the article know this? Is his inquisitorial attentiveness, not just about my books, but also about my private life, so great that he deems it necessary to report about it to the public? And is he adequately informed about this? Since, as I have already shown, the author's truthfulness in this article, so far as I am concerned, does not appear in the best light, if I did not take up this point the public would wonder to what extent the *Evangelische Kirchenzeitung*'s article, [309] also on this particular question, can be trusted. I make this comment only in view of other similar cases where I do not have the oppor-

9. [Original footnote] It would be a very good thing if those who are so opposed to critical studies did not give the impression that their opposition only targets the skeptical kind of criticism, not criticism *per se*. If they wished to speak freely, they should acknowledge that such a distinction cannot be made, in itself or, especially, in relation to their position. A criticism which may not also be skeptical is no criticism at all. Quite often, only doubt leads us to truth, and a theology which axiomatically posits that we should never doubt and inspect anything, would do well to simply suppress historical criticism from the scientific fields which constitute theology.

10. "Vorwort," *Evangelische Kirchenzeitung* 18, no. 1 (January 2, 1836):1–6; no. 2 (January 6, 1936):9–14; no. 3 (January 9, 1836):17–23; no. 4 (January 13, 1836):25–31; no. 5 (January 16, 1836):33–38; no. 6 (January 20, 1836):41–45. The article to which Baur responded, "Die Zukunft unserer Thelogie," also mentioned this long preface ("Die Zukunft," 283).

11. Baur arguably has the word *calumny* in mind here (see above, 125).

tunity and a reason to explain myself. I have no desire to deny conventions and relations, and I have nothing to hide about my behavior from public life. And yet a dispiriting and embarrassing sentiment overwhelms me when I consider how far the overt suspicion has gone, when one is forced to respond before all also about such personal matters. And so I do not deny at all that I stand in a friendly relation with Dr. Strauss. I wish to add to this that, in the long string of years in which I have learned to know him better, until now, as with other similar cases, I have not been able to discern in him the demonic nature which the editor of the *Evangelische Kirchenzeitung*, with the unfailing eyes of his Christian love, wishes to see in him. But what may be implied by such a relation? Does it mean that I am responsible for axioms and assertions which I have not articulated, for books which I have not written? Perhaps one will be able to draw such consequences and account for this before God and one's conscience. To me, only one thing is worth noting, namely the confirmation of the old experience that, wherever inquisitorial attempts to brand others as heretics consolidate themselves and escalate, such attempts never remain limited to the things which are the direct objects of attention; rather, these attempts instantly extend also to all the other objects which are found to stand in looser or more distant relation with the former, primary objects. This is the old, well-documented practice whereby, *in majorem Dei gloriam*, no aspect of life is so frail and holy that it should be spared its venom. It is not the first time that, because of theological opinions, a friendship is perceived as an outrage, or a teacher is tracked with his student; for the sake of the living, even the dead [310] are not granted peace. Since I, for once, must speak of such things, I cannot omit to note that the information which is contained in the same article (p. 285), according to which the Church of Württemberg has decreed the expulsion of this theologian (D. Strauss) from any ecclesial teaching post, is not quite accurate. What the author of the article, following his slogan, would have liked to have occurred, did not quite happen in that way. At a minimum, I do not know whether the change in the author's position, following the publication of the first part of the *Life of Jesus*, is accurately described as an exclusion, decreed by the Church of Württemberg, from any ecclesial teaching position. What I know, however, is that the Church of Württemberg, with regard to what is good and appropriate which it must decree and order, knows its own position well enough to embrace for itself the principles of the *Evangelische Kirchenzeitung*—principles which are inspired by the hate of heretics.[12]

Assuredly, every true friend of the Protestant Church, if he is able to judge very differently such publications, having read the article on "The Future of Our Theology" as well as the "Preface" which accompanies it, will be filled with the dreariest sentiment and outlook concerning the future of our theology and of our Church. Certainly, everyone is compelled to ask: what will happen, in the near future, with the Protestant Church, if such axioms come to expression always [311] more unashamedly and forcefully, if they become always more commonplace? Where is the love of Christ when, as was the case with the treatment of my work, every regard is sacrificed on the altar of the hate of heretics? Where is the freedom of faith and thinking, when the circle within which a theological difference of opinion may occur always become narrower? Where is the faith in an invisible Church, which no one can discern with one's heart amidst the visible Church, when the damning judgment which is issued about actions or books and when the judging gaze penetrate into the most interior reaches of the heart? Indeed, how can there still be, in the Protestant Church, a remnant of assurance for the moral foundations of life, when those who champion the holy cause of the gospel, who dedicate themselves to their journals, who always make sure to claim how "seriously they take Christ," make such a game of the truth (as I have shown to be the case with the article under consideration, insofar as it concerns me), or when means, such as those I have shown, are

12. [Original footnote] *Écrasez l'infâme!* is the openly stated Christian slogan of the *Evangelische Kirchenzeitung*'s editor. On that basis, anyone is invited to decide for oneself what may in fact be said with the expression "friendly rapport." It seems to me to be the proper place, here, to ask the readers of these pages not to forget, anywhere in my declaration, the kind of claim to moral regard which moral principles of this kind, which are openly stated, may make.

put to use in order to reach more surely the goal which has been set? What this amounts to, in one word—as the honorable Neander felt compelled to state, right after having read the said "Preface," its impression on him being fresh and all the more true, and protesting in the spirit of love and freedom—is: "a *papacy*," indeed a new papacy, erected in the midst of the Protestant Church, and already endowed with everything which any papacy must possess if it is not to fail in its highest and ultimate purpose.[13] I will not deny what is good about the *Evangelische Kirchenzeitung*, but no one will deny that the true spirit of Christianity cannot rule where such an impure and un-Christian principle comes to expression (were it the case only in one particular respect), as it does in the presumptuous quest to brand heretics—a quest through which the *Evangelische Kirchenzeitung* would like to suppress every free, spiritual movement in order to create a new tyranny of the spirit. If the editor of the *Evangelische Kirchenzeitung* takes such an activity to be authentically Christian and [312] Protestant, then I can only wish, out of Christian love, that the true light may rise, at the right time, over the awful blindness and self-deception in which he finds himself. May he finally come to realize—he who, with the sympathizers of his *Evangelische Kirchenzeitung* alone, believes to stand so high above the spirit of the age—that this same spirit of the age, and the pernicious trajectories in which in his eyes only others are captive, hold him tightly in their arms. Doesn't his *Evangelische Kirchenzeitung* place itself at the level of some of the daily newspapers which, in his own opinion, are largely responsible for the corruption of our time, when it pays tribute in such a way to factionalism, when it so deliberately lingers with each scandal (made up or not), not in order to warn and to admonish with Christian seriousness and Christian love, or to teach and refute, as is necessary, but above all in order to brand as heretic and to arouse suspicion, to judge and to condemn, and in order to exploit every incident of this kind? Doesn't it fall to the level of daily papers when it sorts every person whom it has selected according to specific names, colors, and parties, when it manages to obfuscate the differences which lie beneath their united points of view, when it does not abstain from expressing political suspicion—including during the decisive year of 1830, which presented so many opportunities of doing so? In all this, with its way of speaking which is always excited, puffing and panting in its fervor and desire for revenge, hoping to stir up the sensuous nature in its readers, doesn't it present itself like these newspapers? May the editor of the *Evangelische Kirchenzeitung*, if he is still ready to make "the weather of the Lord, his terrible thunderstorm, his furious and vengeful wrath"[14] fall on the head of others, if his intent still is to frighten with the lion's roar and to remind of the grave time of the judgment which is close at hand, may he, before it is too late, think about the kind of judge in front of whom he too will have to stand, accounting for all of his words. Every papacy, of whichever kind, carries with itself its own curse, the curse of [313] hubris and egomania. Sooner or later it collapses into its own nothingness. Under a tyranny of spirit which would like to suppress a freer, spiritual life wherever it emerges, under an egomania which always only screams its "No!" (a "No" which contradicts nature) wherever there is the free and joyous love of life of the spirits—the spirits which their eternal Father, from the fullness of his life, sends out so that they may build, with invisible forces and using the whole range of charisms of his Spirit, his Kingdom, according to a plan which mortal eyes seldom notice; under such egomania no one in Germany will accept to bend one's neck, and it will not be possible that, for the sake of the project of establishing a papacy for oneself and for a few others, goes lost for the world what men such as Schleiermacher and Hegel[15] [314] have achieved, in their solemn life work, for the good of Church and State and as a lasting fruit for all who, through their [315] own reflection and research, testing everything and holding fast to every good thing, know they are following in

13. For August Neander's critical comments ("Nachschrift"), dated February 17, 1836, on the *Evangelische Kirchenzeitung*'s preface, see *Dr. Neander's Erklärung in Beziehung auf einen ihn betreffenden Artikel der Allgemeinen Zeitung* (Berlin: Haude und Spenersche Buchhandlung, 1836), 11–12. Also reprinted in *Evangelische Kirchenzeitung* 18, no. 30 (April 13, 1836):col. 233.

14. Jer 30:23 (Baur is quoting Luther's Bible).

15. Here Baur adds a very long footnote, which has been removed.

their footsteps. [316] When someone like Neander openly protests against the *Evangelische Kirchenzeitung*'s chosen standpoint, [317] that is, against an exclusive salvific dogmatics on the basis of which [318] all kinds of different schools are appraised, then the final hour of such papacy has come. [319] And so, at this point, it cannot be concealed, quite naively, that the article we have been dealing with "has turned out to be rather dull." But the consolation comes right away, with the new self-delusion that "the esteemed man, in the Postface of his declaration, expresses what he has to say about Strauss concerning several minor differences with greater affect than against the one who is invalidating the Christian basis, and whom he nevertheless considers as his comrade in faith and spirit,"[16] which means paying tribute to the very papacy against which he so solemnly protests. Considering the heartfelt manner in which he recently wrote about the late Billroth (a person I also highly esteemed) and Billroth's friend, Professor Weisse,[17] I also cannot imagine the esteemed Tholuck being of a different opinion than Neander and refusing, in our current divisions, to broadly recognize with him the unity in spirit—which is suffused with the truth of Neander's weighty words in his Declaration (p. 12): "It is easy to be consistent when one reaches the conclusion and is done quickly; it is, on the other hand, difficult when one keeps one's conscience, in all directions, in a bitter struggle with oneself in order to better assimilate it, open to the truth that all of our knowledge is and remains fragmentary." The *Evangelische Kirchenzeitung*'s appeal to all who take Christ seriously, namely to prepare themselves in all seriousness and faithfulness for the great battle of our time, for the period during which Christ's Church and the Kingdom of Darkness will separate themselves and confront each other in greater ways than ever before: this appeal will nevertheless be issued. May everyone who knows what he wills, wherever he is located in such a battle, may everyone who is earnest about Christ know that [320] even if—in the imminent future—delusional, human predictions are not realized, the Lord's divine word, on the other hand, remains eternally true: *You will know them by their fruits* [Matt 7:16, 20]. May this single saying be the answer to whatever the *Evangelische Kirchenzeitung* might still publish about me.

16. [Original footnote] See the *Litterarischer Anzeiger für christliche Theologie und Wissenschaft überhaupt*, 1836, Nr. 52, p. 249s.

17. [Original footnote] *Litterarischer Anzeiger*, *ibid.*

18.

Søren Kierkegaard (1813–55)

Gotthold Ephraim Lessing had lamented the immense historical gaps between Jesus's remote times and the eighteenth century, between the contingent historical truths and the "necessary" truths of reason. Søren Kierkegaard did not know of any gap at all. As a (critical) reader of Georg Wilhelm Friedrich Hegel and as a Lutheran Christian, he was convinced of the contemporaneity of Christ. Yet this contemporaneity is everything but a soothing presence: it is the very source of the "scandal" that calls for our decision, the decision of faith or non-faith. Where Kierkegaard agreed with Lessing was in the notion of a "leap," which was no more possible according to the Danish philosopher than to Lessing—but according to Kierkegaard it is this impossible act that God asks of human beings and, especially, that God enables humans to do.

The excerpts that follow come from Kierkegaard's book *Practice in Christianity* (written in 1848, published in 1850), trans. Howard V. Hong and Edna H. Hong (Princeton: Princeton University Press, 1991).

PRACTICE IN CHRISTIANITY (1850)

[9–10] No. 1: "Come Here, All You Who Labor and Are Burdened, and I Will Give You Rest." For Awakening and Inward Deepening, by Anti-Climacus

Invocation

It is indeed eighteen hundred years since Jesus Christ walked here on earth, but this is certainly not an event just like other events, which once they are over pass into history and then, as the distant past, pass into oblivion. No, his presence here on earth never becomes a thing of the past, thus does not become more and more distant—that is, if faith is at all found upon the earth; if not, well, then in that very instant it is a long time since he lived. But as long as there is a believer, this person, in order to have become that, must have been and as a believer must be just as contemporary with Christ's presence as his contemporaries were. This contemporaneity is the condition of faith, and, more sharply defined, it is faith. Lord Jesus Christ, would that we, too, might become contemporary with you in this way, might see you in your true form and in the surroundings of actuality as you walked here on earth, not in the form in which an empty and meaningless or a thoughtless-romantic or a historical-talkative remembrance has distorted you, since it is not the form of abasement in which the believer sees you, and it cannot possibly be the form of glory in which no one as yet has seen you. Would that we might see you as you are and were and will be until your second coming in glory, as the sign of offense and the object of faith, the lowly man, yet the Savior and Redeemer of the human race, who out of love came to earth to seek the lost, to suffer and die. . . .

The Halt

[34] He is not the one who by allowing himself to be born and by making his appearance in Judea has presented himself for the examination of history. It is he who is the examiner; his life is the examination, and not for his generation alone, but for the *human race*. . . .

[63–64] In relation to the absolute, there is only one time, the present; for the person who is not contemporary with the absolute, it does not exist at all. And since Christ is the absolute it is easy to see that in relation to him there is only one situation, the situation of contemporaneity; the three, the seven, the fifteen, the seventeen, the eighteen hundred years make no difference at all; they do not change him, but neither do they reveal who he was, for who he is is revealed only to faith. . . .

History you can read and hear about as about the past; here you can, if it so pleases you, judge by the outcome. But Christ's life on earth is not a past; it did not wait at the time, eighteen hundred years ago, and does not wait now for the assistance of any outcome. A historical Christianity is non-sense and un-Christian muddled thinking, because whatever true Christians there are in any generation are contemporary with Christ, have nothing to do with Christians in past generations but everything to do with the contemporary Christ. His life on earth accompanies the human race and accompanies each particular generation as the eternal history; his life on earth has the eternal contemporaneity. And this in turn makes all didacticizing of Christianity (didacticizing that essentially has its mask and refuge in the pastness of Christianity and in the eighteen hundred years of history) into the most un-Christian of all heresies, as anyone would perceive and therefore would abandon didacticizing if he tried to imagine the generation contemporary with Christ—didacticizing. But every generation (of believers) is indeed contemporary.

19.

Albrecht Ritschl (1822–89)

Albrecht Ritschl was perhaps the most prominent Protestant (Lutheran) theologian during the decades between Friedrich Schleiermacher and Karl Barth. He began his theological career as a disciple of Ferdinand Christian Baur before breaking from him and finding his own path. His constructive theology, which is deeply historical, especially with regard to the historical tradition of Christian theology, was very influential, especially in the last quarter of the nineteenth century, but also until the First World War. He attracted some of the best minds among the new generation of theologians and historians of Christianity: scholars such as Adolf von Harnack, Johannes Gottschick, Ferdinand Kattenbusch, Max Reischle, Martin Rade, and Wilhelm Herrmann. Soon after his death, two bright young scholars—namely, Johannes Weiss and Ernst Troeltsch—questioned Ritschl's thought in two ways: Weiss, who had rediscovered the eschatological dimension of Jesus's message, argued that Ritschl's interpretation of the kingdom had in fact very little to do with Jesus's message; Troeltsch, for his part, considered metaphysics to be a good thing for Christian and Protestant theology and thus did not view the development of Lutheran theology, from the first generation to Protestant Orthodoxy, as an intrinsically problematic development.

Writing not long after David Friedrich Strauss, Ritschl was deeply sensitive to the challenge of history. What follows is an expression of Ritschl's attempt to reply to the modern lives of Jesus.

The selections below come from the very first pages of Albrecht Ritschl's *magnum opus*, *The Christian Doctrine of Justification and Reconciliation*, vol. 3: *The Positive Development of the Doctrine*, trans. H. R. Mackintosh et al. (Edinburgh: T&T Clark, 1902), 1–4 (§1). The book's original German title is *Die christliche Lehre von der Rechtfertigung und Versöhnung*, 3rd ed. (Bonn: Marcus, 1888), vol. 3.

THE CHRISTIAN DOCTRINE OF JUSTIFICATION AND RECONCILIATION (1888)

[1]§ 1. The exposition of Biblical Theology contained in my second volume was undertaken in order to ascertain what idea of the forgiveness of sins, justification, and reconciliation—together with their relations—has been called into existence by Jesus as the founder of the Christian Church, and maintained by the apostles as its earliest representatives. In view of the many distortions and obscurations which the intellectual content of Christianity has suffered in the course of history, my aim, in harmony with the theological principles of the Protestant Church, was to discover the conceptions originally held of the religious relation of Christians to God which the abovementioned notions express. Once this authentical exposition of the ideas named has been given, however, the interests of theology are satisfied. For succeeding thinkers have been guided, in part intentionally, in part unconsciously, by the models of the New Testament, or should not be followed when they in point of fact diverge from them.

Now it is not sufficient for my purpose to bring out what Jesus has said about the forgiveness of sins attached to his person and his death. For even if his statements might seem perfectly clear, their significance becomes completely intelligible only when we see how they are reflected in the consciousness of those who believe in him, and how the members of the Christian community trace back their consciousness of pardon to the person and the action and passion of Jesus. For thus we are made aware that Jesus' purpose of pardon has not failed. Its success, however, not only serves to make more clear what his purpose was: it also forms an [2] essential condition of our religious and theological interest in the matter. We should pay no special attention to this purpose of Jesus, nor should we seek to discover its value and its meaning, did we not reckon ourselves part of the *religious community* which first attested, through the writers of the New Testament, its possession of the forgiveness of sins as effected by Christ. On the other hand, the necessity of this connection with the Church is ignored by those who think themselves competent to arrive at or reproduce "the religion of Jesus"; as also by those who acknowledge in Jesus only the Author of new moral legislation, or one of those who have helped to perfect humanity's ideal. Those who comprise in the latter view the results of their historical criticism, either ignore Jesus' sayings about forgiveness as attached to his person and his death, or regard them as merely casual expressions, or content themselves with supposing that in Jesus' view forgiveness flows directly of itself from moral obedience to the law. The advocates of "the religion of Jesus" are quite well aware that some value belongs to the *religious* example of Jesus, apart from his moral legislation and his moral example. But in thinking that his significance can be stated completely in terms of personal imitation, they overlook the very fact that Jesus withdraws himself from imitation when he sets himself over against his disciples as the author of forgiveness. The minds of his disciples are so far responsive to his teaching on this point, that they become convinced that pardon must first be appropriated before it is possible to imitate his piety and his moral achievement.

Authentic and complete knowledge of Jesus' religious significance—his significance, that is, as a founder of religion—depends, then, on one's reckoning oneself part of the community which he founded, and this precisely insofar as it believes itself to have received the forgiveness of sins as his peculiar gift. This religious faith does not take an unhistorical view of Jesus, and it is quite possible to reach an historical estimate of him without first divesting oneself of this faith, this religious valuation of his person. The opposite [3] view is one of the characteristics which mark that great untruth which exerts a deceptive and confusing influence under the name of an historical "absence of presuppositions." It is no mere accident that the subversion of Jesus' religious importance has been undertaken under the guise of writing his life, for this very undertaking implies the surrender of the conviction that Jesus, as the founder of the perfect moral and spiritual religion, belongs to a higher order than all other men. But for that reason it is likewise vain to attempt to re-establish the importance of Christ by the same biographical expedient. We can discover the full compass of his historical actuality solely from the faith of the Christian community. Not even his purpose to found the community can be quite understood historically save by one who, as a member of it, subordinates himself to his person.

Thence follows for our present task, however, that the material of the theological doctrines of forgiveness, justification, and reconciliation is to be sought not so much directly in the words of Christ, as in the correlative representations of the original consciousness of the community. The immediate object of theological cognition is the community's faith that it stands to God in a relation essentially conditioned by the forgiveness of sins. So far, however, as this benefit is traced back to the personal action and passion of Christ, his proved intention to adopt such means makes the mediation of the community more intelligible. Such being the position of affairs, we have now a basis for the practice of theology in attaching its terminology directly to the apostolic circle of ideas. It would be a mistaken purism were anyone, in this respect, to prefer the less developed statements of Jesus to the forms of apostolic thought. Nay more, we are justified in not paring down the most developed forms of the Pauline system, but preserving them in theological usage, for they serve to express most sharply the opposition between Christianity and Judaism. What urges us to this is not solely the predominant custom of the Western Church and the Reformed tradition, but the fact that by means of the Pauline formulas [4] the uniqueness of Christianity is marked off from the Pharisaic falsification of the religion of the Old Testament, and thereby the Christian Church most securely protected against a recrudescence of the latter error.

The precondition, thus indicated as essential for the understanding of forgiveness, justification, and reconciliation, which are assured through Christ, holds good for every part of the Christian circle of thought. We are able to know and understand God, sin, conversion, eternal life, in the Christian sense, only so far as we consciously and intentionally reckon ourselves members of the community which Christ has founded. Theology is bound to take up this point of view, and only so is there any hope of constructing a theological system which deserves the name. For in order to comprehend the content of Christianity, as a totality composed of rightly ordered particular data, we must occupy one and the same standpoint throughout.

20.

Walter Rauschenbusch (1861–1918)

A Baptist pastor and theologian born in Rochester, New York, in a family of German immigrants, Walter Rauschenbusch was well versed in German modern theology. He had been sent to Gütersloh by his parents to attend gymnasium there. In 1891 he was back again in Germany, this time for a study trip of nine months, during which he wrote a manuscript on "the righteousness of the kingdom" (edited in 1968 by Max L. Stackhouse). His interest in the theme of the kingdom of God is not unrelated to the prominence of this theme in Albrecht Ritschl's theology and among Ritschlian theologians in the last decades of the nineteenth century. But Rauschenbusch reinterpreted this theme in ways Ritschl would never have dreamed of. As a Baptist pastor working in the neighborhood of Hell's Kitchen (Manhattan), he became sensitive to the plight of impoverished workers and immigrants and the appalling conditions in which they lived, and he read the Scriptures with this situation in mind. He went on to become one of the most important voices of what became known as the social gospel, that is, of an interpretation of the Christian faith that seeks to uncover the social and political implications of the Bible and the gospel in the context of the massive and rapid industrialization of Western societies, in preparation for the advent of God's kingdom. "Christianizing the social order" was Rauschenbusch's motto and the title of one of his most successful books. He was in contact with like-minded theologians across the West, including Hermann Kutter and Leonhard Ragaz in Switzerland and Wilfred Monod and Élie Gounelle in France. Decades later, Martin Luther King Jr. praised the theologian: "Rauschenbusch has done a great service for the Christian Church by insisting that the gospel deals with the whole man, not only his soul but his body; not only his spiritual well-being but his material well-being. It has been my conviction ever since reading Rauschenbusch that any religion which professes to be concerned about the souls of men and is not concerned about the social and economic conditions that scar the soul, is a spiritually moribund religion only waiting for the day to be buried."[1]

1. Martin Luther King Jr., *Stride Toward Freedom: The Montgomery Story* (New York: Harper, 1958), 91.

The texts below come from *The Righteousness of the Kingdom*, ed. Max L. Stackhouse (Nashville: Abingdon, 1968); and from *A Theology for the Social Gospel* (New York: Macmillan, 1917), lectures given at Yale's Divinity School in April 1917.

THE RIGHTEOUSNESS OF THE KINGDOM (1891)

[280] Insofar as Christianity is identical with righteousness and with the cause of God, its ultimate victory is certain. But I am not asserting that it is victorious at all times and all along the line.

Public thought in America is so far from doubting the value of life and the triumph of right that it is in a perpetual chuckle of satisfaction at "the progress of the world." Hoary wrongs are crumbling; the nations are marching toward popular liberty; steamboats are getting faster, kings rarer, creeds more liberal; what more would you have? Give humanity free play and we shall have the millennium here on schedule time.

This hopefulness is probably due partly to our youthfulness and partly to the idea of evolution which has saturated our thought. We conceive of the world rolling slowly out into the light of day; therefore every step must be day-ward, every change must be an improvement, every new idea must approximate more nearly to the truth than the one it supplants, every tendency must be just. That is the way in which evolution has taken hold of the popular mind.

But this view is not accurate. Evolution—granting it proved—teaches the possibility of change for the better, not the certainty of it. Environment may modify backward as well as forward. Degeneration is as much a scientific fact as development. The forces of death and destruction press hard on the forces of life. The assumption that, on the whole, evolution is moving forward and upward rests partly on sight, but even more on faith.

The matter becomes even more doubtful when the idea of evolution is applied to human history. The nations of the earth have not moved forward with unfaltering march. Concerning some, the proof is wanting that they have ever been lower than they are now. Of others proof is abundant that they have been higher than they are now, and, having come down, they apparently propose to stay down. In Egypt, in Central America, in Asia Minor, in Greece the monuments of a higher civilization look down on a degenerate state. In India and China there is stagnation, if not degeneration. In fact it looks as if [281] every nation had its period of childhood and its teens, and then, when growth is most rapid and life most luscious, it is stung by some hidden disease and sapped of its virility. It declines and henceforth is old. Some nations have collapsed quickly. Others have stood erect for centuries and perhaps, like Italy, have risen to a second period of glory. There are only a few nations whose track through the last two thousand years seems headed toward the Kingdom of God. It is a wavering, lagging line, yet it goes forward. And they seem to have the faculty also of planting new and vigorous societies and of putting a thrill of life into their paralytic sister nations.

In short, while we hold fast our faith in the destiny of humanity and in the capacity of every nation to grow up into an ever higher stature and, for aught we know, into an endless bloom of manhood, yet history solemnly tells us that there are lost nations as well as lost individuals. "Many are called, but few are chosen." The Bible itself tells of a nation, elect of God, which failed in the hour of its visitation, and its vineyard has been taken away from it.

History does not encourage the rollicking optimism which trusts men, especially in the United States, to come down every time feet foremost, like a cat. Nations also have to strive with fear and trembling to be saved. For humanity also the gate is narrow and the way to life is straight.

It is a goodly doctrine, that of human progress. It is very sweet to man. It is delightful to know that, after a few more hampering traditions and worn-out institutions are knocked away, humanity will ride down into the perfect life like a ship from her dock into the sea. The presupposition of this doctrine is that man is by nature good and tends upward, if only he is not dragged down by outward forces. I am frank to confess that I once felt all the attractions of this view of life. But I have been obliged to yield it up and to say now with Browning: "The candid incline to surmise of late that the Christian faith may be false, I find. I still, to suppose it true, for my part, see reasons and reasons; this, to begin: 'Tis the faith that launched point-blank her dart at the head of a lie—taught Original Sin, the Corruption of Man's Heart."

[282] It is not true that man tends by nature upward. It is the downward way that is easy; the upward way is steep and toilsome. It requires no effort for us to yield to temptation; the effort comes when we try to resist. The number of those who overcome even the natural intellectual inertia is small. Educational institutions do not sustain themselves; with few exceptions they would collapse if the benefactions of individuals or the taxing power of the community were withdrawn from their support. We have to pass laws to get children into school and to keep them out of the saloon. In Europe the theatres giving the classic plays have to be subsidized; those rendering adapted French plays need no subsidies.

None of us individually drifts into purity, justice, and unselfishness, as we all know. And humanity as a whole would likewise, if let alone, by no means roll into the millennium, but by a broad and easy track into a hell on earth, into rottenness, beastliness, and self-destruction. What association of men or what human institution does not sag downward? What political party does not grow corrupt? What church does not tend toward formalism and worldliness? What charitable society is not in danger of becoming uncharitable? What educational system or institution does not stiffen into pedantry to the stifling of intellect? What body of law needs no effort to exhume justice buried under its legal decisions like Nero's guests under his shower of roses?

And not only is the natural tendency downward by mere moral inertia. We have to reckon also with the fact that there is such a thing as conscious, determined, malicious love of evil. The natural thing is to do evil because it looks sweet before it is done, then to do it again because it has acquired power, and thus to continue the downward course. But all this while man knows it to be wrong, he wishes that he did not do it, he is pained to see the young and innocent acquiring the same habit. But it seems to be possible for the human spirit to give itself to evil and to love it, to take delight in ensnaring the innocent, to corrupt their minds systematically, to interfere consciously with the efforts to better society, and not only to turn sideward with a hiss at the approach of purity, but to strike a poisoned [283] fang into its heel. If those who have consciously abandoned the principle of selfishness and handed themselves over to love are children of God, then such are children of the devil. They bear the mark of the beast on brow and hand, on intellect and action.

Now, such men and women have power. There are periods of history which, like a forest tract with charred trunks, show the passing of one of these human firebrands. And what these Castilian spirits have been in the larger territory of history, their smaller kindred, smiling behind the saloon bar, button-holing local politicians, promenading on the city streets, telling anecdotes on the kegs of a village grocery, or laying snares in drawing-rooms, are to the social circle within which they move. If a determined good man has power, so has a determined bad man. He can even with the same exertion of force accomplish more, because he appeals to the lower instincts of lust, hate, pride, and needs only to draw out the pegs to set the log rolling. These forces have to be reckoned with. They add momentum to the natural downward drift of humanity. Therefore our wrestling is not merely with the natural weakness of flesh and blood, but "against the principalities, against the powers, against the world-rulers of this darkness, against the spiritual hosts of wickedness."

Let us have no illusions. The world will not evolve into a Kingdom of God by natural processes. It is uphill work. It is a battle. Every inch will have to be fought for.

But neither let us have *any* cowardice, especially no croaking sloth hiding under a religious garb. We *must* conquer. We may use the old crusaders' cry with a purer right than they: *Deus lo volt*—God wills it!

And what, then, shall lift humanity up, if the force that raises it is not naturally inherent in it? Water cannot rise higher than its source. An effect cannot contain more than its causes. One epoch of history cannot be greater and nobler than the one out of which it has grown, unless an additional force has entered into its composition. Whence does that force come in human history?

The same question has been raised concerning the asserted upward evolution of the organic world below man. If the higher forms of [284] life have developed from the lowest, what has pushed them up? Those who believe in God have not hesitated to reply: God. He is immanent in the world, forever active and working. It is his force and his guidance which moulds his existing works into higher forms through his Kingdom.

We take exactly that position concerning the life of humanity. God is in it. "The Father worketh hitherto." His will is set toward his Kingdom on earth. His Spirit works upon the spirits of men and of nations. Within limits known to him, and for reasons known by him, he suffers their disobedience and resistance. But he wearies not. His force is still put forth. And the medium through which it is most exerted is those human spirits who have freely surrendered themselves to the will and service of righteousness. There God gets a purchase on humanity. There he can grip it. Such spirits he fills with the ideas and impulses which their time needs in order to take the next step forward, and through these channels the forces of God flow out into humanity. These are the prophetic souls. In them and in their work lies the hope of humanity's progress. The upward forces communicated through them have to overcome the downward inclination of flesh and blood, as life in the physical world overcomes the force of gravity.

The hope of the world therefore lies in religion. Politics cannot lift man; at its best it removes hindrances to his uplifting or refrains from laying stumbling blocks in his way; at its worst it defeats the aims of justice and lends tools to the leagued interests of oppression. Its power in either direction is immense. But it never creates moral forces, it simply yields to them.

A THEOLOGY FOR THE SOCIAL GOSPEL (1917)

Chapter 14: The Initiator of the Kingdom of God

[146] The social gospel has an inherent interest in history. Individualistic theology sees everywhere countless sinful individuals who must all go through the same process of repentance, faith, justification, and regeneration, and who in due time die and go to heaven or hell. The historical age in which a person lived, or the social class or race to which he belonged, matters little. This religious point of view is above time and history. On the other hand the social gospel tries to see the progress of the Kingdom of God in the flow of history; not only in the doings of the Church, but in the clash of economic forces and social classes, in the rise and fall of despotisms and forms of enslavement, in the rise of new value judgments and fresh canons of moral taste and sentiment, or the elevation or decline of moral standards. Its chief interest is the Kingdom of God and the Kingdom of God is history seen in a religious and teleological way. Therefore the social gospel is always historically minded. Its spread goes hand in hand with the spread of the historical spirit and method.

This dominant interest in the creation and progress of social redemption influences the approach to the theological problems of the person and work of Christ. We [147] want to see the Christ who initiated the Kingdom of God. Theologians have always tried to make their christology match with their conception of salvation. If they believed salvation to consist chiefly in the knowledge of God, they emphasized the personality and the doctrine of Christ as the complete revelation of God. If they made salvation to consist chiefly in the mystic impartation of divine life and immortality, their christology laid chief stress on the union of the divine and human in the incarnation and in the sacraments. If salvation consists above all in the expiation of guilt, the forgiveness of sins, the justification of the sinner, and the remission of his penalties, then we need a Christ who made atonement for our sins, rendered satisfaction to God for our delinquencies, and offset our guilty defects by his infinite merit and divine virtue. Each conception of salvation made a pragmatic selection and construction of the facts. Each was fragmentary, but without necessarily excluding other series of ideas. So now the social gospel, without excluding other theological convictions, demands to understand that Christ who set in motion the historical forces of redemption which are to overthrow the Kingdom of Evil.

This is surely not an illegitimate interest. It is a return to the earliest messianic theology; whereas some of the other christological interests and ideas are alien importations, part of that wave of "Hellenization" which nearly swamped the original gospel.

Being historically minded and realistic in its interests, the social gospel is less concerned in the metaphysical problems involved in the trinitarian and christological [148] doctrines. The speculative problem of christological dogma was how the divine and human natures united in the one person of Christ; the problem of the social gospel is how the divine life of Christ can get control of human society. The social gospel is concerned about a progressive social incarnation of God. . . . The social gospel joins with all modern thought in the feeling that the old theology does not give us a Christ who is truly personal. Just as the human race, when it appears in theology, is an amorphous metaphysical conception which could be more briefly designated by an algebraic symbol, in the same way the personality of Jesus is not allowed to be real under theological influence. If it does stand out vital and resolute, it is in spite of theology and not because of it. Some of the [149] greatest theologians, men who wrote epoch-making treatises about Christ, such as Athanasius, give no indication that the personality of Jesus was live and real to them. When those who have been trained under the old religious beliefs come under the influence of historical teaching, the realization that Jesus was actually a person, and not merely part of a "scheme of redemption," often comes as a great and beneficent shock. He has been made part of a scheme of salvation, the second premise in a great syllogism. The social gospel wants to see a personality able to win hearts, dominate situations, able to bind men in loyalty and make them think like himself, and to set revolutionary social forces in motion.

Every event and saying in the life of Christ has, of course, been scanned intensely and used over and over for edification or theological proof. But in the main the theological significance of the life of Christ has been comprised in the incarnation, the atonement, and the resurrection. The life in general served mainly to connect and lead up to these great events, and to found the Church. The things in which Jesus himself was passionately interested and which he strove to accomplish, do not seem to count for much. The impartation of divine life and immortality to the race was accomplished when he was a babe. The atonement might actually have been frustrated if the life effort of Jesus had been [150] successful, for if the Jews had accepted his spiritual leadership, they would not have killed him.

The social gospel would interpret all the events of his life, including his death, by the dominant purpose which he consistently followed, the establishment of the Kingdom of God. This is the only interpretation which would have appealed to himself. His life was what counted; his death was part of it. The historic current of salvation which went out from him is the prolongation of that life into which he put his conscious energy.

Theology has made the divinity of Christ a question of nature rather than character. His divinity was an inheritance or endowment which he brought with him and which was fixed for him in his pre-existent state. He was divine on account of what took place at one moment in the womb of one Jewish woman rather than on account of all that took place in the inner depths of his spirit when he communed with his Father and fought through the issues of his life. Theology has been on a false trail in seeking the key to his life in the difficult doctrine of the two natures. That doctrine has never been settled. The formula of Chalcedon was a compromise. Any attempt to think precisely about the question results in a caricature; safety lies in vagueness. We shall come closer to the secret of Jesus if we think less of the physical process of conception and more of the spiritual processes of desire, choice, affirmation, and self-surrender within his own will and personality. The mysteries of the spiritual world take place within the will.

To repeat: The social gospel is not primarily interested in metaphysical questions; its christological interest [151] is all for a real personality who could set a great historical process in motion; it wants his work interpreted by the purposes which ruled and directed his active life; it would have more interest in basing the divine quality of his personality on free and ethical acts of his will than in dwelling on the passive inheritance of a divine essence. . . .

[165] The Kingdom of God is not a concept nor an ideal merely, but an historical force. It is a vital and organizing energy now at work in humanity. Its capacity to save the social order depends on its pervasive presence within the social organism. Every institutional foot-hold gained gives a purchase for attacking the next vantage-point. Where

a really Christian type of religious life is created, the intellect and its education are set free, and this in turn aids religion to emancipate itself from superstition and dogmatism. Where religion and intellect combine, the foundation is laid for political democracy. Where the people have the outfit and the spirit of democracy, they can curb economic exploitation. Where predatory gain and the resultant inequality are lessened, fraternal feeling and understanding become easier and the sense of solidarity grows. Where men live in the consciousness of solidarity and in the actual practice of [166] love with their fellow human beings, they are not far from the Kingdom of God. The great thing in the salvation of humanity is that salvation is present. Life begets life.

Yet it is a matter of unspeakable difficulty for the Kingdom of God to make headway against the inherent weakness of human nature and the social entrenchments of the Kingdom of Evil. "The risks of temporary disaster which great ideals run, appear to be directly proportioned to the value of the ideals. Great truths bear long sorrows."[2] The more we do justice to this fact, the more we shall realize that the initiation and perpetuation of the historical movement of redemption was the essential thing. Jesus was the initiator. To show this more and more clearly is the service the social gospel asks of doctrinal and historical theology. By this avenue of approach we shall appreciate the human dimensions of Jesus. The individualistic theology was the creation of people with little historical training and historical consciousness, and to that extent the problems they set were the product of uneducated minds. The full greatness of the problem of Jesus strikes us when we see him in his connection with human history. Our own consciousness of God's love and forgiveness, our inward freedom, our social feeling, the set of our will toward the achievement of the Kingdom of God, our fellowship with the "two or three" in which we have a realization of the higher presence, we owe to our connection with the historical force which Jesus initiated. Where did he himself get what he had? At what fountain did he drink?

2. [*Original footnote*] Royce, "Problem of Christianity," 1:54.

21.

Martin Kähler (1835–1912)

Martin Kähler is an important voice within Protestant theology, with a lasting influence in the twentieth century. As a student of theology, he was especially grateful for what he learned from the New Testament scholar Johann Tobias Beck (1804–78) and from August Tholuck (1799–1877), among others. Kähler began to teach theology at the University of Halle in 1860 before moving to Bonn in 1864. He returned to Halle in 1867, becoming ordinary professor of systematic theology and New Testament in 1879. He died there in 1912.

Kähler wished to be a biblical theologian but without biblicism (Kraus 1988, 511–12). Pietism's influence on his thinking, through Tholuck especially, is unmistakable. And so he criticized a number of theological schools of thought, such as Friedrich Schleiermacher's theology, which he considered too anthropocentric, or Hegelian (speculative) theologies and other idealist approaches. His first major work, titled "The Science of Christian Doctrine" (*Die Wissenschaft der christlichen Lehre von dem evangelischen Grundartikel aus im Abrisse dargestellt* [1883]), with its concentration on Easter, navigates near Ritschlian waters, yet Kähler remained uneasy—in fact, silent—about this proximity (Ritschl 2013, 21–23, 379, and 389n5).

Kähler remains well known for his 1892 book on the historical Jesus controversy—*The So-Called Historical Jesus and the Historic, Biblical Christ* (original title: *Der sogenannte historische Jesus und der geschichtliche, biblische Christus*). This manifesto is a thoughtful theological response to the "lives of Jesus" movement. While critical of the purely biographical approach to Jesus, Kähler considered "the development of criticism as a divine dispensation for the church" (Kähler 1964, 148n). Even if Kähler's results are today often part of the theological vulgate, his book has not lost any of its relevance.

The text below is adapted from the English translation of Kähler's pamphlet *The So-Called Historical Jesus and the Historic, Biblical Christ*, trans. Carl E. Braaten (Philadelphia: Fortress Press, 1964).

THE SO-CALLED HISTORICAL JESUS AND THE HISTORIC, BIBLICAL CHRIST (1892)

[43] I wish to summarize my cry of warning in a form intentionally audacious: *the historical Jesus of modern authors conceals from us the living Christ.* The Jesus of the "Life-of-Jesus movement" is merely a modern example of human creativity, and not an iota better than the notorious dogmatic Christ of Byzantine Christology. One is as far removed from the real Christ as is the other. In this respect historicism is just as arbitrary, just as humanly arrogant, just as impertinent and "faithlessly gnostic" as that dogmatism which in its day was also considered modern. This judgment applies to both of these as "isms" but not necessarily to those who held, or hold, these erroneous views. . . .

[46] I regard the entire Life-of-Jesus movement as a blind alley. A blind alley usually has something alluring about it, or no one would enter it in the first place. It usually appears to be a section of the right road, or no one would hit upon it at all. In other words, we cannot reject this movement without understanding what is legitimate in it. . . .

[48] . . . We do not possess any sources for a "Life of Jesus" which a historian can accept as reliable and adequate. I repeat: we have no sources for a biography of Jesus of Nazareth which measure up to the standards of contemporary historical science. . . .

[92] One cannot make the figure of Jesus the mere object of historical research, as one can other figures belonging to the past. The figure of Jesus has in every age exerted too powerful and too direct an influence on all sorts of people and still makes too strong a claim on everyone to allow a person to suppose that a decisive stand with respect to Jesus is not implicit in a negative attitude to the claim made by the apostolic "recollection" of him, a recollection with which "none of the records of mankind can even remotely be compared."[1] No one can concern himself with this particular slice of history without somehow coming under the influence of its unique significance for the present. Certainly a Christian will always remind himself that the Jesus of history would, or could, be of no concern to him as a Christian if there were not something in this historical reality which concerns him today just as much as it did the contemporaries of Jesus. The way in which the figure of Jesus today confronts people with his claim to be of unique significance for the religion and morality of every person is precisely the way the Gospel accounts portray his encounter with his own contemporaries. It is through these accounts alone that we are able to come into contact with him. They are not the reports of impartial observers who have been alerted to his presence, but, rather, the *testimonies* and *confessions* of believers of Christ. . . .

[96] According to the historical content of the Pauline symbol (1 Cor 15:3–4), it is in the death of Jesus that God has spoken in a language of deeds (*Tatsachensprache*) which remains indelible. We need no source-documents to record these facts, for they are transported through the millennia by confessions born of gratitude. Indeed, these facts, that is, their essential meaning and abiding worth, cannot be established by historical documents at all; only the witness and the faith of Christians can do that. . . .

[113] I have found it equally impossible to accept the logic of the claims which Protestant Orthodoxy, in its much debated doctrine of verbal inspiration, advanced with respect to the "attributes of Holy Scripture." . . . As far as we can see—and in the New Testament we can in some instances go back to the very beginnings—the biblical writings originated in a thoroughly human fashion. Why not assume that the same is true of all the biblical writings, even where we lack specific information to that effect? . . . [114] Here, too, a rigid consistency has led many astray. It was thought that only the inerrancy of Scripture concerning every incidental matter mentioned by the biblical writers could guarantee the trustworthiness of the one and only main point. What was forgotten was that this main point constitutes the one great exception which alone will prevent the grace of God from falling prey to human fallibility. The consequence is that wherever such a view of inerrancy has prevailed, whether clearly or vaguely, one's whole faith in the revelation of God is called into question when the accuracy of any detail recorded in the Bible is cast into doubt. And hence the relation of believing Christians to the Bible suffers greatly from an unhealthy frustration.

1. [*Original footnote*] Leopold von Ranke, *The History of the Popes* (London: H. G. Bohn, 1853).

It is this diseased condition in the life of our church that concerns me. . . . Whether the controversy centers on the problem of the date and authorship of the biblical books, or on their divisions or their sources, or on the reliability of the details of the biblical accounts, the arguments and counterarguments always move within the limited circle of our present historical knowledge and method. Therefore they are never conclusive. Anyone conversant in these matters knows also that today we smile at many things which the historical knowledge and method of an earlier day regarded as incontrovertible. . . .

[123] Our age wants to see everything "historically." Thus the church's canon of Scripture has become a collection of historical documents. To previous [124] generations the Bible was a revelatory document, a document—as the attempted proofs would have it—of incomparable reliability; to recent generations the biblical canon has become a collection of documents which could be read alongside of others, but, like them, first had to be made accessible through scientific research.

I have never doubted that the biblical writings may and, for certain purposes, must be treated in that manner. If what I have written has been understood to contradict this, then it has been misunderstood. . . . For me the more important question is whether we can do justice to the Bible when we view it from the historical perspective alone. . . . [125] The old doctrine of the inspiration of the Bible is much closer than the one currently popular both to the intention which is dominant in the Bible itself and to what the church has experienced as a result of its possession of this collection. . . .

[127] I deny that the purpose of the Gospels is to serve as documents for a *scientifically reconstructed biography* of Jesus. They have not posited such a purpose for themselves, nor may the church or theology force it upon them as their essential purpose. Their purpose is to awaken faith in Jesus through a clear proclamation of his saving activity. . . .

[140] A person who holds this view stands just as solidly upon the authority of the Bible as does any advocate of verbal inspiration—except that he does not have to take upon himself the burden of proving the details of the tradition regarding the biblical books, a burden always acknowledged by the advocates of verbal inspiration. Without apprehension or anxiety he can grant to historical research all the freedom it desires, to investigate the compilation of the biblical canon and the age and literary construction of the books and portions thereof. . . . [141] Once the infallibility of our biblical records is no longer demanded, then their comparatively remarkable trustworthiness will [142] again be appreciated, even the trustworthiness of the legends, so far as this is conceivable. . . . [143] A normative authority of Holy Scripture [144] cannot be the presupposition for acknowledging revelation, but solely an implication of it. . . .

[146] The fact of biblical criticism—a phenomenon now two and one half centuries old—does more than merely present us with problems and tasks. An acquaintance with biblical criticism also makes us, it seems to me, more skillful in resolving these problems than we would if we approached them from the standpoint of our orthodox forefathers. . . . If previously the Bible appeared as a broad homogeneous mass offering in every passage an infallible oracle, today, in continuing response to new developments in criticism, people have become aware of the structure of the Bible's contents. The great facts of the Bible and its vivid personalities have emerged as significant, not only inasmuch as they satisfy our simple desire for the graphic and concrete, but [147] also for our questions and reflections on matters of divine and human import.

22.

Alfred Loisy (1857–1940)

Alfred Loisy's name remains closely associated with the modernist crisis, a crisis that shook the Roman Catholic Church, especially in France, Germany, England, and Italy in the decades preceding the First World War. Sometimes seen as following in Ernest Renan's (1823—92) footsteps, Loisy was the leader of the modernist movement in France. A seminarian since 1874 and a Roman Catholic priest since 1879, he began his career as a teaching assistant in Hebrew, then, after the completion of his doctoral dissertation in 1890, as professor of exegesis at the recently founded (1875) Institut catholique de Paris. His professorship was taken away from him in 1893. But the apex of the crisis unfolded in the six years that separated the publication of Loisy's famous little book *The Gospel and the Church* (1902) from the condemnation of the "modernist errors" in the encyclical *Pascendi Dominici gregis*, issued in September 1907, and Loisy's excommunication six months later. Loisy's books were placed on the Vatican's Index of Prohibited Books at the end of 1903. In 1909, Loisy was endowed with a chair at the Collège de France (Poulat 1962).

Before *The Gospel and the Church*, which was in fact a brilliant Catholic response to Adolf von Harnack's *Essence of Christianity*, Loisy published a critical history of the Hebrew Bible (1892). The following excerpts, translated by the editor, come from his *Histoire critique du texte et des versions de la Bible*, vol. 1, *Histoire du texte hébreu de l'Ancien Testament* [*A Critical History of the Biblical Text and Versions*, vol. 1, *History of the Hebrew Text of the Old Testament*] (Amiens: Rousseau-Leroy, 1892) (two footnotes that are found in the French version have been omitted), and from *The Gospel and the Church*, trans. Christopher Home (New York: Scribner's, 1912).

A CRITICAL HISTORY OF THE BIBLICAL TEXT AND VERSIONS, VOL. 1: *HISTORY OF THE HEBREW TEXT OF THE OLD TESTAMENT* (1892)

Chapter 2: Overall criticism of the traditional text of the Old Testament

[203] This chapter, which is dedicated to the critical examination of the traditional Hebrew text, will serve as a detailed inventory of the facts and conclusions of which the preceding chapter has shown us the origin and concatenation. We will present the method which is required in the criticism of the text of the Old Testament; we will then give a glimpse of the results which have already be reached by implementing this method.

I. Principles of the textual criticism of the Old Testament

Since we are treating a topic which Catholic exegetes have seldom considered in this century, and which barely mentioned in our manuals of biblical studies, we will insist on the legitimacy of this criticism, before showing its resources and articulating its rules. We will answer these three questions: is the use of criticism legitimate? What are the means which are at its disposal? How must these means be applied?

§1. The legitimacy of textual criticism

We do not need to justify here the general implementation of the critical method to biblical studies with regard to the questions of the origin and the interpretation of the holy Books. Such questions pertain to what is often called high criticism, as if to distinguish it from textual criticism, which certainly is something very humble. But [204] textual criticism and real criticism must not be separated: the latter needs the former in order to be applied fruitfully to ancient texts. There is only one criticism, which is neither high nor low, and which is applied to texts in order to determine both their original content and meaning. Here we consider criticism in its material dimension, that is, insofar as it aims at fixing the reading of the documents, not in its formal dimension, which is directed at their interpretation. We are simply wondering whether it is permissible to discuss the details of the biblical text, in particular those of the Old Testament's Hebrew text, following the principles which are being used in the examination of all ancient profane texts.

In theory, no one contests the legitimacy of the critical examination under consideration, especially with regard to the Hebrew text, which, unlike the Vulgate, has never become the object of Church decisions. The scholars who deal with the criticism of biblical texts presuppose that these texts were the object of the kind of alterations which we see in all of the works of Antiquity which have been copied and transmitted to us. The Church has never pretended being infallible in the material preservation of the sacred text, as long as the text's integrity does not stand in a necessary relation with the integrity of the doctrinal substance it contains. The Church could not and did not ever use a text whose alterations would have compromised the doctrine of the faith and morals; but it could have, and did, use texts which, literarily speaking, had endured quite a lot. The text of the Greek Bible was in a rather pitiful state in the 3rd century; various recensions were made of it, which were, in a certain sense, revised [205] editions. The old Latin Vulgate was in a severely corrupted state, in the 4th century. Jerome's Vulgate was notably altered during the Middle Ages: as a consequence of the many errors which found their way in it, the Council of Trent asked the pope to support the preparation of a correct edition. The outcome of this request was the Clementine edition, which does not present itself as perfect, and the Church does not expect anyone to believe that it represents, in its most minute details, Jerome's text. The Church forbids the use, in the liturgy and in theology, of any other version besides the Vulgate; but it does not forbid critics to study, using the means which are available to them, Saint Jerome's original text, to take note of the modifications this text was subjected to in the course of time and which are preserved in part in the official Bible of the Roman Church. Criticism of the Latin Vulgate's text is therefore legitimate, despite the decisions of the Council of Trent, despite the prescriptions concerning the official use of Clement VIII's Bible. It is equally legitimate when dealing with the Septuagint as when it turns it attention to the Greek text of the New Testament. With regard to the Hebrew Bible, no official declaration, nor the use of the Church, confer to it the kind of official authenticity which pertains to ecclesiastical texts, and so the argument could be made, without contravening the principles of theology, that this text was altered even in passages which concern faith and morals.

[206] Catholic theologians, unlike Orthodox Protestants, do not have the same reasons to oppose textual criticism. Orthodox Protestantism, in making holy Scripture the one and only infallible rule of faith, needs a certain and flawless text and cannot afford to wait for criticism to furnish such a text, for doubt would be cast on the current text in use. This explains why, still today, certain Protestant commentators, even while acknowledging in theory the possibility of alterations in the traditional Hebrew text, refuse in practice that there may have been other corrections besides the Masoretic ones, consider all of the variations between the Masoretic text and the ancient versions as coming from the translators, uneasily consent to change a few vowels in the received text, and try to justify the most obvious of the copyists' errors. From a Catholic standpoint, the immediate rule being not Scripture but the official teaching of the Church, possible alterations of the sacred texts are not so consequential. Since the Church's infallibility guarantees that these alterations did not introduce in the ecclesial Bible and in the tradition's teaching any error with regard to faith or morals, since the Church's Bible and its authentic interpretation possess a doctrinal value which comes from tradition itself and from the Church which authorize them, independently of their more or less rigorous conformity with the original and primitive texts of Scripture, the work of the apologist and of the theologian is not seriously hindered by the discovery of alterations which happened in the various texts of the sacred Books.

Nevertheless, most Catholic exegetes [207] consider the text of the Vulgate in the same manner as conservative Protestants consider the Masoretic text. They have difficulties admitting that there might be even slight interpolations in the Clementine Bible. Isn't anyone who contests the authenticity of the verse about the three celestial witnesses in the First Epistle of Saint John perceived up to this day as reckless? People are not content to abide by the Church's declarations concerning the substantial integrity of the Latin Bible. They act, in practice, as if this integrity applies to the most minute details of the text. The entire content of Clement VIII's Vulgate is supposed to have belonged to the Latin version's original text and to the original texts of the Old and the New Testaments. The traditional Hebrew text has profited from the fact that Saint Jerome, for his version, used a text which is almost identical to the Masoretic text (except for the vowel points), and also from the fact that he interpreted it most of the time according to the exegetical tradition of Palestinian Jews. In most of the places where the Septuagint differs from the present-day Hebrew text and proposes a better text, they also differ from the Vulgate, which corresponds to the Hebrew. Abandoning the Hebrew version would mean abandoning the Vulgate. We prefer not to discuss the differences which exist between the Hebrew, the Greek, and the Latin versions. Commentators who mention these differences usually avoid taking sides for or against one of them: they seek to offer a positive interpretation of them all. Similarly, if a passage in a given version is not found in the original texts, it is supposed to be authentic, or an attempt at a demonstration of its authenticity is made, without distinguishing in any way between these passages and the context which is now presented in the original versions.

Our commentaries, in fact, have generally been similar [208] to those of the Middle Ages and even of the 16th century, namely theological commentaries, not historical and critical commentaries of holy Scripture. Scholastic theology was built on the Latin Bible, almost without recourse to the original texts, without taking into consideration the differences which may have existed between these texts and the ecclesial text. Scholars used the Vulgate with the same sense of security as if they had held the autograph manuscripts of the sacred authors in their hands. They were entitled to this, since the authority of the tradition and of the Church was completing the authority which the version possessed through its substantial conformity with the original texts of the Old and the New Testaments. Nevertheless, it is true that such a summary approach clearly differs from the critical investigating method which is becoming more and more the norm in modern exegesis. It must be added that theologians have only recently begun to distinguish with clarity between the Vulgate as text and as Scripture from the Vulgate as a traditional ecclesial document. On the basis of this distinction, the conclusions which were based on the text of the Latin Bible were not threatened by the mere fact that these conclusions could not have been so easily deduced from the original text. This distinction and all its practical implications, it must be admitted, has not yet penetrated exegesis as it is commonly practiced; most of our commentators have hesitated, up to this day, to use the double-edged sword which is called criticism.

It is high time, however, that we learn to use it. A great scientific movement has emerged [209] outside the Church. The entire work of Protestant and rationalistic exegesis cannot be reduced to an unjust attack against the supernatural character of the Bible and against revelation. Criticism cannot be made responsible for the errors of which some wish to make it responsible; and despite the transgressions of some who view themselves as representing it, criticism has contributed to perfecting what could be called the historical intelligence of the holy Books. It has endeavored to study the history of biblical literature, to analyze Israel's religious conscience, to follow the development of the monotheistic idea and of the institutions which sponsored it, since the most remote times to the birth of the Christian Church and even all the way until the present. Criticism has chosen a magnificent program, which it hopes to fulfill. In order to do so, it submits the Bible to a very meticulous examination: it studies history and discusses the texts in order to reach assured conclusions concerning their provenance and the nature of their content. Its method is as necessary as its program is beautiful. But this program must be ours, since the faith, whose history is being narrated, is our faith. We cannot leave it to foreigners, who are sometimes our enemies, to study the origins of our religion. The method, therefore, is a necessity for us too; it is the only way to fulfill the task. Protestant and rationalistic science may have conceived this project; it is important that Catholic science secure the fruits of it. . . .

[210] To prudently correct the text of Scripture does not mean treating it irreverently, it means purifying it from certain elements which human weakness has introduced in it, it means showing the most enlightened [211] respect to the holy Books. This form of respect was put into practice with regard to the biblical text by Origen, Saint Jerome, the council fathers at Trent, Popes Sixtus V and Clement VIII. It is our turn to use it, and in so doing we will not only exercise a right: we will fulfill a command.

THE GOSPEL AND THE CHURCH (1902)

[34] All these hypotheses, more or less probable, which could readily be multiplied, have only one result, to raise before the theologians an interminable series of difficulties, because criticism, giving most of its attention to the literary facts, too often leaves the history unexplained, not only the history of nascent Christianity, but [35] even the history of the composition of the Gospels. The points on which the synoptic Gospels differ from one another; and the differences between John and the synoptics, have been carefully accumulated, and thus limits have been set to the historical authority of the Gospels that believers cannot fail to find exceedingly narrow. The meaning of all that cannot be taken as literal history with regard to Christ escapes them, because to some extent it has escaped the critics themselves, and they have therefore failed to make it clear to believers. Faith is disquieted by conclusions and scientific conjectures that do not entirely satisfy the intelligence. They would have given rise to less trouble if they could have been understood.

But to render the development and character of the evangelical literature quite intelligible, the Gospels must not only be studied in themselves and in their relations as literary works and as simple historical documents, but must also be regarded as a partial expression of the great movement that proceeded from the preaching of Jesus. The literary tradition of the gospel has followed the evolution of primitive Christianity. The two explain one another; and if the critical analysis of the Gospels necessarily precedes [36] the reconstitution of evangelical and apostolic history, it is nonetheless true that, by a sort of reciprocity, it is the primitive history of Christianity that explains the composition of the Gospels, and throws light on those particular points that are most disconcerting for minds unused to criticism. Once understood and presented as a product and a witness of an ancient faith, the Gospels, however critically analyzed, will no longer be a dangerous trial to the faith of our contemporaries.

23.

Adolf von Harnack (1851–1930)

Adolf von Harnack was, in his own day, the world's foremost historian of Christianity. The son of Theodosius von Harnack, a somewhat conservative Lutheran professor of theology who was well known for his studies on Luther's thought, the younger Harnack began his career by studying the history of early Christianity, and especially Gnosticism and its sources. Soon he belonged to a small group of bright young scholars who considered Albrecht Ritschl, whose main works were being published in the 1870s, as *the* thinker showing the way for Protestant theology—namely, a way influenced by Luther's own writings rather than by strict adherence to the Lutheran symbolic (confessional) documents.

A precocious and highly productive scholar, Harnack joined the University of Giessen as full professor at age twenty-eight. Nine years later, in 1888, he moved to Berlin's Humboldt University, where his theological liberalism led to strong opposition, which sought to cancel his nomination. In 1893 Adolf Schlatter, a much more conservative theologian, became his colleague in Berlin—a decision that was meant to counterbalance Harnack's influence. Even Ritschl was worried about Harnack's development as a theologian, fearing that Harnack might tend toward a certain "theological nihilism" (Ritschl 2013, 402–3; Ritschl 2010, 2–4). As a church historian, one of Harnack's highest achievements is certainly his *History of Dogma* (*Lehrbuch der Dogmengeschichte*, 1886–90), which covers almost the entire span of Christian thought.[1] It is from this work that Harnack drew for his yearlong lectures on "the essence of Christianity" in 1899–1900. The book that ensued was an enormous success, with more than one hundred thousand copies sold, and translations in fourteen languages by 1930.

Harnack's intention was to replace metaphysical as well as dogmatic accounts of the Christian faith with a strictly *historical* account. But, unlike Lessing, he was convinced that history, far from being mere contingency, is the reality in which the divine Spirit moves and reveals itself.

1. Harnack's important participation in the edition, in forty-five volumes by the year 1924, of Christian texts from the first century up to 325 (*Texte und Untersuchungen*) must also be mentioned.

Harnack remains famous for this thesis: "Dogma in its conception and development is a work of the Greek spirit on the soil of the Gospel" (Harnack 1901, 17). Dogma is, thus, foreign to the gospel as good news; it does not belong organically with the original message of Jesus. Not that it does not have any value! But with this historical development during the first centuries of Christianity and beyond, what was a simple message—about the kingdom and its coming, about God as Father and the "infinite value of the human soul," about a higher justice and the command of love—became a complex and often abstract doctrine.

Harnack lived long enough to witness the rise of the dialectical school in the 1920s. To say that he was puzzled by this new school and its theology is an understatement, as can be seen from his 1923 letter exchange with Karl Barth (Rumscheidt 1972).

The selections below come from *Christianity and History*, trans. Thomas Bailey Saunders (London: A&C Black, 1896), with minor revisions. For the original German text, see *Das Christentum und die Geschichte: Ein Vortrag* (Leipzig: J. C. Hinrichs, 1895).

CHRISTIANITY AND HISTORY (1895)

[19] . . . I may begin by mentioning the encouraging fact that the great assault made by the eighteenth century on the connexion between religion and history has been repelled. This assault found its pregnant expression in the principle laid down by Lessing: *Historical truth, which is accidental* [20] *in its character, can never become the proof of the truths of Reason, which are necessary.*

The principle may, indeed, be right; everything depends upon the way in which it is construed. But in the way in which it was understood by Lessing's own generation, influenced as that generation was by Rousseau, it is wrong. The whole of the superficial philosophy of the eighteenth century is at the bottom of it. According to that philosophy, everything that has happened in the way of history is of trivial moment; it is an accident; no, it even cramps and embarrasses the mind; and there is no salvation anywhere but in the two forces which that generation described as *Nature* and *Reason*. They were regarded as forces that were invariable and constituted [21] once for all; and no true blessing was to be obtained outside of them. It was believed that every person from the creation downwards possessed in his reason a fixed capital, which was capable of supplying him with everything that might be needful for a virtuous and happy life. It was believed, further, that humanity was fitted into the framework of nature, and was in harmony with it; and that humanity had only to unfold its powers in accordance with nature, in order to become a glorious specimen of its kind.

In this view of the world, history was no longer a necessity; for a human being could receive absolutely nothing from it which he did not already possess. To the consistent adherents of this view, its logical outcome was that history seemed a strange and wrong-headed [22] venture; and the cry was all for renouncing its tyranny, and for returning to the freedom of nature. It is true that Lessing himself made great efforts to do justice to history; but his efforts were uncertain, and they were but little understood. His generation had no concern for anything but the truths of reason, alleged to be eternal, and the "natural religion" which it had rediscovered; and in possession of these blessings, it looked down on "the accidents of history" with contempt, and cut the bond between them and religion. All historical religions, so the eighteenth century taught, are at best only the one true, natural religion in disguise—the religion which always was and always will be—and this religion has no other content but Reason, fixed and unalterable. By the [23] side of it, even Christianity and its founder can make no special or particular claim; for everything that is particular is accidental, superfluous, and intellectually mischievous.

Now today this view of the world is not, it is true, extinct; but it has been refuted. In no respect has the spirit of the nineteenth century so strongly opposed the spirit of the eighteenth, as in this.

It is a change which we owe to Herder and the leaders of the romantic movement; we owe it to Hegel and his great scholar Ranke; we owe it, not least of all, to the powerful reaction of the Christian faith. The illusion of a ready-made reason, existing from the beginning, has been dispelled; the idol of a "divine nature" has been unmasked; the vast problem involved in [24] the facile notion of a "natural religion" has been revealed. In the place of shallow talk about divine nature and profane history, about the "eternal truths of reason" and contingent[2] records, we have arrived at the knowledge of *history*; of the history from which we have received what we possess, and to which we owe what we are. In this process two conceptions, above all, came to the front with increasing clarity: *development* and *personality*. They involve an opposition; but it is an opposition which determines the work of the historian in dealing with his facts.

When the meaning of history came to be accurately understood, religion was restored to its place; for religion is no ready-made structure, but a growth; and [25] it is a growth that falls within the history of humanity. Its developments are no mere outward semblance: they are a reality. Its prophets and founders have been prophets and founders indeed; for they have raised humanity to a higher level. Reverence for the spirit that prevails in history, and gratitude to all those from whom we have received any benefit—and without it we should have been the poorer in our inner and outer life—must, therefore, govern our views of that science.

Here we have a critical spirit very different from that which pervaded the so-called age of Enlightenment. The assault which the eighteenth century directed against the connexion between history and religion has, in fact, been a failure. But other assaults have been taking shape in [26] our own time. There is a whole array of them.

The first proposition that meets us is this: It is just because the Christian religion is a part of history, and consequently of that *development* of which all history consists, that it is no more than a link in that development; and therefore its founder cannot be allowed any peculiar or unique position.

We succeed, let us say, in defeating this attack. A fresh opponent then starts up with the objection that even though the founder of the Christian religion may have been an incomparable man, he lived many centuries ago; and it is therefore impossible to go to him with our troubles and sorrows, and to lay hold of him as the rock of our life: it is not the *person* which we have [27] any longer to consider, but the *doctrine*, the *principle*.

If, in the end, this opponent be also routed, there is still one more. We are told that we may speak of Jesus Christ as we will, and he may have been all that we say, but that we cannot be certain of it; for where our idea of him has not been destroyed by historical criticism, it has been rendered doubtful; and, even though it were more trustworthy than it is, still the facts of history can never be known with a certainty that would entitle us to make them the foundation of our religions belief.

These are the three barriers that have been opposed to the creed of the Church on the score of history; and it is on these three questions that the whole of the controversy turns. Every form of doubt, [28] whether secret or open, deals in the main with these questions; and in some shape or other they are doubts which have been entertained and pondered by us all.

III. Personality and history

[52] That in spite of the eighteen hundred years which separate us from him, Jesus Christ can have, no has, a place in the religious life of the Christian; that his personality, and not his doctrine alone, is still today *set for the rising again of many*—I have tried to show. But a third and final attack confronts us. You may, we are told, talk of Jesus Christ as you will, and he may have been all that you say, but you cannot be certain of it; for where our idea of him has not been destroyed by historical [53] criticism, it has been rendered doubtful; and even though it were more trustworthy than it is, still the facts of history can never be known with a certainty that would entitle us to make them the foundation of our religious belief.

This objection is the most serious of the three; and if it were in all respects justifiable, it would go ill with us.

"Where our idea of him has not been destroyed

2. Revised translation. The original translation has "casual" for the German word "zufällig."

by historical criticism, it has been rendered doubtful." At first sight it looks as if this were indeed the case. I pass over such results of criticism as flourish today, and tomorrow are cast into the oven; I speak only of those which are brought before us again and again with increasing force. If we direct our attention first of all to the external historical facts, we find that [54] the tradition as to the incidents attending the birth and the early life of Jesus Christ has been shattered; and so too has been the credibility of many of the stories which were told of him. We find, too, that criticism cannot lay the ancient doubts raised by the reports of what took place on the first Easter morning. As regards the picture of his life, as regards his discourses and the doctrine he taught, the historical way of looking at them seems to transform them altogether.

The person who reads his Bible in a homely way is likely to treat all the characteristic features which he encounters in that book as above and beyond time. He sees and feels such things only as he takes to form the true kernel of the narrative: things which concern himself; and it was by [55] these that the Christian doctrine was formerly established by the Church. But the historical way of looking at them may not, and will not, overlook the concrete features in and by which the life and the doctrine were actually fashioned in their day. It seeks for points of connexion with the Old Testament and its developments, with the religious life of the Synagogue, with contemporary hopes for the future, with the whole intellectual and spiritual condition of the world of Greece and Rome; and it finds that the evidence of such connexion is unmistakable. The consequence is, that the sayings and discourses of the Lord, and the image of his life itself, not only take their colour—and it is a very definite colour—from the history of the time, but they are also seen to possess [56] certain definite limitations. They belong to their time and their environment; and they could not exist in any other. But they lose no particle of their power and validity, unless it can be shown that the main lineaments of the personality of Christ, and the sense and true point of his sayings, have been altered. I cannot discover that historical criticism has effected any such change.

That same is true of the testimony which he gave of himself. I admit that if historical research had proved that he was an apocalyptic enthusiast or a visionary, whose image and utterances were advanced to the level of pure aim and lofty thought only by the refining influence of later times, it would be another matter. But who has proved that, and who could prove it? For [57] besides the four written Gospels we possess a fifth, unwritten; and in many respects its voice is clearer and more effective than those of the other four—I mean the united testimony of the first Christian community. It enables us to gather what was the prevailing impression made by this personality, and in what sense his disciples understood his words and the testimony which he gave of himself. It is true that his clothes—the outward form of his doctrine—were part of the heritage; but the great and simple truths which he came to preach, the personal sacrifice which he made, and his victory in death, were what formed the new life of his community; and when the apostle Paul with divine power described this life as a life in the Spirit (Rom 8), and again [58] as a life in love (1 Cor 13), he was only giving back the light which had dawned upon him in and through Jesus Christ his Lord. This is a simple matter of fact, which no historical criticism can in any way alter. All that it can do is to place it in a clearer light, and so increase our reverence for the divinity which was revealed in radiance in a Son of Abraham, amid the wreck and refuse of a narrow world. Let the plain Bible-reader continue to read his Gospels as he has hitherto read them; for in the end the critic cannot read them otherwise. What the one regards as their true gist and meaning, the other must acknowledge to be such.

But the facts, the facts! I do not know how there can be a greater fact than the [59] one which I have just been describing. By the side of it, what can any historical detail signify?

We are told, however, that an historical detail has a very obvious significance; that it is only the external fact, no, the miraculous fact, which can afford us the final and only certainty that there exists a reality corresponding to our belief; that the objects of our belief are not mere phantoms of thought, but that God himself governs the course of history, and is leading it to its goal.

I am well aware of the gravity of this assertion, and I am far from disputing the right of everyone to make it if he chooses. If God would but rend the heavens and come down, that we might behold him!—It is a cry that is often [60] heard. But I know, too, that it is not born out of the depth and strength of the faith which the apostle Paul describes, and that it readily falls under the utterance of the Lord: *Unless you see signs and wonders, you will not believe*. Great is the power of external authority in matters of religion; great is the power of signs and wonders; but only where their substance lies can faith and devotion find their ultimate assurance. Their substance is God the Lord; it is reliance on Jesus Christ, whose word and spirit are even today a witness to the heart of the power of God.

Woe to us if it were otherwise; if our faith rested on a number of details, to be demonstrated and established by the historian. It would be more sophistry [61] for any historian to claim that he had achieved such a task; for it is assuredly true that no detail of the past can attain such a degree of evidential certainty that it could form the foundation for bricks and mortar, let alone a whole eternity. Testimonies, documents, assertions—when all is said, to what do they amount?

There is, I admit, a difference between fact and fact. The actual external details are always a matter of controversy; and in this sense Lessing was perfectly right when he warned us against coupling matters of the highest moment with "accidental truths of history," and hanging the whole weight of eternity on a spider's thread. But the spiritual meaning of a whole life, of a personality, is also an historical fact: it has its reality in the [62] effect it produces; and it is here that we find the link that binds us to Jesus Christ. It is a feeling which is one with devotion itself; and this is what the same Lessing meant when he spoke the word of deliverance: "Even though we may be unable to remove all the objections that may be made against the *Bible*, nevertheless, in the heart of all Christians who have attained to an inner sense of its essential truths, *religion* remains steadfast and intact."

But are we to say that such external details as have been handed down are of no significance whatever? Who would be so shortsighted, or so frivolous, as to maintain such a proposition? Because we cannot build upon them, they are far from having no significance. First of [63] all, we have to examine whether they are not actually true after all. Much that was formerly rejected has been re-established on a close investigation, and in the light of comprehensive experience. Who in these days, for example, could make such short work of the miraculous cures in the Gospels as was the custom of scholars formerly?

Then, too, it may be said of all that is told of Jesus Christ, that it is written as a *lesson* for us. That is a consideration which in our controversies is often unduly overlooked; but it is in keeping with the objects of the oldest writers, and the practice of the oldest teachers. In matters of religious tradition it is the peculiarity of much that passes for historical, that the spiritual meaning to be found in it [64] is its most important feature. Where something is maintained as an historical fact, it is more often than not a defense of the article of faith bound up with it. It is through the formula, *conceived of the Holy Spirit*, that the dogma of the divine sonship of Jesus Christ is proclaimed; in and with the message of the Ascension we are taught that he lives and rules with the Father.

This leads us to another aspect of the religious significance of external details, which is closely related to that which I have been mentioning. They have been to faith what the prop is to the vine, or a sheltering screen to the tender plant. They have given it support and guidance, or they have protected its growth from the influence of wind and weather; and the [65] service which they have rendered in the past, they still render today to many. The difficulty is that one man's faith requires a strong stake to prop it, or some kind of protective shelter; while another finds the prop break in his hands, and his faith bloom only in the free light of the sun.

Finally, much in the New Testament that is recorded as history, much that affects us most deeply, is not only told us as a lesson, but, in the form in which it is given, it possesses a deep *symbolical* significance. I know none of the leading events of the narrative of which that cannot be said. The same spirit which unveiled to our eyes the power and the glory of a divine life, so far as mankind is able to grasp it, has also veiled the [66] truth for us with a delicate web of ingenious legend, a poetry that moves the heart, and has thus brought it home in picture and parable.

That the stories which are told of Christ possess this manifold significance, will be obvious to everyone who considers the history of Christianity with an open mind and a humble heart. It is an interpretation of the facts which is not without its dangers; for on the one hand it may readily lead someone to foist his own mind upon history, to confuse the plant with the prop, and so to conjure up grave difficulties; and on the other, it may deaden the force of historical facts as real facts, and the personality of Christ as a real personality. However, the difficulties which have arisen here are [67] not of our making, and we cannot resolve them in any arbitrary fashion of our own. Rather, let us trust to that divine guidance which knows what is good for us; let us proclaim truly, and with a pure mind, the knowledge which we have received; and then let us endeavour to understand the profound saying, that natural strength and the crutch that supports it come from the same source.[3]

It may, perhaps, have been expected that I should speak of other matters: of the changes which Christianity has experienced in the course of its history, or of the blessings which it has spread abroad in the world. But a knowledge of the [68] fundamental question, namely, how far religion and history are connected, and how they are united in the Protestant faith, is more important than anything else. This Protestant faith need fear no test that can be applied to it. It can bear a strict and methodical scrutiny of the facts which form its historical foundation; no, for its own sake it must demand such a scrutiny; for while it has no concern with Pilate's speculative question—what is truth?—yet the knowledge of the truth is assigned as its mission and there, too, its promise will be fulfilled.

3. [*Original footnote*] "Kräfte und Krücken kommen aus einer Hand" (Goethe).

24.

William Wrede (1859–1906)

Born near Hannover, William Wrede began his theological studies in Leipzig in 1877. Appalled by the Lutheran orthodox theology taught by Christoph Ernst Luthardt (1823–1902) and August Kahnis (1814–88), he was encouraged not to give up his studies by Adolf von Harnack, who was also one of his teachers. Wrede then continued his schooling at the University of Göttingen in 1879, where the great master of systematic theology at the time, Albrecht Ritschl, was at the height of his powers. But it is Albert Eichhorn (1856–1926) who influenced Wrede the most in Göttingen. In Göttingen, Wrede belonged to what has been called "the smaller Faculty," that is, the group of younger scholars, among whom Ernst Troeltsch was the main systematician, who constituted a new sort of approach, soon tagged *religionsgeschichtliche Schule*, or "school of the history of religion." This school was determined not to let dogmatic prejudgments influence the study of the past, and also wished to study the history of Christianity in close connection with its broader context, especially in antiquity. After completing his doctoral studies in New Testament, Wrede became a professor in Breslau (1893). He died in 1906, only forty-seven years old, from severe pneumonia.

Before his important study on the "messianic secret in the gospels" and especially in Mark (*Das Messiasgeheimnis in den Evangelien* [Göttingen: Vandenhoeck & Ruprecht, 1901]), and before his book on Paul (*Paulus* [Halle: Gebauer-Schwetschke, 1904]), Wrede published a programmatic text in 1897 titled "The Task and Methods of 'New Testament Theology.'" In the work, he calls for a complete replacement of the traditional way of construing New Testament theology with its focus on key topics, such as faith or love, deduced as it were from revelation, by a *history* of early Christian religion and theology based on textual sources (Morgan 1973, 9). The study of the New Testament and its message must become "a purely historical enterprise" (Morgan 1973, 12). If this seems radical, Wrede had nothing against such radicality, on the contrary he cherished it: "My criticism . . . may be called radical, I have nothing against that. I content myself with the fact that, sometimes, the things themselves are most radical, and when that is the case presenting them as they are should not be seen as a problem" (Wrede 1901, vi; Strecker 1960).

What follows is excerpted from William Wrede, "The Task and Methods of 'New Testament Theology,'" in *The Nature of New Testament Theology: The Contribution of William Wrede and Adolf Schlatter*, ed. and trans. Robert Morgan (London: SCM, 1973), 68–116. The original title is *Über Aufgabe und Methode der sogenannten neutestamentlichen Theologie* (Göttingen: Vandenhoeck & Ruprecht, 1897).

THE TASK AND METHODS OF "NEW TESTAMENT THEOLOGY" (1897)

[69] So long as New Testament theology retains a direct link with dogmatics as its goal, and people expect from it material for dogmatics to work on—and that is a common view—it will be natural for biblical theology to have an eye to dogmatics. Biblical theology will be pressed for an answer to dogmatic questions which the biblical documents do not really give, and will endeavour to eliminate results which are troublesome for dogmatics. . . . I do not intend to dwell on this question of principle for long, but I must state from the outset that my comments presuppose the strictly historical character of New Testament theology. . . . How the systematic theologian gets on with its results and deals with them—that is his own affair. Like every other real science, New Testament theology has its goal simply in itself and is totally indifferent to all dogma and systematic theology. . . .

[70] The first thing which must be required of anyone who wishes to engage scientifically in New Testament theology is . . . that he be capable of interest in historical research. He must be guided by a pure disinterested concern for knowledge, which accepts every really compelling result. He must be able to distinguish between the alien modern ideas of his own thought and those of the past. He must be able to keep his own viewpoint, however precious, quite separate from the object of his research and hold it in suspense. Then he will indeed know only what really was.

One might say that this account of New Testament theology entirely surrenders its specifically theological character. It is no longer treated any differently from any other branch of intellectual history in general or the history of religion in particular. That is quite correct. But in what should the specifically theological type of treatment consist? It would always result in a mixture which included the personal theological viewpoint of the scholar, and that could only obscure things. . . .

[73] On the whole it is not within the historical researcher's power to serve the church through his work. The theologian who obeys the historical object as his master is not in a position to serve the church through his properly scientific-historical work, even if he were personally interested in doing so. One would then have to consider the investigation of historical truth as such as serving the church. That is where the chief difficulty of our whole theological situation lies, and it is not created by individual wills: the church rests on history, but historical reality cannot escape investigation, and this investigation of historical reality has its own laws. . . .

[92] Here again, the method of doctrinal concepts fails to achieve an adequate account of the development. It is bound to fail, today at any rate. In his own way Baur in his day succeeded in treating everything in the form of doctrinal concepts, and from his standpoint this was a meaningful procedure. For in Baur's account of the history, one well-known contrast was absolutely decisive. The different writings were all seen as witnesses to this and were characterized above all by their relationship to it. This meant that the heart of the real historical development in fact coincided with his construction of how the individual writings followed one another. Of course—if in fact this order of the writings was a true reflection of the development. But Baur's edifice was an untenable construction. However, his followers and opponents do not possess this sort of total conception of the development as hinging on *one* main point. This is no longer possible. That means that a particular arrangement of the literature can give only very incomplete expression to the character and content of the development. The successive writings or groups of writings do not strictly correspond to so many characteristic moments of the devel-

opment. They do not express its really significant moments exhaustively or sharply. Yet they give the impression of doing so. Or the intention of giving a historical presentation is at certain points suspended, and in the middle of a generally developmental account things are inserted which are only externally related to it. The resulting impressions are therefore only partly right, and are partly [93] wrong or unclear. Furthermore, so that the less significant writings are not just put one after another, they tend to be given historical labels which are only half appropriate. . . .

[116] One thing cannot be denied. Biblical theology today is much less developed than the history of the apostolic and sub-apostolic age. Yet it belongs with this in the same way that the history of doctrine belongs with church history. It is not yet in the true and strict sense a historical discipline at all. May it become one!

25.

Ernst Troeltsch (1865–1923)

Ernst Troeltsch deserves a very special place in a volume such as the present one. Few have reflected with such depth and originality about the implications of modernity, and the concomitant historicizing process, for religion and especially for theology. Born near Augsburg in 1865, the son of a medical doctor, he began his theological studies in Erlangen in 1884, before moving to Berlin the following academic year and moving again, for the winter semester of 1886, to the University of Göttingen. Two scholars attracted him to Göttingen: Albrecht Ritschl and a younger scholar who would soon become Ritschl's son-in-law: Johannes Weiss. In 1891, Troeltsch completed his doctoral dissertation, which was a study of Johann Gerhard and Philipp Melanchthon (in that order) and which, for all his respect and admiration for Ritschl, amounted to a break with his teacher's way of presenting the history of early Protestant theology and the beginnings of Protestant scholasticism. Whereas Ritschl spoke of a quick decline, from Luther to Melanchthon and later to the scholars of Protestant scholasticism (or Protestant Orthodoxy), Troeltsch was inclined to defend the Protestant scholastics, arguing that their reintroduction of Aristotelian metaphysics and the natural law was a legitimate reply to new challenges.

In the same way, Troeltsch advocated a radical reforming of Protestant theology, which ought in his view to ban its supranaturalist presuppositions through which Christianity is, from the outset, distinguished from the flow of history. Theology must acknowledge the revolution modernity represents and has to begin "from below," that is, from history as such, and not from a "salvation history" or a suprahistory. Troeltsch's program is classically presented and argued in the following article, "On the Historical and Dogmatic Methods in Theology" (1898), as translated and published in Ernst Troeltsch, *Religion in History*, trans. James Luther Adams and Walter F. Bense (Edinburgh: T&T Clark, 1991), 11–32.

In Ferdinand Christian Baur's footsteps, Ritschl had articulated a theological system that was heavily indebted to the study of history. Troeltsch took these approaches a (big) step further, questioning the very legitimacy of dogmatic theology as it was traditionally practiced, namely, as *fides quaerens intellectum* ("faith seeking understanding"), reversing the formula and preferring to say *intelligo ut credam* ("I understand in order to believe"). But, in several writings at the turn of the nineteenth century, Troeltsch ended up affirming many of Christianity's traditional claims; simply, these claims could only be reached, in his opinion, at the end of a close examination of human history broadly conceived.

"ON THE HISTORICAL AND DOGMATIC METHOD IN THEOLOGY" (1898)

[11] In compliance with the kind request of Professor Niebergall and the wishes of the editorial board, I am taking the liberty of adding a few remarks to the essay of this theologian. They are intended to shed additional light on the controversy, and not only to clarify those of my views which he has attacked but also to defend my total position in the philosophy of religion and theology against his strictures. Since Niebergall is essentially espousing the ideas of his teacher, Julius Kaftan, the following remarks also represent my final word in my exchange with that distinguished Berlin theologian and member of the High Consistory.[1] I shall let this be my final word because further discussion would be of little avail in view of the fact that the opposition between us is one of principle.

I have deliberately spoken of my "theological method." For our primary concern here involves methodology rather than apologetics or any particular point of dogma. Apparently Niebergall, because of his presuppositions, has not quite perceived this point; for he takes the authoritarian concept of revelation for granted and regards anything beyond Christianity as merely "natural decor." He and others who share his view do not regard theology as such as problematical; they see only minor problems that can be patched over, and consequently they assume the same attitude on the part of everyone else. Admittedly, such an attitude has its merits and even a certain practical importance, since it reflects a common need. But it is also possible to take an entirely different approach, starting from basic principles, and my labors have more and more led me to this approach. I have not borrowed "grounds against our supernaturalism" from any scholar in order then to meet them by my "view of the history of religion as a continuing revelation."

[12] For some two hundred years these grounds have been readily available. It was not necessary for me to borrow them. Nor was my starting point the competing claims of various revelations or some "pantheistic" concept of evolution. Such vistas are fairly obvious and have been treated often enough—however superficially—in theological apologetics. Instead, I have explicitly called attention to the much deeper ground where the disintegration of the Christian world of ideas actually originates. Though related to these other matters, this ground is still relatively independent and in any case absolutely decisive. I am referring to *the historical method as such*, to the problem of "Christianity and history," which is to be understood not as the defense of Christianity against particular results of historical criticism but rather as the effect of modern historical methodology on the interpretation of Christianity itself. Once applied to the scientific study of the Bible and church history, the historical method acts as a leaven, transforming everything and ultimately exploding the very form of earlier theological methods. I have clearly indicated that this was the starting point of my labors and I have developed in detail the consequences of this position.

Significantly, my efforts in this direction have made no impression whatever upon Niebergall. He proceeds as though no difficulty at all existed in this connection, and as though, with the admission that the historical context played a conditioning role, all difficulties were solved and the old dogmatic method substantially saved. He is astonishingly insensitive to the consequences flowing from the historical method. In comparison, the older apologists of the eighteenth century and the

1. [*Original footnote*] See my essays "Die Selbständigkeit der Religion" and "Geschichte und Metaphysik" in *Zeitschrift für Theologie und Kirche*, as well as Kaftan's essay "Die Selbständigkeit des Christentums," by which he means its supernatural revelation and redemptive power.

few rigid supernaturalists of the present may well be found to have attained a deeper insight.

Yet Niebergall's stance is a common one, perhaps more characteristic of contemporary theology than any other. Only particular problems raised by historical criticism are considered; one by one, they are then either rejected or designated as harmless, as the case may be. When Christianity is treated systematically, the historical-critical approach is abandoned. By focusing only on various needs, postulates, claims, theories of knowledge, or other intangible generalities, contemporary theologians attempt to validate the old authoritarian concept of revelation; and with the help of this concept they weave together a tolerable dogmatic system. Exegetes and historians are left to see for themselves how they may authenticate these purely dogmatic postulates in relation to their research. Historians, for their part, generally prefer to confine themselves to the conditioning role of the historical context and leave the theoretical questions to the dogmatists. In this sort of theology one is constantly being shuttled back and forth between the two groups.

[13] In contrast to the foregoing, I wish most emphatically to call attention to what is signified by the historical method, the historical mode of thought, and the historical sense. I am not thinking here of the earlier historiography, which limited its criticism to particular fragments of history, providing information about interesting foreign lands or accumulating archival material. What I have in mind is the genuine historical scholarship of the present, which involves a definite approach to the whole sphere of culture, constitutes a method of representing the past and the present, and therefore implies some extraordinary consequences. Here we are concerned principally with three essential aspects: the habituation on principle to historical criticism; the importance of analogy; and the mutual interrelation of all historical developments.

The first of these three items indicates that in the realm of history there are only judgements of probability, varying from the highest to the lowest degree, and that consequently an estimate must be made of the degree of probability attaching to any tradition. Accordingly, our overall attitude to the enormous body of material our civilization derives from memory and tradition is fundamentally changed, even when our attitude toward the particular contents of this material has not yet undergone any correction. But the latter, too, is subjected by historical criticism to analysis, correction, and transformation in a thousand ways, with the final result being never more than probably correct.

It is obvious that the application of historical criticism to religious tradition must result in a profound change in one's inward attitude to it and in one's understanding of it. Indeed, such a change has actually taken place. But the operation of historical criticism in this area signifies above all the definitive inclusion of the religious tradition with all traditions that require preliminary critical treatment. If the manner of operation of various traditions is thus shown to be in principle the same, the traditional objects and events (which must first be ascertained critically) will hardly fail to show a corresponding similarity.

The second basic postulate of the historical method is that the instrumentality that makes historical criticism possible is the employment of analogy. Analogous occurrences that we observe both without and within ourselves furnish us with the key to historical criticism. The illusions, distortions, deceptions, myths, and partisanships we see with our own eyes enable us to recognize similar features in the materials of tradition. Agreement with normal, customary, or at least frequently attested happenings and conditions [14] as we have experienced them is the criterion of probability for all events that historical criticism can recognize as having actually or possibly happened. The observation of analogies between similar events in the past provides the possibility of imputing probability to them and of interpreting what is unknown about the one by reference to what is known about the other.

But this omnipotence of analogy implies the similarity (in principle) of all historical events—which does not, of course, mean identity. While leaving all possible room for differences, however, the analogical method always presupposes a common core of similarity that makes the differences comprehensible and empathy possible. Hence, the acceptance of historical criticism entails recognition of the significance of this analogical approach for the investigation of the history of Christianity. Biblical criticism itself is based on analogies to the ways of tradition in which other vestiges of antiquity have come down to us. Similarly, the conditions assumed by historical criticism were in numberless cases ascertainable only through the seeking out of analogies. Jewish and Christian history are thus made analogous to all other history. Actually, fewer and fewer historical "facts" are regarded as exempt from the exigencies of the analogical principle; many would content themselves with placing Jesus' moral character and the resurrection in this category.

We have already seen that the importance of analogy as a method leveling all historical phenomena rests on the assumption of a basic consistency of the human spirit and its historical manifestations. The consequence of this position is the third basic concept of history, namely, the interaction of all phenomena in the history of civilization. This concept implies that there can be no change at one point without some preceding and consequent change elsewhere, so that all historical happening is knit together in a permanent relationship of correlation, inevitably forming a current in which everything is interconnected and each single event is related to all others. Now, the principles of historical explanation and understanding are implicit in this position. At every point there do indeed emerge unique and autonomous historical forces that, by virtue of our capacity for empathy, we perceive to be related to our common humanity. At the same time, however, these unique forces also stand in a current and context comprehending the totality of events, where we see everything conditioned by everything else so that there is no point within history which is beyond this correlative involvement and mutual influence.

There is no need for us to demonstrate that this approach constitutes the foundation of all principles of historical explanation. The [15] historian's craft combines the art of intuiting the original import of the sources with the discovery of correlative and mutually determinative changes. The historian's ultimate problems arise from the attempt to understand the nature and basis of the whole historical context and to arrive at value judgements regarding its various forms.

The scholarly investigation of the Bible has accordingly become involved with the general political, social, and intellectual history of antiquity, and the investigation and evaluation of Christianity has at last been placed within the framework of the history of religion and culture. The exigencies of their own research have gradually compelled the scholars to elucidate the beginnings of the religion of Israel by analogies from the religions of other Semitic peoples and to relate the profound and original transformation of the religion of Yahweh to the general conditions prevailing in Western Asia, especially to its great catastrophes and its general intellectual horizon. Judaism had to be interpreted by reference to the conditions of the Exile and its institutional reorganization, and its profoundly altered conceptual framework had to be explained in terms of ideas absorbed during the Exile. The rise of Christianity had to be related to the disintegration of Judaism, to the political movements and the apocalyptic ideas of the time; and the establishment of the Christian church had to be studied in the light of the interaction of primitive Christianity with the surrounding world of the Roman empire. Indeed, no comprehensive view can any longer fail to see in the mighty movement of Christianity the culmination of antiquity. Major developments in the Near East and the West prepared the way for this culmination. Very different lines of development finally converged in it.

Now, all these necessities were entailed by the historical method itself, which, once admitted at any one point, necessarily draws everything into its train and weaves together all events into one great web of correlated effects and changes. It is not at all necessary here to adopt the distinctly Hegelian notion of Strauss that the Idea does not like to pour all its fullness into a single individual. No general philosophical theory is required to arrive at this result. The historical method itself, by its use of criticism, analogy, and correlation, produces with irresistible necessity a web of mutually interacting activities of the human spirit, which are never independent and absolute but always interrelated and therefore understandable only within the context of the most comprehensive whole.

In its origin, of course, this method was not independent of general theories. No method is. But the decisive test is the usefulness and fruitfulness of a method, its perfection through application, and its [16] contribution to the achievement of continuity and understanding. No one can deny that wherever the historical method has been applied it has produced surprisingly illuminating results, and that confidence in its ability to illuminate previously obscure areas has been consistently vindicated. Such success is its sole—but wholly sufficient—validation.

Give the historical method an inch and it will take a mile. From a strictly orthodox standpoint, therefore, it seems to bear a certain similarity to the devil. Like the modern natural sciences, it represents a complete revolution in our patterns of thought vis-à-vis antiquity and the Middle Ages. As these sciences imply a new attitude toward nature, so history implies a new attitude toward the human spirit and its productions in the realm of ideas. Everywhere the older absolutistic or dogmatic approach, which regarded particular conditions and ideas as simply "given" and therefore absolutized them into unchangeable norms, is being supplanted by the historical approach, which regards even those matters that are alleged to be most obviously "given" and those powers that control the largest number of people as having been produced by the flow of history. Jurisprudence, ethics, sociology, political theory, and aesthetics have been affected to their very depths by the historical approach and have been aligned with historical viewpoints and methods. Whether this historicizing of our entire thinking should be regarded as a boon is not the question here. On this point, Nietzsche's brilliant essay, "On the Use and Abuse of History," contains observations worth heeding. In any case, we are no longer able to think without this method or contrary to it. All our investigations regarding the nature and goals of the human spirit must be based on it. Goethe's words still apply:

> Those who will not account
> to themselves for the past thirty centuries
> may continue to live
> in the dark, day-by-day, grossly ignorant.

Thus, the historical method has also penetrated theology, first subtly and piecemeal with all sorts of limitations and reservations, then ever more energetically and comprehensively, with the result that here also it accomplished what it had done everywhere else, namely, a transformation in principle of our entire mode of thought and our whole attitude toward the subject. To be sure, at first only particular results entered the general consciousness, and with them an uncomfortable insecurity. But subconsciously, the fundamental significance of the historical method is all-pervasive, driven by the logic of an inner necessity. The success of the method in the solution of particular problems urges its extension to the whole field, to the [17] way the subject itself is approached. Here again, direction is not given by some theory or system but by the exigencies of the objects of historical investigation, which seem to come alive and are rendered comprehensible as soon as they are approached with the historical method. Those who expressed objections or reservations about it were compelled to retreat step by step until they were reduced to invoking, as a defense, the uncertainties engendered by deficiencies in the sources and the tradition.

The particular views that resulted from the historical treatment of Jewish and Christian religious traditions are not, however, the most decisive aspect of the development, their intrinsic importance notwithstanding. What is crucial are the consequences of the method as such, which in the nature of the case are two. In the first place, historical criticism brings a measure of uncertainty to every single fact and shows that certainty attaches only to its effects upon the present; the historical link between original fact and present influence must remain at least partly obscure. But this is to loosen the connection between religious faith and all particular facts. To be sure, the connection is not broken, but its character is changed. Now it becomes impossible to base religious faith on any single fact: faith and fact are linked by large and broad connections; their relationship is mediate, not direct.

In the second place, these connections between faith and fact are themselves not isolated and unconditioned but are most closely correlated with a much larger historical context; they arise out of this context, they share its substance, and they must be understood in relation to it. It does not follow, however, that the originality of the particular historical fact is thereby denied. What does follow is that its originality is analogous to others emerging from the common context and is neither more nor less mysterious than these. The creative significance of the personages who dominate the great life-complexes need not be denied. But the personages of Judaeo-Christian history are neither more nor less irrational than those of Greek and Persian history.

One implication of the historical method is extremely important. It follows from the univocity and the total interconnection of historical events that their evaluation and judgement no less than their explanation and description must begin with the total context. Although numerous theologians seek to persuade us that the proper starting point is the isolated claim and judgement of the Christian community, no just estimate of Christianity can be formed except by reference to the total context—even as the self-judgement of the Greeks [18] or the Romans cannot be allowed to determine our estimate of their permanent contribution to the human spirit.

Obviously, this is how the historical method works. It relativizes everything, not in the sense that it eliminates every standard of judgement and necessarily ends in a nihilistic skepticism, but rather in the sense that every historical structure and moment can be understood only in relation to others and ultimately to the total context, and that standards of values cannot be derived from isolated events but only from an overview of the historical totality. This relativism and respect for the historical totality belong together, as indeed they are always conjoined in the practical application of the method. This spirit of historical investigation has gradually permeated every facet of historical theology; Christianity, too, must be regarded as an entity to be explained and evaluated in relation to the total context of which it forms a part. Indeed, only the investigations carried out in this spirit have produced authentic historical knowledge; all the animadversions against the historical method have represented only checks upon it or corrections of particular results, but no viable alternative. For these reasons the old dogmatic method has become untenable for anyone who has become historically sensitive. This fact, and it alone, is the starting point of all theories like the one I am proposing. Once employed, the inner logic of the method drives us forward; and all the countermeasures essayed by the theologians to neutralize its effects or to confine them to some limited area have failed, despite eager efforts to demonstrate their validity.

Indeed, no one is in a position to see these consequences more clearly than the biblical scholar, particularly in the concrete work of his speciality. Even someone who is unable to accept any of our theories is bound to be aware, after the discussions of the idea of the kingdom of God or of Jesus' messianic consciousness, that it is impossible to arrive at some supra-historical core with a method that necessarily raised such problems as these and, precisely through them, has advanced our historical understanding. Conversely, one need only survey the enormously complicated apparatus that Zahn has constructed for the purpose of annulling the results of the historical method to become aware that nothing has been accomplished in behalf of his approach; he has merely matched results with results, rather than method with method. Moreover, it will be apparent that his tortuous deductions can scarcely provide a basis for the old naively secure relationship to tradition that was the presupposition of the old dogmatic method.

If this is the situation, only one consequence appears possible. The [19] historical method must be consistently applied. This implies not only recognition of the relative uncertainty of all historical knowledge (and consequently the awareness that the connection of religious belief with particular historical events is only mediate and relative) and the resolute subjection of the Judaeo-Christian tradition to all the consequences of a purely historical method (without fearing or seeking to bypass the results). Most importantly, it implies that Christianity should be seen in its involvement with general history. The scholarly investigation and evaluation of Christianity must begin with the general context of universal history. Now, to apply the historical method to theology with utter, uncompromising consistency means to base theology on the historical method, which is oriented to universal history; and since our concern is with Christianity as both religion and ethic, the method will have to be that of the history of religion [*religionsgeschichtliche Methode*]. This idea of a theology based upon the history of religion, which was envisaged from the very beginning of historical criticism (first by the Deists and then in various forms by Lessing, Kant, Herder, Schleiermacher, de Wette, and Hegel, and finally by Baur and Lagarde), I have sought to sketch in my previous works, attempting to give it the form required since the elimination of the rationalistic concept of religion-in-general and of the Hegelian dialectic of the Absolute.

I cannot now enter again into the details. That task will have to wait for a more comprehensive work. I only desire to stress that, although many of these specific studies are important, what is decisive for me is the method. I have no doubt that even a presentation of the Christian life-world based on the method of the history of religion will fail to convince the atheist and the religious skeptic. This is not, however, my concern, which is limited to attempting to satisfy the intellectual need for consistency and uniformity of view and approach. Nor do I doubt that this method—only the details of which are my own—will attract but few followers at first, either on the right or on the left; nor does this fact concern me. What is of primary importance is that the scholar should attain a firm conviction by means of the exposition. I have the greatest confidence, however, that the implication of the historical method will necessarily lead through the present confusion and derangement of biblical studies to its full and resolute application. Only then will the worst of our fears (regarding apologetics) be lifted from our hearts, and we shall be able to behold with greater detachment and freedom the glory of God in history.

The need for a consistency that makes possible such detachment and freedom is bound to lead an increasing number of theologians, or at least people [20] who are intellectually concerned about religion, in the direction indicated. The simple result will be, as I have already written, the following:

> All human religion is rooted in religious intuition or divine revelation, which in specifically religious personalities achieves the power to establish new communities; the faithful subsequently enter into this experience, though with diminished originality. The belief in God contained in this intuition (which is concealed in nature religion at the beginning of religious history, when the religious consciousness takes naturalistic forms) decisively breaks through these limits in the religion of Yahweh—notwithstanding many comparable beginnings elsewhere—and in the preaching of Jesus, which, emerging out of the religion of Yahweh, undergoes an infinitely rich development that was impossible to predict at the outset. But in this development the concern was always with life oriented to faith in the living God and with the interpretation of the particular situation in the light of this faith.

This new method in theology would not be adequately characterized, however, unless I contrasted it with the old method, consistently and authentically interpreted. This comparison is especially necessary in view of the remarks of Niebergall and the theologians close to him, who have claimed this method as their own even though they were not very clear about its essential nature. If the new method is to be termed the history-of-religion method, since it subjects all tradition to criticism first and, where a question of principle is involved, always starts from the total historical reality in order to derive its standards of value from this totality, the older one is to be termed the dogmatic method. It starts from a firm point of origin completely beyond the relativity of historical scholarship and thence arrives at absolutely certain positions that, at best, may subsequently be related to the insights and opinions governing the rest of human life. By its principles this method is absolutely opposed to the historical one. Its essence is that it possesses an authority that, by definition, is separate from the total context of history, not analogous to other happenings, and therefore not subject to historical criticism and the uncertainty attaching to its results. The dogmatic method seeks to commit persons to certain particular facts of history, especially insofar as these attest the authority and destroy all historical analogy to it. The dogmatic method can bring about such a commitment because its facts are not those of ordinary history and hence can be neither established nor demolished by historical criticism; they are safeguarded, rather, by a miraculous transmission and sealed by an inward testimony in the heart.

The dogmatic method accordingly lacks the main features of the method of secular historical scholarship, namely, criticism, analogy, [21] and correlation. Indeed, it combats these features most energetically and admits them, at best, only in regard to the most immaterial details. It cannot abide historical criticism, not because it is narrow-minded but because it cannot suffer the uncertainty of results that is connected with such criticism, and because its facts possess a character that contradicts every critical presupposition—indeed, the very possibility of criticism. The dogmatic method cannot admit analogies or make use of them because it would then have to surrender its own innermost nature, which consists in the denial of any analogical similarity between Christianity and other forms of religious development. It cannot submerge itself in the total historical context because its monopoly on dogmatic truth can be recognized only in its antithesis to this context, in the assertion that its own constitutive causality is "wholly other."

To be sure, the dogmatic method also claims to be based upon "history." But this is not the ordinary, secular history reconstructed by critical historiography. It is rather a history of salvation [*Heilsgeschichte*], a nexus of saving facts which, as such, are knowable and provable only for the believer. These facts have precisely the opposite characteristics of the facts that secular, critical historians can regard, on the basis of their criteria, as having actually taken place.

When dogmatic apologetics stresses the "historical" character of Christianity in order to appeal to the secular appreciation of historical and social forces (which generally prevails among us, as over against purely individual efforts and discoveries), this is pure obscurantism. Such apologetics has already caused enough confusion in theology. Today all kinds of things are labeled as "historical" and as "facts" which are nothing of the kind, and which ought not to be so labeled, since they are miraculous in nature and can only be apprehended by faith. The miracles of the Judaeo-Christian tradition are often assigned a label that sounds general and obscures their difference from the secular world. This camouflage is dropped only when the discussion has safely passed to the sphere of theology. Even Niebergall has followed this approach quite freely. Yet, it is apparent that genuine dogmatics is poorly served by such a "historical" force that ultimately is merely fortuitous. It has need, rather, of a history that, by concentrating the necessary absolute truth at one point, sets itself apart from ordinary history, which relativizes all truths by showing their mutual interdependence. To safeguard its own uniqueness, the dogmatic method requires an open rupture with this kind of history: otherwise it would become subject to all of its conditions, the mutual limitations of its phenomena, and the continuing possibility of change.

[22] In all these matters the traditional dogmatic method operates quite consistently and correctly. It claims an authority that is dogmatic rather than historical, intrinsic rather than based on comparison, immutable rather than sharing the conditions of historical existence. It does not seek historical greatness, based on actual strength and influence or on philosophical reflection, but rather a foundation for dogmatic truths, characterized as supernatural by special marks and thus essentially non-historical. Consequently, everything depends on the evident demonstration of this supernatural character that establishes dogma even as it vitiates history. Whether greater emphasis be placed on the internal or the external manifestations or supernaturalism, ultimately, its internal manifestation in the operations of grace always serves to prove the credibility of the external manifestation, which alone vitiates historicity. The miraculous is truly decisive, and, since a miracle confined to the psychological sphere is not sufficiently different from the life of the soul as we encounter it universally in history, such a delicate miracle only becomes useful when solid "physical" miracles can be deduced from it. Ultimately, everything depends on this external manifestation of supernaturalism. It would be better honestly to take one's stand on it rather than to talk of a "history" that is not history at all but rather its opposite.

Only this proof by miracle provides the dogmatic method with a firm foundation and a methodological principle. It will be recalled that the historical method issued from the metaphysical assumption that all things, including the activities of the human mind, are totally interconnected; that it achieved autonomy through elaboration; and that it then had yet again to formulate general theories regarding the essence of history and the principles by which it formed its historical judgements. Similarly, the dogmatic method possesses a general metaphysical principle that was originally only rather implicitly present but which became clearly and precisely explicit in the course of its elaboration. Only the proof for the supernatural character of its authority or for the miraculous provides the decisive metaphysical foundation for the dogmatic method, without which it could be regarded as a knife lacking both handle and blade. The division of the domain of history into one area devoid of miracles and subject to the normal working of historical criticism and another area permeated by miracles and accessible to study only through methods based on inner experiences and the humble subjection of reason is the primary theoretical basis of the dogmatic method. The construction of such a concept of history and the establishment of a separate methodology [23] for the history of dogma or the history of salvation, with special conditions independent of ordinary history, is the basic presupposition of the dogmatic method in theology. Consequently, the theological investigations of recent centuries are replete with this special methodology geared to the history of salvation, which vitiates and distorts the methodology of secular history in various ways, and with distinctive Christian theories of knowledge supposedly based either on the principle of ecclesiastical obedience or on regeneration and inner experience. Only fatigue caused by such fruitless apologetics can excuse the astonishing habit of contemporary dogmatists who believe that they are able to pluck fruit without having a tree or who, after cutting a small, dry twig from an old trunk, expect fruit to grow from this twig.

But ultimately the essence of the problem is not exhausted by this great distinction between two realms of history and between two opposite methods corresponding to these realms. For the duality of the realms of history must be derived from a necessary ground both in the nature of God and in human nature. In the final analysis the duality of history is related to a duality in the divine nature. This duality is therefore regarded and maintained by the dogmatic method as the foundational and primary support of its concepts. God is not part of the nexus of interrelated forces continually affecting one another, nor is God involved in every vital movement only as the purposive will that produces the motion of the total system. God is also capable, rather, of extraordinary activities (as compared to regular modes of operation) which break through and abrogate the ordinary operation of the system. Everything depends on this concept of God.

No less fundamental, however, is the concept of humanity necessitating such a distinctive mode of divine operation, that is, the concept of a hereditary sinfulness due to a fall from the regular, normal, and uniform cosmic order and the concept of a salvation that requires a restoration of this order by extraordinary means. These dualistic concepts of the human and the divine are indispensable presuppositions of the dogmatic method with its dualism of two historical methods—one critical and relativistic, operative in secular history; and the other absolute and apodictically certain, appropriate to the history of salvation. Here, too, weariness with the labors of apologetics has induced many modern theologians to neglect or abandon these theories. In particular, the remarkable discovery of the irrelevance of metaphysics to theology has led to a renunciation of the proof of this dualism, even though the dualism itself necessarily [24] continued to be recognized as valid. As though a non-metaphysical theology were not bound to eliminate this dualism and its consequences! The result would be that theology would turn into the phenomenological and historical study of religion, in which the truth-content of the religious phenomenon must first be ascertained; while a new, more cautious, and more limited metaphysics would emerge, characterized by abandonment of the miracle-dualism and based on moral certitude or sensitivity [*Gefühl*].

For the young theologian beginning to study, nothing is more astounding than the contradiction between the alleged indifference of such fundamental concepts as God, the primal state, original sin, and miracles, on the one hand, and the working assumption of their entire validity (except for some accommodating concessions regarding the influence of the pre-modern worldview), on the other. One can become accustomed to anything and make a virtue out of every necessity; but with any sense for clarity, consistency, and intellectual precision, one can hardly resign oneself to such a virtue with equanimity. For this reason most young theologians will ultimately return to the old metaphysical bases of the dogmatic method; from all their studies they will only retain the impression that the proof of these bases is a matter of no particular importance. The dogmatic method is thus pushed forward by an inner necessity towards the type of theology suggested above, just as the historical method necessarily leads to a theology that is fundamentally based on the history of religion.

It is not my intention to develop in detail the scope of the dogmatic method, but only to sketch it in its essence and to contrast it with the historical method. One might term the old method

"Catholic" because it was created by Catholic theologians and received its classic formulation from them; and one might term the new method "Protestant" because in the last analysis it grew out of the Protestant criticism of the Catholic doctrine of authority. Yet, on the one hand, the old method is so deeply imbedded in the inclinations of human nature to dogmatism and is so necessary a product of historically unsophisticated periods that it would not make sense to term this method specifically Catholic; for it is also employed in Jewish and Muslim theology. On the other hand, Protestant historical criticism was only partial and apologetic in intent; Protestantism arose in an era that was by no means historical in its outlook. It was not until the Enlightenment that an essentially historical outlook emerged; the allegedly unhistorical outlook of the Enlightenment belongs to the realm of legend. To be sure, the Enlightenment began by critically emancipating itself from the recognized authorities and thus its first [25] task was to put everything on one level. But its leveling efforts immediately led to a new task, the task of differentiation and graduation, which required that all the phenomena dealt with be first transformed into purely historical ones. In this transitional stage the Enlightenment made supernatural dogmatism, in part, rational; and where this was not possible, it worked out a new worldview based on history. The latter, of course, had to weave together historical data and materials of general validity, and is entitled to be termed "historical" only *a posteriori*. At this very point the difference between the two methods becomes plain.

Thus, the only appropriate terms are the dogmatic and the historical method. Each has its own foundation and problems; each is consistent within itself. My concern, however, is not to detail the particular problems of each, but only, because of their respective consistencies, to insist on their incompatibility. With this insistence, the main objective of this paper is attained. I only wish to add a few remarks concerning my position in this methodological controversy. These comments will serve to defend my position against some objections of Niebergall and, incidentally, to illuminate the distorted manner in which he himself espouses the dogmatic method.

His first objection to my method is on the score of its difficulty and the subjective conditions of its implementation. It goes without saying that the production of a scale of values among the great cultural types [*Geistestypen*] of history depends on subjective judgements and can never be fully conclusive. I have always stressed this point explicitly. Nevertheless, I am convinced that, given a sharp and penetrating analysis of the nature of these types, people who are seriously concerned about ethical and religious matters—neither frivolous nor trying to be merely clever but really in earnest about finding meaning in life—may arrive at a relative degree of consensus. This conviction is based on a belief that is both religious and ethical, namely, that ultimately the essential uniformity of human nature provides a foundation for consensus in recognizing supreme standards of value and that, because of this foundation, the consensus will prevail. As for Niebergall's strictures concerning the difficulties of implementing my approach, I can say only that no amount of emphasis upon the difficulties in a method that is inherently possible can justify the adoption of a method that is inherently impossible. It only challenges us to greater devotion to the task.

Niebergall also criticizes me for connecting the scale of values I have constructed with a metaphysics of history that makes it possible to deduce values, in a logically progressive and increasingly profound [26] sequence, from the nature of the human spirit or rather from its transcendent ground as it operates in the spirit. I am unable here to consider in detail his remarks about intellectualism and practical reason, which are completely incomprehensible to me in their present form. I only note that no one who considers history to be pure chaos will undertake to derive a scale of values from it by the exercise of reason. For the deduction of such a scale of values it is indispensable to believe in reason as operative in history and as progressively revealing itself. This belief, too, is primarily of ethical and religious origin; but it is a belief that is confirmed, in my judgement, by the deepening of personal life which is constantly taking place in history.

The third objection adduced by Niebergall is the danger of self-deception to which one is exposed in such a production of a scale of values. I do not intend to inquire whether the danger resulting from the application of the historical approach is greater than that arising from the special apologetic conditions of the dogmatic method, geared as it is to the history of salvation, whose practitioners feel no obligation to warn against such a hazard. The point I would emphasize, rather, is that I do not regard the danger as wholly insuperable. Actually, one does not always endeavor to demonstrate a preconceived thesis with all the devices of cunning, yet with the greatest possible appearance of impartiality, as many theologians believe who are absolutely unable to think otherwise. In such an intricately complex and extremely individualistic culture as our own, it is often difficult to know where to take one's stand; and it is actually possible, without any preconceived preference for Christianity, to desire to orient oneself through a comparative survey. If as a consequence one reaches the judgement that Christianity is the highest ethical and religious force, this result need not at all have been antecedently present—not even where there was a relative appreciation for Christianity from the outset, such as any serious person naturally would feel. The ultimate avowal of Christianity as the supreme religious force of history, which is the outcome for me, is something quite different from a relative and preliminary appreciation that is connected, moreover, with a serious intent not necessarily to commit oneself to this initial and immediate judgement.

Finally, Niebergall attacks me for inconsistency inasmuch as I, while ostensibly oriented to historical relativism, yet emerge at the end with the recognition of the "absoluteness" of Christianity, a conclusion that in his judgement is quite impossible for me. It must be admitted that Niebergall has here pointed correctly to vacillations not only in my mode of expression but also in my way of thinking as they appear [27] in various essays spread over several years. It would have been possible for him to observe that I have actually tended to draw the consequences of the historical method ever more strictly and that I have finally come to characterize the term "absoluteness" as only a rationalized and disguised vestige of the dogmatic method. I believe, in fact, that the term is not terribly important—but only because its opposite, the much-maligned "relativism," is not so important to me as it would appear to be from the dogmatic point of view. Indeed, I would say that it is the essence of my view that it thoroughly combats historical relativism, which is the consequence of the historical method only within an atheistic or a religiously skeptical framework. Moreover, my view seeks to overcome this relativism through the conception of history as a disclosure of the divine reason.

It is here that we see the undeniable merits of the Hegelian doctrine, which needs only to be freed of its metaphysics of the absolute, its dialectic of opposites, and its specifically logical conception of religion. The point is that history is not a chaos but issues from unitary forces and aspires towards a unitary goal. For the believer in religion and ethics, history is an orderly sequence in which the essential truth and profundity of the human spirit rise from its transcendent ground—not without struggle and error, but with the necessary consistency of a development that has had a normal beginning. The contrasts are rather superficial and incidental. In essence, the differences among the great historical structures are not very great, and the actual ideas and values in the world are infinitely rarer than is supposed, although their manifestations and ramifications are innumerable. With the great idealists, I believe that in this apparent chaos the divine depth of the human spirit reveals itself from different directions, and that the belief in God, provided only that it is actually belief in God and not self-seeking magic, is at its core identical in all its forms. Moreover, I hold that this belief in God, by the internal consistency of the divine force that empowers it, continues to increase in energy and depth to the degree permitted by the original tie of the human spirit to nature.

Only at one point was this limitation broken through. This point, however, was located at the center of great contemporary and subsequent religious developments, namely, in the religion of the prophets of Israel and in the person of Jesus. Here a God distinct from nature produced a personality superior to nature with eternally transcendent goals and the willpower to change the world. Here a religious power manifests itself, which to anyone sensitive enough to catch its echo in one's own soul, seems to be the conclusion of all previous religious movements and the starting point of a new phase in [28] the history of religion, in which nothing has yet emerged. Indeed, even for us today it is unthinkable that something higher should emerge, no matter how many new forms and combinations this purely inward and personal belief in God may yet enter. Clearly, this position constitutes neither dogmatic absolutism nor the confrontation of historical scholarship by Christianity, nor the exemption of Christianity from the flux, the conditioning, and the mutability of history. But it provides a stopping point that is attainable through a historical mode of thought geared to the philosophy of history, and that is adequate for the religious person. More we do not need, and more we cannot achieve. Here we find the religious support for our life and thought that has constituted the dynamic center of our European civilization, and which remains a vital power capable of further development.

It is true that the relationship of this European religion to the religions of the Orient is still a great and dark question for the future. But insofar as we recognize in the transcendence of nature, which constitutes the faith of the prophets, and in the active and lively love of God and humanity which constitutes the faith of Jesus, the decisive and elevating forces of religion, we can persevere in our traditional faith and leave further developments to the future. In this connection also, Niebergall has measured me by needs that are taken for granted by him. He has not put himself into a religious mood that really finds its rest and support in such thoughts. To his opinion that the reader of my work has to ride through a very cold land and then pass through a dark tunnel before emerging into the smiling fields of home, I might reply that the distant land is not so cold, the tunnel not so dark, nor the ultimate point of arrival so inviting as he supposes.

For my part, I have considerable misgivings about the position of Niebergall. Here again I shall forgo consideration of the epistemological explanations with which he supports his position and the formulation of which he regards as constituting the major part of difference from my own work. These matters are not crucial for the problem as a whole. For if the question to be decided is whether the scale of values in the spiritual life is to be derived from a philosophy of history or from an authoritarian judgement based on supernatural considerations, then it is quite pointless to stress factors of sentiment and will, which naturally enter into every value judgement. One can never base authoritarian supernaturalism on the practical character of all values, since this same practical character applies also to non-Christian and non-religious values. Rather, we are dealing exclusively with the basis of the authority that the dogmatic method requires as its starting point.

[29] In this regard there is no doubt that Niebergall agrees with the intentions of the traditional dogmatic method. He desires the doctrine of a supernaturalistic authority: not a "historical absolute but one that is dogmatic and apologetic," an "absolute apart from and opposed to the history of religion"; that is, apart from and opposed to the views of historical criticism in general. He wants a "realm lying beyond the history of religion"; that is, a realm lying quite beyond secular history. He is concerned with "absoluteness as an immediate derivation from God" in contrast to the merely mediate derivation from God of ordinary history and the history of non-Christian religions, which is based on a "merely natural endowment." He conceives of the absolute as a "faith that absolute values have been supernaturally revealed at one point in history"; that is, values having an absoluteness that is primarily authenticated by their supernatural mode of revelation. Despite all Niebergall's talk about his respect for history and the practical motivation of all faith, one must not permit oneself to be deceived: what he wants is outside of and contrary to history. He wants a history of a higher order, which has different presuppositions from ordinary history and events that are distinguishable by criteria not provided by ordinary history. When he speaks of the "autonomy of Christianity," "practical motivation," or "historical character," such terms are euphemisms for the miraculous, which theologians of his type prefer not to call by its correct name.

The intentions of Niebergall are never fulfilled, however. His mode of thought falls far short of what he aspires to achieve, namely, a "pure and bright supernaturalism." One hears next to nothing from Niebergall concerning a consistent foundation for supernaturalism in the concept of God, the primal state, the Fall, and redemption. His work contains only pitiful vestiges of any other demonstration of supernaturalism actually derived from history, that is, from the miraculous character of sacred history. He intends to establish the biblical revelation as his starting point, a priori authentic and normative for his approach to history. This intention, which he emphatically proclaims, is constantly being crossed, however, by the contrary procedure of starting from general history and searching it for the possible disclosure of absolute values corresponding to human need. He acts as though he knew nothing of Christianity and were seeking, as a universal human postulate, for some absolute, redemptive revelation. From this stance he discovers the historical "fact" of Christianity and rejoices to find it satisfying all his requirements. The historical mode of thought has here produced a deep impression after all. What should have been the starting point of the dogmatist now [30] appears as the contingent result of a search of history. The result has been that, instead of being deduced from the concept of God and Adam's fall, theology is being authenticated by reference to human needs. Everything now depends on the legitimacy of these needs and the fact of their satisfaction, which is no more automatically guaranteed for these needs than for any others.

I do not wish to expatiate further upon these needs—the need (ostensibly demonstrated by Kant) of theoretical doubt for supernatural revelation, or the need of morality for authority, for a guarantee of victory, and for the atonement of sins. All these needs may be legitimate, but it cannot be denied that these needs themselves are in the first instance purely historical forms which do not lead beyond history. Of greater importance is the question why the satisfaction of these needs should be regarded as taking place in Christianity in an absolute manner. Here again the emphasis is not placed upon an inner necessity that enables Christianity alone to satisfy these needs, but recourse is taken—with an apparent objectivity that is very popular in contemporary theology—to the purely factual "claim" of Christianity. Here we meet the same dialectical comedy as before. One comes upon the "historical fact" of a tremendous claim and appears completely surprised by this fact, as though it were something astounding and overwhelming. The claim of Christianity is made into its essence, and the erstwhile theology of miracle now becomes a theology of claim. Christianity claims to be absolute truth and redemption. Without recognition of this claim Christianity is unattainable. But the assertion of claims, of course, no more proves their validity than the existence of needs guarantees their satisfaction—all the less so as various religions advance competing claims that require decision on the basis of some kind of criterion. In all of these expositions a dread of the real roots of the dogmatic method and a superficial accommodation to purely historical arguments are the only operative factors. Actually existing needs and claims are said to form the basis of the theory. But needs and claims are themselves products of history. They are to be understood in their historical context, to be illuminated, and possibly to be corrected, as have a hundred other needs and claims. By no means do needs and claims indicate some higher reality removed from historical relativity and criticism.

Thus everything depends on whether these needs are satisfied not merely by a claim but by a higher reality. In the last analysis Niebergall's views necessarily affirm this position. But how feeble and cautious is his assertion of a higher supernatural reality and causality as opposed to secular history! He stresses "supernaturalism" and [31] "immediacy" as appropriate to revelation, in order to support a distinctive causality that would give special status to Christianity as the means-oriented natural causality would not. But even this emphasis is expressed only in the most general terms. To be absolute, "Christianity must be based upon a special revelation that must somehow be made comprehensible as revelation." This "somehow" is typical of contemporary theology, which in its refinement disdains the concerns of the older apologetics and disposes of them "somehow." If one seeks clues to this "somehow" in Niebergall, only one attempt at more precise definition will be found, along with the crude manipulation of some famous models. The personality of Jesus must be such as to break through the ordinary historical causality. But even in this context Niebergall speaks primarily of the mysterious and underivable essence of the personality, as though the same observations were not true of every personality.

> Here in the ground of the soul there remains a gap in the causal nexus which is the greater, the more unique and developed is the personality. It is this gap that provides full scope for the operation of a higher power. We believe that the revelation that we religiously apprehend and revere sets in at this point, which resists all analysis. . . . Start-

> ing with Jesus, the reservoir of revelation fed both from heaven and by terrestrial streams, we proceed upwards along the course of these tributaries.

And at another point he says, "We resolve to attribute beneficent powers that come to our assistance in deepest need to the intervention of God, because we know of no earthly source from which they could have been derived."

What should one say to such remarks? Should one admire the modesty of a theology that has come to the point of finding its foundation ultimately in a gap? Or should one stress the uncertainty with which even this gap is asserted, in view of the fact that no clear distinction is made between the gaps in the causal nexus which characterize the personal life of ordinary human beings and the particular gap within the personality of Jesus, which is the only one that concerns us at this point? I think that one can only say that such a doctrine of authority and revelation has been deeply affected by the spirit of historical criticism, analogy, and relativity. Indeed, it has been almost destroyed. All that remain are some pathetic and quite general claims. In this respect, the older dogmatic doctrine was better and more understandable.

This judgement is made entirely from a scholarly perspective and refers only to the consistency of the ideas. Practically, such an enervation and edentulation of the old authoritarian doctrine may be [32] a very good thing. In practical life, it is impossible to get along without such mediating positions; and in church affairs, the mediating groups may constitute a very desirable transitional form. In closing these observations, we may stress that *sub specie aeternitatis* all the differences we have noted may be quite unimportant. Consequently, they need not excessively disunite us in our earthly pilgrimage.

26.

Wilhelm Herrmann (1846–1922)

The "lives of Jesus" had shaken many devout Christians in the course of the nineteenth century. It also led to a renewed academic reflection on the role of history, and historical scholarship, in Christian theology. Wilhelm Herrmann is among the thinkers who claimed that, while the Christian faith is intimately related to historical figures and events, it does not depend on historical scholarship. Such a dependence would imply that faith is, first and foremost, a "knowing" or an "accepting something to be true" (*assensus*, or *Fürwahrhalten*), when in fact it is, according to Herrmann, a "lived experience" (*Erlebnis*), a trust (*Vertrauen*) that comes from a personal encounter with the power of God's revelation in Jesus Christ. And so historical scholarship has a positive influence on theology in that it reminds theology, and faith, that its ground is found elsewhere than in scientific results. This may be interpreted as a defensive strategy, as a retreat from the unruly waters of historical scholarship (Sockness 1996). Or it may be interpreted, as I think it may, as a correct reminder of the Christian faith's true ground, which, while found within history, simultaneously exceeds it.

Herrmann studied theology at the University of Halle (1866–71) and discovered in those years the works of Albrecht Ritschl, which enthused him (Herrmann 2013). In the last two decades of his life, it is Friedrich Schleiermacher's *Speeches* that he tended to praise, as he began to focus more and more on the personal experience of God rather than, with Ritschl, on the Christian community. In 1879, having taught in a gymnasium in Halle, he was named professor of systematic theology at the University of Marburg, where he taught until his retirement in 1917. He is among the founders of the *Zeitschrift für Theologie und Kirche* (1891), a significant German theological journal to this day. Herrmann, notably with his christological concentration and his fondness for logical tensions in Christian discourse, had a deep influence on two of the most prominent Protestant theologians of the twentieth century, namely, Karl Barth and Rudolf Bultmann, who both admired him (Barth kept a portrait of Herrmann in his house in Basel). However, his two students developed—unlike him—a crucial *eschatological* interpretation of God's self-revelation, and they were more interested in how God finds God's creature than, as Herrmann put it, on the human person's "way to religion."

What follows is transcribed from Herrmann's most successful book, *The Communion of the Christian with God, Described on the Basis of Luther's Statements*, trans. J. Sandys Stanyon (London: Williams & Norgate, 1906), chapter 2, §5. The original German title is *Der Verkehr des Christen mit Gott, im Anschluss an Luther dargestellt* (Stuttgart-Berlin: Cotta, 1903).

THE COMMUNION OF THE CHRISTIAN WITH GOD, DESCRIBED ON THE BASIS OF LUTHER'S STATEMENTS (1903)

§ 5. It is not through a Historical Judgment that the Person of Jesus becomes a Fact we Ourselves Establish.

[66] The former contention has the greater weight. Human beings must indeed be powerfully moved by the supposition that Jesus himself cannot be held to be an undeniable element in our actual environment, and that it is only the story of Jesus, as vouched for by others, that can be [67] called such an element. Many within the Christian fellowship find this supposition to be a very slave-chain, and for many outside that fellowship it is a drag holding them back from entering. But are the chains as adamantine as they seem? If not, then we, too, can overcome a serious hindrance which the faith of the Reformers reached beyond, but from which they could not get free.

It is true that we would have no certain knowledge of Jesus if the New Testament did not tell us about him. Narratives by others contribute in all cases not a little to the picture we form for ourselves of historical reality. If tradition of some sort did not show us what others have experienced of human life we should lack the most valuable of the interchanges of spiritual possessions. But given this exchange, then the narrative which comes to us, either by word of mouth or in writing, is not the only fact which we incorporate into our picture of historical reality; the content of those narratives may also become a fact for us. This happens only when we can ourselves establish its reality, and we may do this in various ways.

The most elementary form of doing so consists in extending the confidence we place in the trustworthiness of the narrator to that which he narrates. This constantly happens in our daily life, whenever we base our plans of action upon information given by others. We are guided by the content of their report just as by a reality we have grasped for ourselves. But it does not occur to us to offer ourselves as witnesses that things are really as they are said to be. Hence we can remain [68] in this attitude only so long as we are concerned with matters of minor importance. But as soon as the contents of the information affect seriously the most important interests of life, our trust in the mental power and moral goodness of the narrator no longer suffices to assure us that what he reports is a fact beyond all doubt. If even in such a case we are compelled to take action in reliance on the report, our action takes the character of a venture. We are often obliged to act thus when the pressure of necessity does not permit of inaction; under such compulsion we may find ourselves obliged to treat the contents of the narrative as fact. But it is obvious that no such compulsion exists when the information received in any way concerns our religious faith. If we do put confidence in the trustworthiness of a narrator, and are thus led to receive his narration as a fact among the subjects of our religious thought, then, whether the confidence be really felt or be only arbitrarily assumed, it is always very certain that the matter reported is nothing that affects the vital interests of religion. This may be clearly seen in Roman Catholicism. The historical appearance of Jesus is there really accepted on the authority of the narrators, and so we find that that appearance has nothing to do with the highest concern of religious life, namely, how a person is to find God. It serves as a stimulus to the imagination, as an example and as a symbol, but it is not to the Roman Catholic the great fact in which he sees God entering into his own life and revealing Himself to him. Whenever we find the proclamation of the appearance of Jesus thus [69] based entirely on the authority of the narrators, it will also be observed that the Person of Jesus is put on one side so soon as the deepest religious interest comes forward for consideration. A believer cannot base his very existence entirely on what may be given him by other people.

Our mental activity in the matter of receiving reports is certainly greater when we do not form our conception of the actual event from the narrative alone, but seek to obtain it by a combination of the narrative with something else which we know to be real. This procedure is frequently exemplified in daily life, and it has been developed into an art in historical criticism. The contents of the narrative are viewed in the light of the evident character of the narrator as seen through his writings, the position he occupied and its impress on him, and the culture of his age which influenced his way of looking at things. From a consideration of these circumstances we decide how far the contents of the story may be incorporated into our picture of what actually happened. But the decision thus reached of necessity lays claim to nothing more than probability. We are always prepared to modify our results upon more exact examination of the narrative or upon the discovery of new information. It is obvious, then, that such decisions do not give us facts on which our religious faith could be based. Hence it is quite explicable why historical criticism of the sacred records is so much disliked in many quarters. If people will imagine that the reliability of the sacred records is the proper ground of religious faith, then they must necessarily be [70] rendered in the highest degree uneasy by faithful attempts to estimate the historical probability of what is narrated in those records. We have no such anxiety; on the contrary, we declare that the historical appearance of Jesus, insofar as it is drawn into the sphere of this attempt to establish the probable truth, cannot be a basis of faith. It is only a part of that world with which faith is to wrestle.

At this point, of course, the question arises whether we can maintain our position that the historical Christ has become for us the absolutely convincing ground of our faith in God. For how is it at all possible to lift out of the mist of probability the content of a tradition that is subject to historical criticism?

It may be said that we learn with certainty that at least Jesus lived, from the fact of the existence of his church and its historical significance, and that just as little can we question the correctness of certain features in that portrait of Jesus which his followers have preserved in the records of the New Testament. From the standpoint of the mere historian this is certainly the case. A historian may doubt much that the New Testament tells us concerning the glory of Jesus. Because it is possible to attribute it in some measure to the transfiguring enthusiasm of his disciples, it is open to the suspicion of exaggeration. But, on the other hand, the correctness of his portrait in its other features must be admitted by every one who is not prepared to adopt the absurd supposition that in the case of a man who has exerted the greatest influence on history all traces of his earthly life have disappeared. On the strength [71] of those elements in Jesus which, beyond all doubt, are with us today, every reasonable person will hold the more general features of the common story of his life to be correct. Now, one might in theory hold the opinion that we have only succeeded in establishing the probability of those facts concerning Jesus; none the less in practice, even if our interests in Jesus be only historical, we do all include his picture with its well-known features as a part of the historical reality amid which we live, and here we are evidently in no way dependent upon the authority of the chroniclers who give us those features of the life of Jesus. On the contrary, the decision which we reach that these things are facts proceeds from our own independent activity, and is based upon that which we regard as real at present exactly as the decisions of historical criticism are. It is thus perfectly clear that we are quite in a position to detach the content of a narrative both from the narrative itself and from its author, and to regard it as an element of the reality to which we have to adjust our lives.

27.

Hermann Gunkel (1862–1932)

Born near Hannover, the son of a pastor, Hermann Gunkel began his theological studies at the University of Göttingen in 1881, especially under Albrecht Ritschl, spending one year in Giessen (1882–83), where Adolf von Harnack was teaching at the time. In 1895, after one year in Halle, he became a professor at the University of Berlin, moving to Giessen in 1907 and back to Halle in 1920.

Gunkel remains a significant figure in the modern exegesis of the Old Testament, notably with his commentary on Genesis (*Genesis-Kommentar*, 1901). His reflections on the "Goals and Methods of the Explanation of the Old Testament" (Ziele und Methoden der Erklärung des Alten Testamentes; 1904), an article he first published in a journal (*Monatsschrift für die kirchliche Praxis*), as well as the preface to his book of collected essays in which this article was reprinted (*Reden und Aufsätze* [Göttingen: Vandenhoeck & Ruprecht, 1913]), translated here by the editor of the present volume, offer very interesting comments on the nature and methods of biblical exegesis. Gunkel's call for a theological exegesis, and for new methods that the next generation will need to elaborate in this regard, is worth noting. Gunkel is interested not just in the "explanation" of texts but also in our "understanding" them. It could be argued that Rudolf Bultmann and Karl Barth, who both were his students at the University of Berlin, searched precisely for this in their exegetical and theological writings.

REDEN UND AUFSÄTZE

Preface (1913)

[v] . . . The history-of-religion [*"religionsgeschichtlich"*] research has been described as an abyss in which the Bible would be lost. As a result, this scholarly approach has been placed under a ban. But the meaning and purpose of our efforts have thus been badly misjudged, and even the expression "history-of-religion" [*"Religionsgeschichte"*] has been completely misunderstood. This expression, nowadays, designates a research whose main objective is to try to explain the biblical religion in connection with extra-biblical religions. My repeated caveats against this interpretation have remained unheard.[1]

Against this, I consider it my duty to recall always anew the original meaning of this word and the real intention of our scholarship. From the beginning, we did not take "history-of-religion" to mean the history of *religions* [*Religionen*], but the *history of religion* [*die Geschichte der Religion*]. At a time when literary criticism was at its height and led to so many excesses whereby the actual subject matter of all biblical scholarship, namely *religion*, tended to recede behind all kinds of preliminary work, we wanted—even if we welcomed, to an extent, such preliminary work—to turn the attention, once again, to the main thing. We [vi] were fully convinced that the ultimate goal of working on the Bible is to search its figures and their hearts, to develop an inner feeling for their ideas in order to describe them adequately. We were not simply thinking about the biblical books and their criticism; in reading them we sought, rather, to find the living religion. But we were convinced that this living religion is not grasped when one organizes systematically the doctrinal propositions of the biblical authors; the point is, rather, to present the religion in its *movement*, how it surges always anew from the hearts of the great human beings who have been touched by God's Spirit. Hence no "biblical theology" in the old style, but "*history* of religion." A history of religion without abbreviation and obfuscation, following the strict rules of history as a science, a history of religion which shows us the highly intricate picture of the life of a religion, how it is intimately related to political, social, and cultural dimensions, how religious ideas emerge, how they enter into conflict and they unite one with one another, how the religious fabric evolves from one generation to the next, changing and producing new ideas. We spoke of the "history-of-religion" study *in this sense*, trying to offer a complement to the dominant literary critical approach, since we were convinced that certain aspects which had been considered mostly in a literary way would present a very different image if one were to pay attention to the inner laws of the religion and its history.—Now it is certain that the history-of-religion approach studies, not as its main subject but as one unavoidable particular aspect, the people of the biblical religion not in isolation, but in relation with other peoples with which Israel interacted in the various epochs of its history. This facet of our work was particularly noted by the public, not surprisingly since this was a lacuna left by our scientific predecessors and also since in the first years we presented several striking theses in this regard. But we think we have shown, since then, that our intention is in no way to limit our attention only on this point. Church circles have also expressed the worry that with such scholarship the specificity of the biblical religion is curtailed. But even the short time during which this method has been [vii] applied has shown, again and again, that the Bible resists comparative work very well, that the high dignity of the biblical religion becomes clear to any scholar who plunges with seriousness and understanding into the ancient history. Naturally! . . . And so the history of religion and the history of literature [*Literaturgeschichte*] have no other goal than to foster the understanding of holy Scripture's actual religious content. I have absolutely no doubt that these scholarly methods, which penetrate with all their energies toward the center of biblical scholarship, are called in preeminent ways to serve the practical work of the Church. . . .

"Goals and Methods of the Explanation of the Old Testament" (1904)

[11] Biblical exegesis, as we usually practice it in our academic lectures and in commentaries, consists formally in a series of distinct remarks which we make on the text. Once one topic is solved, we treat the next one, which may not have anything to do, as regards the subject matter [*sachlich*], with the first, but which still needs to be mentioned at this juncture, since the text lends itself to it. . . . The worst thing, however, is that with all of various details which the exegete presents, one thing may be [12] left out, namely the text! When one surveys such a commentary once again, after one has read it, one may not always be free of the impression that one has found in it a wealth of valuable details, but that one has not gained a closer rapport to the text. Given all of this, it may not be useless to explicitly ask *what is biblical exegesis*, what is its goal and the means by which it seeks to achieve it. We think that this question should matter to the same extent to all the theological tendencies. . . .

1. [*Original footnote*] See *Deutsche Literaturzeitung* 25 (1904): 1109 and my article "Die Religionsgeschichte und die alttestamentliche Wissenschaft" (1910).

And so here no one should be confused about the actual goal of any exegesis: it is *the understanding* [*Verständnis*] *of the author* and the author's work. The more an exegete keeps this final goal in mind, the more he really fulfills this task, the more he subordinates all the other particular tasks under this one goal, the more he may be called a true exegete. But what is meant by understanding an author, on this anyone who can articulate an opinion will have to agree. It certainly means more than to explain a text sentence by sentence, word by word! Understanding someone as singular and as (in his own way) tremendous as Isaiah obviously means something completely different than explaining [*Erklärung*] his words! For words are never what matters the most [*das Eigentliche*]. They are what is most important only for the pedant [*Kleinigkeitskrämer*]. Words are means of expressing ideas and perceptions. And even these are not ultimate; ideas and perceptions are expressions of the living, moved soul. The soul of human beings, the mysterious inner life which manifests itself to the external world insofar as it expresses itself, that is what is properly of value. . . .

[15] But more. If the power of insight is to become alive in us, we also need, like the artist, inspiration. The artist too creates in times of enthusiasm, when his heart becomes warm and his soul broad. And so it is a deep truth even in daily life that only love confers true understanding. A consideration of history which, proud and cold, looks down at history, which sees in the past nothing but a chain of egoism and abjection, a hodgepodge of error and violence, such consideration cannot penetrate history and recognize its reason. Only love sees what is worthy of love, only idealism sees the ideal. Therefore we must expect that whoever aims to explain a book has achieved a very personal relationship to it. . . .

[18] When purely philological matters fill up the biblical commentary, then it is a misuse. Such preliminary work has taken up so much space in exegesis that now many users of our scientific commentaries turn away from them, for they cannot do anything with them. There have been times when theology had a low standing in the public sphere and when the Old Testament theologian preferred to present himself as an orientalist, as a philologue. Let us be proud of our theology and let us not forget that a commentary of a biblical book which is essentially philological is a deficient commentary, since it leaves out the main thing [*Hauptsache*]! Currently Old Testament scholars, if I see correctly, have taken their distances, to their own damage, from the rest of the theological fields: we can see that in a number of theological conferences, from which they are absent. Against this trend, it seems very important to us that Old Testament scholars too regard themselves as theologians and that they maintain a relation with the other theological disciplines. . . .

[24] We thus come to the endpoint of the task which we have already described several times as the most important within the entire exegetical work: we come to the *theological problem* proper. Our thesis, which is very simple, is that understanding the Bible finds its apex in the understanding of its *religion*. Biblical exegesis is theological exegesis; explaining a biblical book means explaining its religious content. . . .

[25] When someone is concerned too quickly with edification and the needs of the praxis, it is to be feared that, for the sake of a foreign goal, he will not abide by the rigor of historical scholarship.—But what kind of theological exegesis is needed? There have been several different presentations of the Old Testament in the course of the history of this science. On this too there can be only one answer. The *dogmatic* explanation, which in the past was dominant and which sees in the Old Testament just as in the New a source for the Christian doctrine, this explanation, simultaneously with the doctrine of the inspiration, has collapsed. . . . We practice a *historical exegesis*. What does that mean? . . .

[29] Future exegesis, we hope, will possess a high spirit which, even as it cares for the details, does not get bogged down in trivia, which, through all of the details, attains the true, big goals. Future exegesis, we hope, will have a bold and open spirit which, alongside the respect it will show, knows no old or new authority and refuses to be bound to any school. We do not need to inquire about the forms this exegesis will take; when the spirit is there, the spirit himself creates the forms. I am, however, convinced that future commentaries will hardly retain the current form, in which very different questions are treated one after the other without interconnection: an effort will be made, in particular, to separate quite visibly

the comments on the wording of the text from the explanation of its meaning.—At any cost, this exegesis, we are convinced of it, will also serve life. For what the pastor or teacher who reaches for the commentary may legitimately expect from it is that it brings out the religious content of the Old Testament in the full light of knowledge, and that is precisely what this exegesis will do.

28.

Albert Schweitzer (1875–1965)

Albert Schweitzer is a towering figure of twentieth-century Christianity, mostly known for his work as a doctor in Lambarene (Gabon), but his contribution to academic theology, before and after his departure for Africa in 1913, is sometimes passed over or forgotten. And yet, several of his monographs have had a lasting impact in the theological world. His most important contribution is arguably his study of the lives of Jesus: *Von Reimarus zu Wrede: Eine Geschichte der Leben-Jesu-Forschung* (Tübingen: Mohr Siebeck, 1906), titled *Geschichte der Leben-Jesu-Forschung* in its second edition (Mohr Siebeck, 1913). This second edition was translated into English as *The Quest of the Historical Jesus* (ed. John Bowden [London: SCM Press, 2000]), portions of which are printed below, preceded by a new Preface written in Lambarene in 1950. Schweitzer was not the first one to emphasize the eschatological character of Jesus's message concerning God's kingdom: Johannes Weiss (1863–1914) had already signaled the modern, Kantian error of interpreting the kingdom in ethical terms, as if human beings were called, with God's help, to build it, when in fact Jesus expected the imminent coming of God's rule without any aid from human beings. And more than a century before Weiss, Reimarus had seen that Jesus's message was eschatological. But Schweitzer was relentless and thorough in his assessment of the modern lives of Jesus, which, he argued, were for the most part a series of projections of modern values onto the (to us) enigmatic life of the Galilean preacher and healer.

Schweitzer was a liberal theologian who forcefully criticized the liberal theological tradition for its readiness to adjust its portrait of Jesus in ever new ways—none of them adequate to the real historical Jesus, who, after making a brief comeback in modern historical scholarship, had returned to his ancient era (see below, 195).

THE QUEST OF THE HISTORICAL JESUS (1913)

Preface to the Sixth Edition[1]

[xliv] Historical research not only compels us to recognize change; it also shows us what is actually happening, viz., that the type of idea employed for the expression of religious truth becomes increasingly spiritual.

The gospel of the kingdom of God came into the world in its late-Jewish form, which it could not retain. The kingdom, expected to come immediately in supernatural fashion, failed to appear, and so did the Son of man who was to arrive on the clouds of heaven.

Grappling with this compelled believers to take a more and more spiritual view of the kingdom of God and the messiahship of Jesus, the former becoming a spiritual and ethical ideal to be realized in this world, and Jesus the spiritual Messiah who laid its foundation through his ethical preaching. So obvious is this view to faith that it is taken to be the view of Jesus himself, and his preaching is understood in this sense. All this involves overlooking the words of the first two Gospels, which are based on a different presupposition.

Respect for historical truth, however, compels our faith to give up this naivety, and to admit that it has been subject to development. It can do this without being untrue to itself or to Jesus. It has become what it is under the pressure of a higher necessity, under the influence of the Spirit of Jesus. . . .

[xlv] Historical truth not only creates difficulties for faith; it also enriches it, by compelling it to examine the importance of the work of the Spirit of Jesus for its origin and continuance. The gospel of Jesus cannot simply be taken over; it must be appropriated in his Spirit. What the Bible really offers us is his Spirit, as we find it in him and in those who first came under its power. . . . The quest of the historical Jesus is an act of truthfulness on the part of Protestant Christianity. My presentation of its course makes an epoch of scholarly Protestant theology live again for future generations. May these share with their predecessors the determination to be truthful, and thereby be assured that unflinching truthfulness is an essential part of real religion.

Chapter 1: The Problem

[3] When, at some future day, our period of civilization lies closed and completed before the eyes of later generations, German theology will stand out as a great, a unique phenomenon in the mental and spiritual life of our time. For only in the German temperament can there be found in the same perfection the living complex of conditions and factors—of philosophical thought, critical acumen, historical insight, and religious feeling—without which no deep theology is possible.

And the greatest achievement of German theology is the critical investigation of the life of Jesus. What it has accomplished here has laid down the conditions and determined the course of the religious thinking of the future.

In the history of doctrine its work has been negative; it has, so to speak, cleared the site for a new edifice of religious thought. In describing how the ideas of Jesus were taken possession of by the Greek spirit, it was tracing the growth of something that must necessarily become strange to us, and, as a matter of fact, has become strange to us. . . . We have not yet arrived at any reconciliation between modern thought and history—only between half history and half thought. What the ultimate goal towards which we are moving will be, what will bring new life and new regulative principles to coming centuries, we do not know. . . .

[5] The historical investigation of the life of Jesus did not take its rise from a purely historical interest; it turned to the Jesus of history as an ally in the struggle against the tyranny of dogma. Afterwards, when it was freed from this pathos, it sought to present the historical Jesus in a form intelligible to its own time. . . . [6] Thus each successive epoch of theology found its own thoughts in Jesus; that was, indeed, the only way in which it could make him live. . . . The stronger the love, or the stronger the hate, the more lifelike is the figure which is produced. For hate as well as love can write a Life of Jesus, and the greatest of them are written with hate: those of Reimarus, the Wolfenbüttel Fragmentist, and that of David Friedrich

1. Lambarene, 1950.

Strauss. It was hate not so much of the person of Jesus as of the supernatural nimbus with which it was so easy to surround him, and with which he had in fact been surrounded. They were eager to picture him as an ordinary person, to strip from him the robes of splendour with which he had been apparelled, and clothe him once more with the coarse garments in which he had walked in Galilee.

And their hate sharpened their historical insight. They advanced the study of the subject more than all the others put together. But for the offence which they gave, the science of historical theology would not stand where it does today.

[7] . . . The others, those who tried to bring Jesus to life at the call of love, found it a cruel task to be honest. The critical study of the life of Jesus was a school of honesty [*die Schule der Wahrhaftigkeit*] for theology. The world had never seen before, and will never see again, a struggle for truth so full of pain and renunciation as that which the Lives of Jesus of the last hundred years contain. . . . The problem of the life of Jesus has no analogy in the field of history. No historical school has ever laid down canons for the investigation of this problem, no professional historian has ever lent his aid to theology in dealing with it. Every ordinary method of historical investigation proves inadequate to the complexity of the conditions. The standards of ordinary historical science are inadequate here, its methods not immediately applicable. The historical study of the life of Jesus has had to create its own methods for itself. . . .

The cause of this lies in the nature of the sources of the life of Jesus, and in the character of our knowledge of the contemporary religious world of thought. . . .

[10] If old Reimarus were to come back again, he might confidently give himself out to be the latest of the moderns, for his work rests upon a recognition of the exclusive importance of eschatology, such as only recurs again in Johannes Weiss. . . . From Strauss down to the 1890s there was no real progress, if one takes into consideration only the complete Lives of Jesus which appeared. But a number of separate problems took a more clearly defined form, so that in the end the general problem suddenly moved forward, as it seemed, with a jerk. . . . The constructions of Reimarus and Bruno Bauer have no solidity; they are mere products of the imagination. But there is much more historical ability in their clear grasp of a single definite problem, which has blinded them to all else, than there is in the circumstantial works of Beyschlag and Bernard Weiss.

Chapter 2: Hermann Samuel Reimarus

[14] Before Reimarus, no one had attempted to form a historical conception of the life of Jesus. Luther had not even felt the need to gain a clear idea of the order of the recorded events. . . . There had been nothing to prepare the world for a work of such power as that of Reimarus. . . .

[15] To say that the fragment on "The Aims of Jesus and His Disciples" is a magnificent piece of work is barely to do it justice. This essay is not only one of [16] the greatest events in the history of criticism, it is also a masterpiece of world literature. The language is as a rule crisp and terse, pointed and epigrammatic, the language of a man who is not engaged in literary composition but is wholly concerned with the facts. At times, however, it rises to heights of passionate feeling, and then it is as though the fires of a volcano were painting lurid pictures upon dark clouds. Seldom has there been a hate so eloquent, a scorn so lofty; but then it is seldom that a work has been written in the just consciousness of so absolute a superiority to contemporary opinion. And throughout there is dignity and serious purpose; Reimarus's work is no pamphlet.

Lessing could not, of course, accept its standpoint. His view of revelation, and his conception of the person of Jesus, were much deeper than those of the Fragmentist. He was a thinker; Reimarus only a historian. But this was the first time that a really historical mind, thoroughly conversant with the sources, had undertaken the criticism of the tradition. It was Lessing's greatness that he grasped the significance of this criticism and felt that it must lead either to the destruction or to the re-casting of the idea of revelation. He recognized that the introduction of the historical element would transform and deepen rationalism. . . .

[17] [Lessing] called "for someone who should be as nearly the ideal defender of religion as the Fragmentist was the ideal assailant." At one point, with prophetic insight into the future, he says: "The Christian traditions must be explained by the

inner truth of Christianity, and no written traditions can give it that inner truth, if it does not itself possess it."

Reimarus takes as his starting-point the question of the content of the preaching of Jesus. "We have reason," he says, "to draw an absolute distinction between the teaching of the apostles in their writings and what Jesus himself proclaimed and taught in his own lifetime." What belongs to the preaching of Jesus is clearly to be recognized. It is contained in two phrases of identical meaning, "Repent, and believe the gospel," or, as it is put elsewhere, "Repent, for the kingdom of heaven is at hand."

However, the kingdom of heaven must be understood 'according to Jewish ways of thought.' Neither John the Baptist nor Jesus ever explain this expression; therefore they must have been content to have it understood in its known and customary sense. That means that Jesus took his stand within the Jewish religion, and accepted its messianic expectations without in any way correcting them. . . .

[18] If, therefore, we desire to gain a historical understanding of Jesus' teaching, we must leave behind what we learned in our catechism about the metaphysical divine sonship, the Trinity, and similar dogmatic conceptions, and go out into a wholly Jewish world of thought. Only those who carry the teachings of the catechism back into the preaching of the Jewish Messiah will arrive at the idea that Jesus was the founder of a new religion. . . .

[22] We can well understand that [Reimarus's] work must have given offence when it appeared, for it is a polemic, not an objective historical study. But we have no right to dismiss it in a word as a Deistic production, as Otto Schmiedel, for example, does; it is time that Reimarus came into his own, time for us to recognize a historical performance of no mean order in this piece of Deistic polemics. His work is perhaps the most splendid achievement in the whole course of the historical investigation of the life of Jesus, for he was the first to grasp that the world of thought in which Jesus moved historically was essentially eschatological. There is some justification for the animosity which flames up in his writing. This historical truth had taken possession of his mind with such overwhelming force that he could no longer [23] understand his contemporaries, and could no longer assent to their belief that it was directly derived from the preaching of Jesus, as they claimed.

What added to the offence was that he saw the eschatology in a wrong perspective. He held that the messianic ideal which dominated the preaching of Jesus was that of a political ruler, the son of David. All his other mistakes are simply the consequence of this fundamental error. It was, of course, a mere makeshift hypothesis [*Nothypothese*] to derive the beginnings of Christianity from an imposture. Historical science was not at that time sufficiently advanced to show even to the man who had divined the fundamentally eschatological character of the preaching of Jesus the historical solution of the problem; it took more than a hundred and twenty years to fill in the chasm which Reimarus had been forced to bridge with that makeshift hypothesis of his.

Measured by the basic instincts of Reimarus, the whole of theology down to Johannes Weiss appears retrograde. Throughout, it ignores the principles that Jesus, as a historical personality, is to be regarded, not as the founder of a new religion, but as the final product of the eschatological and apocalyptic thought of late Judaism. Every sentence of Johannes Weiss's *Jesus' Proclamation of the Kingdom of God* (1892) is a vindication, a rehabilitation, of Reimarus as a historical thinker. . . . Reimarus was the first, after eighteen centuries of misconception, again to have an inkling of what eschatology really was. Then theology lost sight of it again, and it was not until after the lapse of more than a hundred years that it came in view of eschatology, once more, now in its true form, so far as that can be historically determined, and only after it had been led astray, almost to the last, in all its historical researches by the sole mistake of Reimarus—the assumption that the eschatology was earthly and political in character. . . . Though the solution offered by Reimarus may be wrong, the observations from which he starts out are, beyond question, right, because the primary observation is genuinely historical. . . .

[24] The fact is that there are some who are historians by the grace of God, who from their mother's womb have an instinctive feeling for the real. Through all the intricacy and confusion of reported fact they follow the pathway of reality,

like a stream which, despite the rocks that encumber its course and the windings of its valley, finds its way inevitably to the sea. No erudition can supply the place of this historical instinct . . . .

[25] Reimarus had discredited progressive theology. Students—so Semler tells us in his preface—became unsettled and sought other callings. The great Halle theologian (born in 1725), the pioneer of the historical view of the canon, the precursor of Baur in the reconstruction of primitive Christianity, was urged to do away with the offence.[2] . . .

[26] [Reimarus] had no predecessors; nor had he any disciples. His work is one of those supremely great works which pass and leave no trace, because they are before their time; later generations pay them a just tribute of admiration, but owe them no gratitude. . . . Thus the magnificent overture in which all the motifs of the future historical treatment of the life of Jesus are announced breaks off with a sudden discord, remains isolated and incomplete, and leads to nothing further.

Chapter 25: Conclusion

[478] . . . The study of the Life of Jesus has had a curious history. It set out in quest of the historical Jesus, believing that when it had found him it could bring him straight into our time as a teacher and saviour. It loosed the bands by which for centuries he had been riveted to the stony rocks of ecclesiastical doctrine, and rejoiced to see life and movement coming into the figure once more, and the historical Jesus advancing, as it seemed, to meet it. But he did not stay; he passed by our time and returned to his own. What surprised and dismayed the theology of the last forty years was that, despite all forced and arbitrary interpretations, it [479] could not keep him in our time, but had to let him go. He returned to his own time by the same inevitable necessity by which the liberated pendulum returns to its original position.

The historical foundation of Christianity as built up by rationalistic, by liberal and by modern theology no longer exists; but that does not mean that Christianity has lost its historical foundation. The work which historical theology thought it had to carry out, and which fell to pieces just as it was nearing completion, was only the brick facing of the real immovable historical foundation, a foundation which is independent of any historical knowledge or justification because it is simply there [*weil es eben da ist*].

Jesus means something to our world because a mighty spiritual force [*Strömung*] streams forth from him and flows through our time also. This fact can neither be shaken nor confirmed by any historical discovery.

The mistake was to suppose that Jesus could come to mean more to our time by entering into it as a man like ourselves. But that is not possible. First because such a Jesus never existed. Secondly because, although historical knowledge can no doubt introduce greater clarity into an existing spiritual life, it can never call life into existence. History can destroy the present; it can reconcile the present with the past; it can even to a certain extent transport the present into the past; but to contribute to the making of the present is not given to it.

But it is impossible to overestimate the value of what German research into the Life of Jesus has accomplished. It is a uniquely great expression of truthfulness, one of the most significant events in the whole intellectual and spiritual life of humanity. . . . And yet the time of doubt was bound to come. We modern theologians are too proud of our historical method, too proud of our historical Jesus, too confident in our belief in the spiritual gains which our historical theology can bring to the world. The thought that we could build up by the increase of historical knowledge a new and vigorous Christianity and set free new spiritual forces rules us like a fixed idea, and prevents us from seeing that the task which we have grappled with and in some measure discharged is only one of the intellectual preliminaries of the great religious task. We thought that we had to lead our time by a roundabout way through the historical Jesus, as we understood him, in order to bring it to the Jesus who is a spiritual power in the present. This detour has now been closed by true history.

There was a danger of our thrusting ourselves between people and the Gospels, and refusing to leave the individual alone with the sayings of Jesus.

There was also the danger that we should offer

2. Schweitzer refers here to Johann Salomo Semler's book *Beantwortung der Fragmente eines Ungenannten insbesondere vom Zweck Jesu und seiner Jünger* (Halle: Erziehungsinstitut, 1779), ed. by Dirk Fleischer (Spenner: Waltrop, 2003).

them a Jesus who was too small, because we had forced him into conformity with our human standards and [480] human psychology. . . .

In the process we ourselves have been enfeebled, and have robbed our own thoughts of their vigour in order to project them back into history and make them speak to us out of the past. It is nothing less than a disaster for modern theology that it mixes history with everything and ends by being proud of the skill with which it finds its own thoughts again in the past. . . .

What does the historical Jesus mean for us when we dissociate him from all false justification of the past by the present? We are immediately aware that his personality, despite all that is strange and enigmatic in it, has great significance for us. These is something there for all periods of time, so long as the world exists. However much opinions and knowledge may be transformed, there is something which may profoundly enrich our religion. This elementary feeling must find clear expression. It must not be allowed to lapse into dogmatic assertions and empty phrases, nor mislead historical research into making constant and futile attempts to modernize Jesus, for this merely weakens and misinterprets that element in his message which was determined by the time in which he lived, and cannot increase his greatness for us. . . .

[487] He comes to us as one unknown, without a name, as of old, by the lakeside, he came to those men who did not know who he was. He says the same words, "Follow me!," and sets us to those tasks which he must fulfil in our time. He commands. And to those who hearken to him, whether wise or unwise, he will reveal himself in the peace, the labours, the conflicts and the suffering that they may experience in his fellowship, and as an ineffable mystery they will learn who he is. . . .

29.

Karl Barth (1886–1968)

Since the First World War as a Reformed pastor in a Swiss village, since 1921 as a theology professor teaching in various German universities, and from 1935 until his retirement in 1962 from the University of Basel, Karl Barth, through numerous publications, conferences, and lectures, decisively sought to reorient Protestant (and Christian) theology in the direction of a biblical, reformatory theology. Sound theology, in his eyes, is bound to Scripture, seeks to listen to it and to understand its message. Barth was convinced that modern exegesis had gone astray, losing sight of the content of Scripture and of its interpretation, which must be not only historical but also theological. As a consequence of a retrieval of a theological exegesis, that is, an interpretation that focuses on the "subject matter" (*Sache*) to which Scripture witnesses, Barth was often perceived, incorrectly (even by his former teacher Adolf von Harnack), as an opponent of the modern exegetical methods (Rumscheidt 1972). His view was, rather, that historical and critical exegesis is an indispensable preparation for the understanding of the Bible; but understanding Scripture implies a theological interpretation that wrestles with the text and what it points to or what it gives voice to—without containing it—namely, God's own word. And so Barth lamented that much historical and critical exegesis, in modernity, stops too early in its quest to understand the Scriptures.

Barth's prefaces to the two editions of his *Epistle to the Romans* (1919, 1922), printed below, belong to the classic texts of twentieth-century Christian theology. Especially the preface to the second edition (1922) raises anew the question of what it means to understand the Bible (and any other text), and thus *Romans* has been described by Hans-Georg Gadamer as "a kind of hermeneutical manifesto" (Gadamer 2003, 509).

The publication of the second edition of *Romans* sparked an important discussion between Barth and Rudolf Bultmann, not only on "theological exegesis" (*Sachexegese*) but also on the critical dimension of such an exegesis (*Sachkritik*). Bultmann was convinced that the biblical text, once it has led us to understand what the text means, has to be criticized for what it (inadequately) says. And so, already in the early 1920s, it was clear that

Barth was not ready to criticize Scripture in the same way as Bultmann thought possible and necessary. In Barth's mind, before we ask (critical) questions of Scripture, its truth has already confronted us with its own questions. The subject of criticism is, as it were, inverted or reversed: it is no longer the human interpreter!

Barth, thus, resisted the challenge history posed to theology and vigorously promoted an unapologetically theological interpretation of Scripture. Besides Scripture, Barth wished for theology to rediscover the Christian tradition as a whole, beyond each theologian's proclivities.

In addition to the excerpts from the two prefaces to the Römerbrief, the reader will find, below, some selections from Barth's book *Protestant Theology in the Nineteenth Century: Its Background and History*, trans. Brian Cozens and John Bowden (Grand Rapids: Eerdmans, 2002) and from his *Church Dogmatics* IV/1, trans. Geoffrey W. Bromiley, ed. Geoffrey W. Bromiley and Thomas F. Torrance (Edinburgh: T&T Clark, 1956; 2004).

THE EPISTLE TO THE ROMANS[1]

Preface to the First Edition (August 1918)

Paul, as a child of his age, addressed his contemporaries. It is, however, *far more* important that, as prophet and apostle of the kingdom of God, he veritably speaks to all people of every age. The differences between then and now, there and here, no doubt require careful consideration. But the purpose of such investigation can only be to recognize that these differences are, ultimately, *without* significance. The historical-critical method of biblical investigation has its rightful place: it is concerned with preparatory work for understanding—and this can never be superfluous. But if I was forced to choose between it and the old doctrine of inspiration, I would without hesitation opt for the latter: it has a greater, deeper, *more important* legitimacy, for it orients in the direction of the work of understanding, that is, towards that which, when it is left out, renders all preparatory work useless. I am glad not to have to choose between the two. But my whole attention has been directed at seeing *through* the historical into the spirit of the Bible, which is the eternal Spirit. What was once a serious matter is still serious today, and what today is serious—and not merely accidental or odd—stands in immediate connection with what was once a serious matter. Our questions, if we rightly understand ourselves, are Paul's questions, and Paul's answers, when their light shines for us, must be our answers.

> Truth was found long ago,
> A noble community of souls it bound.
> The old truth— grasp it![2]

The understanding of history is an ongoing conversation, which always strives to become more earnest and penetrating, between the wisdom of yesterday and the wisdom of tomorrow, which is the same wisdom. . . . It is certain that all epochs which hungered and thirsted after righteousness were naturally prone to involve themselves, with regard to the subject matter [*sachlich*], with Paul, instead of standing at a leisurely distance away from him. Perhaps we are now entering such a time. If this turns out to be the case, then this book may, already now, render a certain, though limited, service.

Preface to the Second Edition (September 1921)

. . . I now turn to a different side. I have been accused of being a "resolute enemy of *historical criticism*." Would it not be better to discuss the matter calmly, rather than use such vehement

1. The translations have been modified here and there on the basis of the original German version.

2. From one of Goethe's late poems, *Vermächtnis* ("A Legacy"), §8, found at the end of the second book of *Wilhelm Meister's Journeyman Years* (1821, 2nd ed. 1829).

words? I have, it is true, protested against recent commentaries of the epistle to the Romans. The protest was directed not only against those originating in the so-called "historical-critical" school, but also, for example, against the commentaries of Zahn and Kühl. But it is not historical criticism which I am protesting against. On the contrary, I acknowledge once again explicitly both its necessity and legitimacy. My complaint is that recent commentators confine themselves to an explanation [*Erklärung*] of the text which seems to me to be no explanation at all, but merely the first step towards a commentary. Recent commentaries contain no more than an ascertainment of "what lies there" in the text, through a rendering and a paraphrase of the Greek words and groups of words in their corresponding German equivalents, through philological and archeological elucidations of events, and through a more or less plausible arrangement of each detail in such a way that it may befit a historical and psychological pragmatism. . . . Jülicher and Lietzmann, not to mention conservative scholars, intend quite clearly to press beyond this preliminary work in order to *understand* [*verstehen*] Paul, that is, in order to disclose how what lies in the text, not only can somehow be repeated [*nachgesprochen*] in Greek or in German, but also how it can be thought about [*nachgedacht*] and what may be its *meaning*. It is *at this point*, and not on the obvious need to use historical criticism in the course of the preparatory work, that the difference between us appears. I follow attentively and gratefully the historians as they are occupied with this preliminary explanatory work. . . . When, however, I consider their attempts at a proper *understanding* and *explaining* [*Verstehen und Erklären*], I am again and again astonished by how little they claim for their work. By proper understanding and explaining I mean the practice which Luther exercised with intuitive certainty in his interpretations, Calvin's way of setting a visible, systematic aim for his exegesis, and what was clearly at least attempted by recent scholars such as Hofmann, J. T. Beck, Godet, and Schlatter. . . . Any handling of the text which takes its *subject matter* [*sachlich*] seriously requires the use of the leverages and jacks of a relentless and yet supple, dialectical movement. The critical historians must be *more critical*! *Under*standing "what stands *here*" requires more than a disjointed *appraisal* (an appraisal, moreover, determined by the exegete's own arbitrary point of view) of words and groups of words in the text. One understands the text, on the contrary, only when one traces, with *as much* poise and docility *as possible*, the inner tension [*die innere Spannung*] of the concepts which the text presents with more or less clarity. In relation to historical documents, criticism (κρίνειν) means for me the measuring of all of the words and groups of words by the subject matter [*Sache*] of which these words are manifestly (as it appears) speaking. . . . The relation of the words to the Word in the words ought to be uncovered. . . . I am not a "pneumatic" theologian, as he [Jülicher] has called me. I am no "bitter enemy of historical criticism."

PROTESTANT THEOLOGY IN THE NINETEENTH CENTURY: ITS BACKGROUND AND HISTORY[3]

Foreword (September 1946)

[xii] . . . Secondly, and more profoundly, I have allowed publication because I have constantly had occasion to wish and suggest that the attitude and approach of the younger generation of Protestant theologians to the period of the Church that is just past might be rather different from that which they now often seem to regard, somewhat impetuously, as the norm—misunderstanding the guidance they have received from me. I would be very pleased if they were (to put it simply) to show a little more love towards those who have gone before us, despite the degree of alienation they feel from them. I made a few remarks to this effect in 1932–1933, when I introduced the lectures. I hope that my own approach here will make clear to one and all that the better exegesis and dogmatic theology for which we are striving again today must prove itself by the way in which its advocates acquire not only a sharper but also a more impartial eye for the historical reality of their fellow-theologians of yesterday and the day before. We need openness towards and interest in particular figures with their individual characteristics,

3. Translated by Brian Cozens and John Bowden (London: SCM Press, 2001).

an understanding of the circumstances in which they worked, much patience and also much humor in the face of their obvious limitations and weaknesses, a little grace in expressing even the most profound criticism and finally, even in the worst cases, a certain tranquil delight that they were as they were. *Que voulez-vous? Le bon Dieu l'a fait comme cela*, remarked a Moroccan soldier to me about a human fellow-creature with whom he was not exactly pleased. And after all this, perhaps we ourselves will be portrayed, discussed and assessed by a posterity that is better instructed than ourselves! Above all, such an approach is in accord with the knowledge of the divine judgment on all that is called the flesh, which has rightly and necessarily come alive among us in such a different way. Whence comes historical rectitude, if not from here?

Chapter 1[4]

[1] . . . We know history only when and in that something happens in us and for us, perhaps even happens against us; we know it only when and in that an event concerns us, so concerns us that we are there, that we participate in it. Any knowledge of history that proved to be merely seeing, observing, establishing, is a contradiction in itself. Certainly the knowledge of human action—and that is what history is about—involves seeing, observing, establishing, but [2] not in isolated theory. The theory of practice is the only possible theory where history is concerned. It is a seeing, observing, establishing where we ourselves are taken up in a particular movement, taken up in an action of our own which somehow encounters, corresponds to or even contradicts the action of another. We know history in that another's action somehow becomes a question to which our own action has to give some sort of answer. Without this responsible reaction to being questioned, our knowledge of history would be knowledge of facts, but not of living people; it would not be history but a form of science. . . . Neither the misguided theologian nor even the opponent of theology are excluded as incompetent—it is impossible to be an opponent of theology without being a theologian oneself—but only the idle onlooker who thinks that he can see and talk about something that does not concern him. Here, as anywhere, this onlooker sees nothing at all of history as such, of the event, no matter how carefully and widely the net of things that have happened is spread before him. If his eyes are to be opened and he is to be entitled to join in the discussion, he must be involved in the matter.

Now the matter, theology, is critical and systematic reflection on the presupposition of the Church's ministry of witness. . . . What is involved is always the hearing of the Word of God, documented in the Bible, in any given present, since that necessarily precedes any speaking. Because the present is continually changing, the theologian cannot be content with establishing [3] and communicating the results obtained by some classical period; his reflection must be renewed constantly. For this reason, serious theological work is forced, again and again, to begin from the beginning. However, as this is done, the theology of past periods, classical and less classical, also plays a part and demands a hearing. It demands a hearing as surely as it occupies a place with us in the context of the Church. The Church does not stand in a vacuum. Beginning from the beginning, however necessary, cannot be a matter of beginning off one's own bat. We have to remember the communion of saints, bearing and being borne by each other, asking and being asked, having to take mutual responsibility for and among the sinners gathered together in Christ. As regards theology, also, we cannot be in the Church without taking as much responsibility for the theology of the past as for the theology of the present. Augustine, Thomas Aquinas, Luther, Schleiermacher and all the rest are not dead, but living. They still speak and demand a hearing as living voices, as surely as we know that they and we belong together in the Church. They made in their time the same contribution to the task of the Church that is required of us today. As we make our contribution, they join in with theirs, and we cannot play our part today without allowing them to play theirs. Our responsibility is not only to God, to ourselves, to the people of today, to other living theologians, but to them also. There is no past in the Church, so there is no past in theology. "In him they all live." Only the heretic, indeed only the arch-heretic, the

4. From lectures given in the late 1920s and early 1930s.

one who is totally lost even for God's invisible Church, could really belong to the past and have nothing more to say to us. And we are in no position to identify such arch-heresy. Not even among avowed pagans, much less among Jews or suspect, even very suspect, Christians. All heretics are relatively heretical, so even those who have been branded heretics at one time or another and condemned for their avowed folly and wickedness must be allowed their say in theology. The theology of any period must be strong and free enough to give a calm, attentive and open hearing not only to the voices of the Church Fathers, not only to favourite voices, not only to the voices of the classical past, but to all voices of the past. God is the Lord of the Church. He is also the Lord of theology. We cannot anticipate which of our fellow-workers from the past are welcome in our own work and which are not. It may always be that we have special need of quite unsuspected (and among these, of quite unwelcome) voices in one sense or another. So history, the history of the Church, of doctrine and of theology, enters the theological workshop and becomes a theological task.

CHURCH DOGMATICS IV/1 (1953)[5]

[288] The well-known offence in the fact of the atonement does not exhaust itself in this problem of distance. We ought to be warned against too great or exclusive a preoccupation with this aspect by the fact that this problem which has become so acute within more recent Protestantism has, all things considered, more the character of a technical difficulty in thinking than of a spiritual or a genuine theological problem. In it it is only formally and not in substance, only incidentally and secondarily and not primarily and centrally, that the question concerns God and [289] ourselves, Jesus Christ and his cross and our reconciliation. It is a methodological question. . . . This does not prevent us from taking the problem of distance with the seriousness proper to it. What it does prevent us from doing is stopping at this discussion, as though it was there that we had to, and could, come to the decision which is necessary. What it does enjoin upon us is that we should consider the deeper presuppositions which we have to treat it we are to handle it rightly. . . .

[290] And now we have to ask whether our whole concern about our temporal distance from Jesus Christ, our indirect relationship to him, is not a genuine problem only in the sense that it represents a genuine [291] movement of flight from this encounter. Are we not putting up a technical difficulty, knowing all along that it is not this difficulty which oppresses us, but rather the concern that this difficulty is not so great that it cannot be removed, that it has in fact been removed?

Supposing our contemporaneity with the Word of God made flesh, with the Judge judged in our place, is already an event? Supposing the Christus *pro nobis nunc* is already *Christus pro nobis praesens nunc*, here and now, present with us? Supposing it is in fact incontrovertible, the most certain of all things, that he is present here and now for us in the full efficacy of what, according to the Gospel, he was and did then and there? Supposing that by him and in him our judgment has been accomplished? . . . The assault this makes on us is too violent and incisive. If all this is true and actual, it is clear that we have good reason to close our eyes to it, to keep as far from us as we can the knowledge of this truth and actuality.

And if there is a technical difficulty in the matter—the difficulty of making the contemporaneity of Jesus Christ with us and of us with him conceptually intelligible and perspicuous—do we not have good reason to occupy ourselves with it as much as possible, to see to it that its force remains? As long as we are occupied with this difficulty, we do not really need to worry about what has taken place and been done to us with the incarnation of the Son of God, in his appearance in our place, in his effective action for us now as well as then, and here as well as there. As long as we can question and discuss the presence of that once and for all event, as long as we can make it the most serious question how we can honestly accept as true today that which comes to us as the truth and actuality of something which happened then and which is maintained by others—so long we are obviously protected against the catastrophe which the knowledge of the content, the knowledge of the [292] *Christus pro nobis prasesens*, would mean

5. Translated by Geoffrey W. Bromiley, edited by Geoffrey W. Bromiley and Thomas F. Torrance (London: T&T Clark, 2004).

for us. We do not then have to notice that we are in exactly the same position as Peter in the boat and the women at the empty tomb and the shepherds of Bethlehem, that we can only tremble as on the day of the Lord which has dawned for us, that we can only be afraid and terrified. We find ourselves in a relatively sheltered corner where we can dream that we are still in some way existing *ante Christum* since he is not there for us, where we can imagine that it is not yet all up with us; and all because we think that we are excused and safeguarded by the "broad, ugly ditch" of temporal distance; all because of the existence of Lessing's question. It is understandable that we have a supreme interest in trying to make out that our relationship to Jesus Christ is purely historical and therefore mediated and indirect, that it is a relationship of mere recollection. . . . We need all this because it seems to create a delay. The genuineness of Lessing's question cannot be disputed in that it springs from a very genuine need: the need to hide ourselves (like Adam and Eve in the garden of Eden) from Jesus Christ as he makes himself present and mediates himself to us; the need to keep our eyes closed to that about which we ask with such solemn concern, taking ourselves and our "honesty" with such frightful seriousness; the need to safeguard ourselves as far as this movement of flight allows against the directness in which he does in fact confront us, against his presence, and the consequences which it threatens.

In any other sense than this the question of Lessing, the question of historical distance, is not a genuine question. In a singular way it derives and has its real weight from the very fact that it is soluble and has actually been solved. . . . [293] The movement of flight into Lessing's problem is unnecessary. In and with the overcoming of the real and spiritual problem of the relationship between Jesus Christ and us, the technical problem of the relationship between the then and there and the now and here is also soluble and has in fact been solved.

30.

Rudolf Bultmann (1884–1976)

Rudolf Bultmann is among the twentieth-century scholars who excelled both as biblical exegetes and as systematic theologians. Such scholars were not legion, and he was arguably among the most significant of them. His influence on the study of the New Testament and the interpretation of the Christian faith has been enormous, even if in recent decades (roughly since the 1980s) his influence as a constructive theologian has receded, giving way to a very diverse array of political, liberationist, feminist, contextual, postliberal, revisionist, and public theologies.[1]

Bultmann was trained by some of the best minds in modern Protestant theology and exegesis: Johannes Weiss (who convinced him of the eschatological nature of Jesus's message), Adolf von Harnack, Wilhelm Heitmüller (1869–1926), Adolf Schlatter (1852–1938), and especially, with regard to systematic theology, Wilhelm Herrmann.

But in the early 1920s he became close to the new dialectical school, led by Karl Barth and Friedrich Gogarten, and this led him to clarify his stance relative to the theology he had been taught. Bultmann would eventually articulate an understanding of God's action in history that sought to preserve the indirectness of revelation, which is always hidden—only faith discerns it. He stated this view with the expression "paradoxical identity," by which he denotes the simultaneity between worldly, historical events or realities and God's eschatological act. Bultmann saw a fundamental coincidence between systematic and historical theology, as well as between theology and exegesis, since in his opinion the interpreter's relation to the subject matter that comes to expression in the texts is the same for theology as for history (Bultmann 1968, 253; Morgan 1973, 37). God's word is present "as the one who has become flesh, and only as this one is it now present" (Bultmann 1953, 40; Congdon 2015, 485). This was one way of opposing any objectification of God (one of Bultmann's greatest concerns throughout his life as a theologian). With his demythologizing program of 1941, Bultmann tried to salvage the critical approach of modern, liberal theology against certain biblicist and orthodox theologies—often asso-

1. For an introduction to these theological schools or movements, see David F. Ford (with Rachel Muers), ed., *The Modern Theologians: An Introduction to Christian Theology* (Oxford: Wiley-Blackwell, 2008).

ciated with Barth, or perhaps rather with Barth's disciples—that were dominant at the time within the Confessing Church (*Bekennende Kirche*), but also against the new German mythology and ideology of the National Socialist regime. And so Bultmann fought on two fronts: against a certain modern rejection of theological concerns by "strict" historians of early Christianity (such as William Wrede) or by Ernst Troeltsch, and against a rejection of rigorous historical method by some of Barth's disciples (and perhaps by Barth himself).

The selection below comes from *Faith and Understanding*, trans. Louise Pettibone Smith (Philadelphia: Fortress Press, 1987).

"LIBERAL THEOLOGY AND THE LATEST THEOLOGICAL MOVEMENT" (1924)

[29] I. Liberal theology owed its distinctive character chiefly to the primacy of *historical interest*, and in that field it made its greatest contributions. These contributions were not limited to the clarification of the historical picture. They were especially important for the development *of the critical sense*, that is, for freedom and veracity. We who have come from a background of liberal theology could never have become theologians nor remained such had we not encountered in that liberal theology [30] the earnest search for radical truth. We felt in the work of orthodox academic theology of all shades an urge towards compromise within which our intellectual and spiritual life would necessarily be fragmented. We can never forget our debt of gratitude to G. Krüger for that often cited article of his on "unchurchly theology." For he saw the task of theology to be to imperil souls, to lead people into doubt, to shatter all naïve credulity.[2] Here, we felt, was the atmosphere of truth in which alone we could breathe.

But to what result has the course of historical criticism actually led? If it was at first directed by a confidence that such critical research would free people from the burden of dogmatics and lead to a comprehension of the real figure of Jesus on which faith could be based, this confidence soon proved to be delusion. Historical research can never lead to any result which could serve as a basis for faith, for *all its results have only relative validity*. How widely the pictures of Jesus presented by liberal theologians differ from one another! How uncertain is all knowledge of "the historical Jesus"! Is he really within the scope of our knowledge? Here research ends with a large question mark—and here it *ought* to end.

The error is not that people did this historical work and obtained results which are more or less radical; rather, it is that they did not understand the significance of such work nor the meaning of the inquiry.

[31] . . . There can be no question of discarding historical criticism. But we must understand its true significance. It is needed to train us for freedom and veracity—not only by freeing us from a specific traditional conception of history, but because it frees us from bondage to every historical construction which is within the scope of historical science, and brings us to the realization that the world which faith wills to grasp is absolutely unattainable by means of scientific research.

This truth becomes even clearer when a second error in the historical understanding of liberal theology is recognized. It forgets not only that all the results it presents within its overall picture of reality have merely a relative validity, but also that all historical phenomena which are subject to this kind of historical investigation are only relative entities, *entities which exist only within an immense interrelated complex*. Nothing which stands within this interrelationship can claim absolute value. Even the historical Jesus is a phenomenon among other phenomena, not an absolute entity. Liberal theology has indeed recognized this conclusion up to a certain point. It speaks of the historical Jesus with great assurance, but in terms which do not ascribe an absolute value to him. Again it is Troeltsch who speaks most unambiguously. On page 14 of the work [32] already cited,[3] we read

2. [*Original footnote*] Gustav Krüger, "Die unkirchliche Theologie," in *Die christliche Welt* 14 (1900), col. 804–7.
3. [*Original footnote*] E. Troeltsch, *Die Bedeutung der Geschichtlichkeit Jesu für den Glauben* (1911).

the plain statement that there cannot be a *necessary* binding of the Christian faith to the person of Jesus. Faith in God leads to acknowledgment of the person of Jesus, not vice versa.

But here again the final result is compromise. We are told that, almost as by a law of social psychology, the Christian church, like every religious organization, requires a cult with a concrete center. The figure of Christ is such a center. "The linking of the Christian *idea* to the central position of Jesus in cult and teaching is not a conceptual necessity derived logically from the idea of salvation. But in terms of social psychology it is indispensable for the cult, for action, for proselytizing. That indispensability is sufficient justification for the assertion of the link" (p. 30).

A statement of that kind makes it entirely clear that *Christianity* is understood as *a phenomenon of this world, subject to the laws of social psychology*. It is equally clear that such a conception runs exactly counter to the Christian view. Although Troeltsch's view may to some extent be justified—only orthodoxy would dispute that—certainly it is not *theology*, not if *God* is the subject of theology and the theologian is speaking as a *Christian*.

That such a conception could be offered and accepted as theology is possible partly because no objection was made to the inclusion of the person of Jesus in the complex of general historical interrelations. Indeed, it was acceptable as theology because of the belief that *the revelation of God in history could be perceived precisely within this nexus of relations*. Therefore it is possible to speak of a "pantheism of *history*" in liberal theology, analogous to a pantheism of nature. . . .

[49] It is not surprising that such disregard of what is essentially Christian has not remained unopposed within liberal theology. It is not only research into the history of religion with its attention focused on what is characteristic in historical phenomena which has registered opposition to the unrestrained rationalization and moralization of Christian ideas. Rudolf Otto's book, *The Idea of the Holy*, in particular, resulted from the theological situation very much as did the protest of Barth, Gogarten and their circle. Otto's designation of God as the "wholly Other" and his emphasis on "creature feeling" as the essential element of religious piety are characteristic of that protest. . . .

[52] In view of the whole situation presented here, we can understand why Barth refuses to assume a definite theological position.[4] Naturally when he is engaged in a theological argument, he cannot avoid adopting a position. Yet there are good grounds for his refusal. One reason is that the refusal is an expression of the truth that faith, the exposition of which is theology, is not an actual position which someone, even if he is a theologian, *can* take. In practice faith always happens as an act of God; and seen from the human point of view it is the abandonment of every position. Faith is the supremely paradoxical cry: "I believe, Lord help my unbelief" (Mark 9:24). But then it follows that because theology can be nothing other than the exposition of faith, no concepts of knowledge which have meaning can be gained from it apart from the miraculous actualization of faith. The subject of theology is God. Theology speaks of God because it speaks of the human as he stands before God. That is, theology speaks out of faith.

4. [*Original footnote*] *Zwischen den Zeiten* 1 (1923):3–4.

31.

Marie-Dominique Chenu (1895–1990)

Marie-Dominique Chenu, OP, was one of the most significant twentieth-century specialists on Thomas Aquinas. But unlike some of the scholars specializing in Thomas Aquinas in the late nineteenth and twentieth centuries, he was not a strict Thomist, nor a neo-Thomist. Chenu, who did not believe in any *theologia perennis*, that is, in any theology that is immune to the flux of time, sought to read Thomas Aquinas in his (Thomas's) context. He had, moreover, a deep sense of the religious experience that nourishes Christian theology, and thus refused any theological reflection that severs theology from faith as act. But, in the wake of the modernist crisis, to claim that any theology is historical smacked of relativism and subjectivism among certain Thomist theologians, and thus Chenu got into trouble.[1] His programmatic lecture "A School of Theology: Le Saulchoir," given in 1936 and privately distributed to friends a year later as a text, was placed on the index of forbidden books in 1942, and Chenu lost his position of rector (*régent*) of the Dominican house of studies of Le Saulchoir (formerly near Tournai in Belgium; since 1939, just outside Paris) (Alberigo 1985, 23). Chenu was comforted by the cardinal of Paris, Emmanuel Suhard, who said to him, with deep foresight, "Don't be upset, Little Father, in twenty years time everyone will be speaking as you do now" (Rémond 1985, 8). This was not the end of Chenu's difficulties with Rome: in 1954 he was asked to leave his teaching position and move to Le Havre, in Northern France.

Yves Congar described his fellow Dominican brother well when he acknowledged "his extraordinary capacity toward intellectual awakening" (Congar 1971, 773). Chenu, with his interpretation of the utter historicity of the Christian faith, that is, of the fact that "history is not the temporary scaffold of an eternal contemplation," believed that "the Christian commitment in history is no optional add-on to a pure faith hunched over its divine

1. Claude Geffré mentions "his [Chenu's] struggle to affirm the historicity of theology in the midst of the antimodernist obsession of those years, i.e. at a time when people were soon suspected of relativism and subjectivism when they sought to take seriously human experience and history." Geffré, "Théologie de l'incarnation et théologie des signes des temps," in *Marie-Dominique Chenu: Moyen-Âge et modernité*, ed. Joseph Doré et al. (Paris: Centre d'études du Saulchoir, 1997), 134.

object, for this object is itself God's Word in time" (Chenu 1964, 675). These insights, among others, had a deep influence on Gustavo Gutiérrez (b. 1928), one of the founders and leading thinkers of liberation theology.

Chenu's *Une école de théologie: Le Saulchoir* (1937) was published, with several accompanying essays, in French in 1985 (Paris: Cerf). The present English translation, which follows the French edition's pagination, was made by Fr. Joseph A. Komonchak.

UNE ÉCOLE DE THÉOLOGIE: LE SAULCHOIR (1937)

[132] This is why in organizing the theological task, the study of the sources of faith is the master-discipline. If the speculative theologians showed indifference, even bad temper, towards this study, it was because, unconsciously or not, they regarded their systematic construction as an intelligibility which stood by itself, definitively acquired, the result of an argument that follows an autonomous logic. If a more careful inventory of the given by exegetes, historians, and "positive" theologians discovered something, the speculatives passed over it and sometimes condemned it if they could not find a way to insert it into their closed system, thus committing not only a technical blunder but a sin against the law of their science by cutting it off from its ever fresh and ever active source. In principle at least, a philosopher may without harm overlook the history of philosophy, since it is not historians who furnish him with his material, but things themselves. But the theologian has no object outside of the *auditus fidei*, of which the historian, under the light of faith, furnishes him the inventory—not only a catalogue of propositions registered in some Denzinger, but living, copious material, always alive in the Church to which it is entrusted, pregnant with divine intelligibility.

If Christianity thus draws its reality not from metaphysics but from history, the theologian's first concern—first both in dignity and chronologically—is to know this history and to equip himself for it. This is not a transitory business, which one might hasten to abandon to specialists at the doorway of the laboratory of speculation; it is a permanent application in which the mind may delight. Neither is it a utilitarian apologetic, the science of the valets charged with defending the sacred Ark against the heretics and deniers of dogma; it means being substantively nourished at the very Word of God. Texts in theology are what experience is in science, said St. Thomas; they are the soil in which it is constantly coming alive and progressing in understanding. And even more than in science, this return is required, this "resolution," back to the given as to the *principles*, both light and object, in which any construction has its basis and meaning.

In such a conception of theology, Sacred Scripture and Tradition are not first of all repertoires of arguments for the use of the School and its disputed questions. They are first of all the *given*, which is to be examined, known, loved for itself, and all later speculations would be vain that did not seek to know this given better in all its resources of religious intelligibility. To exploit the texts of [133] St. Paul *in order to* demonstrate the physical causality of the sacraments, is to go backwards; physical causality is simply one way of fully conceiving St. Paul's sacramental realism. If I maintain the unity of being in Christ, it is not in order to apply to this singular case the real distinction between essence and existence; it is to safeguard the magnificent Christological mysticism of the Alexandrians, one of the greatest riches of Tradition in the eastern Churches. These are simple truisms, but they express the inviolable order of values, in contrast to the plan in so many textbooks where it really seems as if the Bible was given to us only to furnish arguments for the schoolmasters. That famous threefold plan by which a "thesis" in theology is established by *probatur ex Scriptura, probatur ex Traditione, probatur ex Ratione*, is simply the residue of a compromise between positive and speculative theology; in fact, it compromises both of them in a false symmetry in which the primacy of the given and the values of speculation are poorly arranged. Above all, by reducing it to the construction of schemes of "proofs," it compromises the full and enjoyable assimilation of the inexhaustible riches of Christian thought and experience, past and present, of which the texts and the institutions are full. . . .

Faith and History

If revelation occurs in time, in the course of history—a sacred history, but a history, centered on the historical fact [135] of the incarnation—, and if thus the revealed given is inscribed and offered in historical facts and texts, then we face a direct and brutal question: is not theology, like the faith which inspires it, subject to the judgements of historical criticism? And does not this in principle abandon the faith to relativism and thus involve the work of theology in a circle within which one can never rejoin the "Word of God"?

This is the whole problem of historical method and of how effectively to arrange exegesis and the history of dogmas in theological knowledge. We know what disquiet has weighed upon theology, for thirty years, not only on its orthodoxy, sorely attacked by Modernism, but on theology's internal working and on the balance in its program of instruction. An integral notion of faith and its economy permit us to deal with this problem and to set up this program with confident serenity.

Theology flows from faith; it is born in it and by it. It arises out of faith's weakness, out of the radical weakness of the mind's assent to propositions it does not see or measure. But theology also arises out of faith's strength, from that strength which the realistic perception of the mysterious divine reality stores in a soul in quest of possessing that reality, *substantia rerum sperandarum*. The arc of the believer does not in fact end at the dogmatic proposition, but at the very divine reality of which it is a human expression. This is not, then, a concept, formulas, a system of thought, but the One in whom I recognize the whole of my life, the delightful object of my happiness. Faith certainly is assent to propositions, authentic vehicles of its religious perception; but that is its misery, or rather the provisional misery of my mind, which only knows the truth, even divine truth, in propositions. Faith is, through them and thanks to them, adherence to what fulfills all desires, the one desire of my soul: happiness in the gift of God himself.

This realism of faith, so vigorously expressed by St. Paul in his witness to salvation in the knowledge of Christ, finds its psychological reason in the strictly supernatural character of the inner light, the "Word of God" in me. Knowledge of God in me, the Word of God is all grace, personal grace, putting me in dialogue and direct contact with Him, mysterious presence to which "the new man" has access, not because his reason led him there, but because God reveals himself, *sibi ipsi testis*. "Anyone who believes in the Son of God, has God's testimony in himself" (1 Jn 5:10). Transcendent and interior, it is not tied to either preaching or manifestation; it is not an historical assertion, [136] it is not entangled in time, even vis-à-vis Christ, since faith is precisely the operation that makes us "contemporaneous" with Christ; and if the Gospel comes to us through the continuity of time, it is not, for the eye of faith, a book of history, but truly the Word of God.

The theologian is a believer; he is a believer par excellence, and his task is carried out formally in the mystery into which his faith introduces him and not in the projection into human words of the Word of God. "Sacred doctrine" is the traditional term, to be taken in its proper sense, without which it will wind up being only a profane science, a profanation of the Word of God. The drama of the theologian's effort is precisely to maintain, in the radical fragility of the propositions in which he embodies it, the realistic perception of the mysterious reality of God: a dialectic in which his strength triumphs over his weakness—in faith. "There is no theology without a new birth." At this point, then, theology is nothing more than faith correlated to time; it is not rooted in history. Thus it is not the happy conclusion of a favorable historical criticism, on whose results one constructs a lovely scaffolding of "reasons." The revealed given, the theological given, is not "scientific": it is revealed. And if I attempt a science of it—what boldness!—this will not be by reinforcing its historical bases or by justifying them apologetically; it will be the "science of a believer." Otherwise, once again, we will have only a rational game played on the surface of the given, a theology without the Word of God. This is a cardinal point on which the organization and the spirit of theology both depend. At Le Saulchoir, Frs. Gardeil and Lemonnyer, fully aware of what was at stake, were the masters of this categorical stance.

Well, then, shall we ever rejoin history? Did we not say that Christianity draws its reality from history? Is it not the paradox of faith that, *substantia rerum sperandarum* [the substance of things hoped for], it only finds its object in a received teaching: *fides ex auditu* [faith from hearing]? The Word of God is given to us *in* human words, and supernatural faith is assent to definite propositions. The dogmatic formula is not a juridical statement, external to the revelation which it presents; it is the embodiment in concepts of the Word of God. This is the economy of this Word: it speaks humanly; it takes on the forms of the human mind and is produced in the mind in accord with all the conditions required by the mechanism of a psychology that is bound to the slow and heavy complexity of notions and judgements, bound to the categories of time and space, as the philosophers put it, engaged in a history. *Cognita sunt in cognoscente* [137] *ad modum cognoscentis* [things known are in the knower according to the mode of the knower]: to exclude God from this natural law of all knowledge, under the pretext that he is transcendent or that he reveals himself, would be to surrender in advance to the spiritual disorder of a false mysticism. If man truly knows God, he knows him humanly. No more than grace within nature is faith a light set on the surface of reason; it lives within it. And faith is not contaminated by this incarnation, any more than the Word is lessened by becoming flesh. The twofold theandric mystery, better: the single mystery, which is the very mystery of Christ, in whom the divine and the human are one: a single Person, in whom faith plants me, the eternal Son of God entered into history. The Christ of faith, in the Christ of history.

All of history goes by here. The theologian does not and cannot have any hope of finding his given [*son donné*] outside of history, outside of that *auditus fidei* spread across time from Abraham, "whose faith was credited to him as justice," to Christ, and in the Church of Christ permanently across the centuries. A sacred history, obviously, but a history whose sacredness does not extract or abstract it from the contexts that are the matter and the law of human history. Otherwise it would not really be an incarnation: if human words were violated in their structure by the entrance into it of the Word of God, they would be unintelligible to man and would no longer reveal that Word of God to him. The Word truly became man when he became man, one of us. The Son of God is an historical personage.

It is, then, upon a history that the theologian works. His given is not the nature of things nor their timeless forms; it is events, responding to an *economy* whose realization is bound to time, as extension is bound to the body, beyond the order of essences. This is the *real* world, and not a philosopher's abstraction. The believer, the believing theologian, enters by faith into this plan of God, and what he seeks to understand, *quaerens intellectum*, is a divine initiative, a series of divine, absolute, initiatives whose essential trait is to be without "reason": the general initiatives of creation, incarnation, redemption as much as the particular initiatives of the predestinations of grace: the sweet and terrible contingencies of a love that does not have to justify its blessings or its abandonments. This is the true world of contemplation and of theological understanding: surrendering to the initiatives of a free God who directs according to his pleasure this immense and indefinable history of which he is the chief protagonist. So that if there is a problem, it is in finding reasons for this freedom from reasons, in "rationalizing" [138] this history and not in knowing it in itself, in its immediate economy. For it is clear that it is in accord with the laws of history that he will have to know it and in it to know the Word of God; it is because of this theandric character of the Word that historical criticism with all its apparatus will become an appropriate instrument for theology.

It was the conjuncture of modernist historicism and of a false theology of faith which provoked, around 1900, such trouble in the study of the sources of revelation and in the development of the method of theology. A modernist historicism regarded history as an absolute when only faith is absolute; a false theology of faith gave up its substantial supernatural character out of fear of no longer being able to provide a rational apologetics for a mystical assent. For a Gardeil, on the contrary, relying on a full Thomist theology of faith, history was no longer the suspect criticism which must be kept on a leash and mistreated, but the precious *ancilla* which by autonomous use of its rules and instruments gave faith a way to adhere more closely to its own given, handed over in the course of time in accord with the progressive economy of revelation, and not in accord with the logical deductions of a Neoplatonic Logos.

That is why Fr. Gardeil's disciples at Le Saulchoir welcomed with such complete and heartfelt confidence the resources of *historical method* whose rights were vindicated and whose results were praised by Fr. Lagrange in his famous conferences at Toulouse.[2] The best witness to this encounter between theology and historical exegesis is the doctrine of inspiration which underlay Fr. Lagrange's method. The incarnation of the Word of God extended even to the letter of the words—"literal inspiration," as it is called—and the very letter with all its grammatical, literary, historical dimensions is precisely what gives access to the understanding of the faith. The Word of God is *in* the human word: the power of God is revealed in this infirmity. Accidents might happen in the course of inept investigations by a philologist, a literary critic, a historian; but they are only accidents, and a method is not based on accidents but on the objective order of realities, here the realities of supernatural faith *in* the mind and language of man. Biblical docetism is only the false modesty of a fearful faith within a poor theology.

We see how on these bases the theological task is organized in accord with the complexity of its methods which, far from reducing it, guarantees the unity of faith. Historical exegesis (the Bible) and the history [139] of dogmas (the Tradition) will be, as their names indicate, works of history, of a history carried out in accord with its laws and procedures and in the light of its resources, in all sincerity and loyalty. On the other hand, positive theology—biblical, patristic, symbolic, etc.—will be developed under the light of faith and in accord with its criteria, since it is a theology in the proper sense. The road from Athens to Piraeus is not the same as the road from Piraeus to Athens. If the discerning of these two ways seems too abstract and their intersection delicate, it is because the intersection of the divine and the human in revelation—revelation of the Word of God at the summit of which is realized the revelation of the Word made flesh—is itself delicate to conceive and to express. As for the apparent subtlety of the discerning, it is these methodological abstractions which, in accord with the law of all scientific work, guarantees the probity of the research and the internal order of the construction. The discipline of formal objects is one of the most precious riches of Thomist pedagogy; the painful confusion of ideas, methods and vocabularies, among the best theologians, during the Modernist crisis, once again underlines its quality and its urgency.

It is this very discipline and spirit that enabled the freedom with which St. Thomas opened himself to Greek science against the philosophico-religious concordism which wanted to forbid access to it to Christendom; and it enables today the wary ease with which a Thomist rejects biblical concordism in all its forms, not only the scientific concordism which burdened the teaching of Scripture for half a century, but ethnological and historical concordisms, compromises unfortunate for both faith and science. It was the same adversaries, in the thirteenth and in the twentieth centuries, who have seen rationalism in this.

If the economy of revelation develops in time, if faith thus finds its authentic expression in statements bound up with history, the particular case—and it is only that—of the development of dogma within the new economy, in the life of the Church, does not disconcert the theologian: it is something natural, a manifestation of the law of incarnation. To want to camouflage it or to reduce it to a mere play of equivalent words, as is desired by a certain "fixism" for which the whole of theology consists in being anti-modernist, is not only to mistreat history (a poor way for preparing a good theology), but also to misunderstand faith. A strange inversion, the mark of an error: it is the same theologians who, because they have lost the sense of the transcendence of the Word of God in faith, transfer [140] its absolute character to authoritative formulations of it and thus remove these formulas from history. "An unintelligent and low conception of the divine real": Fr. Gardeil's harsh comment was aimed at those minds who, because they had rejected the analogy of the divine names, no longer felt the theologian's anxiety before a mystery that is to be found in words that are human, however categorically true they may be. It is faith that is an absolute and escapes history, pure faith in its infused light, and not dogma, *auditus fidei* docile to the magisterium.

2. [*Original footnote*] Marie-Joseph Lagrange, *La Méthode historique. Surtout à propos de l'Ancien Testament* (Paris, Victor Lecoffre, 1903).

Real development, at the heart of the dogmatic reality, and not in some secondary prolongations: is the *quaerens intellectum* of the believer to be exercised at the fringes of the truth? No doubt this opens the door to relativism in dogmatic formulas; but this historical relativism is only the effect in time of their metaphysical relativism. With the vigor and the serenity of a Cajetan, Fr. Gardeil proclaimed this metaphysical relativism, the very expression of the doctrine of analogical knowledge. After so radical a source of relativity, historical contingencies and psychological complexities of dogmatic formulas can be regarded with composure.

To explain dogmatic development in terms of the scientific theory of evolution, as was done around 1900, is not without difficulties. It is a ticklish operation in any circumstances to transfer the words and theories of the physical disciplines to a discipline of the mind; in this case it would be necessary to cleanse "evolution" of its biological transformism or its Hegelian metaphysics. But the image of biological growth long governed theology (Vincent of Lerins, in the fifth century); and the sense of history on which Hegel's speculation rested had already found in Christendom, in a Möhler and a Newman, a rare spiritual quality. It is, then, a fine case of theological "science": it is treated in one of the most careful chapters of *Le Donné révélé*, from which one of the disciples and friends of Fr. Gardeil, Fr. Marin-Sola was soon to draw the inspiration for his great book, *L'Évolution homogène du dogme catholique* (Valencia, 1923; Fribourg-Paris, 1924). Some of the conclusions of the two masters can certainly be discussed, but it remains that the historian of Christian doctrines finds there, in the thesis of the progressive intelligibility of the revealed given, not only a legitimation of his work and his method but the theological reason for his historical observations. Msgr. Batiffol, who benefitted from the friendly criticism of Fr. Gardeil at a difficult moment in his work on the development of the dogma of the Eucharist, was assured that he was on the right track, despite the narrow solution which certain theologians had used to block him. [141] A significant and comforting encounter of two masters who for too long a time, like the disciplines which they were practicing, operated on their own.

This should be noted, however: because this historical "growth" of dogma remains the temporal effect of a faith which remains identical across time in the souls to whom the Word of God speaks, the crises of Christian thought—if one may put it this way—are in the end to be judged, beyond the *successio temporum*, in accord with the spiritual plan of the *propinquitas ad Christum* [nearness to Christ] (St. Thomas, IIa IIae, q. 1, a. 7, ad 2 et 4): a history of souls and no longer only linear evolutions, personal faith and not mere social memory. Such is the history of dogmas, or, better, the history of Christian doctrines which will be for the theologian the matter of Tradition.

32.

Prefatory Note to *Sources chrétiennes*, vol. 1 (1942)

The brief prefatory note to the first volume of *Sources chrétiennes*, published in the middle of the Second World War, can be read as a clarion call, issued to Roman Catholic theologians and laypeople, to broaden the notion of "tradition" so as to overcome a certain narrow neo-Thomism and to retrieve the vast patristic literature, especially in Greek (Gregory of Nyssa's *Life of Moses* was the first volume to be published; the second volume was Clement of Alexandria's *Protrepticus*) and Latin. Most of the prominent theologians and historians of theology at the time of its publication greeted the new collection with joy.[1] Theologians affiliated with neo-Thomism, such as Marie-Michel Labourdette, responded critically to this agenda, initially seeing in it "an anti-intellectual relativism and a vaguely spiritual personalism, accompanied by the abandonment of the great Thomist construction of theology as an organized science, dealing with the ultimate and timeless truth" (Daley 2011, 366; see also Fouilloux 2011, 119–25).

The collection of the *Sources chrétiennes* was an initiative of French Jesuits, especially Jean Daniélou (1905–74) and Henri de Lubac (1896–1991). Their aims are clearly stated in the prefatory note below, which is found in the first volume of the collection, namely, the edition of Gregory of Nyssa's treatise on the life of Moses: *Contemplation sur la Vie de Moïse, ou Traité de la perfection en matière de vertu*.[2] The *Sources chrétiennes* played a significant role in the renewal of Roman Catholic theology and spirituality in the wake of the Second World War, and it all came to fruition, in superb fashion, at the Second Vatican Council (1962–65). The collection is ongoing; its six-hundredth volume was published in 2018.

1. See for instance Henri-Irénée Marrou, "Pour un retour à l'étude des Pères. Sources chrétiennes," in *La Vie spirituelle* (April 1, 1943):383–92. Marrou wrote, "A collection such as this one may become the instrument and the occasion of a renewal of piety through a concrete return to these 'sources' which are our Fathers in the faith" (p. 386). See Étienne Fouilloux, *La collection "Sources chrétiennes": Éditer les Pères de l'Église au XXe siècle* (Paris: Cerf, 2011), 85–88.

2. Introduced and translated by Jean Daniélou (Paris-Lyon: Cerf-L'Abeille, 1942), 7–8. This is the source for the excerpt below. The English translation relies in part on Brian Daley's translation: see Brian Daley S.J., "The *Nouvelle Théologie* and the Patristic Revival: Sources, Symbols and the Science of Theology," *IJST* 7/4 (2005): 368 (362–82).

PREFATORY NOTE TO THE FIRST VOLUME OF *SOURCES CHRÉTIENNES* (1942)

The collection of which this is the first volume presents a very precise character, which it would be good to define from the beginning. It is intended to put at the disposal of the educated public complete works of the Church Fathers, adding to them all the tools that will allow their full understanding. This is, we believe, what is needed at this time in order to serve the cause of the Fathers. The point is to foster, in relation to them, a climate of understanding, to familiarize people with their style of thought, to overcome the still widespread prejudgment among many which leads them to think that it is impossible to read the Fathers. . . . It seems to us that if the Fathers are hard to read, it is because we are completely ignorant of their style of thought. They represent for us a cultural realm almost as distant as that of India or China. What we need to do is to explain that world from within, to introduce people to it, to give a view of its surroundings and a description of its byways, and then to hand the keys over to the reader, leaving him or her the pleasure of discovering treasures that he would not otherwise have guessed exist. . . . Our desire was to include the Greek text. The current circumstances, for various reasons, did not allow us to do so. But we consider this a simple delay and we hope to publish, in the future, the original texts whose translations have been published—some are ready to be published.

We know, by all the encouragement we have received, that our effort corresponds to the expectations of many people. We hope that these expectations will not be disappointed, and that this collection will allow a number of readers direct access to these "sources" of spiritual life and theological doctrine, always springing up new, which are the Fathers of the Church.

The Editors.

33.

Gerhard Ebeling (1912–2001)

Born in Berlin, Gerhard Ebeling was a student at the Finkenwalde seminary, a seminary run by the Confessing Church (*Bekennende Kirche*) during the National Socialist years (and soon closed by the Nazis), where Dietrich Bonhoeffer was serving as director and professor. He also studied in Marburg with Rudolf Bultmann, who became a major influence, and Emil Brunner in Zürich before becoming a pastor within the Confessing Church during the Second World War. Ebeling eventually became a major proponent of the theological school known as hermeneutical theology, which owed much to Martin Heidegger and his disciple Hans-Georg Gadamer, as well as a leading specialist of Martin Luther's theology. His interests were both historical and systematic and conjoined within his hermeneutical approach, since both disciplines rely on interpretation and understanding of the past and present. Ultimately there is "one single process of understanding" (see below, 216). Ebeling began teaching at the University of Tübingen in 1947, first as historian of the church and later as systematic theologian, before spending over two decades as a professor at the University of Zürich (1956–79), with an interlude in Tübingen from 1965 until 1968).

The selections included here, "Preface to the English Edition" and the 1950 article on "The Significance of the Critical Historical Method for Church and Theology in Protestantism," are excerpted from Ebeling's book *Word and Faith*, trans. James W. Leitch (London: SCM, 1963).

WORD AND FAITH (1963)

Preface to the English Edition

[10] As regards method, the thing is to stand up to the tension between the historical and dogmatic approaches and their different ways of working. The conflict between historical and dogmatic theology threatens to tear theology apart today and so have it ruined by its own inner contradiction. My transition from the discipline of church history to that of systematic theology was not meant, however, as a change of front in this internal theological warfare, but as the resolve to observe the responsibilities of the historian and the dogmatician in one person, and thus to take upon myself what is after all really expected of every theological student. The assurance that this was a hopeful undertaking was provided by insight into the

hermeneutical problem, in which the historical and dogmatic tasks ultimately appear as mere aspects of one single process of understanding.

The Significance of the Critical Historical Method for Church and Theology in Protestantism (1950)

[29] . . . The proposition that Christianity stands or falls with the tie that binds it to its unique historical origin . . . contains an assertion which is paradoxical in comparison with all other phenomena in history. For it not only means that the historical origin of Christianity has the peculiarity of a *primum movens* at the beginning of a process of development in history, but it ascribes to this historical origin once and for all abiding, normative, absolute significance for the whole historic phenomenon of Christianity in its entirety. That is, the historical origin of Christianity is assigned the character of revelation. It is thereby withdrawn from the relativity and transience of all historic events. It forms a realm which is once and for all defined, distinguished from all other phenomena of history—a judgment which finds expression in the fixing of the canon of holy scripture. . . .

[37] I began by saying that Christianity stands or falls with the tie that binds it to its unique historical origin. From that there arose the problems, first of the ontological interpretation of the event of revelation, secondly of the view of the testimony to this event of revelation, that is, of holy scripture, and then thirdly of the present actualization of the event of revelation. But now there is still a fourth problem that presents itself—namely, the problem of the historical character of the present actualization of the event of revelation. Christianity is, in spite of the tie that binds it to its unique historical origin—which bond actualizes itself when the event of revelation becomes present, and is thus not only a postulate but a bond that again and again rises in actual fact—Christianity, I say, is for all that not a phenomenon that abides always identical and unchanged, but it exists in history, that is, it is subject to the march of time. It can never simply remain precisely the same as it was at the start; for then it would not exist in history at all. But how, then, can it remain identical with itself in the absolute sense presupposed by the statement that Christianity stands or falls with the tie that binds it to its unique historical origin?—"in an absolute sense," because this [38] unique historical origin claims to be revelation in the utterly absolute sense. It is of course the basic structure of all historic being that it exists in the dialectic of constancy and change. Mutation can take place only in a thing that remains identical with itself. To the essence of the historic there belong not only the several variations of each new moment, but at the same time also continuity of being, not only change but also tradition. But now, does not transience likewise belong to the nature of historic existence? Is it not only the transitory, the relative that can vary? Christianity, however, makes the claim to exist in history as something absolute, intransitory. But what, then, is the relation of the historic mutation to the identity of the absolute?

To this problem, which is presented to us by the simple fact of the history of the Church and of theology, a solution has been sought in the formula that here the divine and the human, the eternal and the temporal, exist side by side. The human and temporal element is said to be the changing forms, the divine and eternal one the content that abides identical and unchanged. But to formulate it that way really only describes the problem here presented—and that, too, by applying the categories of form and content in a highly questionable way. For the distinction of form and content suggests the idea that the content can be separated from the form. But how can for instance the content of a theological statement be separated from its form? That is in fact precisely the difficulty—that the content can be had only in a particular form. If it were desired to separate for instance the content of the Credo from its particular form, then that could really only be done in a new form. There is certainly a problem here that presses for the making of a distinction. But it seems to me the proper distinction here is not one of form and content, but of word and exposition. The problem of how the Church exists amid the mutations of history and yet is bound absolutely to its unique historical origin, constantly changing and yet remaining identical with itself, is thereby set in the light of the hermeneutical question. I consider the category of exposition the only proper one for coming to grips with the question of the nature of the history of Church and theology. For the category of exposition embraces the historical character of the present actualization of the event of revelation. . . .

[56] In the Reformers' view, both revelation and faith are discovered in their genuine historicity, and that quite definitely means that faith is exposed to all the vulnerability and ambiguity of the historical. Only in that way, and only [57] for that reason, can genuine encounter with the historical revelation be attained in faith and only in faith. . . .

[59] The task of even beginning to explore on any wide scale the real theological relevance of the tremendous work of critical historical theology in the nineteenth century is one in which nineteenth-century theology undoubtedly fails and which now, in the general antipathy towards the nineteenth century, threatens to be entirely forgotten. Systematic theology must therefore be required not only to respect the results of critical historical research—even on that point there is still much to be desired—but also to take up fully and completely into its own approach the outlook of the critical historical method. The trouble is—and it is plainly manifest in the history of modern theology—that Protestant dogmatics since the days of the Enlightenment has not succeeded in really squaring up to this task. It is not historical, but systematic theology that makes plain the crisis which has arisen in Protestant theology. To be sure, critical historical theology has also contributed to it in manifold ways. Yet the primary source of the trouble has not at all been its coming, as it often enough did and does, to mistaken conclusions in what are really uncritical ways. The trouble has been above all that its champions have either supposed that systematic theology could and must be abolished, or else considered themselves in a position to produce a doctrine of the Christian faith as a direct result of their critical historical labours, whether in the form of reducing everything to the life and teaching of Jesus or of progressively bringing to light the advances that have taken place in the history of Church and theology itself. The fact that it is precisely in systematic theology that the problems arise with such sharpness points to a real aporia on the part of Protestantism. It will at all events be unable, if it rightly understands its own nature, to develop a dogmatic that is structurally identical with Catholic dogmatics. Yet what the shape of Protestant dogmatics should be, and what method it should go by, is still an entirely open question—one which Schleiermacher certainly perceived with a clarity hardly ever to be attained again later, even if he too, failed to solve it. If systematic theology takes up into its own approach the whole outlook of the critical historical method, then the result will be not only that it will achieve the critical destruction of all supposed assurances, but above all that it will be kept strictly to its proper concern—namely, the historical revelation in Jesus Christ—in full awareness of the historicity of its own systematic theological labours.

34.

Georges Florovsky (1893–1979)

Orthodox theology, to a very large extent, remained foreign to many of the debates about the meaning and uses of the historical and critical method. Steeped in patristic theology, the typically Protestant (but also Roman Catholic) way, in modernity, to search for the literal sense of the Bible did not appear to be necessary or important. On the contrary, it was perceived as a threat to an authentic reading of Scripture. This does not mean, however, that "history" never was a problem for Orthodox theology. One of its greatest minds in the twentieth century, Georges Florovsky, was very much aware of some of the debates on the notion of history and salvation history among Protestant and Roman Catholic theologians and historians of theology in his own day.

The son of an Orthodox priest, Florovsky was born in 1893 in Odessa, where he studied history and philology. He was self-taught as a theologian. Sergei Bulgakov (1871–1944) had pointed out to him the lack of patristic studies and invited him to work in this field (Blane 1993). In 1926 Florovsky moved to Paris to teach at the Institut Saint-Serge, just two years after its creation. Paris was at the time a magnet for Russian emigrés (in addition to Bulgakov, Nikolai Berdyaev and Vladimir Lossky). In the 1930s he published a string of books in Russian on the Eastern fathers of the fourth century (1931 in English: vol. 7 of his Collected Works), the Byzantine fathers of the fifth through eighth centuries (1933 in English: vol. 9 of his Collected Works), and the "ways of Russian theology" (1937 in English: vol. 5 of his Collected Works). Florovsky was an important participant in the ecumenical movement, including at the World Council of Churches' first conference in Amsterdam (1948) as a member of the WCC steering committee. After the Second World War, Florovsky taught at Saint Vladimir's Seminary in Crestwood, near New York City, and at Harvard and Princeton, where he died in 1979. For his approach to theology, he coined the expression "neo-patristic synthesis."

The following selections are transcribed from his article titled "The Predicament of the Christian Historian," in *Christianity and Culture: The Collected Works of Georges Florovsky*, vol. 2 (Belmont: Nordland, 1974), reprinted in *The Patristic Witness of Georges Florovsky: Essential Theological Writings*, ed. Brandon Gallaher and Paul Ladouceur (New York:

T&T Clark, 2019). One footnote has been suppressed. This article was first published in 1959, in a volume in honor of Paul Tillich (*Religion and Culture*, ed. Walter Leibrecht [New York: Harper & Brothers]).

THE PREDICAMENT OF THE CHRISTIAN HISTORIAN (1959)

[61] It has been, in fact, recently suggested that "a Christian history" is simply nonsense. It has been contended that "the message of the New Testament was not an appeal to [62] historical action, but to repentance," and that this message "dismantled, as it were, the hopeless history of the world."[1] This radical eschatologism, which simply "dismantles" all human history, is open to serious theological doubt. Indeed, it is a theological, and not a historical, assumption. It is rooted in a one-sided theological vision in which God alone is seen active, and man is just an object of Divine action, in wrath or mercy, and never an agent himself. But it is this "inhuman" conception of man, and not "the message of the New Testament," which makes nonsense of human history. The message of the New Testament, on the contrary, makes sense of history. In Christ, and by him, Time was itself, for the first time, radically and existentially validated. History has become *sacred* in its full dimension since "the Word was made flesh," and the Comforter descended into the world for its cleansing and sanctification. Christ is ever abiding in his Body, which is the Church, and in her the *Heilsgeschichte* is effectively continued. The *Heilsgeschichte* is still going on. It is obviously true that in practice it is utterly difficult to discern the pattern of this ongoing "history of salvation" in the perplexity of historical events, and historians, including Christian historians, must be cautious and modest in their endeavor to decipher the hidden meaning of the particular events. Nevertheless, the historian must be aware of that new "situation" which has been created in history by the Coming of Christ: there is "now" nothing "neutral" in the human sphere itself, since the Cross and Resurrection, since the Pentecost. Accordingly, the whole of history, even "the hopeless history of the world," appears now *in the perspective of an ultimate, eschatological conflict*. It was in this perspective that St. Augustine undertook his survey of historical events in his story of the "Two Cities." It may be difficult to relate the *Heilsgeschichte* to the general history of the world. On the other hand, the Church is *in the world*. Its actual history may be often distorted by worldly accretions. Yet "salvation" has also a historical dimension. The Church is the leaven of history. As Cyril C. Richardson has aptly observed recently, the history of the Church bears a *prophetic* character, no less than the sacred [63] history of the Bible. "It is a part of revelation—the story of the Holy Ghost."[2] . . .

[64] The Christian historian does not proceed actually "on Christian principles," as is sometimes suggested. Christianity is not a set of principles. The Christian historian pursues his professional task of interpreting human life in the light of his Christian vision of that life, sorely distorted by sin, yet redeemed by divine mercy, and healed by divine grace, and called to the inheritance of an everlasting Kingdom. The Christian historian will, first of all, vindicate "the dignity of man," even of fallen man. He will, then, protest against any radical scission of man into "empirical" and "intelligible" fractions (whether in a Kantian fashion or in any other) of which the former is doomed and only the latter is promised salvation. It is precisely the "empirical man" who needs salvation, and salvation does not consist [65] merely in a kind of disentanglement of the "intelligible character" out of the empirical mess and bondage. Next, the Christian historian will attempt to reveal the actual course of events in the light of his Christian

1. [*Original footnote*] Karl Löwith, *Meaning in History: The Theological Implications of the Philosophy of History* (Chicago: University of Chicago Press, 1949), 196–7; see also his articles: "Skepsis und Glaube in der Geschichte," in *Die Welt als Geschichte*, Jh. X. 3 (1950); "Christentum und Geschichte," in *Christentum und Geschichte. Vorträge der Tagung in Bochum vom 5. bis 8. October 1954* (Düsseldorf, 1955).

2. [*Original footnote*] Cyril C. Richardson, "Church History Past and Present," in *Union Seminary Quarterly Review* 5/1 (November 1949), 9.

knowledge of man, but will be slow and cautious in detecting the "providential" structure of actual history, in any detail. Even in the history of the Church "the hand of Providence" is emphatically hidden, though it would be blasphemous to deny that this hand does exist or that God is truly the Lord of history. Actually, the purpose of a historical understanding is not so much to detect the divine action in history as to understand the human action, that is, human activities, in the bewildering variety and confusion in which they appear to a human observer. Above all, *the Christian historian will regard history at once as a mystery and as a tragedy—a mystery of salvation and a tragedy of sin.* He will insist on the comprehensiveness of our conception of man, as a prerequisite of our understanding of his existence, of his exploits, of his destiny, which is actually wrought in his history.

The task of a Christian historian is by no means an easy task. But it is surely a noble task.

35.

Wolfhart Pannenberg (1928–2014)

Wolfhart Pannenberg played a major part in various attempts, since the late 1950s, to shift Protestant theology in a different direction than the one proposed by Karl Barth, Rudolf Bultmann, Friedrich Gogarten, and Emil Brunner, that is, the main figures of the school known as "dialectical theology." Unlike them, Pannenberg had little patience for Martin Kähler's distinction between *Historie*, the past as past and as object of rigorous historical research, on the one hand, and *Geschichte*, living history, the past as it influences us today, on the other. He also considered the focus on human "historicity" among existential theologians such as Bultmann to be misguided. And so, starting in the late 1950s, Pannenberg began to formulate a program, soon framed under the motto "revelation as history," in which he argued that God's revelation does not simply occur in history but as history—not as a special thread within world history, as in the various proposals of a salvation history (*Heilsgeschichte*), but in history of the world as such and as a whole. This was a remarkable new development, even if the obvious Hegelian and Troeltschian overtones of this program were unmistakable. Pannenberg went on to write a substantive contribution to the field of Christology, aiming to elaborate a Christology "from below," that is, from the historical man Jesus and not from the incarnate *logos*, and arguing that the ultimate disclosure of truth only occurs at the *end* of history, thus positing eschatology as *the* decisive revelatory event, which was anticipated (*prolepsis*) in the resurrection of Jesus of Nazareth.[1] He fulfilled his program with his three volume *Systematische Theologie* (Göttingen: Vandenhoeck & Ruprecht, 1988–93), which were soon translated into English (Grand Rapids: Eerdmans, 1991–96).

What follows is a transcript from the translation of parts of Pannenberg's article "Heilsgeschehen und Geschichte" [Redemptive Event and History], *Kerygma und Dogma* 5 (1959): 218–37, 259–88. For the English translation, see *Essays on Old Testament Hermeneutics*, trans. Shirley C. Guthrie Jr., ed. Claus Westerman (German ed.) and James

1. *Jesus—God and Man*, trans. Lewis L. Wilkins and Duane A. Priebe (London: SCM, 1968); *Grundzüge der Christologie* (Gütersloh: Mohn, 1964).

Luther Mays (English ed.) (Richmond: John Knox Press, 1963). This excerpt is followed by Pannenberg's "Dogmatic Theses on the Doctrine of Revelation" (1960), found in *Revelation as History: A Proposal for a More Open, Less Authoritarian View of an Important Theological Concept*, ed. Wolfhart Pannenberg et al., trans. David Granskou (London: Macmillan, 1968). The third and final excerpt comes from Pannenberg's 1964 Christology: *Jesus, God and Man*, trans. Lewis L. Wilkins and Duane A. Priebe (London: SCM, 1968); first published as *Grundzüge der Christologie* (Gütersloh: Gütersloher Verlagshaus Gerd Mohn, 1964).

"REDEMPTIVE EVENT AND HISTORY" (1959)

[314] History is the most comprehensive horizon of Christian theology. All theological questions and answers are meaningful only within the framework of the history that God has with humanity and through humanity with his whole creation—the history moving toward a future still hidden from the world but already revealed in Jesus Christ. This presupposition of Christian theology must be defended today within theology itself on two sides: on the one side, against Bultmann and Gogarten's existential theology that dissolves history into the historicity of existence; on the other side, against the thesis, developed by Martin Kähler in the tradition of salvation history, that the real content of faith is suprahistorical. This assumption of a suprahistorical kernel of history, which was in substance present already in von Hofmann's delimitation of a theology of salvation history (*Heilsgeschichte*) over against ordinary history (*Historie*), and which is still alive today especially in the form of Barth's interpretation of the incarnation as "original history" (*Urgeschichte*), necessarily depreciates real history, just as does the reduction of history to historicity. Both theological positions, that of pure historicity and that of the suprahistoric ground of faith, have a common extratheological motive. Their common starting point is to be seen in the fact that critical historical research as the scientific establishment of events did not seem to leave any room for salvific events. Therefore the theology of salvation history fled into a harbor supposedly safe from the critical historical flood tide, the harbor of suprahistory, or, with Barth, of original history. For the same reason the theology of existence withdrew from the meaningless and godless "objective" course of history to the experience of the significance of history in the "historicity" of the individual. The historical character of the salvific event must therefore be asserted today in debate with the theology of existence, with the theology of redemptive history, and with the methodological principles of critical historical research.

"DOGMATIC THESES ON THE DOCTRINE OF REVELATION" (1960)

Thesis 2

[132] In apocalyptic thought, the spiritual situation is substantially sharpened. Not only is the decisive event of salvation always in the future, but the meaning of the present event is, in general, totally hidden. Thus, the continuity from the present to the future is not easily discerned. The two æons stand in juxtaposition. For apocalyptic thought, the present is filled with tribulation. It is only in the time of the eschatological inauguration of the new æon that the meaning of the present time is revealed. The destiny of mankind, from creation onward, is seen to be the unfolding according to a plan of God. Apocalyptic thought conceives of a universal history. Thus, the revelation of God and his glory is transferred to the end of all [133] events. That the end will make manifest the secrets of the present is also the presupposition of primitive Christianity.

The history that demonstrates the deity of God is broadened to include the totality of all events. This corresponds completely to the universality of Israel's God, who is not only the God of Israel, but will be the God of all people. This broadening of the *Heilsgeschichte* to a universal history is in essence already accomplished in the major prophets of Israel in that they treat the kingdoms of the world as responsible to God's commands. . . . It is at the end of this chain of world events that God can for the first time be revealed with finality as the one true God. . . . Placing the manifestation of God at the end of history means that the biblical God has, so to speak, his own history. That is, the historical event of revelation cannot be thought of in an outward way as revealing the essence of God. It is not so much the course of history as it is the end of history that is at one with the essence of God. But insofar as the end presupposes the course of history, because it is the perfection of it, then also the course of history belongs in essence to the revelation of God, for history receives its unity from its goal. Although the essence of God is [134] from everlasting to everlasting the same, it does have a history in time. Thus it is that Yahweh first becomes the God of all mankind in the course of the history that God has brought to be.

JESUS, GOD AND MAN (1964)

[28] Christology is concerned . . . not only with *unfolding* the Christian community's confession of Christ, but above all with *grounding* it in the activity and fate of Jesus in the past. The confession of Christ cannot be presupposed already and simply interpreted. Christology cannot take its point of departure from the confessions of the Reformation, for example, from the Christological statements of the Formula of Concord, or from the Christological formula of the Council of Chalcedon, nor can it simply develop the [29] oldest primitive Christian confession, the sentence *Iēsous (Christos) Kyrios* ("Jesus is Lord," Rom 1:4; 10:9; 1 Cor 12:3). This confession itself must be grounded by Christology. . . .

[34] There are three reasons why this method [a "Christology from above"] is not feasible for us:

1. A Christology from above presupposes the divinity of Jesus. The most important task of Christology is, however, precisely to present the reasons for the confession of Jesus' divinity. Instead of presupposing it, we must first inquire about how Jesus' appearance in history led to the recognition of his divinity.

2. A Christology that takes the divinity of the Logos as its point of departure and finds its problems only in the union of God and man in Jesus recognizes only with difficulty the determinative significance inherent in the distinctive features of the real, historical man, Jesus of Nazareth. The manifold relationships between Jesus and the Judaism of his time, which are essential to an understanding of his life and message, must appear as less important [35] to such a Christology, even when it discusses the offices of Christ as well as his humiliation and exaltation. Certainly if one knows from the beginning that Jesus Christ is the Son of God, then these relationships with the Judaism of Jesus' time are not so crucial for the basic Christological questions. . . .

3. There remains one final reason why the methodology of a Christology "from above" is closed to us: one would have to stand in the position of God himself in order to follow the way of God's Son into the world. As a matter of fact, however, we always think from the context of a historically determined human situation. We can never leap over this limitation. Therefore, our starting point must lie in the question about the man Jesus; only in this way can we ask about his divinity. How the divine Logos, the Second Person of the Trinity, would be thought of apart from the incarnation and thus apart from the man Jesus completely escapes our imagination.

36.

Elisabeth Schüssler Fiorenza (b. 1938)

Elisabeth Schüssler Fiorenza, professor of divinity at Harvard Divinity School, is a major contributor to feminist theology. After her studies at the universities of Würzburg and Münster, she moved to the United States and taught at the University of Notre Dame (1970–84) and at the Episcopal Divinity School in Cambridge, Massachusetts (1984–88), before joining Harvard Divinity School in 1988.

As a scholar of the New Testament and early Christianity and as a feminist theologian, Schüssler Fiorenza sought to overcome a certain male bias that passes over the presence of women in Scripture and in the history of Christianity. History's challenge to theology includes the challenge to pay attention to *all* voices of the past and present, including the voices we forget or do not want to listen to. With this program, Schüssler Fiorenza refused to simply reject or abandon the study of Scripture and of the history of Christianity, as some feminist colleagues did who viewed Christianity and the Bible as fundamentally oppressive and thus a lost cause.

Among her most significant contributions is her book *In Memory of Her: A Feminist Theological Reconstruction of Christian Origins* (New York: Crossroad, 1983), which has been translated into thirteen languages. What follows is excerpted from the introduction to that now classic book.

INTRODUCTION TO *IN MEMORY OF HER: A FEMINIST THEOLOGICAL RECONSTRUCTION OF CHRISTIAN ORIGINS*

[xiv] Both Christian feminist theology and biblical interpretation are in the process of rediscovering that the Christian gospel cannot be proclaimed if the women disciples and what they have done are not remembered. They are in the process of reclaiming the supper at Bethany as women's Christian heritage in order to correct symbols and ritualizations of an all-male Last Supper that is a betrayal of true Christian discipleship and ministry.[1] Or, in the words of the artist Judy Chicago: "All the institutions of our culture tell us through

1. [*Original footnote*] Cf. also Elizabeth E. Platt, "The Ministry of Mary of Bethany," *Theology Today* 34 (1977) 29–39.

words, deeds, and even worse[,] silence[,] that we are insignificant. But our heritage is our power."[2]

The explorations of this book have two goals: they attempt to reconstruct early Christian history as women's history in order not only to restore women's stories to early Christian history but also to reclaim this history as the history of women and men. I do this not only as a feminist historian but also as a feminist theologian. The Bible is [xv] not just a historical collection of writings but also Holy Scripture, gospel, for Christians today. As such it informs not only theology but also the commitment of many women today. Yet as long as the stories and history of women in the beginnings of early Christianity are not theologically conceptualized as an integral part of the proclamation of the gospel, biblical texts and traditions formulated and codified by men will remain oppressive to women.

Such a reconstruction of early Christian history as women's history and of biblical-historical theology as feminist theology presupposes historical and theological critical analysis as well as the development of a feminist biblical-historical hermeneutics. Since I am trained in New Testament exegesis, I will limit my explorations to the beginnings of Christianity but not include all of biblical history. Methodologically, however, it will be necessary to go beyond the limits of the New Testament canon since it is a product of the patristic church, that is, a theological document of the "historical winners." To forego such an undertaking because historical critical scholarship and hermeneutics are "male" but not feminist does an intellectual disservice to women. Since it reinforces male-female role stereotypes, such an assumption is not capable of naming the particular oppressive assumptions and androcentric components of such scholarship.

Reconstruction of early Christian history in a feminist perspective raises difficult hermeneutical, textual, and historical problems. Since feminism has developed different theoretical perspectives and models, this reconstruction must also include the formulation of a feminist heuristic framework or model that allows for the oppression as well as for the historical agency of women in early Christianity.

1. A fundamental methodological insight of historical criticism of the Bible was the realization that the *Sitz im Leben* or life setting of a text is as important for its understanding as its actual formulation. Biblical texts are not verbally inspired revelation nor doctrinal principles but historical formulations within the context of a religious community. Although this insight is challenged today by literary formalism as well as textual biblicism, it nevertheless remains basic to any historical reconstruction. Studies of the social world of Israel and early Christianity are in the process of developing heuristic models that comprehend more fully the social-historical context of the biblical texts.

Similarly, feminist theory insists that all texts are products of an androcentric patriarchal culture and history. The current feminist movement has therefore engendered an explosion of scholarly works in all areas of scientific inquiry and research.[3] Historians, philosophers, [xvi] and anthropologists have emphasized that current scholarly theory and research are deficient because they neglect women's lives and contributions and construe humanity and human history as male. Feminist scholarship in all areas, therefore, seeks to construct heuristic models and concepts that allow us to perceive the human reality articulated insufficiently in androcentric texts and research.

The explorations of this book begin therefore with the hope of moving away from the pervasive apologetic that characterizes most treatments of women in the Bible, to a historical-critical reconstruction of women's history and women's contributions to early Christian beginnings. Moreover, I have assumed that the new questions raised by feminist scholarship will enhance our understanding of early Christian history. The attempt to "write women back into early Christian history" should not only restore early Christian history to women but also lead to a richer and more accurate

2. [*Original footnote*] Judy Chicago, *The Dinner Party: A Symbol of Our Heritage* (New York: Doubleday, Anchor Books, 1979), 246–49.

3. [*Original footnote*] *Signs: Journal of Women in Culture and Society*, which was founded in 1975, has regular reviews of scholarship in various areas. Of equal importance are the *Women's Studies International Quarterly* and *Feminist Studies*. See also Dale Spender, ed., *Men's Studies Modified: The Impact of Feminism on the Academic Disciplines* (Oxford-New York: Pergamon Press, 1981).

perception of early Christian beginnings. If scholars employ philosophical, sociological, or psychological analyses for constructing new interpretative models of early Christian development, nothing should prevent us from utilizing feminist heuristic concepts as well, in order to reconstruct an early Christian history in which women are not hidden and invisible. While an androcentric model cannot do justice to those texts that positively mention women's leadership in early Christianity, a feminist model can positively integrate them. . . .

[xviii] When I attempt to explore the history of women who became Christians in the beginnings of Christianity this should not be misunderstood as an attempt to save the Bible from its feminist critics. I simply mean to raise the question: How can early Christian origins be reconstructed in such a way as to be understood as "women's affairs"? In other words, is early Christian history "our own" history or heritage? Were women as well as men the initiators of the Christian movement?

While theologians in the academy refuse to discuss publicly their own political allegiance and preconceived bias and function, many postbiblical feminists are prepared to relinquish their historical roots and their solidarity with women in biblical religion. Recognizing that androcentric Western language and patriarchal religion have "erased" women from history and made them "non-beings," such feminists argue that biblical religion (and theology) is sexist to the core. It is not retrievable for women, since it ignores women's experience, speaks of the godhead in male terms, legitimizes women's subordinate positions of powerlessness, and promotes male dominance and violence against women. Therefore, feminists must move beyond the boundaries of biblical religion and reject the patriarchal authority of biblical revelation. Revisionist interpretations of the Bible are at best a waste of time and at worst a legitimization of the prevailing sexism of biblical religion—therefore, a cooptation of women and the feminist movement. Feminist praxis is rooted in the religious experience of contemporary women but does not derive its inspiration from the Christian past.

Yet such a postbiblical feminist stance is in danger of becoming ahistorical and apolitical. It too quickly concedes that women have no [xix] authentic history within biblical religion and too easily relinquishes women's feminist biblical heritage. Nor can such a stance do justice to the positive experiences of contemporary women within biblical religion. It must either neglect the influence of biblical religion on women today or declare women's adherence to biblical religion as "false consciousness." Insofar as biblical religion is still influential today, a cultural and social feminist transformation of Western society must take into account the biblical story and the historical impact of the biblical tradition. Western women are not able to discard completely and forget our personal, cultural, or religious Christian history. We will either transform it into a new liberating future or continue to be subject to its tyranny whether we recognize its power or not.

37.

Ignacio Ellacuría (1930–89)

Ignacio Ellacuría is not as widely known as other liberation theologians, but his reflections on the relationship between salvation and history are important. Born in the Basque region of Spain, he entered the Society of Jesus (Jesuits) as a seventeen-year-old in 1947. He went on to study with Karl Rahner and Xavier Zubiri, a philosopher who became his doctoral advisor. Starting in the early 1970s, as a professor of philosophy and theology at the Universidad Centroamericana José Simeón Cañas (UCA) in San Salvador, he began to assert that salvation history is always salvation *in* history as well as *of* history. Any dualism that would sever salvation from history—the history of the world—is strictly excluded here: a unity in distinction, following the traditional christological (Chalcedonian) model, is the most adequate way of considering the matter. Indeed, "There is only one history" (Ellacuría 2013, 189). The history of the world is not a separate reality, cut off from salvation history; rather, God's history unites both (Ellacuría 2013, 148). This means that history is much more than "the testing ground" (see below, 232) for human beings, that is, the time and place in which their future potential beatitude may be decided—such relegating of salvation to what comes after time and space needs to be overcome. Certainly, the fullness of salvation, or eternal salvation, is "only consummated beyond death" (Ellacuría 2013, 188). But "salvation is not ahistorical. Salvation must be made present in history," Ellacuría forcefully asserts (see below, 232). How must it be made present? God is the "active subject of salvation par excellence" (Ellacuría 2013, 189). But human beings are also engaged in this process, as they are called to begin embracing and practicing what God offers and commands. It is not God who has become unfaithful to God's promise or covenant. Rather, human beings, including Christians of course, have too often refused to obey God's will.

Ellacuría was one of the six Jesuit priests who, alongside Julia Elba Ramos and Celina Ramos, were murdered on the lawn of UCA by a military squad on November 16, 1989. He remains a witness to the confidence and hope that "in the struggle of history, the lamb will conquer in spite of his sacrifice and death" (see below, 233).

The following excerpts come from Ellacuría's essay "Salvation History," in *Essays on*

History, Liberation, and Salvation, trans. Margaret D. Wilde, ed. Michael E. Lee (Maryknoll, NY: Orbis, 2013), 179–188. He wrote the essay in 1987, two years before his assassination.

SALVATION HISTORY (1987)

Salvation and History

[179] [§3] History itself is the fundamental possibility of salvation because it has been willed as such by God. It is only the possibility because that which is really saved depends on the freedom of God and the freedom of human beings. History itself is the manifestation and always-open presence of God, and it can be so in an always-faithful way to the point where it can be called, and can become, the Reign of God. But how is salvation being made present in history?

We can only verify the kind of salvation that is being made present in history from the standpoint of the salvation announced by Jesus Christ. This does not mean that all salvation, even in the strict meaning of salvation, comes from the historical Jesus by means of direct or indirect causality. There is salvation before Jesus and after Jesus; but that does not mean [180] that this salvation is not always in reference to him or that there is salvation apart from him. The many biblical affirmations that there is salvation only in Jesus must be taken together with many other affirmations that assure us of the presence of the savior God in many people who never explicitly knew of the existence of Jesus or committed themselves personally to him as revealer and savior. Despite this, in order to speak with certainty about who and what is saved, of what are the criteria and the paths of salvation, the Father has chosen the Son as the mediator of salvation by his enlivening Spirit.

From this perspective, we can say that the first gift of salvation to history is the overcoming of sin. History has the fundamental double possibility of being a history dominated by sin or dominated by grace. This is true both in the behavior and in the being of every person as well as in the collective behaviors and institutional structures of different social groups. Indeed although we can recognize the presence of grace in many places and in very different ways, we can also recognize the very extensive and intensive presence of sin with its corresponding absence of grace and with the consequent need for salvation. . . .

[185] Is There Salvation in History?

Anyone who looks with critically realistic eyes at the different scenarios of history can only wonder how we can say that history has already been saved. The coming of Jesus does not appear to have turned history into a history of salvation. It does not seem as if salvation, insofar as it comes from Jesus, has made enough of an impact as to divide history into what [186] came before and after his birth. It might have seemed so when history was confused with Western civilization and during the ten centuries or more when Western civilization was dominated more by ideology than by Christian faith. Even then, without denying the great contribution of faith to improving history, we were far from being able to speak of a human history, let alone a divine history. And if that was true in the times and places where Christian ideology dominated the culture and social structures, the view from a broader perspective in space and time would have to be more pessimistic. . . .

This situation calls for a Christological focus. Did Jesus fail, during his mortal life, in the proclamation and realization of the Reign of God? Did that experience of failure force him to describe the task of realizing the Reign in less historical terms? Was it necessary to resort to an imminent parousia in which a triumphal second coming would correct the failure of his humble first coming? Was it necessary to think of salvation without its own historicity; as something that could only happen in subjective interiority; and, above all, as coming in an existence after history? Is history nothing more than the testing ground for human beings, deciding what will be their eternal destiny beyond time and space in the only place where salvation is fully present? Can the Reign of God preached by Jesus [187] only be fully realized beyond history, so that salvation is offered in history but not promised to history itself?

Jesus' experience in history, and the experience of the Christians who follow his work, apparently leads to the conclusion that salvation, although incipient, is not yet within reach in all its fullness. Not even the whole life of Jesus, before his death, recognizes the totality of the salvific process; only with his resurrection and exaltation are we able to speak fully of salvation, through the communication of divinity to humanity. The logic that led Kant to postulate the immortality of the soul, in order to harmonize the just life with the happy life, can be used here to affirm Jesus' promise of eternal life: the assurance of eternal life for the elect, where the greatest possible communication from God to his creature takes place, is the fundamental point of salvation. Salvation par excellence comes beyond history, after the resurrection of the whole human being. This can only be affirmed in faith, but it must be maintained even in the darkest moments of life and history, when it seems as if God has abandoned his elect and even his own Son, and when it seems as if all history is dominated by the powers of evil.

But salvation is not ahistorical. Salvation must be made present in history. The historical failure of salvation does not prove its historical uselessness. History has not ended. In the hearts of most human beings, there is a yearning for things to improve and a utopia, precisely along the line and in the project reflected by the Reign. That yearning, that hope, that protest against injustice and sin, that getting to work, are good signs among others that salvation is trying to break into history. The Apocalypse, last of the revealed books, dramatically expresses this as the struggle between the faith of the righteous and the power of the empire. It is not only about the struggle of the newborn Church against the Roman empire but also highlights the permanent struggle on which talk of salvation history should focus: the struggle between Christ, the principle of good and salvation, and Satan, the principle of evil and condemnation. In the struggle of history, the lamb will conquer in spite of his sacrifice and death. The tenacious struggle of the powers of evil against good, and more specifically against the good of salvation as proclaimed, lived, and realized by Jesus, shows the powerful intention of that good to be historical, to be present in history; otherwise, the power of evil could simply ignore Jesus' forceful message of salvation.

But it is not and never was so. The power of the world, through flattery and co-optation, tries to overcome the force of the gospel in different ways, as it has done ever since Constantine, or, alternatively, to crush it, as [188] it crushed Jesus, the early Christians, and all authentic Christians, to the point where persecution has become a sign of authenticity. But that persecution, which is at bottom a recognition of the power of salvation, can never eliminate it and cannot keep its small seed from growing, so that in the maturity of history it becomes the great tree that gives its shadow of life to everyone else, to the multitude.

For that reason, the fact that salvation has not reached a satisfying fullness in history is not a definitive proof of its failure. Rather it proves that human beings, especially those specifically called to proclaim and historicize salvation, have failed in their mission. In the covenant, God's promise has not failed, but rather humans' response have failed. Today we must reread from that perspective all the demands that Yahweh makes on his people, especially on their religious and political leaders. We do not need another covenant—in this sense the new covenant is definitive but not closed; what we need is to put into practice what God requires of human beings in order to bring about salvation, both personal and historical salvation.

The Historical Subject of Salvation

Certainly all humanity is the passive historical subject of salvation. All humanity, and to a proportionate degree all creation, has been called to salvation. Although this salvation could have taken different forms, it conforms to the nature of what is to be saved and according to the decisions made by human beings—in relation to which the Trinitarian God remains lovingly free, not only abstractly free.

Concluding Interpretive Postscript

> The sun is not visible at the same instant to every place
> on the same meridian at the same time of year;
> it gleams upon the mountain summits and the high plains
> before it penetrates the lower valleys and the deep ravines.
> No less true is that the historic age dawns not
> upon all people at the same period.
>
> —David Friedrich Strauss (see above, 111)

The emergence of historical consciousness in modernity amounted, and still amounts, to a massive challenge for theology. The most contentious debates, such as the modernist crisis within Roman Catholicism, the battles around Baruch Spinoza, Ferdinand Christian Baur, and David Friedrich Strauss, or the emergence of Christian fundamentalism, are behind us, but we should not fool ourselves: besides the fact that Christian fundamentalism is alive and well in many regions of the world, there is no denying that the critical, historical study of Scripture and of the history of Christianity in its entirety has upended Christian theology. The question is whether this was a good thing or not.

But no simple answer will do here. Complex problems require nuanced answers.

Gerhard Ebeling's statement in 1950 regarding the conflict between historical and dogmatic theology and its threat to theology, which risks being torn apart and ruined "by its own inner contradiction" (see above, 215), may appear to us as overblown—and yet we should not come too quickly to that conclusion. It is true that the historical-critical method (or methods) are now often practiced at best *alongside* other exegetical and interpretive approaches, including synchronic readings. This is a positive development, at least when it is not motivated by a secret marginalizing of historical criticism, for few wish to return to the hegemonic tendencies of these methods at the turn of the twentieth century when a stark alternative was being set forth, especially by certain members of the history-of-religion school: either historical exegesis or (useless) doctrinal, dogmatic, or theological constructs. We cannot afford to abide by such either-or, that is, by exclusivist claims such as William Wrede's program of a strictly historical (read, nontheological) approach (see above, 166–67; Morgan 1973, 9, 24, 26). The point, rather, is to examine how Christian theology relates to historical research. But of course "historical research" is by no means a static, homogeneous reality: it can presuppose a range of things, from a strict naturalistic and immanentist stance to phenomenological views whereby the researcher allows the phenomenon to present itself to him or her.

Reflection about the practice of writing history has taken many turns in the past centuries, thanks to the profound scholarship of luminaries such as Giambattista Vico (1668–1744), Johann Gottfried von Herder (1744–1803), Leopold von Ranke (1795–1886), Wilhelm Dilthey (1833–1911), Benedetto Croce (1866–1952), Raymond Aron (1905–83), Michel Foucault (1926–84), Elizabeth A. Clark (b. 1938), and many others. Theology lives from the study of the biblical letter, and thus from historical and critical scholarship, but it should never cease to search for the spirit in the letter. In the first decade of the sixteenth century, the great humanist Jacques Lefèvre d'Étaples stated: "I consider that, rather than fly away from the matter in this way, we have to aspire to find that letter which is animated by the Spirit, as the colors are by the light."[1]

This means that sound Christian theology is always not just historical or doctrinal but both simultaneously in a complex and uneasy interplay. At the end of the seventeenth century, Jean Le Clerc commented that "the general bent of the last age" was directed "rather towards theological than grammatical learning" (see above, 61). In many ways, especially in the anglophone theological world, we live once again in such an age, in which theology often easily overwhelms (or ignores) history. We have grown tired of the critical, historical minutiae, and especially of the endless speculations of source criticism and its layering of biblical texts—Jean Astruc (1684–1766), with his book *Conjectures sur les Mémoires originaux dont il paroit que Moyse s'est servi pour composer le livre de la Genèse* (*Conjectures concerning the original documents which Moses appears to have used when writing the book of Genesis*), was among the first scholars to inquire about possible sources behind the book of Genesis.

And so we are reminded of Hegel's vehement critique of the theologians of his day who too often wished to treat their subject matter at a distance, neutrally, without personally committing themselves to it. Hegel's critique foreshadows the twentieth-century debates between some of the advocates of religious studies, and their claim to scientificity and objectivity, and those who maintain a hermeneutical and theological posture and who continue to inquire about the Christian faith, as it were, "from within." Again, sound theology, I contend, cannot opt either for rigorous, historical study or for the Anselmian program of *fides quaerens intellectum* ("faith seeking understanding"). The consequences of this stance are manifold, but one of them, very simply, is that the theologian will be, to some degree, both a historian and a believer. How does one go

1. "Non ab re igitur censeo ejusmodi esse fugiendam, et ad litteram illam aspirandum quae ut colores luce, ita spiritu animatur[.]" Guy-Thomas Bedouelle, *Le* Quincuplex Psalterium *de Lefèvre d'Étaples: Un guide de lecture* (Geneva: Droz, 1979), 24, lines 67–69; 28. Robert Morgan, who is one of the most knowledgeable and insightful contemporary scholars on the relationship between New Testament critical exegesis and theology, writes, "A biblical scholarship marked by 'letter' that is *closed* in principle to theological meanings ('spirit') is problematic to Christians. … An exegesis that disallows attention to, or admits no interest in, God and salvation is at best a distraction." Morgan, "Spirit and Letter: Mapping Modern Biblical Interpretation," in *The Spirit and the Letter: A Tradition and a Reversal*, ed. Paul S. Fiddes and Günter Bader (London: Bloomsbury, 2013), 49.

about being both simultaneously? Van A. Harvey's important study *The Historian and the Believer* (Harvey 1966), remains helpful, to a certain extent, even if Harvey appeared (but this impression may have been incorrect) to lean quite heavily in the direction shown by Ernst Troeltsch, and so in the direction of one of the two alternatives of the either-or. Harvey was correct to restate, like Baur long before him, that Christians do not need to be afraid of biblical criticism and of history (Harvey 1996, xx). Spinoza already wondered why the use of reason worried certain Christians (see above 47). The historical and the theological inquiries, with their specific methodologies, must go hand in hand in the course of theological reflection. Werner Kümmel put it this way in the conclusion of his overview of New Testament scholarship: "From the very outset New Testament research was confronted with the problem of how the indispensable *historical* task of examining the New Testament could be brought into harmony with the distinctive demand of these documents on the reader for a decision in response to the divine message they contain" (Kümmel 1973, 405 rev.). That is indeed the question, which has everything to do with the possibilities of reading Scripture simultaneously as a source *and* as a witness that demands "a decision."

The problem of the challenge that history poses to theology has to do with the crucial, but only partial, overlap between history and faith, or between historical scholarship and Christian theology. Both articulate discourses about the past. They do it in closely related but also significantly different ways. Rudolf Bultmann may have somewhat minimized this fact with his emphasis on the coincidence of theology and exegesis (see above, 203).

There is, I think, indeed a "leap" from the historical method to the theological method. This gap has everything to do with differing ways of considering reality, including the past. The presence of this gap explains why even some members of theological departments or faculties, to this day, refuse to be seen as theologians and present themselves as historians. Both Gotthold Ephraim Lessing and, later, Søren Kierkegaard were correct in identifying that "leap." Many forms of Christian apologetics, including Wolfhart Pannenberg's optimistic view of the historical "facts" (such as the empty tomb and thus the resurrection) and results historians can attain strictly as historians, tend to downplay this. At the other end of the spectrum there is another error, namely, certain forms of fideism, which the Christian faith, since it does not overlap with history, can simply ignore: intellectual inquiry, including historical inquiry, is simply pointless. These are twin errors that must be rejected. Neither apologetics nor fideism will do for Christian theology in the twenty-first century. What, then, is the relationship between historical methods and theology, if the two should not be separated or confused? Here is a brief attempt not at a solution but at the beginning of a clarification.

"Truth" matters both to historians and to theologians, but not in the same way. Historians are rightly wary of any claim to absolute or definitive truth: in university contexts they usually work with naturalistic and immanentist presuppositions. Theologians, too, will be hesitant to claim to know *the* truth, and yet at the heart of their subject matter is the claim that truth, more precisely, God's own truth, which God *is*, has manifested itself *in history*. How is such a claim possible? And does it become possible only after a close examination of history as a whole, as Troeltsch argued? Or is it possible already in the here and now, and thus not at the end of human history, to make such a claim concerning truth? It is my contention that Christian theology does not end with the affirmation that God acts in history, but rather that Christian theology *begins* with it—before proceeding to reflect on God's action, on its meaning and possibility, on its modalities, since God is not "some sort of magnified historical agent acting on the same plane as other such agents."[2] But God's action, and God's being as disclosed by God's action, does not exhaust what Christian theology is concerned with: theology is equally interested in the ways in which human beings may or may not discern God's action, as well as how they respond to it or might respond to it. This too is part and parcel of theological discourse.

Locating the starting point of theology in God's action, however, is precisely what modern historical methods reject, since their subject matter is *not* divine acts in history, or history as the reality in which God acts, but history as the reality in which *humans* live and move and have their being (assuredly, historians may agree that claims concerning God's acts may be warranted on other grounds than historical ones; Tilley 2004). From this seemingly obvious fact that theology and history do not have the same object or subject matter follows this other rather obvious fact: namely, that their methods and their criteria for scientificity also differ. Reaching some clarity about this is necessary if we wish to attain a fruitful correlation and collaboration between history and theology. Picking up on Baur's attempt at showing what each discipline might learn from the other (see above, 129-30), I am inclined to say this: in some cases historians may learn from theologians not to lose sight of what texts and other historical artifacts appear to say and mean, thus avoiding to focus too exclusively on the context of production of these sources. Theologians are supposed to remind historians that what the text says or intends to say is what really matters. As Robert Morgan put it, "The independence of biblical scholarship from theological constraints brought some gains. Its isolation from the religious imagination some loss" (Morgan 1986–87, 168).

Conversely, theologians may learn from historians to examine the past with all the necessary rigor: not just the multifaceted context and *Sitz im Leben* of past documents and other objects, but also the complex history of their reception (*Wirkungsgeschichte*) over time; they may learn from historians not to imagine that an informed understanding of the past is easy to achieve; they *need* to learn from historians that *whatever* humans had a hand in creating, such as dogmas and sacred books—even inspired ones—is never immutable or infallible. Finally, the surprise or even the shock that awaits many students who embark in the study of academic theology, and who discover the modern exegetical methods and the historical method as a whole, is actually a very good thing. It may awaken students from a certain dogmatic facility or slumber, from unreflected and unreflective assumptions (academic theology may indeed need to "imperil souls," "lead people into doubt," and "shatter all naïve credulity" (see above, 204).

If that is the case, then the recent and current denigration of the modern historical and

2. John Webster, *God without Measure: Working Papers in Christian Theology, vol. 1: God and the Works of God* (London: Bloomsbury, 2015), 8.

critical methods is not a positive sign for contemporary theology (Barton 2007, 2016). It is not true that "the modern attempt to interpret Scripture 'historically' has been intrinsically self-defeating and has now defeated itself, since it has curiously supposed that to interpret the Bible historically we must abstract from the history for whose attestation the church assembled this collection in the first place, the Incarnation and Resurrection of Christ" (Jenson 1997, 59). The modern attempt to interpret Scripture has in fact yielded many positive results: it has compelled scholars to ask questions about the meaning of texts in relation to their contexts of origin, to consider the symbolic value of narratives and stories, and so also, theologically speaking, how these stories shape human lives and indeed entire communities (Hauerwas 1983; Frei 1993). Historical-critical exegesis helps us see that the divine word is always enfleshed, embodied in the particularities of a people, of a culture (Aletti 1985, 517).

It has, therefore, led us to deeper hermeneutical reflections about texts and their "truth," which should not be reduced to the mere "factuality" and "veracity" of what they convey, even if factuality and veracity do matter—the huge success of Werner Keller's book *The Bible as History*, first published in German in 1955 with the triumphalistic and bombastic title *Und die Bibel hat doch recht. Forscher beweisen die Wahrheit des Alten Testaments* (*The Bible is actually correct. Scholars demonstrate the truth of the Old Testament*), a book that was translated into twenty languages and sold more than ten million copies, shows a deep-seated need for factual, "scientific" confirmation for some of the stories contained in Scripture. Adolf von Harnack was probably right when he wrote this (however elitist it may sound): "The difficulty is that one man's faith requires a strong stake to prop it, or some kind of protective shelter; while another finds the prop break in his hands, and his faith bloom only in the free light of the sun" (see above, 163). And he was no less right to point out the symbolic nature of a number of biblical stories, which Scripture presents as historical events:

> Much in the New Testament that is recorded as history, much that affects us most deeply, is not only told us as a lesson, but, in the form in which it is given, it possesses a deep *symbolical* significance. I know none of the leading events of the narrative of which that cannot be said. The same spirit which unveiled to our eyes the power and the glory of a divine life, so far as mankind is able to grasp it, has also veiled the truth for us with a delicate web of ingenious legend, a poetry that moves the heart, and has thus brought it home in picture and parable. (see above, 163)

Truth is not just factual truth (veracity), it is also symbolic truth, which discloses new, unsuspected depths to reality, life, and human existence and which challenges us to embrace these depths. "There is no objective observation of the truth; for its objectivity is that by which we are observed before ever we have observed anything at all" (Barth 1968b, 287).

Historical criticism has provoked theologians to think anew about the true "ground" of the Christian faith: Is there such a ground, and, if yes, what is this ground's relation to history? Is it suprahistorical? Is it purely historical? I do not see how the Christian faith can answer by choosing one *or* the other: faith orients itself to historical events, more precisely, to an event that is mentioned, in its factuality, in the most important Christian creeds: "[he] suffered under Pontius Pilatus" (*sub Pontio Pilato passus*). And, at the same time, in this event faith discerns God's own intervention (2 Cor 5:19). To put the matter simply, the subject matter of Christian theology is indeed historical, but it cannot be reduced to human history, since it concerns God's history with, for, and in the world. The subject matter of Christian theology is found "in" history, but it is not "of" history (John 15:19).

Surely, if it could be proven that Jesus of Nazareth never lived, the Christian faith would lose much of its meaning. But what about his resurrection? As we consider this question, we need to pay attention to the kind of event that is. In what sense was this an event? Was it an event at all? Not just historians, but also some theologians, would—incorrectly, in my opinion—deny it. Here again we face the different subject matters of history and theology as scholarly practices: whereas history inquires about worldly and human events, ideas, and so on, theology is concerned with humanity *before God*, and with God who *acts in history*, disclosing who God is. Jesus's resurrection clearly escapes the realm of what history seeks to understand, but it becomes a topic, indeed a decisive one, in relation to the subject matter of Christian theology. In Christian theology it is not Jesus himself who raised himself from the dead; rather, it is God, his and our Father, who raised him. How can such an act be discerned by historians? They will, at best, notice certain consequences in human history of the Christian *belief* in Jesus's resurrection. History, as a human inquiry, attains certain external aspects of specific belief systems and traditions; it does not attain the core of what is believed. Theology, on the other hand, while it is interested in better understanding how the belief emerged, what it entailed, what it implied socially, culturally, politically, and so forth, seeks to understand who the agent of this act is. It reflects upon an act that cannot be said to be historical in the usual sense of the term, since no human person, but only God and the power of God's Spirit, stands behind this act.[3]

That being said, Christian theology cannot focus on Jesus Christ proclaimed to the detriment of Jesus of Nazareth as the one who proclaimed the kingdom. On this point Bultmann's stance, with what resembles docetic tendencies due to its focus on the Christ of the kerygma and of the church proclamation to the exclusion of Jesus's message and ministry, needed to be revised—as it was since the 1950s with the works of Ernst Käsemann (1906–98) (Käsemann 1954) and in the "new hermeneutics" of James M. Robinson (1924–2016) (Robinson 1959, 1964). The relationship between historical scholarship and theological construct is analogous to the relationship between the historical Jesus, his own message about the kingdom, his actions, and the proclamation of this historical figure as the Christ in whom God reconciled and reconciles the world. Martin Kähler was right to point out (see above, 150–51) that no text of the New Testament is simply interested in the historical Jesus as such: all of the texts of the New Testament, even those who narrate

3. On the debate between Rudolf Bultmann and Karl Barth on this point, see David W. Congdon, *The Mission of Demythologizing: Rudolf Bultmann's Dialectical Theology* (Minneapolis: Fortress Press, 2015), 182–86.

his ministry (that is, the Synoptic Gospels), are not mere biographies but post-Easter testimonies to God's reconciling act in Jesus, and so proclamations of the gospel. The gap between the proclaimer and the proclaimed cannot be resolved and eliminated. But it is also not an unbridgeable gap when one takes the leap of faith. It is not a blind leap, *contra* Kierkegaard and contemporary Kierkegaardians, but to a certain extent it is an informed one, since the human leap grounds itself on God's own act as witnessed in Scripture and, subordinately, as proclaimed by the Christian tradition. To those who do not take the leap, this all may (but also may not) seem nonsensical. But again, Christian theology does not, at some point, begin to consider God's act in the course of its inquiry. Rather, this act is its alpha and omega, and theology does not stop thinking once it has begun its inquiry in this way, but on the contrary it begins its critical inquiry here. There is a significant similarity with certain versions of hermeneutics, according to which "understanding begins . . . when something addresses us" (Gadamer 2003, 299). As it progresses in this work, Christian theology needs to learn from history, from philosophy, and from other fields of knowledge without being detracted from its proper subject matter and without also seeking to absorb or assimilate these other fields within itself. These fields need to be able to continually criticize theology from their own stances; theology would be in danger if it could not profit from these criticisms (even when these criticisms do not appear warranted).

The work of Paul Ricœur (1913–2005), a philosopher with an obvious Protestant identity and a deep knowledge of the major Protestant theological voices of the twentieth century, on hermeneutics and Scripture as a "polyphony" of literary genres, his reflections on language, on meaning and the "surplus of meaning" in classic and sacred texts, his insights into key notions such as "witness," rightly continues to nourish the work of theologians. Interpreting a text, including a biblical text, for Ricœur, does not mean attempting to attain the original author's intention or the historical background of the text. Rather, it seeks to understand the literary and theological "world" the text unfolds in front of itself as well as in front of us (Ricœur 1976, 36–37). Ricœur rightly pointed out how certain theologies of salvation history (*Heilsgeschichte*), and also certain theologies of Scripture's metanarrative, which were quite important around the middle of the twentieth century (Cullmann 1951) and which are still with us (Frei 1974), tend to level and simplify the variety of biblical literary forms as well as flatten the complex, convoluted—and often tragic—history that it relates and narrates (Ricœur 1993, 44).

Among other recent approaches to Scripture, the canonical approach is important. Brevard Childs (1923–2007) was its most important voice, but it continues to live on (Seitz 2011). Certainly, this approach helpfully reminds us of the qualitative difference of canonical texts compared to other texts. These texts are not just classic texts (they are that too; Tracy 1981): Christian communities, in their worship and life, consider them as different or distinct from all other texts. This is what was meant by the old, now badly battered, "doctrine of inspiration." The canonical approach is also helpful in its comprehensiveness, which seeks to include the historical inquiry without leaving the theological dimension aside (Seitz 2011, 34, 85). But important questions have also been voiced, critiquing the canonical approach insofar as it tends, among other things, to harmonize divergences within Scripture (see Ricœur's critique of salvation history) and, like premodern biblical interpretation, as it tends to read into the Old Testament a whole array of specifically Christian themes.

In sum, we should be very hesitant to assimilate history to theology and thus deny what, in historical scholarship, differs from systematic theology as a constructive and normative effort. But we should be equally wary to assimilate theology to history, perhaps for the sake of reinforcing its scientificity, and thus eliminate what makes theology *theological* and not simply one subfield, alongside other subfields, of historical research or of literary studies. All in all, biblical scholarship may be seen as an expression of the freedom conferred by the gospel: the freedom "to carry out this task, without asking anxiously whether it is useful, whether it disturbs people, whether it is agreeable to the church authorities, whether it accords with the official confession" (Barr 2013, 159; Barton 2016, 266). This, I think, is precisely what Baur already wished to convey in his polemical response to Ernst Wilhelm Hengstenberg and the *Evangelische Kirchenzeitung*'s attack (see above, 128–33).

True biblical criticism and sound theological exegesis must be allowed to proceed, ideally in conjunction with one another. This means that Scripture may be read in various ways: as literature, certainly, but also as kerygma or proclamation. As the French biblical scholar Jean-Noël Aletti concluded:

> It is true that the biblical texts deserve to be characterized as literature, but they are at the same time a Good News and they call to conversion. Seeing in them only literature means losing sight of what is most essential about them. And yet, even if they are addressed to faith and require a reading from within the realm of faith, the fact remains that historical-critical exegesis, duly practiced, has led to convergences among biblical scholars of various Christian backgrounds: the literary dimension, firmly maintained and respected, has destroyed many theological prejudices. (Aletti 1985, 519)

Yes, Christian theology has been in crisis for two centuries or so as it seeks to combine, in one way or another, both historical and theological approaches. As Van A. Harvey put it, "the marriage of theology and criticism has not been a tranquil one. No sooner has a measure of domestic bliss seemed assured that a new disturbing characteristic of one of the mates has emerged and a reappraisal of the relationship has taken place" (Harvey 1996, 8). But trying to overcome this crisis by eliminating the tension would be detrimental to theology itself. Theology must live, and may perhaps even thrive, *in* that tension.

Abbreviations

ET	English translation
EvTh	*Evangelische Theologie*
IJST	*International Journal of Systematic Theology*
rev.	revised
SC	*Sources chrétiennes*
SJT	*Scottish Journal of Theology*
TRE	*Theologische Realenzyklopädie*
TZTh	*Tübinger Zeitschrift für Theologie*
ZNThG/JHMTh	*Zeitschrift für Neuere Theologiegeschichte/Journal for the History of Modern Theology*
ZThK	*Zeitschrift für Theologie und Kirche*

Works Cited

Alberigo, Giuseppe. 1985. "Christianisme en tant qu'histoire et 'théologie confessante.'" In *Une école de théologie: Le Saulchoir*, by Marie-Dominique Chenu et al., 11–34. Paris: Cerf.

Aletti, Jean-Noël. 1985. "Conclusion générale." In *Bible de tous les temps*. Vol. 8, *Le monde contemporain et la Bible*, edited by Claude Savart and Jean-Noël Aletti, 517–22. Paris: Beauchesne.

Armogathe, Jean-Robert, ed. 1989. *Bible de tous les temps*. Vol. 6, *Le Grand Siècle et la Bible*. Paris: Beauchesne.

Ashcraft, Richard. 1992. "Latitudinarianism and Toleration: Historical Myth Versus Political History." In *Philosophy, Science and Religion in England 1640–1700*, edited by Peter Kroll, Richard Ashcraft, and Perez Zagorin, 151–77. Cambridge: Cambridge University Press.

Astruc, Jean. 1999. *Conjectures sur la Genèse*. Paris: Noêsis.

Auvray, Paul. 1968. "Richard Simon et Spinoza." In *Religion, érudition et critique à la fin du XVIIe siècle et au début du XVIIIe siècle*, 201–14. Paris: Presses universitaires de France.

———. 1974. *Richard Simon (1638–1712): Étude bio-bibliographique avec des textes inédits*. Paris: Presses universitaires de France.

Bambach, Charles R. 1995. *Heidegger, Dilthey, and the Crisis of Historicism*. Ithaca: Cornell University Press.

Barr, James. 2004. "'Real Theology' and Biblical Theology." In *Old Testament Theology: Flowering and Future*, edited by Ben C. Ollenburger, 449–62. Winona Lake, IN: Eisenbrauns.

———. 2013. "Biblical Criticism as Theological Enlightenment." In *Interpretation and Theology*, 156–68. Vol. 1 of *Bible and Interpretation: The Collected Essays of James Barr*, edited by John Barton. Oxford: Oxford University Press.

Barth, Karl. 1968a. *Ad limina apostolorum: An Appraisal of Vatican II*. Translated by Keith R. Crim. Richmond, VA: John Knox.

———. 1968b. *The Epistle to the Romans*. Translated by Edwyn C. Hoskyns. London: Oxford University Press.

———. 1993. "Der christliche Glaube und die Geschichte." In *Kleinere Vorträge und Arbeiten (1909–1914)*, edited by Hans-Anton Drewes, Hinrich Stoevesandt, Herbert Helms, and Friedrich-Wilhelm Marquardt, 149–212. Zurich: TVZ.

Barton, John. 2007. *The Nature of Biblical Criticism*. Louisville: Westminster John Knox.

———. 2016. "James Barr and the Future of Biblical Theology." *Interpretation* 70 (3): 264–74.

Baur, Ferdinand Christian. 1847. *Kritische Untersuchungen über die kanonischen Evangelien, ihr Verhältniss zu einaner, ihren Charakter und Ursprung*. Tübingen: Fues.

Bauspiess, Martin, Christof Landmesser, and David Lincicum, eds. 2014. *Ferdinand Christian Baur und die Geschichte des frühen Christentums*. Tübingen: Mohr Siebeck.

Bedouelle, Guy-Thomas. 1979. *Le* Quincuplex Psalterium *de Lefèvre d'Étaples: Un guide de lecture*. Geneva: Droz.

Bedouelle, Guy-Thomas, and Bernard Roussel, eds. 1989. *Bible de tous les temps*. Vol. 5, *Le temps des Réformes et la Bible*. Paris: Beauchesne.

Beiser, Frederick C. 2011. *The German Historicist Tradition*. Oxford: Oxford University Press.

Belaval, Yvon, and Dominique Bourel, eds. 1986. *Bible de tous les temps*. Vol. 7, *Le siècle des Lumières et la Bible*. Paris: Beauchesne.

Bentley, Jerry H. 1983. *Humanists and Holy Writ: New Testament Scholarship in the Renaissance*. Princeton: Princeton University Press.

Bernus, Auguste. 1869. *Richard Simon et son* Histoire critique du Vieux Testament*: La critique biblique au siècle de Louis XIV*. Lausanne: Bridel.

Blane, Andrew. 1993. "A Sketch of the Life of Georges Florovsky." In *Georges Florovsky: Russian Intellectual, Orthodox Churchman*, edited by Andrew Blane, 17–49. Crestwood, NY: St Vladimir's Seminary Press.

Bornkamm, Günther. 1962. "Geschichte und Glaube im Neuen Testament: Ein Beitrag zur Frage der 'historischen' Begründung theologischer Aussagen." *EvTh* 22:1–15.

Bultmann, Rudolf. 1953. *Das Evangelium des Johannes*. Göttingen: Vandenhoeck & Ruprecht.

———. 1968. "The Problem of a Theological Exegesis of the New Testament." In *The Beginnings of Dialectical Theology*, edited by James M. Robinson, 236–56. Richmond, VA: John Knox.

Cameron, Euan, ed. 2016. *The New Cambridge History of the Bible*. Vol. 3, *From 1450 to 1750*. Cambridge: Cambridge University Press.

Cappel, Louis. 1650. *Critica sacra, sive de variis quae in sacris veteris Testamenti libris occurrunt lectionibus libri VI*. Paris: Sébastien and Gabriel Cramoisy.

Castellion, Sébastien. 2005. *La Bible nouvellement translatée*, edited by Marie-Christine Gomez-Géraud, Jacques Roubaud, and Pierre Gibert. Paris: Bayard.

Celenza, Christopher S. 2012. "Lorenzo Valla's Radical Philology: The 'Preface' to the Annotations to the New Testament in Context." *Journal of Medieval and Early Modern Studies* 42 (2): 365–94.

Chenu, Marie-Dominique. 1964. *L'Évangile dans le temps*. Paris: Cerf.

———. 1985. *Une école de théologie*, with contributions by Giuseppe Alberigo, Étienne Fouilloux, Jean Ladrière, and Jean-Pierre Jossua. Paris: Cerf.

Congar, Yves. 1971. "Le Père M.-D. Chenu." In *Bilan de la théologie du XXe siècle*, vol. 2. Edited by Robert Vandergucht and Herbert Vorgrimler, 772–90. Tournai: Casterman.

Congdon, David W. 2015. *The Mission of Demythologizing: Rudolf Bultmann's Dialectical Theology*. Minneapolis: Fortress Press.

Cullmann, Oscar. 1951. *Christ and Time: The Primitive Christian Conception of Time.* Translated by Floyd V. Filson. London: SCM.

Dahlke, Benjamin. 2012. *Karl Barth, Catholic Renewal, and Vatican II.* London: T&T Clark.

Danneberg, Lutz. 2001. "Logik und Hermeneutik im 17: Jahrhundert." In *Theorie der Interpretation vom Humanismus bis zur Romantik: Rechtswissenschaft, Philosophie, Theologie*, edited by J. Schröder, 75–131. Stuttgart: Franz Steiner Verlag.

———. 2003. "Ezechiel Spanheim's Dispute with Richard Simon: On the Biblical Philology at the End of the 17th Century." In *The Berlin Refuge (1680–1780): Learning and Science in European Context*, edited by Sandra Pott, Martin Mulsow, and Lutz Danneberg, 49–88. Leiden: Brill.

Dawes, Gregory W. 1993 *The Historical Jesus Quest: Landmarks in the Search for the Jesus of History.* Louisville: John Knox.

———. 2001. *The Historical Jesus Question: The Challenge of History to Religious Authority.* Louisville: Westminster John Knox.

Dean, William. 1988. *History Making History: The New Historicism in American Religious Thought.* Albany: State University of New York Press.

Delforge, Frédéric. 1989. "Les éditions protestantes de la Bible en langue française." In *Bible de tous les temps.* Vol. 6: *Le Grand Siècle et la Bible*, edited by Jean-Robert Armogathe, 325–40. Paris: Beauchesne.

Denzinger, Heinrich. 2007. *The Sources of Catholic Dogma.* 30th ed. Translated by Roy J. Defaerrari. Fitzwilliam, NH: Loreto Publications.

Drey, Johann Sebastian. 1994. *Brief Introduction to the Study of Theology: With Reference to the Scientific Standpoint and the Catholic System.* Translated by Michael J. Himes. Notre Dame: University of Notre Dame Press.

East, Brad. 2017. "The Hermeneutics of Theological Interpretation: Holy Scripture, Biblical Scholarship and Historical Criticism." *IJST* 19 (1): 30–52.

Ellacuría, Ignacio. 2013. *Essays on History, Liberation, and Salvation.* Edited by Michael E. Lee. Maryknoll, NY: Orbis.

Erasmus, Desiderius. 1967. *In novum testamentum praefationes / Vorreden zum Neuen Testament. Ratio / Theologische Methodenlehre.* Translated by Gerhard B. Winkler. In *Ausgewählte Schriften: Ausgabe in acht Bänden, lateinisch und deutsch*, edited by Werner Welzig. Vol. 3. Darmstadt: Wissenschaftliche Buchgesellschaft.

Evans, Christopher H. 2004. *The Kingdom Is Always but Coming: A Life of Walter Rauschenbusch.* Grand Rapids: Eerdmans.

Fouilloux, Étienne. 2011. *La collection "Sources chrétiennes": Éditer les Pères de l'Église au XXe siècle.* Paris: Cerf.

Frank, Günter, and Stephan Meier-Oeser, eds. 2011. *Hermeneutik, Methodenlehre, Exegese: Zur Theorie der Interpretation in der Frühen Neuzeit.* Stuttgart-Bad Cannstatt: Frommann-Holzboog.

Frei, Hans W. 1974. *The Eclipse of Biblical Narrative: A Study in Eighteenth and Nineteenth Century Hermeneutics.* New Haven: Yale University Press.

———. 1985. "David Friedrich Strauss." In *Nineteenth Century Religious Thought in the West*, edited by Ninian Smart, 1:215–60. Cambridge: Cambridge University Press.

———. 1993. *Theology and Narrative: Selected Essays*. Edited by George Hunsinger and William C. Placher. New York: Oxford University Press.

Gabler, Johann Philipp. 1790. "Vorrede." In *Johann Gottfried Eichhorns Urgeschichte*, edited by J. P. Gabler, 1:iii–xxviii. Altdorf: Monath-Kussler.

Gadamer, Hans-Georg. 2003. *Truth and Method*. Translated by Joel Weinsheimer and Donald G. Marshall. New York: Continuum.

Geffré, Claude. 1997. "Théologie de l'incarnation et théologie des signes des temps." In *Marie-Dominique Chenu: Moyen-Âge et modernité*, edited by Joseph Doré and Jacques Fantino, 131–53. Paris: Centre d'études du Saulchoir.

Gibert, Pierre. 2008. "Introduction à la présente édition." In Richard Simon, *Histoire critique du Vieux Testament, suivi de Lettre sur l'inspiration*, edited by Pierre Gibert, 11–63. Paris: Bayard.

Grafton, Anthony. 1983. *Joseph Scaliger: A Study in the History of Classical Scholarship*. Vol. 1, *Textual Criticism and Exegesis*. Oxford: Clarendon.

Greenslade, S. L., ed. 1963. *The Cambridge History of the Bible: The West from the Reformation to the Present Day*. Cambridge: Cambridge University Press.

Groetsch, Ulrich. 2015. *Hermann Samuel Reimarus (1694–1768): Classicist, Hebraist, Enlightenment Radical in Disguise*. Leiden: Brill.

Hardy, Nicholas. 2017. *Criticism and Confession: The Bible in the Seventeenth Century Republic of Letters*. Oxford: Oxford University Press.

Harnack, Adolf. 1901. *History of Dogma*. Vol. 1. Boston: Little, Brown.

Hartlich, Christian, and Walter Sachs. 1952. *Der Ursprung des Mythosbegriffes in der modernen Bibelwissenschaft*. Tübingen: Mohr Siebeck.

Harvey, Van A. 1996. *The Historian and the Believer: The Morality of Historical Knowledge and Christian Belief*. 2nd ed. Urbana: University of Illinois Press.

Hauerwas, Stanley. 1983. *The Peaceable Kingdom: A Primer in Christian Ethics*. Notre Dame: Notre Dame University Press.

Hauser, Alan J., and Duane F. Watson, with Schuyler Kaufman, eds. 2009. *A History of Biblical Interpretation*. Vol. 2, *The Medieval through the Reformation Periods*. Grand Rapids: Eerdmans.

———, eds. 2017. *A History of Biblical Interpretation*. Vol. 3, *The Enlightenment through the Nineteenth Century*. Grand Rapids: Eerdmans.

Hill, Harvey. 2002. *The Politics of Modernism: Alfred Loisy and the Scientific Study of Religion*. Washington, DC: Catholic University of America Press.

Hornig, Gottfried. 1961. *Die Anfänge der historisch-kritischen Theologie: Johann Salomo Semlers Schriftverständnis und seine Stellung zu Luther*. Göttingen: Vandenhoeck & Ruprecht.

———. 1996. *Johann Salomo Semler: Studien zu Leben und Werk des Hallenser Aufklärungstheologen*. Tübingen: Niemeyer.

———. 2000. "Johann Salomo Semler." *TRE* 31:142–48.

Howard, Thomas Albert. 2000. *Religion and the Rise of Historicism*. New York: Cambridge University Press.

Jenson, Robert W. 1997. *Systematic Theology*. Vol. 1, *The Triune God*. Oxford: Oxford University Press.

Kähler, Martin. 1964. *The So-Called Historical Jesus and the Historic, Biblical Christ.* Translated by Carl E. Braaten. Philadelphia: Fortress Press.

Käsemann, Ernst. 1954. "Das Problem des historischen Jesus." *ZThK* 51 (2): 125–53. ET by W. J. Montague, *Essays on New Testament Themes*, 15–47. London: SCM, 1964.

Koester, Helmut. 1975. "New Testament Introduction: A Critique of a Discipline." In *Christianity, Judaism and Other Greco-Roman Cults: Studies for Morton Smith at Sixty. Part One: New Testament*, edited by Jacob Neusner, 1–20. Leiden: Brill.

Köpf, Ulrich. 2014. "Ferdinand Christian Baur und David Friedrich Strauss." In *Ferdinand Christian Baur und die Geschichte des frühen Christentums*, edited by Martin Bauspiess, with Christof Landmesser and David Lincicum, 3–51. Tübingen: Mohr Siebeck.

Kramer, Wolfgang. 1972. "Ernst Wilhelm Hengstenberg, die *Evangelische Kirchenzeitung* und der theologische Rationalismus," PhD diss., Erlangen.

Kraus, Hans-Joachim. 1988. "Martin Kähler." *TRE* 17:511–15.

Kroll, Peter, Richard Ashcraft, and Perez Zagorin, eds. 1992. *Philosophy, Science and Religion in England 1640–1700.* Cambridge: Cambridge University Press.

Kümmel, Werner Georg. 1973. *The New Testament: The History of the Investigation of Its Problems.* Translated by S. McLean Gilmour and Howard C. Kee. London: SCM.

Laplanche, François. 1986. *L'Écriture, le sacré et l'histoire: Érudits et politiques protestants devant la Bible en France au XVIIe siècle.* Amsterdam: APA Holland University Press.

———. 1994. *La Bible en France entre mythe et critique: XVIe–XIXe siècle.* Paris: Albin Michel.

Law, David R. 2012. *The Historical-Critical Method: A Guide for the Perplexed.* London: T&T Clark.

Le Clerc, Jean. 1686. *Défense des Sentimens de quelques théologiens de Hollande sur l'*Histoire critique du Vieux Testament*, composée par le P. Richard Simon de l'Oratoire. Où on remarque les fautes de cet auteur, on donne divers principes utiles pour l'intelligence de l'Écriture Sainte.* Amsterdam: H. Desbordes.

———. 1705. "Éloge de feu Mr. Locke." In *Bibliothèque choisie, pour servir de suite à la Bibliothèque universelle*, 6:342–411. Amsterdam: Henry Schelte. ET by T. F. P. Gent. *The Life and Character of Mr. John Locke, Author of the* Essay Concerning Human Understanding. London: John Clark, 1706.

Liebing, Heinz. 1967. "Historical-Critical Theology." *Journal for Theology and the Church* 3:55–69.

Linde, Cornelia. 2012. *How to Correct the* Sacra Scriptura*? Textual Criticism of the Latin Bible Between the Twelfth and Fifteenth Century.* Oxford: Society for the Study of Medieval Languages and Literature.

Loisy, Alfred. 1912. *The Gospel and the Church.* Translated by Christophe Home. New York: Scribner's.

Marlé, René. 1960. *Au cœur de la crise moderniste: Le dossier inédit d'une controverse.* Paris: Aubier.

Mayeur, Jean-Marie, Charles Pietri, Luce Pietri, André Vauchez, and Marc Venard, eds. 2001. *Histoire du christianisme: Des origines à nos jours.* Vol. 14, *Anamnèsis (Origines – Perspectives – Index).* Paris: Desclée.

McKitterick, Rosamond. 2008. *Charlemagne: The Formation of a European Identity.* Cambridge: Cambridge University Press.

Meyer, Lodewijk. 1666. *Philosophica S. Scripturae interpres* [...]. Amsterdam.

Michalson, Gordon E., Jr. 1985. *Lessing's "Ugly Ditch": A Study of Theology and History*. University Park: Pennsylvania State University Press.

Morgan, Robert, ed. 1973. *The Nature of New Testament Theology: The Contribution of William Wrede and Adolf Schlatter*. London: SCM.

———. 1986–87. "Gabler's Bicentenary." *Expository Times* 98 (6): 164–68.

———. 2013. "Spirit and Letter: Mapping Modern Biblical Interpretation." In *The Spirit and the Letter: A Tradition and a Reversal*, edited by Paul S. Fiddes and Günter Bader, 47–73. London: Bloomsbury.

———. 2016. "Albert Schweitzer's Challenge and the Response from New Testament Theology." In *Albert Schweitzer in Thought and Action: A Life in Parts*, edited by James Carleton Paget and Michael J. Thate, 71–104. Syracuse, NY: Syracuse University Press.

Nisbet, H. B. 2013. *Gotthold Ephraim Lessing: His Life, Works, and Thought*. Oxford: Oxford University Press.

Oberman, Heiko Augustinus. 1966. *Forerunners of the Reformation: The Shape of Late Medieval Thought Illustrated by Key Documents*. Translated by Paul L. Nyhus. London: Lutterworth.

Pitassi, Maria Cristina. 1987a. *Entre croire et savoir: Le problème de la méthode critique chez Jean Le Clerc*. Leiden: Brill.

———. 1987b. *Le problème de la méthode critique chez Jean Le Clerc*. Leiden: Brill.

Popkin, Richard H. 1987. *Isaac La Peyrère (1596–1676): His Life, Work and Influence*. Brill: Leiden.

———. 1996. "Spinoza and Bible Scholarship." In *The Cambridge Companion to Spinoza*, edited by Don Garrett, 383–407. Cambridge: Cambridge University Press.

———. 2003. *The History of Scepticism: From Savonarola to Bayle*. Oxford: Oxford University Press.

Poulat, Émile. 1962. *Histoire, dogme et critique dans la crise moderniste*. Paris: Casterman.

Preus, J. Samuel. 2001. *Spinoza and the Irrelevance of Biblical Authority*. Cambridge: Cambridge University Press.

Rémond, René. 1985. Preface to *Une école de théologie: Le Saulchoir* by Marie-Dominique Chenu et al, 7–8. Paris: Cerf.

Reventlow, Henning Graf. 2010a. *History of Biblical Interpretation*. Vol. 3, *Renaissance, Reformation, Humanism*, translated by James O. Duke. Atlanta: Society of Biblical Literature.

———. 2010b. *History of Biblical Interpretation*. Vol. 4: *From the Enlightenment to the Twentieth Century*, translated by Leo G. Perdue. Atlanta: Society of Biblical Literature.

Reventlow, Henning Graf, Walter Sparn, and John Woodbridge, eds. 1988. *Historische Kritik und biblischer Kanon in der deutschen Aufklärung*. Wiesbaden: Harrassowitz.

Riché, Pierre, and Guy Lobrichon, eds. 1984. *Bible de tous les temps*. Vol. 4, *Le Moyen Âge et la Bible*. Paris: Beauchesne.

Riches, John, ed. 2015. *The New Cambridge History of the Bible*. Vol. 4, *From 1750 to the Present*. Cambridge: Cambridge University Press.

Ricœur, Paul. 1993. "Herméneutique: Les finalités de l'exégèse biblique." In *La Bible en philosophie: Approches contemporaines*, edited by Dominique Bourg and Antoine Lion, 27–51. Paris: Cerf.

———. 1976. *Interpretation Theory: Discourse and the Surplus of Meaning*. Fort Worth: Texas Christian University Press.

Ritschl, Albrecht, and Adolf Harnack. 2010. *Albrecht Ritschls Briefwechsel mit Adolf Harnack (1875–1889)*. Edited by Joachim Weinhardt. Tübingen: Mohr Siebeck.

Ritschl, Albrecht, and Wilhelm Herrmann. 2013. *Briefwechsel (1875–1889)*. Edited by C. Chalamet, P. Fischer-Appelt, and J. Weinhardt with Th. Mahlmann. Tübingen: Mohr Siebeck.

Robinson, James M., ed. 1959. *A New Quest of the Historical Jesus*. London: SCM.

———. 1964. *The New Hermeneutic*. New York: Harper & Row.

Rousseau, Jean-Jacques. 2013. *Émile or On Education*. Translated by Barbara Foxley. Mineola, NY: Dover.

Ruggieri, Giuseppe. 1985. "Foi et histoire." In *La réception de Vatican II*, edited by Giuseppe Alberigo and Jean-Pierre Jossua, 127–55. Paris: Cerf.

Rumscheidt, H. Martin. 1972. *Revelation and Theology: An Analysis of the Barth-Harnack Correspondence of 1923*. Cambridge: Cambridge University Press.

Sandys-Wunsch, John, and Laurence Eldredge. 1980. "J. P. Gabler and the Distinction Between Biblical and Dogmatic Theology: Translation, Commentary, Discussion of His Originality." *SJT* 33:133–58.

Sarisky, Darren. 2015. *Theology, History, and Biblical Interpretation: Modern Readings*. London: Bloomsbury.

Savart, Claude, and Jean-Noël Aletti, eds. 1985. *Bible de tous les temps*. Vol. 8, *Le monde contemporain et la Bible*. Paris: Beauchesne.

Schleiermacher, Friedrich. 1998. *Hermeneutics and Criticism: And Other Writings*. Edited by Andrew Bowie. Cambridge: Cambridge University Press.

Schultze, Harald. 1997. "Hermann Samuel Reimarus." *TRE* 28:470–73.

Seckler, Max. 2007. "Pour comprendre la 'Brève introduction' de Johann Sebastian Drey." In *Aux origines de l'école catholique de Tübingen. Johann Sebastian Drey*, Brève introduction à l'étude de la théologie *(1819)*, edited by Max Seckler, 61–143. Paris: Cerf.

Seitz, Christopher R. 2011. *The Character of Christian Scripture: The Significance of a Two-Testament Bible*. Grand Rapids: Baker Academic.

Sider, Robert D. 2009. Preface to Erasmus. In *Paraphrases on the Epistles to the Corinthians, the Epistles to the Ephesians, Philippians, Colossians, and Thessalonians*. Edited by R. D. Sider. Translated by Mechtilde O'Mara and Edward A. Phillips Jr., ix–xiv. Collected Works of Erasmus 43. Toronto: University of Toronto Press.

Simon, Richard. 1682. *A Critical History of the Old Testament*. Translated by Henry Dickinson [?]. London: Walter Davis.

———. 2008. *Histoire critique du Vieux Testament, suivi de Lettre sur l'inspiration*. Edited by Pierre Gibert. Paris: Bayard.

Sockness, Brent W. 1996. *Against False Apologetics: Wilhelm Herrmann and Ernst Troeltsch in Conflict*. Tübingen: Mohr Siebeck.

Spinoza, Baruch. 2007. *Theological-Political Treatise*. Edited by Jonathan Israel. Translated by Michael Silverthorne and Jonathan Israel. Cambridge: Cambridge University Press.

Strecker, Georg, ed. 1960. "William Wrede. Zur hundertsten Wiederkehr seines Geburtstages." *ZThK* 57 (1): 67–91.

———. 1975. *Das Problem der Theologie des Neuen Testaments*. Darmstadt: Wissenschaftliche Buchgesellschaft.

Theobald, Christoph. 2010. "L'apologétique d'Alfred Loisy. Enjeux historiques et théologiques d'un livre inédit." In *La crise de la foi dans le temps présent* by Alfred Loisy. Edited by François Laplanche, 587–693. Turnhout: Brepols.

Theodulf of Orleans. 2002. "On Baptism." In *Water and the Word: Baptism and the Education of Clergy in the Carolingian Empire*, edited by Susan A. Keefe. 2 vols. Notre Dame: University of Notre Dame Press.

Tilley, Terrence W. 2004. *History, Theology, and Faith: Dissolving the Modern Problematic*. New York: Orbis.

Tracy, David. 1981. *The Analogical Imagination: Christian Theology and the Culture of Pluralism*. New York: Crossroad.

Troeltsch, Ernst. 2008. *Der Historismus und seine Probleme. Erstes Buch: Das logische Problem der Geschichtsphilosophie. Teilband 1*. Kritische Gesamtausgabe 16. Edited by Friedrich-Wilhelm Graf with Matthias Schlossberger. Berlin: W. de Gruyter.

Verheyden, Jack C. 1975. "Introduction." In Friedrich Schleiermacher, *The Life of Jesus*, xi–lxii. Philadelphia: Fortress Press.

Wainwright, Arthur W. 1987. Introduction to *A Paraphrase and Notes on the Epistles of St Paul to the Galatians, 1 and 2 Corinthians, Romans, Ephesians*, by John Locke, 1–88. Oxford: Clarendon.

Wischmeyer, Oda, ed. 2016. *Handbuch der Bibelhermeneutiken: Von Origenes bis zur Gegenwart*. Berlin: W. de Gruyter.

Wrede, William. 1901. *Das Messiasgeheimnis in den Evangelien: Zugleich ein Beitrag zum Verständnis des Markusevangeliums*. Göttingen: Vandenhoeck & Ruprecht. ET by James C. G. Grieg. *The Messianic Secret*. Cambridge: James Clarke, 1971.

Zac, Sylvain. 1965. *Spinoza et l'interprétation de l'Écriture*. Paris: Presses universitaires de France.

List of Original Sources

Chapter 1. Erasmus of Rotterdam

Ratio seu compendium verae theologiae. Basel: Froben, 1519. ET Donald B. Conroy, "The Ecumenical Theology of Erasmus of Rotterdam: A Study of the *Ratio Verae Theologiae*." PhD diss., University of Pittsburgh, 1974.

Chapter 2. Sebastian Castellio

De arte dubitandi et confidendi, ignorandi et sciendi. 1563. French translation by Charles Baudoin. Geneva-Paris: Jeheber, 1953.

Chapter 3. Louis Cappel

Critica sacra, sive de variis quae in sacris veteris Testamenti libris occurrunt lectionibus libri VI. Paris: Cramoisy, 1650.

Chapter 4. Thomas Hobbes

Leviathan. 1651. Edited by Noel Malcolm. Vol. 3, *The English and Latin Texts (ii)*, 588–92. Oxford: Clarendon Press, 2012.

Chapter 5. Baruch Spinoza

Theological-Political Treatise. 1670. Edited by Jonathan Israel. Translated by Michael Silverthorne and Jonathan Israel. Cambridge: Cambridge University Press, 2007.

Chapter 6. Richard Simon

A Critical History of the Old Testament. 1678, 1685. Translated by Henry Dickinson [?]. London: Walter Davis, 1682.

Chapter 7. Jean Le Clerc

"On the Best Manner of Interpreting the Bible. Dissertation II." In *Twelve Dissertations Out of Monsieur Le Clerk's Genesis, Concerning the Hebrew Tongue, the Manner of Interpreting the Bible, the Author of Pentateuch. ...* 1693. Translated by Thomas Brown. London: R. Baldwin, 1696.

Chapter 8. John Locke

Preface to *A Paraphrase and Notes on the Epistles of St. Paul*. 1705–07, in *An Essay for the Understanding of St. Paul's Epistles, by Consulting St. Paul Himself* (London: Black Swan, 1707).

Chapter 9. Johann Salomo Semler

Abhandlung von freier Untersuchung des Canon. 1771, 2nd ed. 1776. Edited by Heinz Scheible. Gütersloh: Gütersloher Verlagshaus Gerd Mohn, 1967. 2nd ed. 1980.

Chapter 10. Gotthold Ephraim Lessing

"On the Proof of the Spirit and of Power." 1777. In *Lessing's Theological Writings*. Edited and translated by Henry Chadwick. Stanford, CA: Stanford University Press, 1956.

Chapter 11. Hermann Samuel Reimarus

"Concerning the Intention of Jesus and His Teaching"; "On the Resurrection Narratives"; "On the Intentions of Jesus and His Disciples." 1777–78. In *Reimarus: Fragments*. Edited by Charles H. Talbert. Translated by Ralph S. Fraser. Philadelphia: Fortress Press, 1970.

Chapter 12. Johann Philipp Gabler

"An Oration on the Proper Distinction Between Biblical and Dogmatic Theology and the Specific Objectives of Each." 1787. Translated by John Sandys-Wunsch and Laurence Eldredge. *SJT* 33 (1980): 134–58.

Chapter 13. Friedrich Schleiermacher

Brief Outline of Theology as a Field of Study. 3rd ed. Revised translation of the 1811 and 1830 editions by Terrence N. Tice. Louisville: Westminster John Knox, 2011.

On the Glaubenslehre*: Two Letters to Dr. Lücke*. 1829. Translated by James Duke and Francis Fiorenza. Atlanta: Scholars Press, 1981.

Chapter 14. Johann Sebastian Drey

Brief Introduction to the Study of Theology. With Reference to the Scientific Standpoint and the Catholic System. 1819. Translated by Michael J. Himes. Notre Dame: University of Notre Dame Press, 1994.

Chapter 15. Georg Wilhelm Friedrich Hegel

Lectures on the Philosophy of Religion. Vol. 1, *Introduction and The Concept of Religion.* 1824, 1827. Edited by Peter Hodgson. Translated by R. F. Brown, P. C. Hodgson, J. M. Stewart, J. P. Fitzer, and H. S. Harris. Berkeley: University of California Press, 1984.

Lectures on the Philosophy of Religion. Vol. 3, *The Consummate Religion.* 1824. Edited by Peter Hodgson. Translated by R. F. Brown, P. C. Hodgson, J. M. Stewart, and H. S. Harris. Berkeley: University of California Press, 1985.

Chapter 16. David Friedrich Strauss

The Life of Jesus Critically Examined. 1835. Translated by George Eliot. Philadelphia: Fortress Press, 1972.

Chapter 17. Ferdinand Christian Baur

"Abgenöthigte Erklärung gegen einen Artikel der *Ev. Kirchenzeitung*, herausgegeben von Dr. E. W. Hengstenberg." First published in *TZTh* 8, no. 3 (1836): 59–178. Reprinted in *Ausgewählte Werke in Einzelausgaben*, edited by Klaus Scholder, 1:267–320. Stuttgart-Bad Cannstat: Frommann-Holzboog Verlag, 1963.

Chapter 18. Søren Kierkegaard

Practice in Christianity. 1848, 1850. Translated by Howard V. Hong and Edna H. Hong. Princeton: Princeton University Press, 1991.

Chapter 19. Albrecht Ritschl

The Christian Doctrine of Justification and Reconciliation. Vol. 3, *The Positive Development of the Doctrine.* 1888. Translated by H. R. Mackintosh and A. B. Macaulay. Edinburgh: T&T Clark, 1902.

Chapter 20. Walter Rauschenbusch

The Righteousness of the Kingdom. ca. 1891. Edited by Max L. Stackhouse. Nashville: Abingdon Press, 1968.

A Theology for the Social Gospel. New York: Macmillan, 1917.

Chapter 21. Martin Kähler

The So-Called Historical Jesus and the Historic, Biblical Christ. 1892. Translated by Carl E. Braaten. Philadelphia: Fortress Press, 1964.

Chapter 22. Alfred Loisy

A Critical History of the Biblical Text and Versions, vol. 1, *History of the Hebrew Text of the Old Testament* [*Histoire critique du texte et des versions de la Bible.* Vol. 1, *Histoire du texte hébreu de l'Ancien Testament*]. Amiens: Rousseau-Leroy, 1892.

The Gospel and the Church. 1902. Translated by Christopher Home. New York: Scribner's, 1912.

Chapter 23. Adolf von Harnack

Christianity and History. 1895. Translated by Thomas Bailey Saunders. London: A&C Black, 1896.

Chapter 24. William Wrede

"The Task and Methods of 'New Testament Theology.'" 1897. In *The Nature of New Testament Theology: The Contribution of William Wrede and Adolf Schlatter.* Edited and translated by Robert Morgan. London: SCM Press, 1973.

Chapter 25. Ernst Troeltsch

"On the Historical and the Dogmatic Methods in Theology." 1898. In *Religion in History.* Translated by James Luther Adams and Walter F. Bense. Edinburgh: T&T Clark, 1991.

Chapter 26. Wilhelm Herrmann

The Communion of the Christian with God, Described on the Basis of Luther's Statements. 1903. Translated by J. Sandys Stanyon. London: Williams & Norgate, 1906.

Chapter 27. Hermann Gunkel

Preface, 1913, and "Goals and Methods of the Explanation of the Old Testament." 1904. In *Reden und Aufsätze.* Göttingen: Vandenhoeck & Ruprecht, 1913.

Chapter 28. Albert Schweitzer

The Quest of the Historical Jesus. 1913. Edited by John Bowden. London: SCM, 2000.

Chapter 29. Karl Barth

Prefaces to *The Epistle to the Romans*. 1919; 2nd ed., 1922. Translated by Edwyn C. Hoskyns. Oxford: Oxford University Press, 1933.

Foreword to and chapter 1 of *Protestant Theology in the Nineteenth Century: Its Background and History*. 1946. Translated by Brian Cozens and John Bowden. Grand Rapids: Eerdmans, 2002.

Excerpts from *Church Dogmatics* IV/1. 1953. Translated by Geoffrey W. Bromiley. Edited by Geoffrey W. Bromiley and Thomas F. Torrance. London: T&T Clark, 2004.

Chapter 30. Rudolf Bultmann

"Liberal Theology and the Latest Theological Movement." 1924. In *Faith and Understanding*. Translated by Louise Pettibone Smith. New York: Harper & Row, 1969.

Chapter 31. Marie-Dominique Chenu

Une école de théologie: Le Saulchoir. 1937. Paris: Cerf, 1985.

Chapter 32. Prefatory note to *Sources chrétiennes*

Prefatory note to *Sources chrétiennes*. Vol. 1. Paris-Lyon: Cerf-L'Abeille, 1942.

Chapter 33. Gerhard Ebeling

Preface to the English edition and "The Significance of the Critical Historical Method for Church and Theology in Protestantism." 1950. In *Word and Faith*, translated by James W. Leitch. London: SCM, 1963.

Chapter 34. Georges Florovsky

"The Predicament of the Christian Historian." 1959. In *Christianity and Culture: The Collected Works of George Florovsky*, vol. 2. Belmont: Norland, 1974. Reprinted in *The Patristic Witness of Georges Florovsky: Essential Theological Writings*. Edited by Brandon Gallaher and Paul Ladouceur. New York: T&T Clark, 2019.

Chapter 35. Wolfhart Pannenberg.

"Redemptive Event and History." Translated by Shirley C. Guthrie Jr. In *Essays on Old Testament Hermeneutics*, edited by Claus Westermann (German edition) and James Luther Mays (English edition). Richmond: John Knox, 1963.

"Dogmatic Theses on the Doctrine of Revelation." 1960. In *Revelation as History: A Proposal for a More Open, Less Authoritarian View of an Important Theological Concept.* Edited by Wolfhart Pannenberg et al. Translated by David Granskou. London: Macmillan, 1968.

Jesus—God and Man. 1964. Translated by Lewis L. Wilkins and Duane A. Priebe. London: SCM, 1968.

Chapter 36. Elisabeth Schüssler Fiorenza

In Memory of Her: A Feminist Theological Reconstruction of Christian Origins. New York: Crossroads, 1983.

Chapter 37. Ignacio Ellacuría

"Salvation History." 1987. In *Essays on History, Liberation, and Salvation.* Edited by Michael E. Lee. Translated by Margaret D. Wilde. Maryknoll, NY: Orbis, 2013.

Index of Names

NB: Names that appear in *italics* are found in the footnotes of the book

Index of Subjects

Permissions

Excerpt from Thomas Hobbes's *Leviathan* used by permission of Oxford University Press.

Excerpt from *Lessing's Theological Writings*. Henry Chadwick, copyright © 1956 by A & C Black Ltd. All rights reserved Used by permission of the publisher, Stanford University Press, www.sup.org.

Excerpt from Reimarus's "Concerning the Intention of Jesus and His Teaching" used by permission of Hymns Ancient & Modern.

Excerpt from Hegel's *Lectures on the Philosophy of Religion* used by permission of Oxford University Press.

Baur, Ferdinand Christian: *Ausgewählte Werke. Band II: Arbeiten zur Kirchengeschichte I. Mit einer Einleitung von Ernst Wolf*. 1963. XXV, 310 S. Ln. Stuttgart-Bad Cannstatt: frommann-holzboog Verlag. Used by permission.

Walter Rauschenbusch, *A Theology for the Social Gospel*, first published by Macmillan in New York in 1917; reprint by Martin Fine Books (Eastford: Connecticut, 2010). Used by permission.

Excerpt from W. Wrede's "The Task and Methods of 'New Testament Theology'" used by permission of Hymns Ancient & Modern.

Excerpt from Karl Barth's *The Epistle to the Romans* used by permission of Oxford University Press.

Excerpt from Karl Barth's *Protestant Theology in the Nineteenth Century* used by permission of Hymns Ancient & Modern.

Excerpt from Karl Barth's *Church Dogmatics* IV/1. Copyright © Karl Barth, 2004, *Church*

Dogmatics IV/1, T&T Clark, an imprint of Bloomsbury Publishing Plc. Used by permission.

Excerpt from Marie-Dominique Chenu's "Une école de théologie" translated and used by permission of Joseph Komonchak.

Excerpt from Gerhard Ebeling's "Significance of the Critical Historical Method for Church and Theology in Protestantism" used by permission of Oxford University Press.

Excerpt from *Ignacio Ellacuria: Essays on History, Liberation, and Salvation* edited by Michael E. Lee. Reprinted by permission of Orbis Books, Maryknoll, New York.